Date: 9/2/21

780.9 MUS V.3
Music around the world.
a global encyclopedia /

PALM BEACH COUNTY
LIBRARY SYSTEM
3650 SUMMIT BLVD.
WEST PALM BEACH, FL 33406

Music around the World

Music around the World

A Global Encyclopedia

VOLUME 3: Q–Z
Andrew R. Martin and
Matthew Mihalka, Editors

ABC-CLIO®

An Imprint of ABC-CLIO, LLC
Santa Barbara, California • Denver, Colorado

Copyright © 2020 by ABC-CLIO, LLC

All rights reserved. No part of this publication may be reproduced, stored in a retrieval system, or transmitted, in any form or by any means, electronic, mechanical, photocopying, recording, or otherwise, except for the inclusion of brief quotations in a review, without prior permission in writing from the publisher.

Library of Congress Cataloging-in-Publication Data

Names: Martin, Andrew R., editor. | Mihalka, Matthew, editor.
Title: Music around the world : a global encyclopedia / Andrew R. Martin and Matthew Mihalka, editors.
Description: 1st edition. | Santa Barbara : ABC-CLIO, 2020. | Includes bibliographical references and index.
Identifiers: LCCN 2019042635 (print) | LCCN 2019042636 (ebook) | ISBN 9781440846366 (v. 1 ; cloth) | ISBN 9781440846373 (v. 2 ; cloth) | ISBN 9781440846380 (v. 3 ; cloth) | ISBN 9781610694988 (cloth) | ISBN 9781610694995 (ebook)
Subjects: LCSH: World music—Encyclopedias.
Classification: LCC ML100 .M894 2020 (print) | LCC ML100 (ebook) | DDC 780.9—dc23
LC record available at https://lccn.loc.gov/2019042635
LC ebook record available at https://lccn.loc.gov/2019042636

ISBN: 978-1-61069-498-8 (set)
　　　978-1-4408-4636-6 (vol. 1)
　　　978-1-4408-4637-3 (vol. 2)
　　　978-1-4408-4638-0 (vol. 3)
　　　978-1-61069-499-5 (ebook)

24 23 22 21 20   1 2 3 4 5

This book is also available as an eBook.

ABC-CLIO
An Imprint of ABC-CLIO, LLC

ABC-CLIO, LLC
147 Castilian Drive
Santa Barbara, California 93117
www.abc-clio.com

This book is printed on acid-free paper ∞

Manufactured in the United States of America

Contents

Alphabetical List of Entries   vii

Preface   xiii

Introduction   xv

Entries: A–Z   1

About the Editors   965

Contributors   967

Index   973

Alphabetical List of Entries

VOLUME ONE
Acadian Music
Accordion (Americas)
Accordion, Types of
Adé, "King" Sunny
African Spirituals
Afrobeat (Afropop)
Afro-Cuban Jazz
Ahmad, Fadzil
Amadinda
Amish Hymns (*Ausbund, Gesangbuch*)
Andalusian Music
Andean Region, Music of the
Arab Classical Music
Armenian Music
Armstrong, Louis
Ashkenazi Jews, Music of
Astatke, Mulatu
Austro-German Dances
Bağlama
Bagpipes
Bandoneón
Banjo
Bariu, Laver
Bartók, Béla
Bashir Brothers (Munir and Jamil)
Basque, Music of the
Batá Drums
Beatles, The
Bebop
Bedouin Music
Bélé
Belly Dance
Berimbau
Björk
Bluegrass
Blues
Bol
Bolivia, Music of
Bollywood Music
Bomba, Ecuador
Bomba, Puerto Rico
Bones (Britain and Ireland)
Brazil, Music of
Buena Vista Social Club
Bunraku
Cajun Music
Calypso
Candomblé
Cantopop
Caribbean Art Music
Carmody, Kevin Daniel "Kev"
Carnival, Music of
Carter Family, The

Čechomor
Celtic Music
Chamarrita
Chanson (Urban/Modern)
Chinese Pop
Chopi People, Music of the
Chutney
Chutney Soca
Classical Music, European
Claves and Clave Rhythm
Cohan, George M.
Colometry/Colometric
Coltrane, John
Concerto
Congo Square
Conjunto
Conjunto (Norteños)
Corrido
Cossacks, Music of
Country Music
Cretan Lyra
Cruz, Celia
Cuatro
Cumbia
Dancehall
Darbuka
Dastgah
Davis, Miles (Dewey, III)
Densmore, Frances
Dhol
Dhrupad
Didgeridoo
Dixieland
Djembe
Dmitri Pokrovsky Ensemble
Dorsey, Thomas A.
Duduk
Dulcimer
Dylan, Bob
Eastern Woodland Native American Music
Emmett, Dan (Daniel Decatur)
Enka Music
Erhu
Eurovision Song Contest
Fado
Fairuz
Fiddle
Field Hollers
Flamenco Music
Folkways Records
Foster, Stephen Collins
French Folk Dances
Fujara
Funk
Gagaku
Gamelan Orchestra (Balinese)
Gamelan Orchestra (Javanese)
Ganga
Ganga Singing
Gender Wayang
Gimbri
Gospel Music
Greek Popular Music
Gregorian Chant
Griot
Guitarrón Mexicano
Gumba
Guoyue
Guthrie, Woody
Guzheng
Gyil

Alphabetical List of Entries

VOLUME TWO

Handy, W. C.
Harana and Kundiman
Hardanger Fiddle (Hardingfele)
Harmonium
Hawaii, Music of
Highlife
Hōgaku
Hornbostel, Erich Moritz von
Huayno
Huqin
Icelandic Ballads
Indian Folk Songs
Indonesian Pop Music
Iranian Classical Music
Irish American Vocal Music
Irish Dance Music
Irish Step Dancing
Italian Folk Music (Various Regions)
Jackson, Mahalia
Jali
Janggu
Japan, Music of
Jazz
Jehan, Noor
Jingju (Beijing Opera)
Johnson, Robert
Joik
Joplin, Scott
J-Pop
Kabuki
Kalthoum, Umm
Kamancheh
Karnatic Music
Kayokyoku
Kebyar
Kecak
Kendang
Khaled, Cheb
Khan, Nusrat Fateh Ali
Khayal
Khene
Kidjo, Angelique
Klezmer
Kodály, Zoltán
Kora
Koto
K-Pop (Korean Pop)
Kulintang
Kuti, Fela
Ladysmith Black Mambazo
Ländler
Launeddas
Lead Belly
Lenya, Lotte
Lithuanian Music
Lomax, Alan and John
Madrigal
Makam
Makeba, Miriam
Malay Music
Malhūn
Malouf
Mambo
Mande Music
Manu Chao
Mariachi
Marimba
Marley, Bob
Marshall Islands, Music of
Masakela, Hugh
Mbalax
Mbila
Mbube

Alphabetical List of Entries

McPhee, Colin
Medieval Secular Song
Mento
Merengue
Mestizo Music
Mexican Regional Music
Mikagura
Min'yô
Moravian Music
Morin Khuur
Mridangam
Musafir
Musicals
Native American Church Music
Native American Flute
Native American Music
Native American Popular Music
Navajo, Music of
Ney
Nisiotika
Nô Theater
Nongak
Nordic Jazz
North Korea, Music of
Norwegian Folk Music
Nueva Canción
Nyckelharpa
Olatunji, Babatunde
Opera
Original Dixieland Jazz Band
Ottoman Classical Music
Oud
Owiyo, Suzanna
Pakistan, Music of
Pansori (P'ansori)
Parker, Charlie
Pashto Music

Philippines, Music of the
Piazzolla, Astor
Pimba
Pipa
Piphat
Polish National Dances
Polka
Polynesia, Music of
Polynesian Hymns
Presley, Elvis
Psaltery
Puente, Tito

VOLUME THREE

Qānūn
Qin (Guqin)
Qraqeb
Quadrille
Quelbe
Race Records
Raga
Ragtime
Rai
Rainey, Ma
Rakha, Alla
Rancho Folclórico
Rap/Hip-Hop
Rap/Hip-Hop in Africa and the Middle East
Rara
Rebab
Redzepova, Esma
Reggae
Reggaetón
Rímur
Riq
Rock and Roll

Alphabetical List of Entries

Rodgers, Jimmie
Rodrigues, Amália
Romani Music
Rumba
Runo Song
Russian Orthodox Church Music
Salsa
Samba Instruments
Samba Music
Sanjo
Schlager
Schottische
Schrammelmusik
Scotch Snap
Seeger, Peter
Sephardic Music
Shajarian, Mohammed-Reza
Shakuhachi
Shamanic Music in Mongolia and Inner Asia
Shamisen
Shankar, Ravi
Shape-Note Singing
Shômyô
Singspiel
Sitar
Ska
Smith, Bessie
Soca
Soul
Steel Guitar
Steelpan
Sufism, Music of
Swing
Symphonic Poem
Symphony
Tabla

Tagore, Rabindranath
Taiko
Taiwanese Opera
Taiwanese Traditional and Popular Music
Tala
Tamboo Bamboo
Tango
Taqsīm
Tar
Tassa Drumming
Tejano Music
Thumri
Tibetan Buddhist Chant
Tibetan Singing Bowls
Tin Pan Alley
Tin/Pennywhistle
Tombak
Touré, Ali Farka
Turbo-Folk
Tuvan Popular Bands
Tuvan Throat Singing
Ukulele
Vaudeville
Veena
Villa-Lobos, Heitor
Virginia Minstrels
Vocables
Waltz
Wayang Kulit
Xalam
Yodeling
Yuman Music
Zajal
Ziegfeld, Florenz, Jr.
Zither
Zouk
Zydeco

Q

Qānūn

Qānūn refers to a trapezoidal, zither-like plucked stringed instrument which is played using plectra attached to both index fingers. The Turkish spelling is *kanon*; the Armenian, *k'anon*. The etymology of the word "qānūn" refers to rule, law, or custom. Edward Lane described the *kánoon* he observed in Cairo in the early 19th century as made of walnut wood with sides of beech, as was the "piece in which the pegs are inserted" and the "ridge along its interior edge, through which the chords [strings] are passed." The pegs themselves were made of poplar wood. The bridge, face, and back were "of fine deal" (perhaps referencing the British usage of fir or pine). The two circular pieces of wood "of a reddish colour, pieced with holes" on the qānūn's face are termed *shemseh* ("sun"). Modern Egyptian qānūns are made of walnut or maple wood, whereas earlier ones were crafted of mahogany or plum. The Turkish kanun is walnut, plane, pine, or ebony. Lane's engraving depicts a turbaned *qānūnji* seated on the floor, with the instrument horizontally balanced on his knees (Lane, 1860, pp. 67–68). Contemporary performers are seated, with the qānūn, now measuring in length between 30–40 inches, similarly placed across the lap or on a stand.

Curt Sachs (1940) traces historical references to the qānūn to a story in the 10th-century *Arabian Nights*, which attributed its provenance to Egypt (calling it *qānūn misrī*); at the time, the instrument was held in a vertical position. The qānūn was introduced to Europe via Spain, where it was termed *caño*. Sachs notes that the dulcimer, of Persian/Iraqi origin (which is struck rather than plucked), was called *santir* (cf. *santūr*) after the Greek *psalterion*; Scheherazade Qassim Hassan writes that the instrument is termed *sintir* in the Old Testament, having evolved from an "ancient Babylonian horizontal harp that was struck with two sticks, as the modern instrument still is" (Hassan, 2002, p. 411). Sachs states that the santir also migrated to Spain, via North Africa. A depiction of a psaltery was carved on the relief of the church of Santiago de Compostela in 1184. Sachs observes that after 1300, "[struck] dulcimers seem to have prevailed in the north, and [plucked] psalteries in the south" (Sachs, 1940, p. 292).

Christian Poché identifies the designer of the "new" qānūn as Istanbul instrument maker Mahmut Usta, who in 1876 installed small brass levers near the pegbox (termed *orab* or *'urab* in Arabic, meaning "carriage," or *mandal*, "that which supports," in Turkish). Two to five levers per every three strings is the norm for the Arab qānūn, with five to nine for the Turkish instrument and 10 for the Aleppine. Intervals can thus be "minutely adjusted by rotating the levers, which control the tension of the strings" (Poché, n.d.). Sachs cites a 14th-century Persian treatise, *Kanz al-tuhaf*, which describes the qānūn as having 64 strings in sets of three.

The Egyptian qānūn currently has 78 strings, with 72–74 for the Turkish instrument. In Lane's account, the strings were made of lamb's gut, and the plectra from buffalo horn. Poché notes that strings are now nylon, with plectra made of metal or bone; Habib Hassan Touma mentions tortoise-shell plectra. The range of the qānūn varies between three and four octaves. Arab qānūnjis play in octaves or double-octaves, with the bass and treble clefs notated for the left and right hands; the Turkish method is limited to the treble clef.

Hassan observes that the qānūn is considered an "aristocratic instrument," known as "the sultan" (Hassan, 2002, p. 411). It is revered for its brilliant sound but is rarely played as a solo instrument. The qānūn is included in the traditional five-instrument *takht* ensemble prevalent in Egypt and the Levant, which performs the vocal genres *dawr, qasīda, muwashshah, layālī,* and *mawwāl* in addition to the instrumental genres *bashraf, samā'ī, tahmīlah,* and *dūlāb*. Regional ensembles incorporating the qānūn include *nūbah* ensembles in North Africa, small *k'anon* ensembles in Armenia, and *čalgije* ensembles of Macedonia and Kosovo.

Hicham Chami

See also: Qin; Zither

Further Reading

Hassan, Scheherazade Qassim. 2002. "Musical Instruments in the Arab World." In Virginia Danielson, Dwight Reynolds, and Scott Marcus (eds.), *Garland Encyclopedia of World Music; Vol. 6: The Middle East*, 401–424. New York: Routledge.

Lane, Edward William. 1860. *An Account of the Manners and Customs of the Modern Egyptians*. London: John Murray.

Poché, Christian. n.d. "Qānūn." *Grove Music Online*. https://www.oxfordmusiconline.com.

Sachs, Curt. 1940. *The History of Musical Instruments*. New York: W. W. Norton.

Touma, Habib Hassan. 1996. *The Music of the Arabs*, trans. Laurie Schwartz. Portland, OR: Amadeus Press.

Qin (Guqin)

The *qin* or *guqin*, a seven-stringed plucked zither, has been the musical instrument of the Chinese literati for more than 2,000 years. The significance of the qin in Chinese culture was demonstrated by proclamation of its music as one of the Masterpieces of the Oral and Intangible Heritage of Humanity by UNESCO in 2003.

There have been numerous references to the qin in classic writings, paintings, and poetry in China in the past. The function of the instrument is to nurture the character of the literati rather than to entertain an audience. Qin music, which is usually played solo, is characterized by serenity and subtlety. Its aesthetic is closely related to the other art forms of the literati, and is deeply affected by Confucian and Daoist philosophy. The qin player strives for a spiritual state of mind and plays with an upright posture without excessive bodily movement.

The instrument is composed of an upper and a lower wooden board. Compared to other forms of zithers, the boards are relatively thick and the sound box is relatively small; thus, it produces only a small sound volume. There are 13 studs on the upper board, which indicate harmonic positions. The seven strings are traditionally made of silk, and are usually tuned along a pentatonic scale. Three types of tones can be produced on the qin: open string notes, stopped notes, and harmonic notes. The main plucking movements are made with right fingers, whereas a left finger stops the string for a stopped note or lightly touches the string for a harmonic note. There are no frets or bridges on the qin, and a left finger playing stopped notes can glide freely on the upper board to produce gliding notes and fine ornamentations.

Titles of qin pieces are often programmatic, depicting scenes of mountains and rivers, life of hermits, allusion to classic stories, memory of old friends, or the mood of disillusioned literati. The melody is monophonic, but the melodic line is characterized by the interpolated use of open string notes, stopped notes, harmonic notes, left-hand plucks, and gliding notes, each having different tone colors. This is coupled with fine nuances of the faint gliding notes and ornamentations. A piece often begins and ends slowly in free rhythm. The pulsed section usually starts very slowly and then gradually accelerates inconspicuously to a moderate pace, often without a regular meter. One does not indulge in a beautiful melody or an intense rhythm, but rather tries to pursue a poetic and meditative mood.

Various past scholars have discussed the aesthetics of qin music in their writings. "The Xishan Treatise on the Aesthetics of *Qin* Music" published in 1673 is one of the most important pieces of literature on this subject (Xu, 2015). Twenty-four aesthetic qualities were defined and elaborated upon, allowing readers to gain a better understanding of the sophisticated aesthetic views of the literati on the qin.

In addition to its music, a good instrument itself is also highly regarded. The crafting of a good instrument require many hours of refined work by an expert qin maker. The oldest instruments surviving in China were crafted in the Tang Dynasty (618–907 CE), and are still playable. Older instruments are valuable not only for producing a good sound, but also as antiques sought after by keen collectors.

The scores of qin pieces were often recorded in qin handbooks. Many handbooks have been passed down from the Qing Dynasty (1644–1911). The scores in the handbooks use a special tablature notation that does not notate the musical notes directly. A tablature is formed by combining simplified components of Chinese characters and numerals to indicate the fingering movement and position. Following the fingering instruction would produce a musical note. A series of such tablatures would form a musical phrase. One special point is that time elements, such as the duration of the individual notes and the tempo, are not indicated in the score (Yung, 1994). The transmission of a qin piece thus normally depends not only on the score, but also very much on the master's teaching of the pupils, as in oral traditions.

As with other oral traditions, details of a qin piece often changed upon transmission from one generation to another. The changes were not limited to the non-notated time elements, but might occur with the notated fingering positions, implying changes in the melodic line as well. When the changes in the fingering positions became significant, a qin master of a later generation would record the new version of the piece in a handbook of his or her own. As a result, many different versions appeared after a widely played piece had been transmitted for several generations.

A number of important handbooks from a more distant past have been discovered in the past century, the earliest extant one having been published in the early Ming Dynasty (1368–1644) in 1425 CE. In addition, it became known to Chinese qin masters that a Tang Dynasty manuscript of a qin piece survived in Japan. Upon discovery of these old scores, masters of the last generation attempted to reconstruct the music. The process is called *dapu* (Yung, 1985)—and it is not an easy process. Without time elements notated, qin masters had to "compose" these elements in order to make the series of notes musically meaningful. Through hard work of the past generation of qin masters, important old pieces have been reconstructed, including *Youlan* (secluded orchid), *Guangling San* (melody of Guangling), and *Jiukuang* (drunken elation).

Qin music passed down from the Qing Dynasty is mainly pentatonic, using *do, re, mi, sol, la* in the melody. Upon detailed studies of qin scores of the distant past, it was realized that qin music in the past was often nonpentatonic, utilizing up to 11 tones within an octave (Tse, 2009). The tonal characteristics steadily changed during transmission from one generation to another, and became mostly pentatonic in the late Qing Dynasty. The surviving qin scores serve as a rich source of information about characteristics of Chinese music in the distant past, of which surviving scores of other genres are scanty.

Though highly regarded, throughout its history the qin has not been commonly played outside of the literati or elite circles. Entering the 20th century in China, the survival of the qin culture was further threatened by the impact of modern Western culture and political turmoil. However, dedicated qin masters worked hard not only to transmit this important cultural heritage to the younger generation, but also to explore the past upon the discovery of old qin handbooks, and to venture into new developments of the living tradition. Important contributors in the 20th century include Zha Fuxi (1895–1976), Guan Pinghu (1897–1967), Zhang Ziqian (1899–1991), Wu Jinglue (1907–1987), and Yao Bingyan (1921–1983) in Mainland China; Sun Yuqin (1915–1990) in Taiwan; and Tsar Teh-yun (1905–2007) in Hong Kong.

New developments since about 1960 have caused controversies and debates (Yung, 2009). Many qin players in Mainland China now use metal/nylon strings, which give a louder and brighter sound, instead of the traditional silk strings. Music institutions in Mainland China train young qin players to become professional performers rather than playing to nurture the personality. New qin pieces composed by professional composers may sound incompatible with the traditional subtle and serene style. After the UNESCO proclamation in 2003, there has been a surge of qin players among the educated young generation in big cities. However, some may just view this as a stylish trend and may not fully understand the aesthetics of the music. Instead of "modernization" or "popularization," some qin players may prefer to "hold onto what we have so that the spirit of our civilization may continue into the future" (Yung, 2009, p. 163).

Tse Chun Yan

See also: Qānūn; Zither

Further Reading
Gulik, Robert Hans van. 1940. *The Lore of the Chinese Lute*. Tokyo: Sophia University.

Tse Chun Yan. 2009. "From Chromaticism to Pentatonism: A Convergence of Ideology and Practice in Qin Music of the Ming and Qing Dynasties." PhD diss., The Chinese University of Hong Kong.

Xu Shangying. 2015. "The Xishan Treatise on the Aesthetics of Qin Music" (trans. Chun Yan Tse and Shui Fong Lam). *Renditions* 83, 89–111.

Yung, Bell. 1985. "*Da Pu*: The Recreative Process for the Music of the Seven-String Zither." In Anne Dhu Shapiro (ed.), *Music and Context: Essays in Honor of John Ward*, 370–384. Cambridge, MA: Harvard University Press.

Yung, Bell. 1994. "Not Notating the Notatable: Reevaluating the Guqin Notational System." In Bell Yung and Joseph S. C. Lam (eds.), *Themes and Variations: Writings on Music in Honor of Rulan Chao Pian*, 45–58. Cambridge, MA: Department of Music, Harvard University/Hong Kong: Institute of Chinese Studies, Chinese University of Hong Kong.

Yung, Bell. 2008. *The Last of China's Literati: The Music, Poetry, and Life of Tsar Teh-yun*. Hong Kong: Hong Kong University Press.

Yung, Bell. 2009. "Historical Legacy and the Contemporary World: UNESCO and China's Qin Music in the Twenty-First Century." In Andrew N. Weintraub and Bell Yung (eds.), *Music and Cultural Rights*, 140–168. Chicago: University of Illinois Press.

Qraqeb

Qraqeb (also spelled *qaraqab*) is an instrument used by the Gnawa (a mystical group of Sufis in North Africa with roots in West African traditions) and in the form of music called *daqqah Marakshiyyah* (Aydoun, 2001, p. 13). The instruments are made of metal sheets that are cut into discs at both ends and are played like castanets in both hands. Unlike castanets, qraqeb are double headed; they are held by a connecting bar in the palm and both ends are played to produce a metallic scraping or clacking sound (Ewens, 1991, p. 53). In Morocco, for both the *daqqah* and the Gnawa, they are played in such a way as to sound more "crisp" with distinct beats; in Tunisia, among the *Bori* (a Hausa word) or *Istanbuli* (named for the Turkish Bey of Tunis who owned the African slaves), they prefer a less clear sound and more of a scraping sound.

As the Gnawa of Morocco became better known in the West, primarily among jazz musicians, their instruments also became better known, and today qraqeb are made in large numbers for tourists. Although simple in construction, the qraqeb are not easy to play. They are held together by a cord that goes around the hand and they have to be kept apart, but because they are double, with both the tops and bottoms being played, they are difficult to master (Aydoun, 2001, p. 135). In addition, the Gnawa use them as part of their ceremonies called *awald Bambara* (sons of Bambara—a people in Mali), during which they are expected to make spectacular leaps and twists while playing the qraqeb.

John A. Shoup

See also: Sufism, Music of

Further Reading

Aydoun, Ahmed. 2001. *Musiques du Maroc*. Casablanca: EDDIF/Autres Temps.

Ewens, Gaeme. 1991. *Africa O-Ye!: Celebration of African Music*. London: Guinness.

Quadrille

A ballroom couple's dance, the quadrille was fashionable throughout the 19th century. The term *quadrille* may derive from the Italian *squadra*, a troop of armed horsemen formed into a square for defense and tournament games. In the Baroque period, the French associated the term both with dance and with a popular card game. The square-dance form on which the quadrille was based is at least 400 years old: three "squares for eight" are described in John Playford's first edition of *The English Dancing Master* (1651).

Le Quadrille des Nations (1662) was an elaborately costumed French masque, including horses, held at the Louvre. Quadrille dancers dressed alike when presenting the dance as one of the "entrées" in a court ballet. Rousseau's court ballet *Les Fêtes de Polyhymnie* (1743) called for a quadrille by a chorus of dancers in groups of four, making a formal entrance by performing symmetrical dance patterns. English country dance, called *contredanse anglaise* by the French, allowed dancers to stand "at will" in two long lines with the gentlemen facing the ladies.

In the 18th century, square dances took two forms: pairs of couples standing in straight lines, facing other pairs, and four couples standing in a square, with each man's partner on his right. Both of these formations were called *contredanses françaises* (or cotillon/cotillion, outside of France). The action was a kind of *rondeau*, moving across or around the square; the figure (floor pattern) was alternated with a refrain or change. Ten standard changes were fashionable. In 1765, French dancing master Claude-Marc Magny published directions for six ballroom dances in which two couples executed a variety of geometric patterns, and one of these was entitled *le quadrille*.

After the French Revolution, the old cotillon was replaced by the 19th-century quadrille (still called cotillon or cotillion by music publishers), in which five different figures were combined to form one dance. After 1815, when the quadrille was introduced into London society, the most popular form was known as the French Quadrille, or "First Set"; this consisted of four popular figures (*Pantalon, L'Été, La Poule,* and *La Trenis*) combined into one dance. Names of figures were usually derived from melodies, but "Pantalon" referred to the longer trousers worn by its inventor, a French courtier named Vincent. This new quadrille was observed by Lady Jersey on a visit to Paris and introduced by eight couples selected and led by her in the Assembly Rooms at Almack's on Kings Street, St. James. Thomas Wilson's *Quadrille and Cotillon Panarama* (1822) records 50 different configurations that could be strung together in "sets of quadrilles." Records of royal court balls indicate that the quadrille became the preferred dance in Queen Victoria's court from 1837.

Carlo Blasis's *The Code of Terpsichore* (1828) defined quadrille steps (three *chassés, jette,* and *assemblé*), and gave a list of additional decorations, intended to display grace and agility in solo passages for both women and men. The waltz, polka, and schottische were introduced in the 1830s, and they caused a radical simplification in quadrille steps. Heinrich Heine, writing from Paris in 1832, refers to figures "only executed while walking, and the feet are only moved in an indifferent and dull and almost sulky manner" (Heine, 1895, p. 355). Henri Cellarius's

The Drawing-Room Dances (1847, p. 63) lamented, "Our [British] young people no longer dance the quadrille but rather walk the figures with a certain nonchalance."

Music for the Romantic quadrille was arranged to fit the dance form precisely, and it drew on popular operas, ballets, songs, and anthems of the day. Composers wrote for string quartet with flute, cornet, harp, and piano, and tempos averaged around 112 beats per minute, but varied with each figure and were separated by pauses of 20 seconds. These pauses were considered to be one of the chief attributes of the quadrille, as they provided an opportunity for respite and conversation, in contrast to the more energetic waltzes and polkas. Johann Strauss, Jr., allowed 15 to 20 minutes for the quadrille on his court dance programs.

By 1850, the five-figure Lancers quadrille (with disputed claims as to its origin around 1820) rivaled the French quadrille in popularity: its last figure, dedicated to the Royal Lancers Regiment, included a march in single and double files. Similar specialty quadrilles enjoyed brief popularity (the Saratoga, the Polo, the Double Lancers, and the Caledonians), but waltz and polka figures began to be incorporated therein. The *Parisian Varietées* quadrille (danced without side couples) of 1865 includes a waltz, a polka, a mazurka, and a tyrolienne among its figures. Due to the proliferation of so many forms, "calling" became necessary to prompt the dancers. The quadrille finally fell out of fashion following World War I, though the American square dance of today has preserved some of its basic forms.

Laura Stanfield Prichard

See also: Austro-German Dances; Schottische

Further Reading

Cellarius, Henri. 1847. *The Drawing-Room Dances*. New York: Dinsmore.

Heine, Heinrich. 1895. *The Salon*. London: William Heinemann.

Richardson, Philip. 1960. *The Social Dances of the Nineteenth Century in England*. London: Herbert Jenkins.

Quelbe

Quelbe is a form of folk music indigenous to the U.S. Virgin Islands. Both a vocal and an instrumental style, quelbe (called "fungi music" in the British Virgin Islands) is performed by scratch bands. In 2004, quelbe was named the official traditional music of the U.S. Virgin Islands. The same legislation requires that quelbe be taught in all the territory's public schools.

As with many of the music styles native to the Caribbean, quelbe evolved by combining elements from various European and African musical traditions. Quelbe originated in colonial times among the slaves who worked the economically crucial sugar plantations. Slaves throughout the Caribbean were typically forbidden from practicing their native music and dance. In consequence, slaves began to adapt the music of European colonizers, in particular imported ballroom music (such as quadrille, minuet, and jig), and military fife and drum music. *Bamboula* rhythms and *cariso* melodies, both examples of older, virtually extinct musical traditions, were added.

Quelbe music was further transformed by the sounds of the instruments used in performance. The earliest scratch bands played on homemade instruments constructed from local materials. These instruments included bamboo flutes, drums built from barrels or kegs, and homemade percussive instruments such as squash (dried gourds), steel triangles, and discarded automobile exhaust pipes. The classic quelbe instrumentation was flute, guitar, banjo, triangle, gourd, and metal pipe. Over time, modern instruments replaced the homemade. Alto saxophone was added, often in place of the flute, and the electric bass replaced the pipe.

The repertoire of quelbe bands also expanded over time, adding popular music forms such as calypso, merengue, and bolero. Despite these changes in instrumentation and repertoire, quelbe bands still retain their original rustic and percussive sound. Quelbe music often accompanies the quadrille dance, a form descending from European ballroom dances brought to the islands in colonial times by plantation owners. During the 1960s, a brief revival of quadrille dance led to renewed interest in and popularity for quelbe music.

Popular quelbe groups include Stanley and the Ten Sleepless Knights, Blinky and the Roadmasters, Joe Parris and the Hotshots, Koko and the Sunshine Band, and Jamesie and the Happy Seven. "Jamesie," James Brewster (1929–), from St. Croix, is often called the "King" of quelbe music and is the subject of the film *Jamesie: King of Scratch*. The album *Perpetuation* (2013) from Flambo Combo, the student cultural ensemble at the Bertha C. Boschulte Middle School on St. Thomas, is particularly notable for featuring authentic, rather than electronic, instruments.

Christine Gangelhoff and Cathleen LeGrand

See also: Calypso; Soca; Steelpan; Tassa Drumming

Further Reading

Bilby, Kenneth, and Daniel Neely. 2009. "The English-Speaking Caribbean: Re-embodying the Colonial Ballroom." In Peter Manuel (ed.), *Creolizing Contradance in the Caribbean*, 231–270. Philadelphia: Temple University Press.

Copemann, Dimitri L. 1991. "Quelbe: The Folk Music of the Virgin Islands." *The Voice* 2, 40–41, 50.

Francis, Dale. 2012. *The Quelbe Method: Music Fundamentals in Quelbe Ensembles*. Bloomington, IN: iUniverse.

Gangelhoff, Christine, and Cathleen LeGrand. 2011. "Art Music by Caribbean Composers: U.S. Virgin Islands." *International Journal of Bahamian Studies* 17, 53–59. http://journals.sfu.ca/cob/index.php/files/article/viewFile/131/187.

Leland, Andrea E. n.d. "The Jamesie Project: The Music of Jamesie & the All-Stars." http://www.jamesieproject.com.

"Stanley & the Ten Sleepless Nights: Performing Quelbe Music for 40 Years." 2010. *St. Croix Source*, June 9. http://stcroixsource.com/content/arts-entertainment/music/2010/06/08/stanley-ten-sleepless-knights-performing-quelbe-music-40.

R

Race Records

"Race music" and "race records" originally were terms used to classify most types of African American music. Race records were the initial examples of popular music recorded by and marketed to black Americans. Before World War II (1939–1945), African Americans enjoyed little representation on radio, and live performances were largely limited to segregated venues. As a result, race music and records served as the principal means of African American musical expression during the 1920s and 1930s. Approximately 15,000 titles were released on race records: roughly 10,000 blues, 3,250 jazz, and 1,750 gospel songs were produced during this time period. Race records constitute significant historical documents of early 20th-century African American music and remain influential with artists, audiences, and researchers. Most 20th-century white, popular music—notably jazz, swing, blues, rock and roll, and country—has its roots in race music.

"Race music" and "race records" had conflicting connotations. They were indicative of segregation in the 1920s, separated from the recordings of white musicians and records released based solely on the race of the artists. The terms also represented a growing awareness by the recording industry of African American audiences. According to William Barlow, the term "race" was not pejorative; in fact, "race was symbolic of black pride, militancy, and solidarity in the 1920s, and it was generally favored over colored or Negro by African-American city dwellers" (Barlow, 1990, p. 38). "Race records" first appeared in the *Chicago Defender*, an African American newspaper, within an advertisement in 1922. Race music and records in the 1920s were distinguished by the popularity of two important varieties of music and the preeminence of three race-record labels.

Jazz and blues became part of the American musical idiom in the 1920s, popularized in large part through recordings released on Columbia, Paramount, and OKeh. Jazz became the national—and eventually international—popular music both in practice and popularity. In the United States, the blues emerged from the South and Southwest, with both rural and urban styles. Vaudeville blues became popular in the North in the early 1920s, building upon the success of Mamie Smith's 1920 recording. Black female blues artists such as Ma Rainey, Bessie Smith, Mamie Smith, and Sippie Wallace were very successful during the early 1920s. These artists, along with Alberta Hunter, who recorded for Paramount, and Sean Martin, who recorded for OKeh, developed large followings through their recordings. Rural blues enjoyed popularity in the late 1920s, represented by artists such as Blind Lemon Jefferson, Huddie Ledbetter, and Robert P. Johnson, all of whom influenced later generations of blues artists. Other rural blues artists of note who recorded for

Paramount during this period were Charley Patton (a/k/a "The Masked Marvel") and Son House.

The stock market crash and Great Depression during the 1930s had a strongly negative impact on the commercial success and expansion of race music and records. Prior to the Depression, in 1927, sales of race records had reached $100 million; by 1933, they had dropped drastically to $6 million. To compensate for the financial losses, the record companies reduced record prices from an average of 75 cents in the 1920s to 35 cents in the 1930s. Few new songs were released, and recording came to a standstill until the mid-1930s. To keep costs at a minimum, the recording industry re-released titles and songs that had been previously unreleased. After the repeal of Prohibition in 1933, the demand for live music increased and the invention of the jukebox stimulated sales of records.

Three race-record labels dominated the production of recordings in the 1930s and reflected the impact of the Depression on the music industry: Columbia, Bluebird (RCA-Victor's entry into the race-record market), and Decca. Columbia, which had acquired OKeh in 1926, was profitable until 1938, at which time it was sold to CBS. The RCA-Victor label had emerged from RCA's purchase of Victor in 1928. Decca, a new entry into the race market, was a subsidiary of London-based Decca.

Despite the economic downturn, the 1930s were a creative period for race music, a development directly attributable to swing music. Swing music of the 1930s increased the popularity of race music. Swing, which developed out of big-band jazz ensembles in the 1920s, was exemplified by the Fletcher Henderson Band, which featured Louis Armstrong on trumpet, Coleman Hawkins on tenor saxophone, and arranger Don Redman. Other prominent swing bands of the time included Chick Webb's band (which had vocalist Ella Fitzgerald), Jimmy Lunceford's Band, Duke Ellington's Orchestra, Count Basie's Orchestra, and Cab Calloway's Orchestra.

The United States involvement in World War II reduced the production and consumption of recorded music, and race records as a separate catalog of recordings ended. The government's rationing of shellac in 1942, a primary component in the manufacturing process of records, severely limited the number of releases. Also in 1942, the American Federation of Music instituted a ban on all recording in a dispute over recording royalty payments to its members and, the studios were closed for two years. After the war and the removal of the recording ban, recording resumed, but the industry focused on mass-market sales and neglected its race catalogs. Independent labels that featured African American music emerged in the Midwest and South and grew enough to challenge the status of the major labels. These labels—namely Chess, King, and Vee Jay—did not employ the term "race records." Race music during this period expanded to include a diversity of styles, collectively known as "rhythm and blues," and although race music was still produced for and consumed by black audiences, the segregated status of the music and recordings continued to decline.

Eldonna L. May

See also: Blues; Field Hollers; Jazz

Further Reading

Barlow, William. 1990. "Cashing In: 1900–1939." In Jannette L. Dates and William Barlow (eds.), *Split Image: African Americans in the Mass Media*, 25–56. Washington, DC: Howard University Press.

Brackett, David. 2014. *The Pop, Rock and Soul Reader. Histories and Debates*, 3rd ed. New York: Oxford University Press.

Charlton, Katherine. 2013. *Rock Music Styles. A History*, 6th ed. New York: McGraw-Hill.

Foreman, Ronald Clifford, Jr. 1968. "Jazz and Race Records, 1920–1932: Their Origins and Their Significance for the Record Industry and Society." PhD diss., University of Illinois.

Southern, Eileen. 1997. *The Music of Black Americans: A History*, 5th ed. New York: W. W. Norton.

Raga

Ragas are melody types consisting of specific pitches, patterns of ascent and descent, and extramusical features. Along with *talas* (rhythmic cycles), ragas form a core component of South Asian classical music, providing the melodic foundation for composed works and improvised performances in both the Hindustani (north Indian) and Carnatic (south Indian) classical traditions.

Creation mythologies claim a divine and nonhuman origin for ragas, and some musicians maintain that ragas are timeless and unchanging, passing through generations from teachers to students. Research shows, however, that ragas have been filtered through centuries of oral transmission and have undergone considerable changes over time. One consequence is that no precise number of ragas can be determined. A traditional answer drawing from a medieval system of classification states that there are 36 ragas. Other recent surveys vary widely, placing the number of Hindustani ragas at 186 and Carnatic ragas at 2,000 (Qureshi, Powers, and Widdess, 2015). Roughly a couple of hundred ragas are in practical use today, and performers will have a working command of a considerably smaller number of these; for example, Hindustani musicians typically know 40 to 50 ragas (Qureshi, Powers, and Widdess, 2015).

The categorization and organization of ragas has been a perennial concern within Indian musical theory since the ninth century CE. Vishnu Narayan Bhatkhande (1860–1936) proposed one of the most widely known systems, arranging Hindustani ragas into ten *thats* (frameworks). Despite numerous problems accounting for and categorizing many ragas, Joep Bor believes that Bhatkhande's work will not likely be replaced by a comprehensive system "until the history of ragas has been traced through a detailed and comparative study of both historical literature and oral traditions" (Bor, 2002, 4). In the 17th century, Venkatamakhin arranged the core Carnatic ragas into a collection known as *mēḷakarta*. These 72 ragas are divided into 12 groups and are foundational collections, as other ragas can be created from this core group.

Hindustani thats are based on seven primary notes (*svaras*) that can be divided into 12 total notes. Carnatic ragas are based on a 12-note scale with 16 total divisions, emphasizing the microtones (*sruti*) between these pitches. Because each vocalist and instrumentalist selects a fundamental pitch according to that person's or instrument's range, no fixed pitch is accepted as a uniform standard in either tradition. Instead, the notes are often sung and referenced using *sargam*, a solfège system assigning syllables to the names of seven primary scale degrees: Sa, Re/Ri, Ga, Ma, Pa, Dha, and Ni (the second degree is called Re in Hindustani music and Ri in Carnatic music). These natural (*shuddah*) notes are equivalent to the Western solfège syllables do, re, mi, fa, sol, la, and ti and the pitches C–D–E–F–G–A–B. In both systems, Sa and Pa are fixed notes whose position cannot be altered, whereas Ri/Re, Ga, Ma, Dha, and Ni are movable. One key difference between northern and southern traditions is that Hindustani music uses two Ri, Ga, Dha, and Ni in two positions, whereas Carnatic music uses four, thus allowing for enharmonic equivalents.

The three main octave registers are represented with dots above or below the syllable: Ṣa (low), Sa (middle), and Ṡa (high). Hindustani conventions represent lowered (*komal*) notes in lower case (re as opposed to Re) or underlined (R̲) and *tivra* (raised) Ma with a line above the syllable (M̄). The additional microtones in Carnatic music are represented with subscript numerals (Ri$_1$, Ri$_2$, etc.).

Every raga has its own unique defining traits. Even different ragas using identical notes can be distinguished through differences in stressed notes, types of accents or ornaments, and extramusical characteristics. While ragas include the specific pitch collections a performer uses, the concept includes more than the notes itself, extending beyond Western ideas of scales. Some ragas are presented differently in ascending and descending forms. The order of ascent-descent (*āroh-avaroh*) can stress certain notes and omit or de-emphasize others. A raga typically includes several key pitches, called the *vādī* and *saṃvādī* in the Hindustani tradition and the *jīva-svara* in the Carnatic. These notes help define the raga and establish its character. They are frequently emphasized in performance, often through the use of characteristic motives called *pakaḍ* (Hindustani) or *rāga-chāya-sañcāra* (Carnatic), or through longer patterns and phrases called *chalan* (Hindustani) or *prayogas* (Carnatic). Certain notes can also be ornamented in specific ways, typically with a series of shakes or oscillations (Hindustani *andolan*, Carnatic *kampita*) and bends or slides (Hindustani *mind*, Carnatic *jāru*). These *gamaka* (ornaments) are integral parts of the raga. As a general rule, Hindustani musicians favor "pure tones and slides" and Carnatic musicians prefer "widely ornamented tones" (Kassebaum, 2000, p. 95).

Ragas also encompass a range of extramusical factors. The Sanskrit root of "raga" is *rañj*, which means "to be colored" or "to redden." This translates more practically as "to be affected, moved, charmed, or delighted." As Qureshi, Powers, and Widdess write, a raga is "that quality of an object that arouses feeling or delight," and use in early literature suggests that "it refers in a non-technical sense to the beauty of a song, its passion" (Qureshi, Powers, and Widdess, 2015). Because ragas are typically considered to have divine, rather than human, origins, they are associated with deities and allegedly exhibit mystical, therapeutic, or supernatural power over the world. The Hindustani tradition especially associates ragas with one of six particular seasons (*ṛtu*) and one of eight times of day (*pahar*), and they can also exhibit specific moods, emotions, and feelings. These extramusical associations are particularly important when they serve to differentiate two or more ragas that share some or all of their pitches or other features.

For example, sargam for the raga known as Bhupali (Hindustani; alternative spellings include Bhopali and Bhoopali) or Mohanam (Carnatic) is Sa–Re/Ri–Ga–Pa–Dha–Sa. This raga is melodically identical to the Western major pentatonic scale, rendered in Western pitches as C–D–E–G–A. Bhupali retains the same form in both ascending and descending motion, and emphasizes Ga as the *vadi* and Dha as the *samvadi*. The raga is associated with early nighttime performances (9–12 p.m.) and is characterized by a devotional or regal mood.

One raga fundamental to both traditions is called *Yaman* (Hindustani) or *Kalyāṇ* (Carnatic; alternative spelling includes *Kalyāṇī*). This raga has different ascending and descending forms. In sargam, the ascending form is Ṇi–Re/Ri–Ga–Ma–Dha–Ni–Sa and the descending form is Sa–Ni–Dha–Pa–Ma–Ga–Re/Ri–Sa. The *āroh* typically begins a half-step below the tonic and omits that note until the higher octave is reached in the ascent, while the *avaroh* presents the full collection. Yaman/Kalyāṇ stresses Ga as the vādī and Ni as the saṃvādī. The raga is intended for early nighttime performances (9–12 p.m.) and its *rasa* has been described as peaceful or tranquil. Two distinctive pakaḍs for this raga ornament Sa, skipping it on the lower ascent (moving Ṇi–Re/Ṛi–Ga) and circling it on the higher ascent (Ni–Ṛe/Ṛi–Sa). These examples both show parallelism between Hindustani and Carnatic ragas, but there can be marked differences between the two traditions. Certain ragas (such as Todi) use completely different scales in each system, and others are interpreted in very different ways in each system (e.g., the Hindustani Kafi and Carnatic Kaapi).

In addition to adhering to the raga's pitch collection and characteristic motions, performers are responsible for manifesting the raga's extramusical factors to audiences, who are likewise expected to exhibit the high levels of stylistic competence necessary to understand and appreciate a performer's interpretative choices and nuances. Outside of *jugalbandi* performances (a duet featuring two equal soloists), ragas are customarily presented by a solo artist. The performer is supported by a drone supplied by a *tanpura* or *tambura*, a four-string chordophone plucked independently behind the soloist.

Although these conventions can change based on medium (voice or instrument), tradition (North or South), genre, *gharānā*, and performer's preference, performances typically contain several distinct sections that guide the musician and shape his or her approach to presenting the raga's structure. In general terms, Hindustani ragas unfold in several distinct sections that get progressively faster and denser; in contrast, tempo changes are less common in Carnatic music. Performances in both traditions begin with a long, textless, nonmetrical exploration of the raga's distinguishing patterns and phrases (Hindustani *alap*, Carnatic *ālāpana*). After an introductory phrase establishing the tonic note in a middle register, an alap gradually expands downward to a low register before moving upward to a high one. In these sections, musicians introduce and present the raga to the audience and display how deeply they understand and can manifest the raga's distinctive qualities. In instrumental music, this section can be followed by the medium-speed *jod* (or *jor*) and faster tempo *jhala*, which introduce a steady, rhythmic pulse (although meter is still absent). Jhala sections are also sometimes heard at the end of performances on string instruments, as the player alternates a slower-moving melody on the main string with rhythmic accents and cross-rhythms on the high strings.

These precede the core of a raga performance, the vocal song (*bandish* or *chiz*) or instrumental composition (*gat*) that a performer uses as the basis for improvisations. This song or composition returns throughout the performance, serving as an aural touchstone for both performer and audience and as a basis for the performer's improvisations. Although the style of song or composition can vary depending on many factors, these elements are expected to present the core essence of its raga and provide structure and inspiration for the performer's improvisations. Meter is established in this section by the entrance of a tabla player, who performs a set accompanimental pattern in the tala (rhythmic cycle) of the composition. Soloists signal a return to the bandish or gat following the end of a series of improvisations through *tihais*, a cadential pattern that is repeated three times.

Ragas were transmitted through oral tradition, customarily in a hereditary teacher-disciple relationship (*guru-shishya parampara*). After committing to learning from an established player and demonstrating this commitment through a formal ceremony, a pupil would often move into his mentor's home, earning his way by working for his teacher in order to receive lessons, learn techniques for practice (*riyāz*), and witness his master's own playing. Such immersion within the musical tradition meant that the student was constantly surrounded by the music, which helped impart the specific compositions and performance idioms that serve as a hallmark of a certain specific school or lineage (*gharānā*). Oral traditions remain the primary way students learn ragas. Generally, a guru sings or plays for a pupil, who is expected to pick up passages by ear and repeat them until they are internalized.

This system served to safeguard the compositional and stylistic secrets that provided the family's livelihood as performers and thus their economic security. Due to many factors—including a shift away from royal patronage in courts employing many musicians to a larger, paying public audience—this tradition has given way in part to training at music schools. Additionally, technology has also played a role in both weakening and strengthening the gharānās, and the South Asian diaspora has impacted this process by spreading Indian classical music to new performers, listeners, and patrons. Despite these shifts, specific pieces and styles of developing a raga remain connected with certain gharānās.

John Hausmann

See also: Dhrupad; Khayal; Shankar, Ravi; Sitar; Tala

Further Reading

Arnold, Alison, ed. 1999. *Garland Encyclopedia of World Music; Vol. 5: South Asia: The Indian Subcontinent.* New York: Routledge.

Bor, Joep. 2002. *The Raga Guide: A Survey of 74 Hindustani Ragas.* Monmouth, UK: Wyastone Estate.

Kassebaum, Gayathri Rajapur. 2000. "Karnatak Raga." In Alison Arnold (ed.), *The Garland Encyclopedia of World Music; Vol. 5:* South Asia: The Indian Subcontinent, 89–109. New York: Taylor & Francis.

Qureshi, Regula, Harold S. Powers, and Richard Widdess. 2015. "India, §III: Theory and Practice of Classical Music." *Grove Music Online.* https://www.oxfordmusiconline.com.

Ragtime

Ragtime describes a late 19th-century American syncopated musical style, with origins in African American folk music. The name derives from an originally pejorative term, "ragged," which was used to imply an uncouth, messy style of playing. A "rag" thus came to indicate a piece of music played in this style (similar to the early use of the term "jazzed up," as in "a jazzed-up version" of an old folk song). The ragtime style is associated with dance music, and it has structural similarities with waltzes, foxtrots, and even marches of the late 19th century. Today, the style is primarily associated with piano music, although instrumental dance band tunes and songs exist in sheet music.

The style was popular from approximately 1880 to 1918; by the end of World War I, jazz took over as the dominant syncopated American style. In the 20th century, there were several ragtime revivals, most notably in the 1970s. In that decade several pianists and musicians (including Joshua Rifkin and Gunther Schuller) made new, high-fidelity recordings of the repertoire. The 1973 film *The Sting* featured an all-ragtime soundtrack and brought the music to a wide audience. A popular book by E. L. Doctorow used the style name as its title, and it was made into a film in 1981.

The ragtime piano style is characterized by an "oom-pah" bass pattern, which requires the player's left hand to repeatedly leap more than an octave for almost the entire composition. It alternates between a bass note on the beat, and chords off the beat, giving the music a jumpy, danceable feel. Above that, the right hand plays melody and harmony, often in the syncopated rhythm that gives the style its most characteristic feature. Ragtime was primarily a notated music, although elements of the rhythm were certainly used in improvisations in barrooms, minstrel shows, vaudevilles, and silent film accompaniment. The pianistic style was an important influence on later styles, such as jazz, stride piano, boogie-woogie, and the Piedmont blues guitar style.

The most notable ragtime composer was the African American Scott Joplin (1868–1917). His "Maple Leaf Rag" (1899) is one of the most recognizable melodies of the era, not to mention "The Entertainer," "Fig Leaf Rag," and "The Easy Winners." Joplin was born to a poor but musical family of railroad workers, and against all odds became a professional itinerant musician before publishing his first piano compositions. When the sheet music for his "Maple Leaf Rag" became a success, selling more than a million copies, Joplin became the most successful African American composer up to that point. He spent the rest of his career trying, largely unsuccessfully, to duplicate the earnings that he made on "Maple Leaf Rag." Joplin even wrote two operas, the second of which, *Treemonisha*, is now considered his masterpiece, despite its poorly received premiere performance in 1915.

Another notable African American composer of rags is Ernest Hogan (1865–1909). Hogan's "La Pas Ma La" of 1895 is considered to be the first published ragtime composition. Even though he himself was black, some of Hogan's ragtime songs included racial stereotypes and lyrics that are now considered extremely offensive. The cover art of this subgenre of song literature (called "coon songs" at the time) included grotesque caricatures of African Americans, influenced by blackface minstrel show performers. Hogan himself, after the phenomenal success of his song "All Coons Look Alike to Me" (1895), felt ashamed of this song for the rest of his life. Other important ragtime composers include Ben Harney (1872–1938), Joseph Lamb (a white composer, 1887–1960), May Aufderheide (1888–1972), and Tom Turpin (1871–1922).

Ragtime instrumental pieces largely follow the formal structure of the march, which was a popular contemporaneous genre, made famous by composers and their bands such as John Philip Sousa and Henry Fillmore. The typical rag is comprised of several independent, contrasting melodies ("strains") that may return later in the piece. Some of these strains may be in a different key than the opening key. Some rags include short introductions or transitions into a new strain or section.

In the 20th century, classical composers used and adapted the style in new compositions. Claude Debussy included a rag in his piano suite *Children's Corner*, Igor Stravinsky included a rag movement in his chamber work *The Soldier's Tale*, and Erik Satie included one in his ballet *Parade*. Later in the century, composers William Bolcom and William Albright composed new rags, using elements of the style but not the traditional form or tonality.

Christopher Gable

See also: Bebop; Original Dixieland Jazz Band; Swing; Virginia Minstrels

Further Reading

Abbott, Lynn, and Doug Seroff. 2007. *Ragged but Right: Black Traveling Shows, "Coon Songs," and the Dark Pathway to Blues and Jazz*. Jackson: University Press of Mississippi.

Berlin, Edward A. 1980. *Ragtime: A Musical and Cultural History*. Berkeley: University of California Press.

Berlin, Edward A. 2016. *King of Ragtime: Scott Joplin and His Era*, 2nd ed. New York: Oxford University Press.

Hasse, John Edward, ed. 1985. *Ragtime: Its History, Composers, and Music*. New York: Schirmer Books.

Rai

At once a specific Algerian musical genre and a global "pop phenomenon," *rai* (*raï*, literally "opinion") emerged from indigenous musical traditions combined with eclectic influences from the Arab world and the West. Simultaneously fostered by the youth culture of the post-independence years and censored by the government, rai would be exported across the Mediterranean to thrive in France and beyond, taking its lead from the undisputed king of the genre, superstar Cheb Khaled.

Bezza Mazouzi traces the origins of rai to early 20th-century western Algeria, as an amalgam of the folk music of Bedouin shepherds and Arab love poetry. Rai would take hold in the ethnically diverse port city of Oran (Wahran) in the 1920s, complemented by the genre of *hadharī*, performed on the traditional instruments *rabāb* (spike fiddle), *gumbrī* (lute), and the percussion instruments *tār* and *darbūka*. Along with the rest of the Arab world, North Africa experienced the flood of Egyptian pop music emanating from film giants Muhammad 'Abd al-Wahhāb, Umm Kulthūm, and Farid al-Atrāsh during the golden age of the 1930s and 1940s. Hadharī transformed into *wahrāni*, indicating its Oranaise roots; the *'ūd* would replace the gumbrī, and the *kamanja* (violin) the rabāb.

A cohort of male and female elders sang traditional rai in the 1950s. The status of "la mamie du Rai" (the mother of rai) belonged to Saadia El Ghizania, an orphaned native of Relizane who was dubbed Cheikha Remitti after singing out a memorable phrase in a bar-tent during the annual festival in Sidi Abed: "Remettez panaché madame, remettez!" She became known for fearless and outspoken improvised lyrics delivered in a raspy dialect and her flirtatious manner, accompanied by *guellal* drums and *gasba* (flute). Her 1954 song "Charrak Gattà!" ("Tear, lacerate!") advocated the loss of virginity. Nonetheless, Cheikha Remitti garnered another title—that of *hadja*—following her pilgrimage to Mecca in 1975. Her voice is heard on a 1994 recording of Sidi Mansour with Robert Fripp and Flea from Red Hot Chili Peppers. Her final album, *N'ta Goudami*, was recorded at the age of 83 in Oran despite a government ban on her songs.

"THE RAI OF THE YOUNG"

The real demarcation for the genre, however, came with what Mazouzi terms the "triumphant" stage of rai: *chāb rai*, "the rai of the young," in the 1980s (Mazouzi, 2002, p. 270). The rapid cultural dissemination of rai through cassette technology was one result of the burgeoning youth culture, coinciding with the new generation of Algerians born around the time of independence in 1962 "seeking a sharp separation from their elders" (Mazouzi, 2002, p. 271). Singers would in fact be referred to as *Cheb* or *Chaba* to emphasize the youth connection.

As a demonstration of synchronicity, it is useful to draw a parallel with another culture in flux, just prior to this time frame but illustrating an analogous dynamic. Across the Atlantic in the United States, the decade of the 1960s exploded with musical and cultural expressions of the post-World War II "baby boomers" who were then coming of age. On a commercial level, television ads in 1963 touted the "Pepsi generation," which represented a new and energetic element in American society. This theme was reinforced by a popular new TV show in 1966, *The Monkees*, with a theme song that proclaimed, "We're the young generation, / And we've got somethin' to say." Barry McGuire's 1965 hit protest song "Eve of Destruction" mirrored social unrest surrounding civil rights, voting age, and the military draft, with lyrics referring to Selma, Alabama, and the recent assassination of President John F. Kennedy. The year before, the Beatles launched the "British Invasion" with their appearance on the Ed Sullivan Show, attracting a full third of the U.S. viewing audience and mobilizing preteens and teenagers in a trans-Atlantic frenzy.

Back in Algeria, Tony Langlois depicts the youth-oriented pop-rai that prevailed in the mid-1980s, then limited to the immediate milieu and produced in Oran for the local market and sung in regional dialect. In fact, it is this specifically local focus that explains Jonathan Shannon's observation that far from enjoying a pan-Arab audience, North African music "was not appreciated widely in Syria" during the time of his fieldwork, in either its classical or popular form. Shannon points to rai which, he notes, "enjoys broad appeal in North Africa, the North African diaspora, and among World Music fans," but "is rarely appreciated in Damascus and Aleppo, where only a few . . . listened to such stars as Cheb Khaled and Cheb Mami." Shannon explains this in terms of "language barriers" (Maghrebi, or North African, colloquial Arabic as opposed to Levantine and Egyptian) and general concerns about the "distribution and consumption of cultural and commercial materials from elsewhere in the Arab world within Syria" (Shannon, 2006, p. 205). On another plane, Marc Schade-Poulsen (1999) identifies one of the chief barriers to a Western embrace of rai as preferred rhythms for dance: for Westerners—four beats per bar as followed by the feet—rather than the Algerian triplets that promoted leading with the hips.

Instrumentation for pop-rai incorporated both traditional and electric forms, generally darbūka and synthesizer. In 1985, the government reversed its position that rai was subversive to the regime and stopped suppressing its broadcast; that year saw Algeria's first Festival of Rai, organized by the Algerian Ministry of Culture. The compilation recording *Rai Rebels*, produced by Rachid Baba Ahmed in his Tlemcen studio, was released in 1988 on the Earthworks label. Prominent rai artists of the time appearing on the recording were husband-and-wife Chaba Fadela and Cheb Sahraoui, singing *"N'sel Fik"* (You are mine); Cheb Hamid, Khadidja; Chaba Zahouania, and Cheb Khaled, *"Ya Loualid"* (Oh my child); Houari Benchenet, *"Foug-e-Ramla"* (On the sand); Cheb Sahraoui, *"Deblet Gualbi"* (My heart wilts without her); Chaba Zahouania, *"Sahr Liyali"* (Going out every night); and Cheb Khaled, Sidi Boumedienne, and Houari Benchenet, *"Mal Galbi"* (What happens to my heart). "N'sel Fik" alternates lyrical testaments of love between husband and wife.

The same year as *Rai Rebels*—with its many love-oriented songs such as "N'sel Fik"—a much edgier song by Cheb Khaled served as the "anthem" of the "Black October" riots that took 500 lives. *"El Harba Wayn?"* (To flee but where?) exemplifies the politicized lyrics of the rai genre.

American influence filtered back to Algeria in the form of Don Was from Los Angeles, who had produced recordings for Bob Dylan and the Rolling Stones. Was worked with Khaled on five tracks for the artist's debut solo album *Khaled*, released in France in 1992, verifying Tony Langlois's theory regarding the "increasing stylistic difference between the Rai produced on each side of the Mediterranean" (Langlois, 1996, p. 260). In an interview with Paul Tingen, Was recalls Khaled's initial interest in "incorporating American R & B [rhythm and blues]" and "creating a different, more American sound." The blockbuster hit "Didi" resulted from this cross-cultural collaboration. Khaled's Americanization did not end with the recording itself, but extended into its marketing. Schade-Poulsen relates the efforts that would propel Khaled into the world music scene: not only unprecedented press coverage and a TV video of "Didi," but intentionally designing the record cover so that it "shows Khaled photographed from the same angle as Stevie Wonder on one of his records." Schade-Poulsen notes that "for the first time in the history of raï," the song lyrics were printed inside, in Arabic and without translation (Schade-Poulsen, 1999, p. 36).

Khaled's next recording, *N'ssi N'ssi*, was disappointing due to what was considered "bad pressing," but *Sahra*, in 1996, took even more diverse directions: Tingen lists reggae, ska, calypso, jazz, French chanson, Egyptian strings, Latin, funk, and African music as "seamlessly woven together" with Algerian rai (Tingen, 1997). The reggae tracks were created in Jamaica with Clive Hunt; Parisian producer Philippe Eidel wedded Western and Arabic music with the waltz-like rhythms of "Wahrane Wahrane," a melancholy tribute to marginalized Algerian emigrés. A bilingual version of the best-selling song "Aïcha" also appears on this album. Khaled commented on the diversity of styles in *Sahra* as a "political statement," serving to "break many barriers" and "give the world a beautiful image of Arabia" (Tingen, 1997).

BACKLASH AND FUTURE DIRECTIONS

During the years of Khaled's initial recordings while exiled in France, the reality of life in Algeria was anything but beautiful for rai musicians. In March 1991, the conservative Front Islamique du Salut (FIS; Islamic Salvation Front) campaigned against music performance during Ramadan on the basis of its so-called illicitness and immorality, leading to violence at concert venues. Elections in December 1991 favoring the FIS (whose campaign included an "anti-rai" plank) had draconian consequences for the rai community. The FIS banned the vulgarity perceived in this music, prompting an exodus of musicians to France, including Chaba Zahouania, Cheb Mami, Chaba Fadela, and Cheb Sahraoui. Two prominent casualties among those who stayed behind were rai-sentimentale vocalist Cheb Hasni, gunned down by a fundamentalist in 1994 at age 26; and Ahmed, the producer of Rai Rebels, shot to death in 1995 (despite his prior efforts to clean up rai lyrics). Cheb Hasni's post-election song "Le Consulat" presciently laments, "My country is a flower which they have devoured."

Rai-in-exile would keep the genre alive, due to the high-level talent of those who had fled Algeria coupled with Khaled's successful track record in France. Langlois notes: "No longer was Rai's authenticity the sole property of one or two cities in North Africa" (Langlois, 1996, pp. 264–265). Yet this migration would in effect de-localize the Oran experience at the core of the genre. Chaba Zahouania, who had recorded the controversial song *"Beraka"* (The shack) with Cheb Hasni, released *Formule: Rai* in France in 1995. The *Rough Guide* describes Cheb Mami's 1998 release, *Meli Meli*, as an eclectic mix fusing rai with rap, flamenco, and funk from "an older and maturer prince of rai." Chaba Fadela and Cheb Sahraoui, by now separated, recorded *Live in 2000*, with their signature song "N'sel Fik" along with the nostalgic tune "Algeria My Home." Cheb Sahraoui released his solo album *Un Homme Libre* (A free man) the same year. Khaled's oeuvre continued to develop, with the releases of *Kenza* in 1999, *Ya-Rayi* in 2004, *Liberté* in 2009, and *C'est la Vie* in 2012. Contrasting Khaled's early lyrics with his 2012 title hit indicates a new optimistic tone, devoid of controversy and almost hedonistic. The simple pulsating rhythm erases any cultural barriers to movement. Although Khaled was now in the 50-plus age range, the energetic choreography evidenced on YouTube recaptures the lively youth culture that has continually informed the genre.

The role of the Algerian government in silencing the practitioners of rai—from its refusal to provide air time to cold-bloodedly using the ultimate weapon of murder in its arsenal—cannot be underestimated. The involuntary exile of some of rai's brightest stars (many featured in the seminal recording *Rai Rebels*) introduced increasingly Western elements into the genre, expanding the sound and garnering new audiences, facilitated by the accessibility of the music in digital format. Dwight Reynolds reminds us of the topsy-turvy nature of rai itself, which makes it difficult to pin down exactly "what rai is and is not, means or does not mean." Reynolds surmises: "At best it represents an innovative new sound blending a half dozen or more traditions, at worst it sounds like rehashed sound effects left-over from Europop hits of a decade ago" (Reynolds, 1995, p. 20).

It must be remembered that these very divergent influences on rai derive, in part, from geography. JaFran Jones points out the "ethnic tapestry" of North Africa resulting from its positioning as a crossroads of civilization: encompassing pre-Islamic Punic, Greek, Roman, and Vandal cultures as well as Berber, Arab, Ottoman Turkish, Spanish Muslim, Jewish, African, Maltese, Sicilian, Spanish, and European influences. These rich cultural overlays would form the basis for hybridization of art forms throughout the region's history. Rai songs have long blended languages, both French and Arabic dialects. Instrumentation has paired traditional percussion with the synthesizer. An aesthetic and ideological kinship was drawn between reggae and rai in a 1985 *Actuel* article cited by Schade-Poulsen: "Raï is at one and the same time Algeria's punk, blues, reggae and funk. . . . Oran is the Kingston of this underground, secret, lyrical explosion. Cheb Khaled is the Bob Marley" (Schade-Poulsen, 1999, p. 29).

Hicham Chami

See also: Khaled, Cheb

Further Reading

Broughton, Simon, et al., eds. 1994. *World Music: The Rough Guide; Vol. 1: Africa, Europe and the Middle East.* London: Rough Guides.

Gross, Joan, David McMurray, and Ted Swedenburg. 1992. "Rai, Rap, and Ramadan Nights: Franco-Maghribi Cultural Identities." *Middle East Report* 178, 11–24.

Jones, L. JaFran. 2002. "North Africa: Overview." In Virginia Danielson, Dwight Reynolds, and Scott Marcus (eds.), *Garland Encyclopedia of World Music; Vol. 6: The Middle East*, 429–439. New York: Routledge.

Langlois, Tony. 1996. "The Local and Global in North African Popular Music." *Popular Music* 15, 259–273.

Mazouzi, Bezza. 2002. "Rai," trans. Beth Raps. In Virginia Danielson, Dwight Reynolds, and Scott Marcus (eds.), *Garland Encyclopedia of World Music; Vol. 6: The Middle East*, 269–272. New York: Routledge.

Noor Al-Deen, Hana. 2005. "The Evolution of Rai Music." *Journal of Black Studies* 35, 597–611.

Reynolds, Dwight. 1995. "Musics of Algeria: Selected Recordings." *Middle East Studies Association Bulletin* 29, 16–21.

Schade-Poulsen, Marc. 1999. *Men and Popular Music in Algeria: The Social Significance of Raï.* Austin: University of Texas Press.

Shannon, Jonathan Holt. 2006. *Among the Jasmine Trees: Music and Modernity in Contemporary Syria.* Middletown, CT: Wesleyan University Press.

Tingen, Paul. 1997. "Khaled: Algerian Rai Music." *Sound on Sound*, October. https://web.archive.org/web/20150606111944/http://www.soundonsound.com/sos/1997_articles/oct97/khaled.html.

Rainey, Ma (Gertrude Pridgett) (1886–1939)

Gertrude Pridgett "Ma" Rainey was known as "The Mother of the Blues." She was one of the earliest known professional female blues vocalists in the United States, and was one of the first to record her music. Rainey was known for her powerful, deep singing voice, skillful phrasing, and energetic performances as well as her style of moaning a feeling of pathos into her songs. Her lyrics often touched on previously taboo subjects such as racism and sexuality. She is credited with expanding the popularity of the blues in America and directly influencing other blues singers such as Bessie Smith.

Rainey was the second of five children born to the poor family of Thomas and Ella Allen Pridgett in Columbus, Georgia. She began singing at the First African Baptist Church where she was a member, and by her early teens had gained attention for her singing at a local talent show called "Bunch of Blackberries," which took place at the historic Springer Opera House in Columbus. In 1904, when she was around 20 years old, Rainey married vaudevillian William Rainey, whose stage name was Pa Rainey.

The duo sang and danced together in African American minstrel shows such as The Rabbit Foot Minstrels, where she was billed as "Madame Gertrude Rainey." Their travels with various performing troupes led to exposure to the blues. From 1914 through 1916, the couple toured with Tolliver's Circus and Musical Extravaganza, billed as "Rainey and Rainey, Assassinators of the Blues." Their increasing popularity coincided with that of the blues itself in America. W. C. Handy was

---

Ma Rainey and Elvis

Elvis Presley is well known for his eclectic and changing song repertoire throughout the course of his long career, though he is best known for his pioneering work in early rock and roll in the 1950s. Elvis, however, was particularly fond of covering blues and rhythm and blues songs written for black female artists. Two of his most famous recordings are "Hound Dog," originally recorded by Big Mama Thornton, and "See See Rider" written and recorded by Ma Rainey. "Hound Dog" catapulted Elvis into the stratosphere of popularity when it was released in 1956, and "See See Rider" became one of Elvis's most lasting and enduring songs and was a highlight of his "Aloha: Live from Hawaii" comeback concert in 1973. Unfortunately, Elvis gave little credit during his lifetime to either female artist, and even claimed to have never actually heard Big Mama Thornton's version of "Hound Dog," despite the similarities of both recorded versions.

Nicknamed the "Mother of the Blues," Ma Rainey recorded more than 100 songs during the peak of her popularity in the 1920s. (Donaldson Collection/Getty Images)

expanding the reach of the blues by writing and publishing his compositions, including "The Memphis Blues," as sheet music. Both white and black audiences responded to the new musical form.

The minstrel shows that the Raineys traveled with usually spent the winter months in New Orleans. There she met blues and jazz artists such as Joe "King" Oliver, Louis "Satchmo" Armstrong, and Sidney Bechet, and she sometimes performed with local musicians. Rainey perfected her stage presence, accompanying her singing with self-deprecating humor. Rainey was short, heavyset, and dark-skinned, with her mouth full of gold teeth, and she flaunted flamboyant jewelry and gowns. However, those who knew her said that her tremendous talent, sweet temperament, and maternal nature made people forget her looks. Though Rainey was only in her late twenties, she was often older than the rest of the troupe with which she and "Pa" Rainey toured; hence, she became known as "Ma" Rainey. It was said she was "like a mother" to young Bessie Smith, a fellow blues singer.

By 1917, Rainey was headlining with her own band, Madame Gertrude Rainey and Her Georgia Smart Set, having separated from Pa Rainey. Later she toured with Ma Rainey and Her Wildcats Jazz Band. Though a popular live act, she became one of the most influential blues singers of the early 20th century through the new medium of recording. Rainey made her first record in 1923, and within five years had recorded about 100 songs, including "See See Rider" (1924) and "Black Bottom" (1927). She recorded exclusively for Paramount, who billed her as "The Mother of the Blues."

During the 1920s, Rainey established a professional home base in Chicago, coinciding with what was called the Great Migration of African Americans from the South. Black audiences understood the blues and liked the way Ma Rainey sang them and she, in turn, was influenced by the blues singers and jazz musicians who migrated north, and was able to perform with a wide variety of musicians.

In 1928, Rainey was dropped by Paramount, citing changing musical tastes that veered away from her "down-home style." With smaller audiences due to the Great Depression, she retired to Columbus, Georgia, in 1933. There, she managed two theaters that she bought with her savings. On December 22, 1939, at age 53, she died of heart disease in Rome, Georgia, and was buried in Columbus.

Nancy Hendricks

See also: Armstrong, Louis; Blues; Jazz; Vaudeville

Further Reading

Davis, Angela Y. 1999. *Blues Legacies and Black Feminism: Gertrude "Ma" Rainey, Bessie Smith, and Billie Holiday.* New York: Vintage.

Harrison, Daphne Duval. 1988. *Black Pearls: Blues Queens of the 1920s.* New Brunswick, NJ: Rutgers University Press.

Lieb, Sandra R. 1983. *Mother of the Blues: A Study of Ma Rainey.* Amherst: University of Massachusetts Press.

Rakha, Alla (1919–2000)

Ustad Alla Rakha Qureshi (also known as Ustad Allarakha Khan Saheb, 1919–2000) was a prominent *tabla* drum virtuoso who popularized the solo tabla drumming style and introduced tabla drumming to the West. He was the main accompanist for *sitarist* Pandit Ravi Shankar, and together they introduced Indian classical music to the West through their world tours in the 1960s, 1970s, and first half of the 1980s. Major performances included the Woodstock festival and the Concert for Bangladesh. He performed with both North Indian Hindustani and South Indian Karnataka classical musicians, bridging the gap between the two musical worlds. Though he is best known as a virtuoso tabla drummer, he had a previous career as a film director, composing the music for 25 films and playing in many. His drumming influenced many American musicians, including rock musicians such as Mickey Hart, the drummer for The Grateful Dead.

He was born Alia Rakha Qureshi on April 29, 1919, in the village of Phagwal in the Jammu region of the Kashmir state of India. His family were Muslim members of the Dogra ethnic group, and his native language was Dogri. His father, Hashim Ali Khan, was a farmer and amateur actor who respected music but had no particular interest in it. He allowed Alla Rakha to study *dhrupad* classical singing with a local teacher. When he was 12, Rakha moved to his uncle's home in Raton Gore village in the east Punjab district of Gurudaspur. At first he started learning tabla from Ustad Jhun du Khan. When he was 16 he joined a theater company near Pathankat as an actor. There he met famous artist Ustad Lal Muhammad Khan, disciple of Ustad Quadir Bakshi (Mian Khadarbakhsh) of the Punjab Gharana (drumming style of the Punjab area) at Pathankat and started learning tabla from him. At the same time, he continued learning dhrupad (classical singing) from Pathankat's famous dhrupad artists, and he studied the vocal styles *khyal* and *thumri* with Patiala Gharana's famous artist Ustad Ashiq Ali Khan.

Once on a visit to Lahore, Rakha heard the master Ustad Quadir Bakshi Khan's tabla. He was amazed by the experience and resolved to become a permanent and devoted disciple of Ustad Quadir Bakshi, so he participated in the bracelet ceremony known as *ganda–banda shagrid* (in which a student symbolically ties himself to his teacher as a show of devotion) and began studying seriously with Bakshi. He spent a few years studying and then began working as an accompanist in Lahore.

In 1937, at age 18, Rakha moved to Bombay and secured a job as a tabla accompanist at All India Radio, where he worked until 1942. He also worked in the Bombay film music industry. His music industry name was AR Qureshi and he worked as a music director, composing, arranging, directing, and recording music for films. His first film was the 1942 *Khandaan,* followed by *Ma Baap* in 1944, *Madari* in 1950, *Sabak* in 1950, *Beiwafa* in 1952, *Saki Hatim* in 1955, *Alam Ara* in 1956, *Parveen* in 1957, *Shan-e Hatim* in 1957, and many more. He stopped composing in 1958 because, according to him, musical tastes changed at that time.

Rakha was a consummate musician in the Hindustani classical music style of North India. Tabla was primarily an instrument that accompanied solo instrumentalists or vocalists. It is technically demanding, and training takes many years of dedicated study with a *guru* master. The tabla player provides the *tala* or rhythmic cycle that is the foundation for instrumental improvisation. The tabla drums make a variety of pitches and tone colors with the combination of the two drums, which are played with the hands. All rhythmic cycles and frameworks for complex *ragas* are memorized as part of the training process. Alla Rakha said in an interview, "It takes between 10 and 20 years to memorize the *bol* (recitation of oral mnemonics) of tabla before one can learn to improvise on them . . . I was determined to be a tabla player so I ran away from home to achieve my ambition. God put me on this earth to be a tabla player."

Starting in 1958, Rakha began performing actively all over the world as an accompanist to sitarist and musical ambassador Pandit Ravi Shankar. In 1958, they performed at the Royal Festival Hall in London. Later that year, they performed in Japan. The duo returned to Japan to perform in 1960 at the UNESCO Music Conference, and in 1967 they appeared at the San Francisco and Monterey Pop Festivals. In 1969, the two performed at the world's largest concert at the Woodstock Music Festival, where many prominent musicians of the time heard Rakha's phenomenal tabla skills and were influenced by his playing in some way. In 1971, Shankar and Rakha performed at Madison Square Garden in the "Concert for Bangladesh" organized by Beatles member George Harrison to benefit the victims of the civil war in Bangladesh at that time. They played alongside the biggest names in American popular music of the era.

Rakha recorded extensively, including an album in 1968 with American jazz drummer Buddy Rich, *Rich à la Rakha*, which was an early exploration of the possibilities of fusion between drum set and tabla. The recording *Ravi Shankar in San Francisco* illustrates the perfect symmetry between Shankar and Rakha, two consummate musicians who challenged each other technically and musically with an extended *sawal-jawab* musical conversation.

In the following decades, Rakha performed all over the world. In addition to being the accompanist to Ravi Shankar for three decades, he performed with other major vocal and instrumental artists such as Ustad Bade Ghulam Ali, Pandit Nikil

Banerjee, Pandit Bhim Sen Joshi, Panna Lal Ghosh, Ustad Ali Akbar Khan, and Khan Abdul Karim Khan.

Rakha's three sons were his students, Zakir Hussain (1951–), Fazal Qureshi (1961–), and Taufiq Qureshi (1962–), all active tabla performers. Other notable students were Mary Johnson Khan, Ray Speigel, Yogesh Samsi, and Anurandha Pal, the first female tabla virtuoso from India. Zakir Hussain was a child prodigy and has continued the family business as a tabla virtuoso. Zakir is based in the United States and maintains an active schedule of international performances. Alla Rakha and Zakir Hussain performed around the world and recorded together as a father-son duo.

In 1985, Rakha created a school of tabla drumming in Bombay, the Ustad Alla Rakha Institute of Music. He visited the United States regularly and taught in San Francisco at the Ali Akbar College of Music and in Los Angeles. Rakha was married to Bavi Begum (d. 2009). They had two daughters, Razia and Khurshid Aulia; and three sons, Zakir Hussain, Fazal Qureshi, and Taufiq Qureshi. In February of 2000, Rakha died suddenly of a heart attack.

Abdur Rahman

See also: Dhrupad; Harmonium; Sitar; Tabla

Further Reading

Alla Rakha Foundation. n.d. "Alla Rakha: Biography." www.allarakhafoundation.org.

Feldman, Jeffrey. 1983. *Learning Tabla with Alla Rakha: A Manual of Drumming & Recitation*. North Hollywood, CA: Digitala.

Hunt, Ken. 2000. "India—East/West Fusion: Meetings by the River." In Simon Broughton and Mark Ellingham (eds.), *World Music Rough Guide; Vol. 2: Latin and North America, Caribbean, India, Asia & Pacific*, 107–116 (2nd ed.). London: Rough Guides.

Lavezzoli, Peter. 2007. *The Dawn of Indian Music in the West*. New York: Continuum.

Pareles, John. 2000. "Ustad Alla Rakha, Master of Hindustani Classical Music." *New York Times*, February 6. http://www.nytimes.com/2000/02/06/nyregion/ustad-alla-rakha-80-master-of-hindustani-classical-music.html.

Rancho Folclórico

Rancho Folclórico (literally, folklore group) is a formally organized group of nonprofessional Portuguese musicians, singers, and dancers that seeks to preserve and revive Portuguese regional folk music traditions through performance. As such, *ranchos folclóricos* do not constitute a singular musical tradition or style, but rather encompass the vast regional variety of folk music traditions across Portugal. Since the 1970s, these ensembles have proliferated and continue to constitute the most widespread groups for the performance of Portuguese folk music, both in Portugal and in Portuguese emigrant communities across the world.

Ranchos folclóricos are typically comprised of nonprofessional musicians, singers, and dancers, and fluctuate widely in ensemble size and composition. In general, each rancho folclórico has between two and 10 instrumentalists (though exact instruments represented vary according to region), one or two vocal soloists, a chorus (normally up to 10 members), and five to 10 pairs of dancers. As an effort toward the preservation and revival of regional music traditions, ranchos folclóricos typically perform the music of a given region in festivals and folklore celebrations across Portugal. In these performances, the rancho folclórico most often highlights characteristic musical selections from regional practice, such as music used in religious festivals, weddings, or other celebrations, while wearing the representative traditional costumes of the region. Ranchos folclóricos are often organized under the leadership of an artistic director, who organizes the group's performing repertoire, adapts stage performances of regional music, and directs the ensemble's rehearsals and performances. Men and women participate in various ways according to tradition, with some musics being exclusive to a single gender, but largely men and women perform across the various musical and dance elements of a rancho folclórico presentation. Children also often learn and perform with regional ranchos folclóricos from a young age.

Across nearly all traditions, the focal point of most rancho folclórico productions is regional songs and dances, performed with and without instrumental accompaniment. Many of the texts and melodies of the vocal music are anonymous and have been passed down through oral tradition. Textually, most song poetry deals with themes of rural life, articulated in a wide variety of terms such as life/death, love, work, or nature. The dances performed by ranchos folclóricos are most often couple and round dances, which vary widely in choreography, tempo, musical accompaniment, and traditional costume. Many regions boast unique local dance styles, such as the *corridinho*—a fast-paced dance in which couples remain embraced while executing rapid turns and virtuosic footwork—in Portugal's Algarve (southernmost) region. Other dances are more widespread, such as the *vira*, which can be found throughout Portugal, especially the north and central regions. Popularized in the Minho (northwest region) of Portugal, the vira most commonly constitutes a couple dance in which the partners move while facing each other, without touching, to a three-step, waltz-like rhythm.

Among the many instruments represented in regional rancho folclórico performances, the most common are various types of accordions, stringed instruments, and percussion. Accordions predominate in much Portuguese folk music, and among the various nonprofessional instrumentalists in a rancho folclórico, accordionists are usually the only members to receive pay for performances. Regarding stringed instruments, guitars of all shapes and sizes are utilized, including classical guitar (*viola*) and its regional varieties, as well as bass guitar (*viola baixo*) and smaller guitar types (the *cavaquinho*, for instance, which resembles a ukelele). Alongside various typical percussion instruments, such as snare drum (*caixa*) and bass drum (*bombo*), a wide variety of Portuguese idiophones are also utilized, such as frame drums (*pandeiro*), triangles (*ferrinho*), and wood scrapers (*reque reque*).

The concept of the rancho folclórico proliferated largely between the 1930s and 1950s, as a by-product of the cultural policy of the Portuguese Prime Minister—and veritable dictator—António de Oliveira Salazar (1889–1970). Salazar's regime, which was known to regulate musical and artistic performance as propagandistic maneuvers, utilized the concept of *folclore* (folklore) as a means to control national cultural expression. Several national organizations and government agencies promoted specific ranchos folclóricos and organized large-scale competitions in which the groups competed for prizes by representing their local customs and musical traditions. To participate, a town had to have an organized and functioning rancho folclórico, a requirement that caused an enormous growth in such groups across Portugal. Since the overthrow of the regime in 1974, the rancho folclórico tradition has thrown off much of its political past, and today more than 2,000 groups participate in folklore festivals and competitions each year. The rancho folclórico has also become particularly important in Portuguese American emigrant communities along the U.S. East Coast, where Portuguese cultural centers often support a local rancho folclórico.

Danielle M. Kuntz

See also: Chamarrita

Further Reading

Brucher, Katherine. 2009. "*Viva* Rhode Island, *Viva* Portugal! Performance and Tourism in Portuguese-American Bands." In Kimberly DaCosta Holton and A. Klimt (eds.), *Community, Culture, and the Makings of Identity: Portuguese-American Communities along the Eastern Seaboard*, 201–224. Dartmouth: University of Massachusetts Dartmouth Center for Portuguese Studies and Culture.

Castelo-Branco, Salwa El-Shawan. 1997. *Portugal and the World: The Encounter of Cultures in Music.* Lisbon: Don Quixote.

Castelo-Branco, Salwa El-Shawan, Cohen, Judith. 2008. "'This Drum I Play': Women and Square Frame Drums in Portugal and Spain." *Ethnomusicology Forum* 17(1), 95–124.

Holton, Kimberly DaCosta. 2005. *Performing Folklore: Ranchos Folclóricos from Lisbon to Newark.* Bloomington: Indiana University Press.

Music Traditions of Portugal [CD]. 1994. Recordings by Max Peter Baumann and Tiago de Oliveira Pinto; notes by Salwa El-Shawan Castelo-Branco. Smithsonian Folkways Recordings: Traditional Music of the World, vol. 9. SF40435.

Rap/Hip-Hop

Rap music originated in the United States, though there are flourishing rap scenes outside of the United States around the world. The genre of rap music traces its roots back to the youth movement of hip-hop culture, which originated in the South Bronx, New York, in the mid-1970s. Within the United States, there are many regional variations of rap music: East Coast rap, West Coast rap, Southern rap, and Chicano rap, to name just a few examples. Within Canada, there are also many regional variations. Some of the more notable differences are those between the Toronto-, Vancouver-, and Halifax-based musical scenes, though there are also ethnolinguistic variations, with flourishing Francophone and First Nations rap music. South America also hosts many regional variations of rap music; some of the more popular rap music scenes are within Colombia, Cuba, and Mexico.

Rap music is one element of a subculture known as hip-hop, which consists of the four elements of DJing, MCing (later to become rapping), graffiti artistry, and breakdancing. This youth culture arose in the mid-1970s in the South Bronx among predominantly African American, Puerto Rican, and Latino youth, primarily as a response to the difficult socio-economic conditions of the time. The roots of rap

> **Rapper's Delight**
>
> Upon its release in 1979, The Sugarhill Gang (Michael "Wonder Mike" Wright, Henry "Big Bank Hank" Jackson, and Guy "Master Gee" O'Brien) likely had little idea that their song "Rapper's Delight" would become one of rap/hip-hop's most celebrated and popular releases. Since its release, in addition to introducing rap/hip-hop to the American cultural mainstream audience, the song (and subsequent album) were the first rap/hip-hop album to reach platinum and double-platinum status in sales. *Rapper's Delight* reached the no. 1 position on various album charts throughout the globe and reached no. 36 on the *Billboard Top 100*—the first rap/hip-hop album to break the top 40. "Rapper's Delight" was included in National Public Radio's 100 most important American musical works of the 20th century, put on the National Recording Registry by the Library of Congress, and made *Rolling Stone* magazine's list of 500 Greatest Songs of All Time.

music and hip-hop culture can be traced to a variety of African American and Afro-diasporic cultural traditions, such as African bardic traditions, storytelling, and toast traditions; blues, soul, and funk music, especially the music of James Brown; ritualized games, such as hopscotch and double dutch; North American black churches, and in particular call-and-response forms of worship; the Black Arts Movement and the music of Gil Scott Heron; and Jamaican Sound System culture. Although hip-hop culture began as a localized youth subculture, it was through the commodification of elements of that youth culture that hip-hop became a more national and eventually global phenomenon.

Within the United States, there are different regional variations of rap music, most notably the distinctions among East Coast, West Coast, Southern, and Chicano rap styles. In 1979, The Sugarhill Gang released "Rapper's Delight" on Sugarhill Records. This was the first rap single to become a Top 40 hit. It also paved the way for the element of rapping to eventually overshadow the elements of DJing, breakdancing, and graffiti artistry. Artists such as Grandmaster Flash and the Furious Five, Marley Marl and the Juice Crew, KRS-One and Boogie Down Productions, and Run-D.M.C. were important early figures in the East Coast rap scene. These artists were followed by artists such as MC Lyte, De La Soul, A Tribe Called Quest, Queen Latifah, and Public Enemy, among others. The musical roots of East Coast rappers such as Public Enemy and the subgenre known as "message rap" are often traced back to H. Rap Brown, Amiri Baraka, The Last Poets, and Gil Scott-Heron (Cross, 1993, pp. 47–48), who were all members of the Black Arts Movement of the 1960s, one of the direct precursors of message raps (Allen, Jr., 1996, p. 161).

In the West Coast, the musical roots of "gangsta rap" may be traced back to several key recordings from 1984–1986. These recordings included artists such as Schoolly D, Toddy Tee, and Ice T. Philadelphia-born Schoolly D is credited as the first gangsta rapper (Forman, 2002, p. 170), and in 1984 he released the single "Gangster Boogie." In 1985, Toddy Tee released "Batteram," which was a rhyme about the newly unveiled batteram, an armored vehicle used in Chief of Police Daryl Gates's "war on drugs" (Cross, 1993, p. 26). In 1986, Ice-T, born Tracy Marrow, released "Doggin' tha Wax," a 12-inch single, with the B-side "Six in the Morning." This track was released at a time when the Los Angeles Police

Department (LAPD) was involved in many early-morning raids, arresting thousands of young people of color, harassing them, and then releasing roughly 90% of them without any charges (Cross, 1993, p. 24). The significance of all these tracks was that they provided detailed accounts of life in the ghetto. These early artists were followed by important artists such as N.W.A., Ice Cube, Dr. Dre, and Tupac Shakur.

Southern rap is a subgenre within the United States that emerged in New Orleans, Houston, Atlanta, Memphis, and Miami. The Geto Boys, a hip-hop group from Houston, Texas, was one of the first rap groups within this subgenre to gain mainstream popularity within the United States. The height of Southern rap's popularity was reached in the early 2000s with artists such as Outkast, Ludacris, and L'il Jon from Atlanta; Rick Ross from Miami; and Lil Wayne from New Orleans.

Chicano rap is a subgenre of rap music that embodies West Coast rap styles and Southwest Mexican American culture. The Sugarhill Gang's "Rapper's Delight," along with the 1980s films *Wildstyle, Breakin', Breakin' II,* and *Beat Street,* introduced many youth of Mexican descent in the Southwest to hip-hop culture. However, it was not until 1990 that Kid Frost released the first recorded Chicano rap album, entitled *Hispanic Causing Panic* and containing the hit song "La Raza." The mid- to late 1990s saw a flourishing of Chicano rap (McFarland, 2006, p. 944). One of the most important rap groups within the Chicano rap subgenre is Cypress Hill, who formed in the late 1980s and espouse the multi-ethnic and multiracial character of hip-hop culture in their music (McFarland, 2006, p. 950).

Within Canada, the rap music scene began to develop in the 1980s in Toronto among members of the Afro-Caribbean diaspora. However, like Canadian society, rap music in Canada is as diverse as the regions of the country. In Toronto, two of the most important early Canadian rappers were Michie Mee and Maestro Fresh Wes. Michie Mee is a Jamaican-Canadian rapper from Toronto who was the first Canadian rapper to sign an American record deal; her 1991 debut album was entitled *Jamaican Funk-Canadian Style*. Maestro Fresh Wes is a Toronto rapper who was the first Canadian rapper to have a Top 40 radio hit, with his 1989 track entitled "Let Your Backbone Slide." Though neither of these rappers gained international success, they are important figures in the early rap music scene in Canada.

One of the most significant moments in rap music in Canada was the release of the 1998 track entitled "Northern Touch" by Vancouver-based The Rascalz, in collaboration with Choclair, Checkmate, Kardinal Offishall, and Thrust. This song is credited as transforming rap music in Canada from a largely underground subculture to a potentially mainstream commercial genre. However, it was not until Kardinal Offishall's 2008 collaboration with American rapper Akon on the track "Dangerous" that a Canadian rapper had a major chart hit outside of Canada. This was followed by Drake's 2009 single "Best I Ever Had," which reached no. 2 on the Hot 100 within the United States; and Somali-Canadian rapper K'naan's single "Wavin' Flag," which was the Coca-Cola theme song of the 2010 FIFA World Cup. Drake remains the most successful Canadian rap artist outside of Canada.

Though much of early mainstream Canadian hip-hop culture first started in Toronto, there are thriving hip-hop scenes in Montreal, Halifax, and the Prairies. Since the 1980s there has been a thriving hip-hop scene in Quebec. Similar to Toronto, the earliest practitioners in Quebec were from Caribbean immigrant communities. The French Bastards are credited with the first Quebec rap release in 1989, entitled "Je M'en Souviens." However, it was Dubmatique's 1999 album release, entitled *La Force de Comprendre* (The strength to understand), that was the first Quebec rap album to receive mainstream radio play (Jones, 2011, p. 181). Dubmatique was followed by acts such as Muzion, Loco Locass, and Atach Tatuq, among others. Radio Radio, an electro hip-hop band from Nova Scotia, is also popular in Quebec. The trio raps in Chiac, a variety of Acadian French that is heavily influenced by English. Other popular East Coast rap artists from Nova Scotia include Classified and Buck 65. In the Prairies, there is a strong and growing community of First Nations rappers, such as the now-defunct War Party from Alberta; Team Rezofficial, consisting of former members from War Party; and Eekwol from Saskatchewan, who is Canada's first solo female aboriginal hip-hop artist.

There are also diverse rap music scenes within South America. Similar to the formative years within the South Bronx, hip-hop in Cuba, Colombia, Mexico, and Brazil expresses racial and ethnic experiences of discrimination, marginality, poverty, violence, and hardship (Tickner, 2008, p. 128). Similar to the spread of hip-hop culture across the United States, movies such as *Wild Style* and *Beat Street* exposed Colombian and Mexican youths to hip-hop culture. The spread of hip-hop culture was also made possible by both Colombian and Mexican immigrants (documented and otherwise) who interacted with Latino and black communities in New York and Miami (for Colombia) and Los Angeles (for Mexico) (Tickner, 2008, p. 129). Until the mid-1990s, the production and consumption of hip-hop culture in Colombia, Cuba, and Mexico remained a local phenomenon.

Athena Elafros

See also: Rap/Hip-Hop in Africa and the Middle East

Further Reading

Allen, Jr., Ernest. 1996. "Making the Strong Survive: The Contours and Contradictions of Message Rap." In William Eric Perkins (ed.), *Droppin' Science: Critical Essays on Rap Music and Hip Hop Culture*, 159–191. Philadelphia: Temple University.

Cross, Brian. 1993. *It's Not About Salary . . . Rap, Race and Resistance in Los Angeles*. New York: Verso.

Forman, Murray. 2002. *The 'Hood Comes First: Race, Space and Place in Rap and Hip Hop*. Middletown, CT: Wesleyan University Press.

Jones, Christopher M. 2011. "Hip Hop Quebec: Self and Synthesis." *Popular Music and Society* 34, 177–202.

McFarland, Pancho. 2006. "Rap Roots: Black-Brown Cultural Exchange and the Making of a Genre." *Callaloo* 29, 939–955.

Tickner, Arlene B. 2008. "Aqui en el Ghetto: Hip-Hop in Colombia, Cube and Mexico." *Latin American Politics and Society* 50, 121–146.

Rap/Hip-Hop in Africa and the Middle East

The origins of hip-hop culture date back to the early 1970s in the Bronx borough of New York City. Developed by African Americans and Latino youth, hip-hop is comprised of various artistic forms and practices, including rap, turntablism or

DJing, breakdancing, and graffiti art. Rap especially became an easy vehicle for socio-political commentary as an expression of everyday minority struggle. In the late 20th and early 21st centuries, due to growing globalization, the genre of hip-hop spread across national borders, cultures, and peoples more than ever before. Because hip-hop has adapted to many global cultures, including the Middle East and Africa, it represents an intersection of cultural exchange, as hybridized forms of hip-hop borrow from global, and specifically American, culture as well as local music traditions. Western rhythms merge with indigenous rhythms and musical structures, songs often include Western and traditional local instruments, and both English and native languages are used. Technology has increasingly made this possible, particularly the internet, which has allowed for an upsurge in musical communications across these borders through music websites, blogs, and social networking.

Hip-hop has been popular in Africa almost since its beginnings in the early 1980s, through the expansion of American influence on the continent. As African youth frequently listened to American artists, they often copied a Western hip-hop style, both in music and appearance. Since the 1980s and 1990s, though, African rap has evolved to reflect national identity and culture in conjunction with its roots in African American hip-hop culture. In Angola, for instance, rap groups such as SSP (South Side Posse) utilize an American hip-hop style combined with Portuguese and African rhythms as well as a Caribbean influence. In the case of Nigeria, a growing hip-hop scene has been overtaking Western music in popularity, backed by early artists such as Plantashun Boyz and Junior & Pretty, as well as newly emerging ones such as Ice Prince & Jesse Jagz and Nikki Laoye. Nigeria is also home to some prominent hip-hop publications, such as *Hip-Hop World Magazine* and *African Beatz*. In the Democratic Republic of Congo, hip-hop consists of a pan-African mix of styles that includes rumba, *soukous*, and *kwassa kwassa*, which can be seen from rappers ProfetZion and Kaysha. *Rap dogba* has become popular as a form of "gangsta" rap-influenced hip-hop in Côte d'Ivoire (the Ivory Coast), named after the hip-hop outfit Angelo and the Dogbas. In Zambia, rappers use *ragga*, a Zambian form of reggae, alongside Western hip-hop style combined with local languages.

Prominent hip-hop communities exist particularly in Senegal and South Africa. Dakar, Senegal, has produced many well-known artists, such as MC Solaar, Positive Black Soul, and Lory Money. Many began rapping by copying popular American artists, but since the 1980s, a national genre of dance music known as *mbalax* has become integral to Senegalese and Gambian hip-hop; mbalax combines Western hip-hop with West African pop music and often uses national languages. In Johannesburg, South Africa, *Kwaito* emerged in the 1990s as a local form of hip-hop which uses Western beats and melodies alongside local rhythms. Cape Town also developed a hip-hop community based on a musical exchange between cultures, which includes graffiti and breakdancing, as well as influences from West Indian and South African cultures.

Although many African hip-hop musicians rap in English, they are increasingly integrating indigenous languages in their rap as well. In Ghana, rappers rhyme mostly in English, but sometimes other native languages are used, such as Twi,

Ewe, Ga, or Hausa. Ugandan hip-hop typically uses Luganda, the native language of Ugandans. A rising number of Namibian artists, including the rapper Shikolo, rap in native languages such as Afrikaans, Oshiwambo, and Damara-Nama.

Many African rappers use their lyrics to reinforce social messages relevant to their local or regional surroundings. The internationally renowned Sengalese singer Youssou N'Dour has incorporated rap into some of his songs, in which he often addresses local or regional social and political issues. Senegalese rapper M'Backe Diou raps in his native language of Wolof on one of N'Dour's tracks from his 1994 album *The Guide (Wommat)*, which chronicles the dates when African countries gained independence from colonial rule: "Now that we're independent let's show it . . . we're all in this together. . . ." South African rappers have been politically and socially active since the late 1980s, with early groups such as Black Noise and Prophets of Da City, who participated in apartheid resistance, promoting political and social awareness, national youth identity, and messages of hope to the South African people.

Hip-hop also flourishes as a form of youth expression across the Middle East and North Africa, despite the struggle to gain acceptance by some government officials who deem it an immoral symbol of Western corruption. Censorship and government crackdowns have slowed the development of hip-hop in the Middle East, mostly in the area of live performance, as there are limited venues and often official permission must be gained to use them. It can be difficult to find hip-hop recordings as well, whether Western or local, but in many areas, a thriving black market, various underground scenes, and access to the internet make this possible.

Arab hip-hop became a genre popularized primarily through the work of Northern African hip-hop artists residing in France in the early 1990s. It combines styles from Western hip-hop, classical Arab singers, Algerian rai, and regional folk sources. Many Arab rappers have used their music as vehicles for political protest and have become increasingly active in times of political and social conflict. Palestinian hip-hop began to emerge in the mid-1990s, and is often focused on the ongoing Israeli-Palestinian conflict. The Arab-Israeli hip-hop group DAM was formed in 1998 by Palestinian members who also hold Israeli citizenship. Their songs use a combination of Arabic, Hebrew, and English to reach wide international audiences, and often contain messages of protest, criticizing the Israeli government for its treatment of Palestinians in Israel.

Israeli hip-hop was developed in the mid-1980s by pioneers such as Yair Nitzani and Nigel Haadmor, and gained further popularity in the 1990s, mostly due to the efforts of Quami de la Fox and DJ Liron Teeni, who collaborated to produce the first Israeli hip-hop radio show in 1996, known as *Esek Shachor* (Black business). Through this program, Shabak Samech became one of the most popular groups in Israel, encouraging hip-hop to stay in a native Hebrew tongue. Today, many Israeli rappers reference personal struggles, economic hardship, and religious themes.

In Tehran, Iran, a still-evolving hip-hop underground community emerged in the 1990s, highly influenced by Western hip-hop. Hichkas, known as the "Godfather of Persian Rap," continues to be an influential figure, producing rap in Farsi that uses both Western and Persian rhythms. Although hip-hop is generally forbidden by the Iranian government, it continues to find new ways to be heard through a growing underground that circulates various forms of media, including underground cassettes and CDs, as well as through social networking websites and YouTube. Many rappers, such as Shahin Najafi, have emigrated to the West to freely continue their art and avoid the dangers of arrest in Iran—sometimes at the risk of never being able to return. Others, including Hichkas and rapper and graffiti artist Salome, frequently tour internationally because they are unable to perform legally in Iran.

In recent years, hip-hop has become a prime site for socio-political youth expression and nationalistic messages throughout the Middle East and North Africa. Rappers have channeled their lyrics toward social and political issues, domestic struggles, and global issues of foreign policy or nations at war. In 2009, after a controversial presidential election in Iran, opposition supporters protested the outcome in what became known as the Green Movement, accusing the government of voter fraud. Many musicians, including hip-hop artists from within Iran as well as the Iranian diaspora, reacted to the election and subsequent violent protests through their music by posting messages on Twitter and videos on YouTube.

The Arab Spring, which witnessed a series of uprisings across North Africa and the Middle East beginning in late 2010, was also supported by hip-hop musicians across the region and its diaspora. Many spread their music online through Facebook, Twitter, and YouTube, to create global awareness of the socio-political situation of youth under authoritarian regimes in Tunisia, Egypt, Libya, Syria, and Yemen, addressing issues of youth unemployment, poverty, and the lack of social freedoms. In November 2010 in Tunisia, El Général's song "Rais Lebled (Mr. President)," pointed out the mounting corruption and poverty among Tunisian youth. The song quickly became an anthem of the Arab Spring revolutions as it spread across the region. El Général's efforts encouraged other musicians in neighboring regions, including the rapper Deeb in Egypt, to release further social-commentary songs as protests ensued throughout the Arab world.

Theresa Steward

See also: Iranian Classical Music; Kuti, Fela; Rap/Hip-Hop

Further Reading
Ansen, Josh, and Jennifer Needleman, dirs. *I Love Hip-Hop in Morocco.* 2008. Documentary. Rizz Productions.
Dabashi, Hamid. 2012. *The Arab Spring: The End of Postcolonialism.* London: Zed Books.
Halachmi, Anat, dir. *Channels of Rage.* 2003. Documentary. Ruth Diskin Films.
Taylor, Timothy. 1997. *Global Pop: World Music, World Markets.* New York: Routledge.
Winder, Rob. 2004. "Rival Rappers Reflect Mid-East Conflict." *BBC News,* November 26. http://news.bbc.co.uk/2/hi/middle_east/4039399.stm.

Rara

Rara is an annual Haitian festival that begins in January following Carnival and lasts until Easter. This Afro-Caribbean tradition reflects Haiti's colonial legacy, blending Euro-Christian and Afro-Haitian cultural practices, including music and

> **Rara and Vuvuzela**
>
> The Kònè horn and *vaksin* (bamboo trumpets) are musical instruments integral to Haitian rara music and festival celebration. The South African horn called a *vuvuzela* is a distant cousin to these Haitian instruments and is traditionally made from the horn of a kudu—though the origins of the instrument are within the past two decades. Whereas the Kònè horn and vaksin are celebrated in Haiti, the vuvuzela gained the ire of international audiences during the 2010 FIFA soccer World Cup held in South Africa, where the instrument was sold to stadium goers as a local musical instrument commonly found at South African soccer matches. The constant drone of the vuvuzela permeated soccer matches and television broadcasts for entire month-long World Cup, much to the chagrin of viewers, attendees, and players.

dance. Rara may be performed a capella with body percussion, or by bands. Wind instruments commonly found in this tradition include tin horns called *kònè*, and bamboo trumpets of various sizes called *vaksin*. Each vaksin tube is able to produce one pitch and its corresponding octave, which are used to create interlocking rhythmic and melodic hocketing patterns when combined en masse. Percussive rhythms may also be beaten on the sides of the bamboo instruments to create a timeline that will help keep the band in sync. Other percussive instruments in rara include struck bamboo idiophones called *banbou*, single-headed hand drums called *tambou petro*, double-headed stick-beaten drums called *kès*, and frame drums called *graj*, as well as a series of rattles and shakers.

Three contexts of rara (each with its own style of music) include religious ceremonies, stationary tributes to patrons, and marches. The most iconic rara performances process for miles across neighborhoods and draw locals out to the streets at night, many of whom will join the parade. Audiences will sing and dance along with the instrumentalists, dancers, majorettes, and actors who enact the roles of sorcerers, queens, and priests, and collect money for the musicians.

Although this tradition is explicitly religious as part of Lent, it serves an even greater social function as a venue to engage with Haiti's legacy of slavery and racial oppression. Rara is a quilted soundscape of fragmented socio-historical memory. Its music and song texts are best interpreted as coded speech acts that respond to the frustrations and desires of the lower classes from which it emerged.

Rara is one of the few times of year when the poor assemble (relatively) freely in crowds that range from a dozen to a thousand people. Through these performances, Haitians are able to reaffirm community boundaries and cultural values while advancing public discourse about the wealth disparity and elitism that are intricately tied to race and ethnicity. These performances pay homage to generations of poor and disenfranchised, to indigenous populations who were killed during colonization, to those who were displaced from the African continent by slavery, and to the majority of contemporary Haitians whose social-economic woes are largely due to that past.

These musical conversations have been excused by the social elite, in part, because of its musical coding. Similar in appearance to preceding carnival celebrations, rara *sounds* festive; its song texts may be humorous or vulgar and therefore are not interpreted by outsiders to be overtly political. For this reason, rara is a subversive art form, a type of grassroots activism, and a method of empowerment (however temporary) that permits the lower classes to take control of the streets.

Elizabeth Ozment

See also: Carnival, Music of; Caribbean Art Music

Further Reading

Avril, Gage. 1997. *A Day for the Hunter, a Day for the Prey: Popular Music and Power in Haiti.* Chicago: University of Chicago Press.

McAlister, Elizabeth. 2002. *Rara! Vodou, Power, and Performance in Haiti and Its Diaspora.* Berkeley: University of California Press.

Rebab

The *rebab* (also spelled *rabāb*, *ribāb*, *rubāb*, *rbeb*, *rabāba*) is a bowed, stringed folk instrument indigenous to many Eastern cultures. Rebab corresponds to the spike fiddle or short-necked fiddle in North African/Arab countries and Southeast Asia; in Iran and Central/South Asia, the word refers to plucked lutes. The Moroccan rbeb has two strings; itinerant Berber poet-musicians of the High-Atlas, *rwais*, play the ribāb with a short bow made from strands of beads. The Iraqi rebab has four strings and is called jōze or *jawza*. The European *rebec* was derived from the Arab rebab and Byzantine *lūrā* (lyre) in the late 10th/early 11th century. The rebab belongs to the category of instruments known as chordophones, which produce sound by the vibration of strings. The rebab is held upright on the knee or lap, or on the floor, held in place by a spike (hence "spike fiddle").

References to the instrument appear in early literature: Al-Jāhiz mentions the rebab by name in a medieval Arabic text, and *Grove* cites the description of the rebab in al-Fārābī as played "by strings drawn on other strings" (Dick et al., n.d.). The Persian scholar Ibn Sīnā (Avicenna) developed a rudimentary classification scheme for musical instruments based on their methods of generating sound in his work *Kītāb al-Shifā'* (The book of healing, ca. 1020). He included two categories for wind instruments and one for idiophones. Four categories are provided for strings: fretted or plucked; nonfretted; lyres and harps; and bowed (including the rebab). Margaret Kartomi observes that whereas Ibn Sīnā elevates the stringed instruments to a "high rating" in his scheme, a century earlier, al-Farabi had followed the practice of "giving supremacy to the human vocal instrument and to instruments producing sounds resembling it" (Kartomi, 1990, p. 128). She discusses al-Kādirī's early 17th-century classification based on "national character," which placed the Arab rabāb, Kurdish *kemandje* (fiddle), European *ifrandj* or *būk* (trumpets), and Turkish *nāy* (flute) among the stringed and wind instruments "typically used by various nationalities when at war" (Kartomi, 1990, p. 131).

Curt Sachs (inventor, with Erich Moritz von Hornbostel, of the revolutionary classification system for musical instruments bearing their names) writes of the cross-fertilization that occurred as a result of the Islamic unification of the

Near East and its subsequent cultural expansion to "an immense zone between the Malayan Archipelago and Spain" beginning in the seventh century. Among the influences on instrumentation due to this migratory phenomenon was a "loss of regional character," as the Kurdish spike fiddle "was found in the Balinese gamelan as well as in the hands of the Egyptian bard" (Sachs, 1940, p. 246).

The rebab is an essential component in Andalusi music, the genre that originated in Moorish Iberia and was diffused throughout North Africa following the Reconquista in the 15th century. Rather than duplicating the classical *takht* ensemble (*'ūd, qānūn, kamanjah, nāy, riqq,* and *darabukkah*), Habib Hassan Touma explains that the Andalusi ensemble had its "own special formations" comprised of an 'ūd, kamanjah violin, darabukkah (goblet-shaped drum), rebab, viola, and *tār* (small tambourine). *Grove*, in fact, deems the rebab the ensemble's pivotal instrument and "pre-eminent as leader of the nawbāt repertory" (Dick et al., n.d.). Philip Schuyler observes that in contemporary Morocco, the instrumental composition of the *malhūn* ensemble is identical to that performing *al-ala al-andalusiyya*—with the exception of the rebab, which is absent from malhūn. For this reason, he notes that urban Andalusian orchestras can readily incorporate the malhūn repertoire into an evening's entertainment to "lighten the mood," simply by omitting the rebab (Schuyler, 2002, p. 499).

Guillaume-André Villoteau identified two sizes of two-stringed rebab during the 1798 Napoleonic expedition to Egypt. Edward Lane, a British Orientalist, documented the use of the rebab in Cairo *kahwehs* (coffee shops or houses) during a series of visits from 1825 to 1828. In the chapter on music in his 1860 *Account*, he defines the instrument as "a curious kind of viol . . . much used by poor singers" and distinguishes between the "'rabáb el-mughannee' (or singers' viol), and the 'rabáb esh-shá'er' (or poet's viol); which differ from each other only in this, that the former has two chords, and the latter but one" (Lane, 1860, p. 75). Lane also notes that the dance of the Ghawázee was accompanied by either the *kemengeh* or the *rabáb*, along with the *tár* "in the hands of an old woman" (Lane, 1860, p. 96). A. J. Racy describes the rebab that Lane would have seen in 19th-century Egypt as an "upright fiddle that had a quadrilateral soundbox with the front side covered with skin" (Racy, 2003, p. 46). Racy reports that the *kamanjah* replaced the rebab in Egyptian folk music by the 20th century. *Grove*, however, verifies the usage of the single-stringed *rabāba al-shā'ir* as the "main instrument of the nomads and rural populations," including the Bedouin in Iraq and Jordan (Dick et al., n.d.). Scheherazade Qassim Hassan links poetry and musicianship in the Bedouin context since their music is "based on the word" and "a rabāba player is expected to be primarily a poet, capable of memorizing poetry and of improvising it instantly" (Hassan, 2002, p. 410).

Hicham Chami

See also: Iranian Classical Music; Pashto Music

Further Reading

Dick, Alastair, et al. n.d. "Rabāb." *Grove Music Online.* https://www.oxfordmusiconline.com.

Hassan, Scheherazade Qassim. 2002. "Musical Instruments in the Arab World." In Virginia Danielson, Dwight Reynolds, and Scott Marcus (eds.), *Garland Encyclopedia of World Music; Vol. 6: The Middle East,* 401–424. New York: Routledge.

Kartomi, Margaret J. 1990. *On Concepts and Classifications of Musical Instruments.* Chicago: University of Chicago Press.
Lane, Edward William. 1860. *An Account of the Manners and Customs of the Modern Egyptians.* London: John Murray.
Racy, A. J. 2003. *Making Music in the Arab World: The Culture and Artistry of Tarab.* Cambridge: Cambridge University Press.
Sachs, Curt. 1940. *The History of Musical Instruments.* New York: W. W. Norton.
Schuyler, Philip D. 2002. "Malhūn: Colloquial Song in Morocco." In Virginia Danielson, Dwight Reynolds, and Scott Marcus (eds.), *Garland Encyclopedia of World Music; Vol. 6: The Middle East,* 495–500. New York: Routledge.
Touma, Habib Hassan. 1996. *The Music of the Arabs,* trans. by Laurie Schwartz. Portland, OR: Amadeus Press.

Redzepova, Esma (1943–2016)

Esma Redzepova, better known simply as Esma, is an important figure for gypsy (Roma) vocal music in Macedonia. With her group, the Ansamble Teodosievski, Esma performed songs from the Roma tradition in folk style as well as in Western jazz and pop styles. Among Romani, she achieved an unprecedented level of excellence in music and dance performances, becoming a world-class artist and a cultural icon, recognized not only for her professional achievements but also for her tireless social engagement (Silverman, 2012).

Esma was born on August 8, 1943, to a Muslim-Gypsy family, in Skopje, today the Republic of Macedonia, but at that time a region of the former Yugoslavia. In 1956, Pece Atanasovki discovered Esma's talent, and invited her to sing for an amateur radio program, during a time in which gypsy female singing in public was considered suspicious and reprehensible. Supported by her brother, she was then introduced to Stevo Teodosievki, a non-Roma musician, who became her teacher, mentor, and later husband. Although the stigma attached to a female gypsy singing publicly was challenging, Stevo planned her career strategically, creating a new category of gypsy concert artist from the unique style of music which evolved within the Roma population over many centuries of migration.

Singing in the Romani language made available to large audiences a traditional and very often discriminated-against art of making music, singing, and dancing, which had been limited to gypsy families and weddings, and at the same time was the sign of Esma's pride in her own heritage. In the early 1960s, she was the first Roma performer to make traditional gypsy music popular for a non-Rom audience, with her hit song *"Chaje shukarije"* (Beautiful girl). Esma Redzepova composed and choreographed most of her songs, which are the musical expression of her gypsy Macedonian roots. Instruments such as violin, clarinet, and accordion provide her melodies with the typical sound environment of the Balkans and of gypsy music, but her songs integrate influences from various other regions of the world as well.

In 1969, Esma and her ensemble made a first trip to India, as Roma in Macedonia were developing a more international identity, reconnecting ties to other Roma groups around the world and recognizing their historical roots in India. Later, in 1976, Esma and her husband Stevo were crowned "Queen and King of Romani

Macedonian vocalist of Roma ethnicity Esma Redzepova performing in 2009. Redzepova was known for her distinctive voice and promotion of Romani music and culture. (Hayley Madden/Redferns)

music" during the First World Festival dedicated to Romani songs and music, which took place in Chandigarh, India. As result of the development of this Pan-Romani movement, Esma included in her repertoire Hindi songs, while continuously promoting and performing the song "*Džįelem, Džįelem*" (a song composed by Žarko Jovanović), which eventually became the Romani anthem.

At the turn of the 21st century, at the "Festival of Roma Experiences" in Moscow, Esma was proclaimed Roma Singer of the Century. Esma and the Ansambl Teodosievski have performed for many heads of state and have toured for more than four decades. Throughout her career, Esma's music was enriched by collaboration with many Roma and non-Roma musicians working in different genres. She is credited with hundreds of recordings, which contributed to her popularity far beyond the borders of Macedonia and the former Yugoslavia.

Starting in the 1960s, Esma and her husband have fostered in their own home 47 children coming from disadvantaged families, and educated them in music. She became involved in Macedonian political life during the 1990s, supporting the Roma parties, and demonstrated her social engagement by donating her time and talent to benefit several charities. She was nominated for the Nobel Peace Prize twice, in 2003 and in 2005, and received numerous awards for her humanitarian work: Esma founded the "Home of Humanity and Museum of Music Esma and Stevo Teodosievski," an institution which she later donated to the city of Skopje. She was a major contributor to advocacy and assistance programs for underprivileged Roma, and was honorary president of the Macedonian Red Cross. During her lifetime, Esma created a new niche for Roma music and dance, giving dignity to a gypsy female singer and fighting discrimination through her commitment to the Roma tradition. Esma is considered a legend among Macedonians.

Antonella Di Giulio

See also: Flamenco Music; Pimba; Romani Music

Further Reading

Marritz, Ilya. 2010. "Esma Redzepova: "Queen of the Gypsies."' *NPR Music: 50 Great Voices*, April 5. http://www.npr.org/templates/story/story.php?storyId=125580636.

Silverman, Carol. 2012. *Romani Routes: Cultural Politics and Balkan Music in Diaspora*. Oxford: Oxford University Press.

Slobin, Mark. 1996. *Retuning Culture: Musical Changes in Central and Eastern Europe*. Durham, NC: Duke University Press.

Reggae

Reggae is the national popular music of Jamaica. As with many popular music styles, its present form is influenced by several types of music that came before it. The history of reggae is almost unique in the 20th century, however, because this music relates to several important facets of Jamaican culture, including religion, colonialism, technology (or the lack of it), poverty, social justice, and violence, as well as incorporating influences from the surrounding Caribbean islands. Jamaica is often called "the loudest island in the Caribbean," and many of the performances of this music were actually created by disc jockeys and "sound system men."

Reggae's characteristic layered rhythm has fascinated musicians all over the world. The reggae beat has three general elements: (1) the "one-drop" bass drum hit on beat three of every measure; (2) the "skank" off-beat rhythm, usually played by the rhythm guitar or the piano; and (3) the "bubble," which denotes the faster syncopated 16th-note off-beats, played by the organ. Not every reggae track will have the bubble element, but the other two musical features are crucial to the sound. Many songs have a rhythmically active bass part; they may also include African percussion instruments, a brass section, and backing vocalists.

Prior to the year in which reggae was first "born" (1968), two previous styles existed that contributed to the birth of the new style: *rocksteady*, which was popular from about 1966 to 1968; and *ska*, which was a primarily instrumental style that developed in the early 1960s. Reggae developed most directly from rocksteady, which was essentially a slowed-down version of ska. Ska was a truly Jamaican dance beat that had its origins in an even earlier colonial style called mento. Mento is often confused with the Trinidad-based style of calypso, as it was often marketed under this more familiar genre name, even though much of it was actually Jamaican in origin. In fact, American singer Harry Belafonte, widely credited with bringing calypso music to an international audience in the 1950s, is of Jamaican descent, and many of his early hits are technically in the mento style.

This earliest style, mento, was a folk style rooted in party music played by Jamaicans of African descent. It dates from approximately the late 19th century and included acoustic instruments (such as guitar) and percussion. Many of the songs

> ### Military Bands and Colonialism
>
> Despite shedding their colonial tethers some decades ago, several former colonies of Britain still embrace cultural vestiges of the colonial past. This is no more evident than the collection of military bands that still exist in places such as Jamaica, Antigua, South Africa, India, and other former British colonies. For centuries, military bands in colonial Britain were used as important public displays of the British cultural and military control over the colonies, and the practice continued into the 20th century. Though these military bands often relied on local musicians as rank-and-file members, very few (if any) local musical styles were ever performed; classic British military music was the norm. In places such as Jamaica and Barbados, for example, the military bands wear a *zouave* uniform that features plumed feathers, a head wrap/turban, and billowing cassocks with knee-high pants. The uniform was a favorite of Queen Victoria, which she discovered during her world travels and demanded that her West Indian regiments adopt—a lasting vestige of colonialism still present today.

were light-hearted or sarcastic commentaries on colonial life, as Jamaica did not gain independence from the United Kingdom until 1962. The 1950s were the heyday of the mento style, although it did not become internationally popular under that name (mostly because it was marketed as "calypso").

After Jamaican independence in 1962, ska became the leading national style. This was a faster, simpler version of mento, performed as a mostly instrumental genre that included instruments such as trombone, trumpet, and electric guitar. This new (for Jamaicans) instrumentation was a direct result of listening to radio broadcasts of rhythm-and-blues music from the southern coast of the United States. The sounds of Fats Domino and Chuck Berry could be heard from radio stations in New Orleans and the Gulf Coast. Ska was thus an updated version of mento, with electric and brass instruments added to the mix. The classic "old school" Jamaican ska band was the Skatalites, made up of former swing band musicians such as trombonist Don Drummond. Significantly, many Jamaican expatriate musicians formed ska bands in London in the early 1960s.

The next style that arose on the island was rocksteady. It is essentially a slower version of ska, and it was popular only from about 1966 to 1968. Interestingly, rocksteady bands used electric bass instead of the upright acoustic bass that ska adopted. This gave the music more punch on recordings, which contributed to its success as a recorded style. The rise of rocksteady is also attributed to its renewed focus on singers; its slower tempo allowed for vocals to become primary in the mixes. One of the foremost rocksteady singers was Alton Ellis (1938–2008), whose romantic, crooning style owed much to contemporary American singers such as Jackie Wilson and Otis Redding. Ellis and his original band the Flames recorded what is considered the first rocksteady hit in 1967: "Girl I've Got a Date."

Rocksteady eventually led to reggae, which is a more political and more serious style. Reggae sometimes includes elements of rock (guitar distortion, synthesizers), and it continues to evolve in the 21st century, even though it is seen as old-fashioned in comparison to newer styles such as dancehall and dubstep. Reggae is even slower than rocksteady, and the slower tempo leaves more room for florid and active bass guitar parts, as well as improvisation and ornamentation in the lead guitar part. The song lyrics' subject matter is often related to the Rastafarian religion (a Christian-based faith originating in Jamaica).

Rastafarianism can be a mysterious subject to those who are unfamiliar with it. The religion has on occasion been seen as a cult, but it is open to anyone who believes in its tenets. Many "Rastas" believe that the Emperor of Ethiopia, Hailie Selassie (1892–1975), was the Second Coming of Jesus Christ, and they see that country as "Zion," or the Promised Land. Thus, the African diaspora all over the world who live outside of Ethiopia live in "Babylon." The ultimate goal of Rastafarians is to have all Africans return to Africa one day, and usher in a new age. Traditionally, the religion is quite patriarchal, with women not even allowed to participate in worship meetings ("groundings"). Rastafarians have also modified the English language to suit their own purposes. Because English was the language of their oppressors (the British), its modification is seen as an act of resistance and empowerment. The word "I" is used frequently, even when "me" is called for by traditional English grammar. One of the sacraments of Rastafarianism is the use of cannabis (*ganja*) for ceremonies and for groundings. Strict Rastas are vegetarian, and abstain from alcohol and tobacco. Another tradition is the "dreading" of the hair: strands of hair are allowed to grow long and are matted or braided together using various oils and waxes. This signifier traditionally set Rastas apart from non-Rastas, although dreadlocks are currently popular with professional athletes and musicians who are not necessarily of the faith.

The most famous exponent of reggae was Bob Marley (1945–1981). His adoption of Rastafarianism had a large influence on his music and served to spread the faith's ideas internationally as his fame grew. Marley was born in St. Ann's Parish in central Jamaica to a black mother (Cedella) and a white father (a plantation manager). He was raised by his mother and grandmother, and at one point during his childhood became lost in Kingston (the large Jamaican capital city) for a year. It turned out he had been living with an aunt, unbeknownst to his mother, who had assumed that he had died.

After the family moved to Kingston, Marley continued to make music with his childhood friend, Bunny Wailer (whose real name was Neville Livingston). With the addition of Peter Tosh and Beverley Kelso, they formed a vocal group that eventually called themselves the Wailers. Marley and his friends largely stayed away from the constant violence that surrounded them in Trenchtown, one of the poorest neighborhoods of Kingston. Rather, they listened to American radio broadcasts and fanatically collected rhythm and blues and early rock and roll records. The Wailers successfully combined doo-wop-style vocal harmonies with ska music, under the guidance of Kingston record label owners and producers Clement Dodd and Lee "Scratch" Perry.

The Wailers, while achieving moderate success in their home country, traveled to London to record new songs in the hopes of gaining more exposure. London was the home of many Jamaican expatriates, and the group luckily came into contact with record executive Chris Blackwell of Island Records. Blackwell, who is white, was born and raised in Jamaica during the colonial period, and always had a love for the island's musical traditions. Blackwell had previously signed Jimmy Cliff, who broadened the appeal of reggae music via the soundtrack for the film *The Harder They Come* (1972).

Once Bob Marley and the Wailers were signed to Island Records, the group recorded the album *Catch a Fire* back home in Kingston, and their reputation grew. 1973 saw the release of the *Burnin'* album, with its hit single "Get Up, Stand Up." That song has one verse sung by Wailers member Peter Tosh, who left Marley's group in 1974 over differences with Blackwell and forged his own solo career. This was followed by the Wailers' breakthrough international hit "No Woman No Cry" in 1975. Several later releases were even more successful, and Bob Marley became the first international superstar from the Third World. After surviving a politically motivated assassination attempt in 1976, he died of cancer in 1981.

Peter Tosh, after leaving the Wailers, always struggled to become as successful as his friend Marley. Tosh teamed up with Mick Jagger and Keith Richards of the Rolling Stones, and in 1978 recorded a cover of the Temptations' song "Don't Look Back." Sadly, in the middle of a resurgence of interest in his career, Tosh was murdered in a Kingston home invasion in 1987.

Bob Marley's family has continued the legacy of this scion of reggae music. In particular, his widow Rita Marley continued as a solo singer and converted the family home into the Bob Marley Museum. Of his children, son Ziggy Marley has found the most success as a recording artist, both with his band the Melody Makers and as a solo artist. His younger brother, Stephen Marley, also records and tours actively.

After Bob Marley's death, traditional reggae took a back seat to newer Jamaican styles such as dub and dancehall. A few reggae artists continued to find success in the 1980s, such as Toots & the Maytals, Aswad, and British band UB40. However, Reggae continues to be popular and adapted into new contexts in many parts of the world. Central and South African countries and England, in particular, have both developed their own reggae-influenced styles. *Ragga* is the name of an East African reggae-derived style, popular in Tanzania and Uganda. *Reggaetón* is a Puerto Rican style that arose in the 1990s, featuring mostly Spanish-language artists who rap and sing over sampled rhythms derived from reggae and other Caribbean styles.

The influence of reggae and ska on popular music can hardly be overstated. Several American and British artists incorporated reggae-derived beats into hits of the 1970s, including Paul Simon ("Mother and Child Reunion," 1972), Eric Clapton (a cover of Bob Marley's "I Shot the Sheriff," 1974), and of course seminal punk and New Wave bands such as the Police and the Clash. Later, in the 1980s, ska became fashionable in certain sectors of the New Wave market, exemplified by Madness and the English Beat. Ska developed further into ska-punk, which ironically has been associated with the skinhead movement and their espousal of racial violence.

Christopher Gable

See also: Calypso; Jazz; Marley, Bob; Mento; Reggaetón; Ska

Further Reading

Barrow, Steve, and Peter Dalton. 2004. *The Rough Guide to Reggae Music*, 3rd ed. London: Rough Guides.

Bradley, Lloyd. 2001. *This Is Reggae Music: The Story of Jamaica's Music.* New York: Grove Press.

Manuel, Peter. 1990. *Popular Musics of the Non-Western World.* New York: Oxford University Press.

White, Timothy. 2006. *Catch a Fire: The Life of Bob Marley*, rev. ed. New York: Henry Holt.

Reggaetón

Reggaetón is popular dance music that fuses Spanish-language rapping and singing, reggae/dancehall riddims hip-hop style, and Caribbean culture. With roots in Panamanian *reggae en español* and United States hip-hop of the 1980s, the genre coalesced in the dance club-based Puerto Rican underground scene of the 1990s. Reggaetón rose in popularity with hard-hitting raps about violence, crime, and poverty in Puerto Rico's barrios, combined with an iconic dance beat based on the "Dem Bow" riddim from Jamaican dancehall star Shabba Ranks's (Rexton Rawlston Fernando Gordon) hit of the same name. By the late 1990s and early 2000s, the term "reggaetón" itself emerged as the standard label among several others that referred to the same style of music, including "reggae en español," "dembow," "underground," "melaza," and others, and there has been continued debate on the spelling of "reggaetó/on" in popular media and official Spanish-language organizations.

Ignored by national radio stations in the 1990s, reggaetón spread through cassette compilations and mix tapes that were originally sold from the very apartments of the disc jockeys who produced the recordings, eventually making their way to street vendors and dance clubs. After government crackdowns, including seizures of recordings and public hearings on the obscene nature of reggaetón lyrics, videos, and the *perreo* ("doggy style") dancing style, artists and producers began making more commercial and "clean" material. By the early 2000s, reggaetón was crossing into international markets, first to the United States and Caribbean hip-hop/dance music scenes, and then eventually the corporate music and radio industries. With the release of Daddy Yankee's (Raymond Ayala) "Gasolina" in 2004 by a subsidiary of the Universal Music Group, reggaetón began a period of dominance in record sales through the late 2000s.

In the last three decades of the 20th century, musical styles from Jamaica, Panama, and New York City came together in a new Puerto Rican club scene known as "underground." As early as the 1970s, centers for reggae and dancehall production outside of Jamaica emerged in the diasporic communities of London and New York City, as well as *reggae en español* scenes in Central America and the Spanish Caribbean. Many Panamanians traced their roots to Jamaican migrant workers from the 19th and early 20th centuries, and a vibrant Afro-Panamanian reggae scene produced artists such as El Général (Edgardo Franco), whose 1988 hit "Tu Pum Pum" is considered an early example of reggaetón (Samponaro, 2009,

> **"Gasolina"—Daddy Yankee**
>
> If not for a stray bullet that lodged in his hip, Puerto Rican reggaetón pioneer Daddy Yankee (Ramón Luis Ayala Rodríguez) would likely be known for his prowess as a professional baseball player rather than his skills with a microphone. Yet, it was out of these struggles that he forged a new musical style that combined many cultural elements of the United States and Puerto Rico. Daddy Yankee's 2004 hit "Gasolina" catapulted the artist to the top of the Latin song charts and firmly established reggaetón as a lasting Latin style. The song was released first as a single and then became the feature track on Daddy Yankee's *Barrio Fino* album, in which the artist combined reggaetón's aggressive synthesized beats with a singable chorus, thus allowing the song a new degree of crossover appeal. *Barrio Fino* was the top-selling Latin album of the 2000s decade and in part because of its success, reggaetón has since shed its "Latin dance craze" status and joined salsa as a globally known Latin music style.

pp. 490–491). Reggae and dancehall tunes are often composed using the same "riddim" or beat/refrain combined with new lyrics, a process known as "versioning." Panamanian reggae en español artists, like El Général, Aldo Ranks (Aldo Vargas), and Renato (Leonardo Renato Audler), were known for versioning dancehall hits with Spanish lyrics.

Like reggae, the sound and style of New York City hip-hop spread throughout the Americas. Beginning in the 1980s, U.S. rap acts performed in Puerto Rico and recordings flowed rapidly via cassette dubs and mix tapes between Puerto Ricans in New York and those on the island. A burgeoning Spanish-language rap scene emerged, feeding off the influences of both hip-hop and reggae en español. Early Puerto Rican rapper Vico C (Luis Armando Lozada Cruz) was a pioneer in the layering of Spanish rhymes over hip-hop beats and dancehall riddims. Prolific producers like DJ Negro (Felix Rodriguez) and DJ Playero (Pedro Gerardo Torruelas) assembled dozens of cassette compilations with future reggaetón stars Daddy Yankee, Ivy Queen (Martha Ivelisse Pesante Rodríguez), Mexicano 777 (Israel Perales Ortiz), among others, and the Puerto Rican "underground" formed as a subcultural club scene of barrio youth.

The Dem Bow riddim, the de facto reggaetón beat, was originally recorded by Jamaican producer Bobby "Digital" Dixon and performed by Wycliffe "Steely" Johnson and Cleveland "Clevie" Browne for Shabba Ranks's 1991 *Dem Bow*. Early Spanish-language versions of the riddim appeared in Panamanian El Général's "Son Bow" and Nando Boom's "Ellos Benia." Over time, the *boom-ch-boom-chick* riddim has served as both a unifying musical characteristic for the genre and the main focus for reggaetón's detractors.

Dem Bow blends several rhythms that anchor other Caribbean and Latin American musical styles, some directly connected to the historical trajectory of reggaetón and others less so. The classic 3+3+2 dancehall beat is spliced between high and low drums (synthesized bass and snare drums), similar to Trinidadian *soca*. On its own, the high drum mimics the montuno-style, anticipated bass of salsa, and the syncopated interplay with a steady low drum is reminiscent of Dominican *tambora* rhythms in merengue, as well as electronic dance music. With the standardization of reggaetón's iconic beat, what started as mixing of several contemporary popular music styles has developed into a recognized autonomous musical genre, as opposed to a subgenre of a larger style, like other Spanish-language hip-hop from Mexico, Cuba, and the United States.

Originally a promotional strategy with the Puerto Rican club scene, the early focus on compilations in underground played a key role in bringing the sound of reggaetón to the mass markets. Some of the artists that appeared in early compilations were among the first to be offered recording contracts. Daddy Yankee's *Barrio Fino*, released on his own El Cartel Records label and distributed by Universal Music Group, would become the first reggaetón album to debut at no. 1 on the *Billboard* Top Latin Albums chart on July 1, 2004, thus beginning an era of popularity for reggaetón that lasted through the late 2000s. Artists such as Tego Calderón (Tegui Calderón Rosario), Don Omar (William Landrón Rivera), and Luny Tunes (Francisco Saldaña and Víctor Cabrera) soon joined Daddy Yankee with major record deals of their own. To satisfy the new market trend, many radio stations switched to a "Hurban" (Hispanic-urban) format: a mix of reggaetón, Spanish-language hip-hop, and Latin pop. United States pop acts such as R. Kelly, Sean Paul, and Britney Spears hired reggaetón production teams such as Luny Tunes, not only to create reggaetón remixes of already popular singles, but also to pen original tunes. Although reggaetón has built its reputation as one of the first Latin popular genres to find lasting record sales in the English-speaking markets, controversy still exists surrounding portrayals of sexual violence and exploitation of women.

Jack W. Forbes

See also: Calypso; Reggae; Salsa; Soca; Zouk

Further Reading

Fairley, Jan. 2006. "Dancing Back to Front: Regeton, Sexuality, Gender, and Transnationalism in Cuba." *Popular Music* 25(3), 471–488.

Marshall, Wayne. 2010. "The Rise and Fall of Reggaeton: From Daddy Yankee to Tego Calderón and Beyond." In Jiménez Román, Miriam and Juan Flores (eds.), *The Afro-Latin@ Reader: History and Culture in the United States*, 396–403. Durham, NC: Duke University Press.

Rivera, Raquel Z. 2002. "Hip-Hop and New York Puerto Ricans." In *Latino/a Popular Culture*, 127–143. New York: New York University Press.

Rivera, Raquel Z., Wayne Marshall, and Deborah Pacini Hernandez, eds. 2009. *Reggaeton*. Durham, NC: Duke University Press.

Samponaro, Philip. 2009. "*Oye mi canto* (Listen to My Song): The History and Politics of Reggaetón." *Popular Music and Society* 32(4), 489–506.

Rímur

Rímur (literally, rhyme) is a type of epic poem similar to other Nordic "skaldic" poetry. These long, rhymed texts are derived from Nordic mythological sagas, with hundreds of rímur still in existence today. The earliest stanzas known to exist date from the early 14th century CE, and it is estimated that the genre of poetry became popular 100 years after. Rímur is a variation of Norse heroic ballad-style poetry, which dates back to the Viking era in Iceland, between the ninth and 11th centuries CE. Rímur remained the most popular Icelandic literary form until the 19th century CE. As of late, rímur has seen a resurgence of interest in Icelandic popular culture, and has become emblematic of Icelandic medieval heritage.

The earliest rímur known today, *Óláfs Ríma Haraldssonar*, is found in the *Flateyjarbók* manuscript (the *Flatey Book*), dating from approximately 1390 CE. It appears under the heading *Óláfs ríma Haraldssonar er Einar Gilsson kvað* (translating to "*ríma* about Ólafur Haraldsson [in reference to Saint Óláf], composed by Einar Gilsson") (Ólason, 2006, p. 56). Ólason argues that, though this *ríma* appears 100 years earlier than any other extant source, it displays a fully developed style and literary command, thus suggesting that the rímur genre must have existed prior to the 14th century. Because no rímur until the 16th century had authors' names, placing them into the chronology of Icelandic literature is a daunting and sometimes impossible task (Ólason, 2006, p. 56).

Little is known of what melody in rímur is necessary to preserve, as the performance practice of rímur is rather limited in melodic scope. This may be due to their recitational structure, prosodic nature, and content length. Rímur were recited by the performer (*kvæðamaður*) during shepherding, fishing, and for gatherings of family and friends, who would come together to listen to the epic poems recited by the chanter. Performers use a guttural voice, akin to a throat-singing technique, and sing at a slow tempo (Hopkins, 2000, p. 507).

The most notable sagas that Icelanders set to rímur are the prose romances known as the Knights' Sagas (*riddarasögur*). Syllable lengths and couplings vary, although rhyme schemes are limited to four stanzas, typically in ABAB or AABB form. The *ferskeytt* meter features four plus three syllables in the rhyme scheme ABAB. The *Stafhent* meter is based on a four plus four syllable phrase, with an AABB rhyme scheme. Other stanza forms exist, but they are most common for poetry originating outside of Iceland (Ólason, 2006, p. 56).

An example of the *ferskeytt ríma* is the first verse of *Óláfs ríma Haraldssonnar*. The poem, 65 ferskeytt verses in length, features the ABAB rhyme scheme (*fríðr* and *blíðr*; *ráða* and *náða*, respectively). It also features the cumulative seven-syllable phrase structure, divided into four and three with three stressed syllables (bold emphasis to show stress, italics to show the separation): "**Ól**afr **kóngur örr** og fríðr, **átti** *Noregi* að ráða; **gramr** var æ við **bra**gna blíðr, **borinn til sigrs** og náða."

Rímur also begin with non-narrative stanzas known as *mansöngr* (literally, love song). Read as occasional poetry, each mansöngr is attached to the beginning of each *canto*, or section, of a given rímur. The canto functions much like a chapter in a book. A late 17th-century rímur may have 30 or so cantos in its construction, with eight stanzas per canto; the addition of mansöngr may add an additional one to 12 stanzas. Jorgensen specifies that this number applies to the bulk of mansöngr, although this can range as much as 80 stanzas in some of the more elaborate rímur (Jorgensen, 1993, p. 536). Content of the mansöngr would focus on internal emotions or feelings. The mansöngr, unlike the rímur, are freely composed rather than paraphrased material from skaldic prose. Thus, authors of mansöngr are free to explore the limits and varieties of Icelandic prose.

Today, 78 intact rímur have survived that are pre-1600 CE; 148 from the 17th century, and 248 from the 18th century. Because the purpose of rímur in earlier times was to keep spirits up during long, dark winters; or to entertain, before the industrialization of the 20th century, its role within Icelandic society has significantly diminished. Several folklorists are attempting to change the fate of rímur, most notably an Icelandic musician, Steindór Andersen. Born in 1954, Andersen has collaborated with renowned Icelandic band Sigur Rós, which led to his own international fame.

John Forrestal

See also: Icelandic Ballads; Medieval Secular Song; Norwegian Folk Music

Further Reading

Harris, Joseph, ed. 1991. *The Ballad and Oral Literature.* Cambridge, MA: Harvard University Press.

Helgason, Jón. 1986. *Kvæðabók.* Reykjavík: Mál og Menning.

Magnason, Andri Snær. 2012. "Voices—Old Recordings of Icelandic Folkmusic." Blog. *Andri Magnason.* http://www.andrimagnason.com/cds-and-other-projects/voicesraddir-cd-with-old-recordings-of-icelandic-folkmusic/.

McTurk, Rory, ed. 2005. *A Companion to Old Norse-Icelandic Literature and Culture.* Malden, MA: Blackwell.

Ólason, Vésteinn. 1982. *The Traditional Ballads of Iceland: Historical Studies.* Reykjavík: Stofun Árna Magnússonar.

Ólason, Vésteinn. 2006. "Old Icelandic Poetry." In Daisy Neijmann (ed.), *A History of Icelandic Literature.* Lincoln: University of Nebraska Press.

Valgardson, William D. 2013. "Rímur: Your Literary Heritage." Blog post, June 8. http://wdvalgardsonkaffihus.com/blog/2013/06/08/rimur-your-literary-heritage/.

Riq

The *riq* (also spelled *riqq*) is a type of tambourine popular in Egypt, Iraq, the Levant, and Sudan. It is derived from the *duff* (or *daff*), with geographically widespread usage and pre-Islamic origins; and the *tār*, which Poché assesses as a "less virtuosic instrument" than the riq despite the fact that it "lends a glitter to the orchestration of music of the Andalusian nawbāt" (Poché, n.d.). A. J. Racy describes the riq as a "small, but relatively heavy tambourine with five sets of brass cymbals and thin fish skin (more recently plastic)." Its function in an ensemble is to "produce a variety of timbral effects that are used to form the beat patterns, namely īqā'āt, or 'metric modes'" (Racy, 2003, p. 78).

Racy explains the timbral-acoustical aspect of the riq and its contribution to the classical *takht* ensemble as resulting from the combination of "membranophonic skin sounds" with the "idiophonic vibrations of the cymbals," making the riq the "tarab percussion instrument par excellence" (Racy, 2003, p. 78). Although Racy acknowledges the inclusion of the *tablah* (*darabukkah*) in current practice, he incisively comments that the "loud, high-strung modern tablah has created a new sound aesthetic that shifted riqq playing somewhat from the artful subtleties of the takht-based style toward a more percussive approach that gives more prominence

> **Riq and Frame Drum**
>
> The Arabic *riq* has an ancient history in the Middle East and north African region, and the instrument is likely a predecessor for the tambourine, the riq-like frame drum with jingles instrument common in the West—which is known as *tof* in Egypt and was played by Hebrews there during ancient times. Despite the ubiquitous nature of the tambourine in nearly all forms of Western art and popular music, the riq and other forms of frame drums have only recently begun to gain in popularity. Percussionist Glen Velez is largely responsible for the instrument's newfound popularity. Velez is a well-known New York based musician who has worked tirelessly to integrate frame drums of various cultures into musical projects in the West, including work with Steve Reich and Pat Metheny. In addition to the riq, Velez has studied the traditional Irish *bodhrán*, Brazilian *pandeiro*, and North African *bendir*, and developed his own playing techniques and methodology for integrating these instruments into music of various cultures.

to the brass cymbals" (Racy, 2003, p. 78). As a result, ensembles are forced to add instrumental variety and/or critical mass, altering the layered timbral balance of the takht. Beyond the timbral component, the riq is essential in maintaining rhythmic integrity. In fact, the musician who plays the riq is not considered a "percussionist" only, but is called *dhābit al-īqā'*, "officer of the rhythm."

British Orientalist Edward Lane describes the mid–19th-century riq in his *Account* but refers to it as a *tár*, measuring 11 inches in diameter (making this earlier version slightly larger than the 20–25 cm diameter normally found today). The engraved illustration shows five sets of cymbals, as used today. Lane indicates the method of performance as holding the instrument in either hand while beating it with both hands—the hand holding the tár "striking only near the hoop, produc[ing] higher sounds than the other hand, which strikes in the center" (Lane, 1860, p. 77). In percussive parlance, the higher sounds are termed *tak* and the lower sounds *dum*.

Hicham Chami

See also: Tar

Further Reading

Hassan, Scheherazade Qassim. 2002. "Musical Instruments in the Arab World." In Virginia Danielson, Dwight Reynolds, and Scott Marcus (eds.), *Garland Encyclopedia of World Music; Vol. 6: The Middle East*, 401–424. New York: Routledge.

Lane, Edward William. 1860. *An Account of the Manners and Customs of the Modern Egyptians*. London: John Murray.

Poché, Christian. n.d. "Riqq"; "Tār." *Grove Music Online. Oxford Music Online.* Oxford University Press.

Racy, A. J. 2003. *Making Music in the Arab World: The Culture and Artistry of Tarab*. Cambridge: Cambridge University Press.

Rock and Roll

Since its inception in the late 1940s, rock and roll has profoundly transformed American music and is now one of the most popular musical forms in the world.

Rock not only altered American culture but also continues to spawn new musical forms—heavy metal, funk, punk, rap, techno, and so on. This continual evolution is what has kept rock and roll relevant through more than five decades.

INFLUENCE OF AFRICAN AMERICAN PERFORMERS

Modern rock enthusiasts owe a great debt to African American performers of the 19th and 20th centuries, especially such blues musicians and singers as Charley Patton and Robert Johnson, whose music directly shaped the growth of rock and roll in the late 1940s. Recordings of blues songs sold well among African Americans in the 1920s and 1930s, and U.S. record companies marketed them under the category of "race" records. Many writers suggest that rock stemmed from a combination of African American blues, slave musical styles, black spirituals, and the rhythm and blues (R & B) of the 1940s. Black R & B songs from the late 1940s included Wild Bill Moore's "We're Gonna Rock, We're Gonna Roll" (1947) and Wynonie Harris's "Good Rockin' Tonight" (1948). Most experts agree that the "rock and roll" references in these early songs referred to sex.

The popularity of rock and roll grew quickly following the Great Migration of African Americans during the 1940s. Trapped in the agricultural South since the end of slavery, the majority of African Americans lived within the sharecropper system and under Jim Crow laws that mired them in poverty and segregation. Freedom on their minds, millions of African Americans migrated to Northern cities and brought with them the Delta blues, the root of rock music. Meanwhile, aspects of other musical genres were incorporated with some blues and rhythm and blues (R & B) music. For example, Bill Haley, who started as a country musician, covered R & B songs such as "Shake, Rattle, and Roll" with a higher tempo. Haley had discovered jazz and blues when he toured St. Louis and New Orleans.

Seeing a potential profit, white record companies set out to popularize African American music in the early 1950s. Sam Phillips established his Sun Records in Memphis, Tennessee, and gave anyone the opportunity to produce a record for $4. Disc jockeys heard the music and began to popularize it. Ironically, racist white record companies and radio stations at first called black rhythm and blues "rock and roll" in order to hide its connection to African Americans.

Some whites were fearful of what they perceived as the music's ability to bring white women and black men together in places that played it. Others argued that the National Association for the Advancement of Colored People used the genre to convince white teenagers to support black social and political equality with whites. The challenge, then, became for the record labels to make this so-called race music palatable to white audiences, preferably by finding white singers to perform it. In the early 1950s, major record labels issued recordings of white singers performing renditions of songs previously released on independent labels by African American singers, which often featured tamer lyrics than those heard in the original performances. In Elvis Presley, Phillips found what he had been looking for: "a white man with the Negro sound and the Negro feel."

THE BABY BOOM: GROWTH OF CONSUMER CULTURE

The growth of the younger portion of the American population due to the "baby boom" (the era of enormous population increase following World War II), created a gigantic segment of young people hungry for entertainment. The upward drive of the American economy led to the growth of consumer culture and new developments in technology, both of which helped facilitate the rise of rock and roll during the postwar period.

Presley arrived on the scene just at the right time with a sound that was unique to most white teenagers: a mix of Southern blues, country, and gospel. He was the first rock-and-roll star, and parents hated him. He swiveled his hips in a sexually provocative way, danced with the microphone, and combed his hair in a pompadour. Presley became a national star in 1956 after releasing the no. 1 singles "Heartbreak Hotel," "Hound Dog" (a remake of Big Mama Thornton's blues song), "Don't Be Cruel," and "Love Me Tender" that year. Popular music was forever changed.

Following in Presley's footsteps were the so-called "bubblegum" rockers of the late 1950s and early 1960s, a slew of groups made up of young men and women who sang songs relevant to the large teenage population. Many of the songs were crafted by such songwriters as Carole King, Gerry Goffin, and Don Kirshner, all of whom worked out of the Brill Building in New York City. African American performers appeared on the charts in singing groups such as The Supremes. Many African Americans were not seen during the early days of rock, however. Such gifted rock and rollers as Chuck Berry and Little Richard, though heard increasingly on the radio, were literally invisible to the American public. With the growth of television and the success of films that featured rock and roll, however, popular African American musicians began to be seen as well as heard.

Meanwhile, the reckless spirit of rock and roll strained at the seams of teenagers' poodle skirts and penny loafers. It was just a matter of time before rock was again redefined, this time not by Americans but by British acts who worshipped such early American blues and rock artists as Berry, Carl Perkins, and Buddy Holly.

THE BEATLES

With the arrival of the Beatles on American shores in 1964, rock and roll became a mass movement for the first time. More than 30 years after their breakup, the Beatles remain the most influential group in rock music. Their first successful song in the United States, "I Want to Hold Your Hand" (1964), was followed by increasingly experimental albums, symbolizing rock's constant need for reinvention. The success of the Beatles launched a "British invasion" of North America, and such white British rock bands as the Rolling Stones introduced a new and more boisterous brand of blues-based rock and roll to America. Ironically, these British musicians, particularly Rolling Stones guitarist Keith Richards and Eric Clapton, helped popularize the work of American blues artists who went largely unrecognized in their own country.

As British rock acts influenced Americans and vice versa, rock and roll had its golden era in the 1960s. American groups such as the Beach Boys pushed recording technology to new limits, and folk singers such as Bob Dylan experimented with rock and roll for the first time, bringing new depth to rock lyrics. The folk rock invented by such groups as the Byrds was embraced by the counterculture movement which was developing in reaction to the civil rights movement and U.S. involvement in Vietnam. The counterculture stamped the rock music explosion with its most salient features: a rejection of traditionalism, complacency, and social mores, along with an acceptance of sexual freedom and drug experimentation. Rock and roll became a badge of identity for young Americans.

WOODSTOCK

That combination of music, sexual freedom, and drug use was nowhere more evident than at the Woodstock Music Festival in the summer of 1969. There, the rock music of the 1960s reached its peak, with stellar performances by such artists as Joan Baez, Sly and the Family Stone, Jefferson Airplane, the Who, the Grateful Dead, Santana, Jimi Hendrix, and Janis Joplin. However, after the height of Woodstock, rock experienced profound losses. A free Rolling Stones concert near San Francisco in December 1969 led to violence that ended in one homicide. The Beatles broke up in April 1970, and before the end of the year, Joplin, Hendrix, and Jim Morrison (leader of the Doors) had all suffered alcohol- or drug-related deaths. Young people who had been defined by rock and roll were disillusioned by those events and the assassinations of Martin Luther King Jr. and Robert F. Kennedy two years earlier. Many wondered if rock had a future.

THE 1970s to 1990s

Rock and roll trudged on, however, albeit less inspired than in its early days. The music became harder and more glamorous in the 1970s and again was heavily influenced by British acts. Led Zeppelin and the Who were two of the most popular groups of the decade. They laid the foundation for the invention of punk music by the British group the Sex Pistols, who felt rock and roll had become complacent and irrelevant to the common man and said so on their 1977 release *Never Mind the Bollocks*. Women became more popular performers, a result of the feminist movement. Songs for the first time reflected the political realities of liberated women in American culture, particularly Helen Reddy's "I Am Woman" (1972). Also, there began to be some overlap between American country music and rock. The Eagles created a style of country rock filled with haunting, disillusioned lyrics. Other groups, such as Rush and Yes, tried to steer rock in more artistic directions, a genre known as progressive rock.

One of the most important American rock acts to begin recording in the 1970s was New Jersey's Bruce Springsteen, who released his first album, *Greetings from Asbury Park, N.J.*, in 1973. Heavily influenced by Dylan, Springsteen combined plain-spoken songwriting and working-class ethics to create a style of rock reflective of everyday American life. His songs resonated with people in cities and rural communities, making him a superstar in the 1980s. Springsteen reached his highest chart success with 1984's *Born in the U.S.A.*, the title song of which told the story of a Vietnam War veteran who had reached a dead end. Many, including President Ronald Reagan, nevertheless took the song for a patriotic anthem. Springsteen's bare-bones rock songs shared the charts in the 1980s with songs by long-haired groups like Guns 'N' Roses, who took rock and roll to its furthest extremes.

Those extremes were now for the eye as well as the ear, as MTV had begun broadcasting on televisions across the nation in 1981. At this point the success of many rock stars depended on the production of popular videos to accompany their songs. Pop star Michael Jackson revolutionized music video with 1983's "Thriller," produced like a mini-movie. However, the excesses of glamour rock and the extreme popularity of such pop acts as Jackson and Madonna led many critics to predict another reinvention of rock and roll. That reinvention finally came from two unlikely places: the American ghetto and Seattle, Washington.

Employing highly politicized lyrics that called into question the racist treatment of African Americans in inner cities, rap music drew controversy for its anger toward the white establishment. Performer Ice-T in the early 1990s called on America's youth to resist police powers in his controversial song "Cop Killer" (1992). It seemed, however, that rock and rap would forever exist in their own orbits, with rock largely the realm of white performers and rap the realm of black performers. The first crossover came in 1987, when rock group Aerosmith and hip-hop music group Run-D.M.C. together released a cover version of Aerosmith's 1977 hit "Walk This Way." Then heavy metal group Anthrax joined with rap group Public Enemy in 1991 for a recording and video of "Bring the Noise." That rock and rap hybrid found intense popularity in the late 1990s with the rise of such groups as the Beastie Boys and Rage against the Machine.

With a few exceptions (among them Springsteen, U2, and the Police), the 1970s and 1980s were a rock wasteland. Much of the best rock and roll was produced not by major record labels for popular radio and MTV, but by small independent labels for college and independent radio stations. Some of those acts were eventually recognized by the mainstream, like R.E.M., but most toiled away in clubs for a small handful of fans. One hotbed for such groups was Seattle, Washington, the home of the independent Sub Pop record label.

In 1987, Sub Pop released the album *Bleach* by Nirvana, which began a major-label bidding war for the band. The release of *Nevermind* in 1991 brought the fury and disillusionment of the Sex Pistols' punk rock bursting into the mainstream, and the members of Nirvana became megastars. Following fast behind were such other Seattle bands as Pearl Jam and Soundgarden, as well as college radio favorites such as the Smashing Pumpkins. To many, rock and roll was new again. The suicide of Nirvana singer Kurt Cobain in 1994 was just another tragedy for rock to rebound from.

21ST CENTURY

The beginning of the 21st century saw little change in the rock landscape. Rock, rap, and pop groups still sat atop the music charts, though more rap albums are now sold in the United States than rock albums. Country artists following the lead of superstar Garth Brooks had incorporated enough elements of rock into their music that by 2000, there was little distinction between the two. It is that ability to morph into almost any type of American music—jazz, folk, country, and rap—that has kept rock and roll almost constantly new for more than five decades.

During those decades, rock moved from the white country blues of Presley to the love songs of the Beatles, the anger of punk, the rhyming of rap, the thumping beats of techno, and everything in between. It somehow managed to retain its relevance and transformed many aspects of American society. Rock and roll has inspired new breakthroughs in American film, television, publishing, and sound technology and is still a multimillion-dollar industry. Though sometimes controversial for its cutting-edge critiques of American culture, rock and roll is one of the most diverse and democratic forms of music in the world.

Jason Newman

See also: Beatles, The; Dylan, Bob; Presley, Elvis

Further Reading

Altschuler, Glenn C. 2003. *All Shook Up: How Rock 'n Roll Changed America.* New York: Oxford University Press.

Bertrand, Michael T. 2000. *Race, Rock, and Elvis.* Urbana: University of Illinois Press.

Szatmary, David P. 2007. *Rockin' in Time: A Social History of Rock-and-Roll.* Upper Saddle River, NJ: Pearson/Prentice Hall.

Ward, Brian. 1998. *Just My Soul Responding: Rhythm and Blues, Black Consciousness, and Race Relations.* Berkeley: University of California Press.

Rodgers, Jimmie (1897–1933)

Along with the Carter Family, the most famous of the landmark Bristol Sessions discoveries, Mississippi native Jimmie Rodgers, established the commercial sound of American country music in the 1920s. He gained fame as "America's Blue Yodeler" and has been called the "Father of Country Music."

Rodgers was born James Charles Rodgers on September 8, 1897, in Pine Springs, Mississippi. Because Rodgers's father, Aaron, worked as a foreman on the Mobile & Ohio Railroad, and his mother, Eliza, died in 1904, Jimmie knew little stability during his youth, living mainly with relatives. The most influential of these was his maternal aunt Dora, a former music teacher who introduced him to a variety of musical styles and tried to curb his smoking and truancy. He sang and played stringed instruments with customers of the pool halls and barbershops of Meridan, Mississippi, and won a talent contest at age 12 singing "Steamboat Bill" and "Bill Bailey, Won't You Please Come Home." He performed with traveling tent and medicine shows in his teens, but was usually retrieved by his father after a few weeks. He also worked a variety of railroad jobs from Mississippi to the Pacific Coast. This put him in frequent contact with black musicians, from whom he learned to play blues music.

After a failed two-year marriage to Sandra Kelly, which resulted in his first daughter Kathryn, Rodgers married Carrie Williamson in 1920. Carrie gave birth to two daughters (one died in infancy while Rodgers was traveling); she remained with him for the rest of his short life and promoted his musical legacy after his death. In the early 1920s he met Goebel Reeves (1899–1959), "the Texas Drifter," who claimed to have taught Rodgers to yodel; however, Reeves was a master of the speed and triple yodel, whereas Rodgers made his name with a slower, blues-influenced style.

Rodgers was diagnosed with tuberculosis in 1924, but refused hospitalization. He formed a trio with his sister-in-law Elsie McWilliams (piano) and Slim Rozell (fiddle) to play local dances and blackface minstrel shows. McWilliams and Rodgers continued to collaborate on new songs throughout the 1920s. As his disease worsened, he preferred southern climates (working on the Florida East Coast Line and in Tucson, Arizona, on the Southern Pacific), but found railroad work increasingly difficult.

In early 1927, he relocated (alone) from Mississippi to Asheville, North Carolina, where he attempted to launch a full-time music career. On April 18, 1927, he first performed on radio (WWNC), and the next week he traveled across the North Carolina border to perform at a Rotary Club event in Johnson City, Tennessee. Also at that event was a string trio called the Ten[n]eva Ramblers, made up of brothers Claude and Jack Grant and Jack Pierce. They discussed their respective ambitions, and Rodgers persuaded the others to join him in Asheville as his (free) backup band.

The initial performance of this new combo, the Jimmie Rodgers Entertainers, was on May 30, 1927, over WWNC, but the group soon left Asheville to play regularly at the affluent North Fork Mountain Resort. In July 1927, Rodgers traveled with Jack Pierce to Bristol, Tennessee, where Pierce asked his father Murray, a local barber, to purchase a car that the group might use to drive to gigs. Coincidentally, Ralph Peer of the Victor Talking Machine Company was conducting recording sessions a short distance from both Murray Pierce's barbershop and the boarding house run by Carrie Pierce, Jack's mother, at 411 1/2 State Street, across from the Taylor-Christian building.

Rodgers and Jack Pierce met with Peer, who encouraged the Jimmie Rodgers Entertainers to audition. The full group probably arrived in Bristol on August 3, 1927, yet, for reasons that scholars continue to debate, Rodgers recorded as a solo act (the next afternoon, accompanying himself on guitar), while the other three musicians, joined by another Bristolian, banjoist Claude Slagle, recorded as the Ten[n]eva Ramblers (in the evening of the same day). Neither of the two songs that Rodgers cut that day for Peer—"The Soldier's Sweetheart" and "Sleep, Baby, Sleep"—sold well when released by Victor on October 7, 1927, yet Peer invited Rodgers to make further recordings at the Victor studio in Camden, New Jersey, in late November. One of these songs, "Blue Yodel (T for Texas)," coupled with Kelly Harrell's song "Away Out on the Mountain" sold more than 1 million copies and immediately made him a national star.

That winter, Rodgers moved his family to Washington, and appeared on a weekly radio show (WTFF) billed as the "Singing Brakeman." He dressed the part when appearing publicly until 1929. Rodgers continued to record "blue yodels" for Victor, and his 1928 version of "In the Jailhouse Now" has become a country classic. Peer preferred that Rodgers work with Julian Ninde (guitar) and Ellsworth Cozzens (steel guitar, mandolin, ukulele, and banjo).

After 1929, he started to receive significant royalties from his recordings and tours, appearing in tuxedo and bowler hat, and billing himself as "America's Blue Yodeler." During most months, he participated in more than a dozen recording sessions and maintained a hectic performing schedule on the major Radio-Keith-Orpheum Interstate Circuit (RKO) of Southern cities. The musicians who collaborated with him in the 1930s were much more eclectic, including Lillian Hardin Armstrong (piano) and the young Louis Armstrong (trumpet) on "Blue Yodel #9," and Lani McIntyre's "Hawaiians" on "Moonlight and Skies" and "For the Sake of Days Gone By."

In 1931, Rodgers's first wife sued him for child support, and the court granted his daughter Kathryn a monthly stipend of $50 per month (paid until her death at age 19, seven years later). He worked with Will Rodgers on a Red Cross tour to raise money for drought-affected families in Texas and Oklahoma, and increased his recording schedule, sometimes earning as much as $250 per side. On June 10, 1931, he met with Sara and Maybelle Carter in Louisville to cut his only recordings with a female vocalist (and his only gospel recordings).

Rodgers died from tuberculosis on May 26, 1933, at the age of 36, but he lived long enough to make more than 100 recordings for Victor. He is celebrated as the most important and influential performer in the history of early country music. Countless tribute recordings have been made to him, and several stars, including Gene Autry, Jimmie Davis, Hank Snow, and Ernest Tubb, started their careers essentially as Rodgers impersonators before launching their own styles.

Laura Stanfield Prichard

See also: Carter Family, The; Guthrie, Woody; Seeger, Peter; Yodeling

Further Reading

Mazor, Barry. 2009. *Meeting Jimmie Rodgers: How America's Original Roots Music Hero Changed the Pop Sounds of a Century*. Oxford: Oxford University Press.

Paris, Mike. 1977. *Jimmie the Kid: The Life of Jimmie Rodgers*. London: Da Capo.

Porterfield, Nolan. 1979. *Jimmie Rodgers: The Life and Times of America's Blue Yodeler*. Urbana: University of Illinois Press.

Rodgers, Mrs. Jimmie [Carrie Williamson]. 1975. *My Husband Jimmie Rodgers*. Nashville, TN: Country Music Foundation Reprints.

Rodrigues, Amália (1920–1999)

Amália Rodrigues was a Portuguese singer and actress, who became famous for her interpretation of Portuguese *fado* (a traditional style of Portuguese song). Largely considered the foremost figure in the internationalization and popularization of fado across the globe in the mid-20th century, Rodrigues—known widely as the "Queen of Fado"—is heralded for her soulful voice and impassioned style of fado singing. Rodrigues remains a Portuguese cultural icon and symbol of Portuguese national identity. Her musical style continues to be emulated by younger generations of Portuguese fado vocalists.

Born Amália da Piedade Rodrigues to a poor family in Lisbon, Portugal, Rodrigues gained formative musical experiences throughout her youth in the city's amateur musical scene. She began her musical career as a singer in neighborhood fado venues (known as *casas do fado*, or "houses of fado," which are restaurants or bars where singers perform traditional and improvised fado songs). Her soulful voice (a powerful, wide-ranging chest voice) and dramatic singing style (intense, impassioned interpretation of poetry; compelling use of dynamics and physical gesture) gained quick attention thereafter, as Rodrigues pursued a professional singing career in Portugal and abroad. Performing at professional venues from the late 1930s, Rodrigues went on to perform several successful international tours in the 1940s and produced her first professional recordings in 1945 on the Brazilian label Continental. Rodrigues also achieved some success as an actress throughout her early and middle career, as in the popular films *Capas Negras* (1946), *Fado* (1947), *Les Amants du Tage* (1955), and *Sangue Toureiro* (1958).

During the height of her career, Rodrigues became popular for pushing the conventional boundaries of fado and enlarging the possibilities for fado performance and composition. For instance, she encouraged more lush instrumental accompaniments for her singing (in addition to the more traditional guitar accompaniment). Moreover, she expanded the traditional repertoire through collaborations with contemporary Portuguese and international poets and musicians. Her partnership with Portuguese composer Alain Oulman (1928–1990) exemplifies many of these groundbreaking impulses. Rodrigues's mature works, such as the album *Com Que*

Amália Rodrigues was a Portuguese singer and actress. She is best known for popularizing *fado*, a style of Portuguese song that can be traced back to the early 19th century. (Gamma-Keystone via Getty Images)

Voz (1969), produced with Oulman, reveal a broader conception of fado that strayed from the simpler folk melodies and traditional accompaniment of older fado songs toward more artistic orchestrations and expansive melodies. Rodrigues was also interested in creating expressive, new poetry, much of which she penned herself, as in the popular song *"Estranha forma de vida"* (Strange way of life).

Rodrigues's popularity was largely the result of her exceptional transformation of traditional fado into a modern genre that engaged audiences around the globe, but she also played an important role in negotiating Portuguese national identity in music amid the social and political upheavals in Portugal throughout the mid-20th century. In her early career, her dynamic voice and captivating stage presence enabled her to draw new Portuguese audiences to traditional fado poetic themes—such as the Portuguese concept of *saudade*, which is a deep nostalgia or longing for the past. In voicing such themes, she became the cultural figure of a generation searching for a renewed sense of national identity during the period leading up to the overthrow of Portugal's authoritarian regime in a bloodless coup on April 25, 1974 (Carnation Revolution). The widespread popularity and deeply nationalistic nature of fado, with Rodrigues as its leading figure, was complicated, however, by this same political strife. Under the control of António de Oliveira Salazar (1889–1970; Salazar ruled the country in the manner of a dictatorship as Prime Minister of Portugal from 1932–1968), the regime had utilized fado as propagandistic art, and following the revolution, Rodrigues was implicated briefly—and falsely—in the work of the deposed fascist government. While fado retained some of its association with the dictatorship, and declined severely in popularity among the Portuguese immediately thereafter, Rodrigues returned to the scene with her highly acclaimed 1977 album *Cantigas numa Lingua Antiga* (Songs in an ancient tongue), and her immense former reputation remained largely intact.

In her late career, Rodrigues continued to tour and achieved increasing recognition as a symbol of Portugal's musical and cultural patrimony. Though illness eventually resulted in her retirement from stage performance by 1994, Rodrigues's legacy grew through numerous high-profile honors, such as a national tribute at Lisbon's 1998 World Expo. The Portuguese government declared three days of national mourning following Rodrigues's death on October 6, 1999, and gave the singer the honor of a state funeral. Moreover, she was also the first woman to be buried at the National Pantheon in Lisbon, alongside generations of famed Portuguese royalty, prime ministers, and poets. Consistently regarded as one of the greatest Portuguese musicians to date, her legendary status and musical legacy remain a vibrant part of Lisbon's cultural life, with numerous monuments and museums dedicated to her memory across the city.

Danielle M. Kuntz

See also: Fado; Pimba

Further Reading

Almeida, Bruno de, dir. 2004. *The Art of Amália* [CD]. EMI.
Santos, Vitor Pavao Dos. 1987. *Amália: Uma Biografia*. Lisbon, Portugal: Contexto.
Vernon, Paul. 1998. *A History of the Portuguese Fado*. Aldershot, UK: Ashgate.

Romani Music

Romani or "gypsy" music is the music of the Romani (gypsy) people that has roots in Indian music and contains elements of Greek, Slavic, Spanish, and Turkish music. There is no pure Roma music: it is more an adaptation of the music of the country in which a Roma group lives. The main instruments used in Romani music are the *tzimbal*, bagpipes, oboe, violin, flute, accordion, and Spanish mandolin and castanets. The only instrument that is used exclusively by Romani musicians is the tzimbal, the harmonious sound of which is created by playing with two small hammers on the instrument's many strings. In different countries, Romani musicians favor particular instruments: for example, the violin in Hungary, the accordion in Poland, and castanets and mandolin in Spain.

The Roma has a population of 7 to 9 million in Europe and another 3 to 4 million worldwide. Two-thirds of the Romani population in Europe lives in central and eastern Europe, the Balkans, and Spain. The distribution of the Romani population in Europe and worldwide, as well as the variations in its social positions and the issues facing it in central and eastern Europe compared with western Europe, are the result of deep historical processes.

Scholars suggest that the discrimination against Roma that continues into the present day persists because "a people without a country must forever be guests in another homeland, and at worst unwelcome intruders. In modern times, people without a country receive less attention and lack an international arena in which to make their voices heard" (Hancock, 2002, p. 55).

In the course of their travels, Roma have come into contact with a great variety of musical traditions, which was inevitable since many of them were professional providers of music for the host country's population. Other "nonprofessional" Roma also provided musical services on special occasions such as weddings or birthdays. Their musical idiom has preserved traces of diverse influences that were merged with the music of the country they stayed in during their travels. Over time, these markers became very vague, and some disappeared completely with the assimilation of certain groups. In musical terms, there is no "typical" Roma style. The occurrence of music varies considerably. In some Roma communities, music has the status of a principal occupation, like trading or peddling. There are also Roma communities in which there are no institutionalized forms of musical activity; in these groups people invent and improvise performances upon request by encompassing regional folk and Romani music.

In most countries Romani music is a variation or integration of the natural and regional style of folk music, which is distinguishable from the original but not specifically of Romani composition or definable as purely gypsy music. However, Spain is the one country where Romani music and dance are a clearly defined and identifiable musical form that has emerged from the Romani/gypsy people and culture. To a large extent this has come to define what the world considers to be gypsy music. Though it may be erroneous for the world to believe that Spanish flamenco incorporates the full panoply of Romani music, it has come to be a recognized and instantly recognizable form of gypsy music.

Historically, Roma were unwelcome in Europe, because they were feared and rumored to be thieves, baby snatchers, criminals, and murderers, and as such they were constantly marginalized. Roma were associated with fortune telling, with song and dance, and with magic. The word *gitanos* (gypsies) also came to be applied to beggars, escaped criminals, slaves, and persecuted Moors and Jews, who became fused with the groups of Roma. Following the Catholic reconquest in 1462, the Moors, after nearly 700 years of domination in Spain, had to abandon their land, together with persecuted Jews, in 1492—unless they converted to Catholicism. Those *conversos* (converts) who stayed in Spain quite naturally settled into the gypsy communities where they were able to maintain and practice their original religious rituals in secret.

Nomadic Roma were persecuted, but their suffering was alleviated through spontaneous expression in song and dance. A *cantaor* (singer) shared his hurt and pain with the listening audience in the *tavernas* (taverns), which were smoky, dark rooms made for drinking. These songs developed into *gitano* style and from the 19th century onward were called "flamenco."

This development of flamenco song might have taken place in more settled communities, where a strong sense of communal anguish and marginalization also existed. One such city was Triana, located in the province of Seville in the 17th century. Triana was largely inhabited by Roma, but it was also a refuge for many other unfortunate people who were unjustly treated and who expressed their hostility toward the dominant powers through song. They sang in a rough, raw manner appropriate to their feelings of rejection—in short, a style which acquired the name of the people who sang it: *cante gitano* (gypsy song) and subsequently *cante flamenco* (flamenco song). This dramatic style was not the creation of the Roma alone, but rather the result of collaboration between a mixture of marginalized people from many centuries. By the time specific evidence of what we now call flamenco existed, in the 1770s, the Roma had largely appropriated this style of singing.

The first recorded reference to Roma in Spain (specifically in Barcelona) dates back to 1447. The second wave of Roma, who arrived soon afterward in the south of Spain, had originally migrated from India to different parts of Europe, Africa, and Asia around 1000 CE.

Roma, with their nomadic lifestyle, found the south of Spain, especially the Andalusian countryside and its warm climate and Moorish music, very attractive. The name *gitanos* was given to Roma who had arrived in Andalusia from Egypt. "Gitanos" is a distortion of *egiptianos* (Egyptians). This terminology has since been applied to all the Roma living in Spain who also came from India.

Flamenco dance is so closely associated with flamenco song that now it is seen outside the gypsy community that the dance is flamenco with the music and song in the magical atmosphere. Historically, flamenco dance parallels flamenco song, in the sense that it has clear connections with India, especially with the Indian classical dance forms of Katak, Kathakali, and Bharata Natyam, all of which involve footwork and hand movements that are reminiscent of flamenco. It is likely that Hindu dancers entered Spain by way of Cadiz as early as 500 CE in order to perform for royalty and at particular festivals. Their dances, of an essentially religious nature, later became part of the ceremonies enacted in Roman temples. Later still, during the Visigoth domination of Spain from the fifth to the eighth century, these dances were incorporated into the practices of the Christian Church. Thus, by the time the Roma began arriving in Spain in large numbers, in the 15th century, there already existed a form of dance with which they, given their Indian background, could identify. Add to this the coexistence of the Roma and the persecuted Moors in close-knit communities, and it becomes clear that what later came to be known as flamenco dance developed in much the same way as flamenco song, though the latter was more important.

For other nations, flamenco became a source of fascination. The Spanish "gypsy" became an archetype of beauty and passion and the flamenco dance was seen as a colorful, powerful, and sensual performance. Roma are fascinating, colorful, and passionate people to the eyes of outsiders, but they have always formed a subculture in the countries in which they live, never being fully accepted by the dominant culture and usually being subject to persecution and discrimination. Romani music focuses on the desire, passion, and fascination with the dance and traditions experienced by the "other." It has become a commercially successful, exotic, and very popular form of entertainment.

Some well-known Romani musicians are the Gypsy Kings, a band from Spain; Carmen Amaya (1913–1963), a Spanish flamenco dancer; Saban Bajramovic (1936–2008), a Serbian singer; Joaquin Cortes (1969–), a Spanish flamenco dancer; Lola Flores (1958–), a Spanish singer and actress; Kal, a Romani band from Serbia; Carlos Montoya (1903–1993), a Spanish flamenco guitarist; Johnny Raducanu (1931–), a Romanian jazz musician; Esma Redzwepova (1943–), a Macedonian singer and songwriter; and Sotis Volanis (1971–), a Greek pop folk singer.

Roma music transcends both musical and geographical borders. The Romani, with no homeland, still pass down their music, their lyrics, and their history by oral tradition.

Anna Hamling

See also: Flamenco Music; Polish National Dances; Redzepova, Esma

Further Reading
Hancock, F. Ian. 2002. *We Are the Romani People*. Hatfield, UK: University of Hertfordshire Press.
Hayes, Michelle Heffner. 2009. *Flamenco: Conflicting Histories of the Dance*. Jefferson, NC: McFarland.

Rumba

Rumba is a Cuban dance, music, and poetic art that formed in the mid-19th century among Afro-Cuban communities of various African origins. Up to the early 20th century, many styles of rumba emerged, of which three dominant forms exist today: *columbia, yambú,* and *guaguancó*. Though its name is a complex and contested term among scholars, rumba developed in the Cuban provinces of Matanzas and Havana, from which it subsequently spread to other parts of the

> **Rumba**
>
> In the United States, the rumba enjoyed a brief, but meteoric, popularity in the 1930s. With its roots in Cuban dance, the rumba was one in a long string of Latin and African American musical styles that enjoyed fad status during the 20th century, including the cakewalk, jitterbug, twist, locomotion, lambada, macarena, and dab, to name only a few. The most notable rumba artist was Don Azpiazu and his Havana Casino Orchestra. Well-known for his race records and work in the Cuban music scene, Azpiazu burst onto the American cultural consciousness with his hit "The Peanut Vendor (*El Manisero*)" in 1930, which launched a rumba craze. "The Peanut Vendor (*El Manisero*)" is widely credited as the first American recording of a Latin dance music style to reach mass popularity. The rumba craze was short-lived; however, the "The Peanut Vendor (*El Manisero*)" and other rumba songs left an indelible mark on American music history.

country. Today it is among Cuba's most important social dances and a potent symbol of Cuban national culture.

Although rumba is a distinctly Cuban performing art, its origins are found in a confluence of dance expressions from Western and Central Africa. However, it is danced like the *makuta* and *yuka* of Central African origin, which still survive in Cuba today, that have had the deepest impact on the genre. Enslaved Africans of BaKongo, Lunda, and Luba origins brought dances sharing similar characteristics to Cuba, that survive to varying degrees in contemporary rumba performance. This includes paired dancing in a circle formation where dancers move independently but in relation to one another, dancing to the accompaniment of three drummers and a wooden box, the inclusion of commenting spectators during performance, and dancers touching their stomachs or thighs in performance.

The etymology of the word *rumba* connects the art with its original performing context. The term is of Spanish ancestry, although it is synonymous with words of African origin used in Cuba, such as *tumba*, *macumba*, and *tambo*, that describe a type of social gathering where music and dance occur. Prior to the abolition of slavery in Cuba, music and dance performances were an important context where enslaved and marginalized black populations could gather to express themselves and their frustrations. After abolition, many former slaves as well as poor whites migrated from the hinterlands to urban Havana in search of work and economic prosperity. Living together in *solares* (barracks-like houses) and sharing a low-class and politically marginalized status, Cubans participated in communal performances and gatherings from which rumba eventually emerged and evolved.

Musically, rumba is closely connected with both its Spanish and African heritage; rhythmically, however, it is deeply rooted in Congolese drum-dance music and the rhythms of Palo spiritual expression in Cuba that also share this ancestry. Instruments first used to play rumba were either regular household items or made from such items, likely reflecting the impact of colonial prohibitions on music-making among many slave societies in the African Diaspora for fear of rebellion. Afro-Cuban *rumberos* (term given to those who sing, dance or play rumba) would use the sides of cabinets or overturned drawers during performances in place of animal-skin drums, or spoons and pans as substitutes for bells or other types of idiophones. This early type of rumba was called *rumba de cajón*, or "box rumba." The cajón has since been refined into a mass-produced instrument and one can still find it being incorporated into contemporary rumba performances.

Today, rumba is connected with a specific set of instruments. *Claves* is the term given to the pair of wooden sticks used in many types of Cuban popular music, and essential for forming the *clave* timeline that establishes the rhythmic structure of rumba from which the rest of the instruments follow. Today drums are mainly used to play rumba, and the combination of their beats forms a dynamic rhythmic structure that supports the innovation and improvisation that are at the heart of good rumba performance. The largest and lowest-pitched drum in the ensemble has multiple names, such as *tumbador* or *hembra* (female), and is typically the first to enter with its anchoring ostinato pattern. The middle-pitched drum is called the *segundo* (second) or *macho* (male), which typically enters second, and whose pattern complements that of the *hembra*. The *quinto* is the highest-pitched instrument, whose name derives from its tonal properties, as it is typically tuned to a major fifth above the *hembra*. Its role is to create the lively and dynamic improvisational rhythms and melodies that add excitement and creativity to the rumba drum ensemble.

Improvisation is an essential feature of good rumba performance that is realized in all the drums, but the quinto's role is unique in this respect. Two struck idiophones are also typically used in addition to the clave and drum ensemble. The *madruga* is a shaker that is found in many types of African and Cuban popular and sacred music types, and in rumba is often made of metal or tin. Sometimes drummers wear shakers on their wrists during performance, an instrument referred to as *muñecas*. Early rumba ensembles would include a musician beating the clave pattern or *cáscara* part on the side of the drum with a pair of sticks. In more contemporary contexts, this part is played on a hollowed-out piece of wood or bamboo called *catá*.

Over time, rumba grew in popularity and spread throughout the island, and by the mid-19th century distinct styles began to crystallize, with each connected to a particular location. As with music and dance in general, some styles of rumba grew very popular, others gained marginal or only local popularity, and others faded into obscurity. Although rumba is a dynamic and evolving tradition, today there are three main styles of rumba, each of which has a unique type of dance movement and rhythmic organization associated with it, thereby making them easily identifiable to connoisseurs of the tradition. These differences aside, all good rumba is marked by the gradual increase in tension and dynamics among the musicians, dancers, singers, and audience.

Yambú was the first style of rumba to be established. As a result, it is connected with an older generation of rumba performers and enthusiasts and connected with the original performing traditions of the rumbas de cajón. It is characterized by its slower tempo and seductive qualities. Men and women dance yambú together in a flirtatious and sensuous style, and use scarves to accentuate pantomime.

Columbia is a style of rumba reserved for male dance soloists who display their skill, power, and virtuosity through a type of dance competition. It is the fastest of the three rumba types, and scholarship suggests that its rhythm is connected to the music of the Cuban Abakuá spiritual brotherhoods and secret societies, whose members are descendants of slaves originating from the Calabar region of modern-day Nigeria and Cameroon. One of the important features of columbia is the close relationship between the quinto player and the dancer who tries to mimic or relate his movements to the rhythmic phrasing of the drummer. *Columbia* is also unique from the other styles with respect to the music's metrical organization that is composed in 6/8 or 12/8.

Guaguancó is the most popular form of rumba; it is in duple meter, and performed at a faster tempo than yambú. As a dance of sexual seduction between a man and a woman, the goal in guaguancó is the *vacunao* (meaning "vaccination" or "injection"), which is characterized by the male dancer thrusting his hand, foot, or (most commonly) his pelvis toward the female dancer, whose dance tries to evade the male gesture through movements known as *botao*. While the dance may exhibit sexual tension, it is always performed with grace, and in a light-hearted and humorous manner. As with columbia, the quinto player and dancers perform in collaboration with one another, especially during moments when the male dancer displays the vacunao that the drummer responds to rhythmically. Some scholarship suggests that due to the "African sound" of guaguancó, its overtly sexual themes, and its close association with the Cuba's marginalized black population, it never received any commercial recording interest in Cuba until the 1960s. Like most African-derived musical expressions in Cuba, it was largely suppressed and ridiculed by white Cuban elites.

Singing in rumba reflects the dynamic process of creolization that marks many Cuban artistic forms. Singing is organized in both solo and call-and-response modes, and texts composed in Spanish or words from various languages found in Africa present humorous, sad, or topical issues. Rumba functions as a means of expression among enslaved black and marginalized Cubans, with lyrics that are deeply critical of power and their subjugation. As improvisation is essential to good rumba performance, there are moments when lead singers (typically male) draw on nonsense syllables to carry out highly elaborate improvised sections.

Song form varies among the different types and is typically organized in a two-part structure consisting of the main primary verse followed by a call-and-response section. For yambú and guaguancó, an introductory phrase called the *diana* (sometimes called *lalaleo*) is also included. This playfully sung opening section, built on nonsense syllables or words of African origin whose meaning has been lost, helps to establish the song's key and choral refrain for the response singers. Singers then move into the *canto* section, which is characterized by the recitation of extended texts revolving around the song's main theme. Although this section is precomposed, often including songs that are part of an established repertoire, the singer may loosely improvise during this section. The final part of the form, called the *montuno* or *estribillo*, is based on a call-and-response song structure that alternates between the lead singer and the chorus. Here the rumba "breaks loose" (locally referred to as *rumba rompe*), with the interactions among the lead singer, chorus, drummers, and dancers growing in intensity and level of improvisation.

Rumba performance contexts underwent significant transformation after the Cuban revolution in 1959, as the new Cuban government sought to extend its control on the arts. No longer was it a marginalized (like so many features of black musical expression during the colonial period) and spontaneous mode of expression for the disenfranchised or limited to private street or backyard performances; now it was a symbol of Cuban nationalism and an important mode of expression for tourists and/or paying audiences. Professional ensembles enjoying state patronage added rumba to their repertoire of Cuban dance forms, shifting the typical venue for experiencing rumba from the street corner to the concert stage. This new context required changes to rumba performance norms. It required groups to perform abbreviated versions of rumba to fit the stage setting and expectations of a theater audience, it standardized various dimensions of rumba performance, it provided audiences with a romanticized visual representation of "typical" rumba performance through idealized stage designs and props, and it limited individual artistic expression to a prescribed set of performance expectations dictated by administrators or artistic directors of the state ensembles. Prior to the Cuban revolution, other forms (e.g., ballet) had been the most widely celebrated and officially supported of the performing arts. The revolution, with its egalitarian values and embrace of the lower classes of Cuban society, caused a shift in official consciousness and the affirmation of rumba as a dance that touched the widest cross-section of the population and was communal in nature, and therefore a new symbol of national identity.

Rumba has also transformed many styles of global popular music since its commercialization and internationalization, particularly since the late 1920s and early 1930s, and the period of the "rumba craze" in the United States and elsewhere. The commercialization of rumba began in Cuba when the music and dance were integrated into the *teatro variedades*, a type of popular theater in Cuba resembling American minstrelsy. There the typical rumba ensemble was replaced by European instrumentation, and actors (mainly white) donned the *guarachera* costumes that later became associated with cabaret rumba. Commercial sheet music catering to middle-class audiences also was an important means through which rumba was commercialized and spread, although once again in a diluted form. Similarly, at this time there emerged a proliferation of compositions that drew on rumba or other styles connected with Afro-Cuban music culture by well-known composers such as Copland or Gershwin. The rumba craze from the 1930s that deeply impacted American dance music was actually based on Cuban *son* music, the Cuban popular style that many suggest was the first true blending of African and European elements in the country. Later, by the 1940s, this craze hit Africa and transformed the development of popular music in countries such as Senegal and the Congo.

Gavin Webb

See also: Afro-Cuban Jazz; Claves and Clave Rhythm

Further Reading

Crook, Larry. 1982. "A Musical Analysis of the Cuban Rumba." *Latin American Music Review* 3(1) (Spring-Summer), 92–123.

Daniel, Yvonne. 1995. *Rumba: Dance and Social Change in Contemporary Cuba*. Bloomington: Indiana University Press.

Manuel, Peter, ed. *Essays in Cuban Music: North American and Cuban Perspectives*. New York: University Press of America.

Moore, Robin. 1995. "The Commercial Rumba: Afrocuban Arts as International Popular Culture." *Latin American Music Review* 16(2) (Autumn-Winter), 165–198.

Runo Song

Estonian *runo* song is a genre of Estonian folksong similar to other genres of song indigenous to the Balto-Finnic region (Finland, Latvia, Lithuania, Estonia). Like its Finnish counterpart, the Estonian runo song is strictly metric (referred to in the Balto-Finnic region as *regivärss*, or "runic meter"). The amount of runo songs indicating female performance practice is outstanding, thus indicating that the genre is largely a female one (Bousfield, 2011, p. 379). Songs feature a variety of topics, including (but not limited to) mythic stories (typically from the *Kalevala*), work songs, songs with spiritual content, and songs based upon harvesting or the calendar year. The aesthetics of the songs gravitate toward a sense of "stoic sadness," as indicated by their harmonic stasis, repetition, and lyric content (Bousfield, 2011, p. 379).

Around the 19th century, Estonian runo song traditions began to be replaced by other end-rhymed Germanic folksong traditions. By the 20th century, runo song was almost completely phased out of existence. The occupations of Estonia by Germany and the Soviet Union worked to suppress any uniquely Estonian traditions, and to replace them with German or Russian culture. Recently, there has been an upsurge of interest in restoring the runo song tradition in Estonia. In some areas of Estonia, the runo song tradition continues to flourish: mostly in the areas of Setumaa, along the Estonian-Russian border; and the island of Kihnu, located in the Baltic Sea, north of the Gulf of Riga and south of the Pärnu Bay.

Estonian runo song has much in common with the Finnish variety of Karelian epic poetry. It is believed that the earliest runo songs date back to the first millennium BCE. Ingrid Rüütel argues for the premillennial origin of runo song, because the Balto-Finnic tribes at this time spoke the same proto-language, and had not yet split into separate ways (Rüütel and Lippus, 2001, pp. 342–343). *Vemmalvärs*, a Germanic-influenced folk song, eventually replaced Estonian runic song (O'Connor, 2006, p. 175). Musicologists and Estonians themselves divide the Estonian runo song tradition into two categories, "old" and "new." Old refers to the pre-German "*Kalevala* songs," whereas the latter refers to the more recent phenomenon inspired by Germanic traditions.

Runo song is characterized by several features: a small range, typically to the extent of a perfect-fifth interval; the use of alliteration, or the beginning of each word with the same consonance; the use of parallelism; and the incorporation of trochaic tetrameter, or the use of four trochées (four long syllables, each succeeded by a short syllable). An example of trochaic tetrameter is the first two lines of the 13th-century Latin *Dies Iræ*: "Dies iræ, Dies illa, Solvet sæclum in favilla." The stress of a long or short syllable is not fixed in runo song; long syllable is not stressed simply because it is long. Thus, the eight-syllable meter may be changed from steady groupings of 2-2-2-2, to groupings of 2-3-3, 3-2-3, or 3-3-2. Metslang argues for parallelism as the "[nature of] arrang[ing] subsequent verses into a whole, namely a parallel group in which the meaning of one verse and also of the form conveying it, is partly repeated, [and] partly varied in the other parallel verses. Thus a complete meaning, a poetical picture, is formed" (Metslang, 1981, p. 50).

An example is: "sail, boat, make way, boat / sail, boat, to the shore" (*sõua, læva, jõua læva / sõua, læva, sinna maale*) (Daitz and Tormis, 2004, p. 49). The phrases "make way" and "to the shore" imply motion, both in regard to the story the poem is conveying and to the forward propulsion of the text; the text "sail, boat" acts as a textual anchor; and *sõua læva / jõua læva* serves an alliterative function. Similarly, the text "I went to the forest for a broom / a silver broom from below the yard / a gold broom from the paddock / a copper broom from the field" (*läksin metsast luuda tooma / hobeluuda oue alta / kuldaluuda koppelista / vaskiluuda vainiiulta*) uses terms belonging to the same "semantic field." All three terms—different words for different types of expensive metals—connote a shared idea of wealth (Kelertas, 2006, p. 437).

Contemporary Estonian composers—in particular, Veljo Tormis—are known for their inclusion of runo song in contemporary Estonian music. Tormis's work *Eesti kalendrilaulud* (Estonian calendar-songs) derives its name and content from Estonian runo song. In the 1960s, Tormis became one of the most critical avenues for the re-engagement, proliferation, and dissemination of Estonian runo song, and his work is supremely influential in the scope of runo song scholarship.

John Forrestal

See also: Classical Music, European; Medieval Secular Song; Norwegian Folk Music

Further Reading

Bousfield, Jonathan. 2004. *Baltic States*. New York: Rough Guides/Penguin Group.

Bousfield, Jonathan. 2011. *The Rough Guide to Estonia, Latvia and Lithuania*. New York: Rough Guides/Penguin Group.

Broughton, Simon, Mark Ellingham, and Richard Trillo, eds. 1999. *World Music: Africa, Europe, and the Middle East*. London: Rough Guides/Penguin Group.

Daitz, Mimi S., and Veljo Tormis. 2004. *Ancient Song Recovered: The Life and Music of Veljo Tormis*. Hillsdale, NY: Pendragon Press.

Eesti Kirjandusmuuseum. n.d. *Eesti Regilaulude Andmebaas* [Estonian runic songs database]. http://www.folklore.ee/regilaul/andmebaas.

Kelertas, Violeta. 2006. *Baltic Postcolonialism*. New York: Rodopi.

Koskoff, Ellen, et al., eds. 2008. *The Concise Garland Encyclopedia of World Music*. Hoboken, NJ: Taylor and Francis.

Metslang, Helle. 1981. Некоторые синтаксические аспекты стихового параллелизма в эстонской рунической песне. [The verse parallelism of the Estonian runo songs from the syntactic point of view]. Tartu Ülikool, Tartu, Estonia.

O'Connor, Kevin. 2006. *Culture and Customs of the Baltic States*. Westport, CT: Greenwood Press.

Ross, Jaan, and Ilse Lehiste. 2001. *The Temporal Structure of Estonian Runic Songs*. Berlin: Mouton de Gruyter.

Rüütel, Ingrid, and Urve Lippus. "Estonia." In *Grove Music Online*. http://www.oxfordmusiconline.com. https://www.oxfordmusiconline.com.

Sarv, Mari. *Regilaul: Clearing the Alliterative Haze*. http://www.folklore.ee/folklore/vol10/alliter.htm.

Russian Orthodox Church Music

The Russian Orthodox Church (ROC) is an autocephalous branch of Eastern Orthodox Christianity that practices in full communion with the other 14 branches of Eastern Orthodoxy. The ROC is altogether separate from other branches of Eastern Orthodoxy—the Greek Orthodox Church of Alexandria, for example—and does not operate under a higher branch of religious authority, although the branches do recognize their shared doctrinal values and participate as "One Holy, Catholic, and Apostolic Church" (Whitehead, 1995). Unlike Catholic or Protestant traditions, Orthodoxy makes use of cantillation throughout its entire liturgy. This practice may stem from the ROC's potential roots in the Byzantine Church, or relations with other Byzantine-influenced churches at the time of its inception.

The ROC was officially declared in 988 CE, after the Christianization of the Kievan *Rus's*—a loosely knit coalition of Eastern Slavic tribes to whom present-day Belarus, Ukraine, and Russia claim relations. In 988 CE, Prince Vladimir the Great (958–1015) introduced Christianity to the Rus's population at large, through relations with the Byzantine Empire (ca. 330–1453). One year earlier, Prince Vladimir had traveled to Constantinople, then a brilliant, powerful city and patriarchate of the Christian Church. He attended a great service at the Hagia Sophia, and was overcome with emotion, unsure whether he was in Heaven or on Earth (Krautheimer, Ćurčić, and Beckwith, 1993, p. 237). Utilizing the Byzantine Church structure, he introduced Christianity to the Rus's civilization. Moss states that the Byzantine and South Slavic influences that Prince Vladimir brought back to the Rus's helped create an elite Rus's culture, "[producing] literary and artistic works of considerable merit" (Moss, 2002, p. 14). This could have been because of the very influential trade routes that passed through Kiev, through which both Byzantines and Scandinavians (who followed to the Latin rite) passed (Gardner, 1980, p. 6).

Like the ROC's doctrinal roots, the musical roots of the ROC are also found within the Byzantine Church. Byzantine music is itself a composite musical heritage, drawing features from plainsong traditions from nearby countries, as well as from the Greco-Roman classical age beginning some 1,000 years earlier. The majority of the Byzantine repertory consists of manuscripts dating from the 12th to the 15th centuries CE (Steib, 2013, p. 144). Of course, this time period coexists alongside the chant practices of the Slavic repertories, so it becomes difficult to determine and differentiate who influenced whom in this relationship. Additionally, performance practices surrounding the Byzantine rite are historiographically debated, as many scholars attempt to recreate a history working from the present day backward, using the contemporary Greek Orthodox Church as a model for early Byzantine performance practice (Steib, 2013, p. 144).

The influence of the Byzantine rite might have come through the Bulgarian Orthodox Church, judging from the use of Old Church Slavonic as the liturgical parlance of the ROC. Church Slavonic, closely related to "Old Bulgarian," might be a sign of the relationship between the Bulgarian Orthodox Church and the Byzantine rite. The Church Slavonic language was introduced by Saints Cyril and Methodius from Moravia—the language itself a development of the Bulgarian

Empire (681–1018 CE). The Bulgarian Orthodox Church may have appropriated Byzantine customs and liturgical singing, and translated the hymns from Greek—the common language at the time both in the Orthodox Church and in the Latin rite of the Germanic west—into Church Slavonic (Gardner, 1980, pp. 10–11). Scholar Palikarova-Verdeil argues that Bulgarian singers were trained under the auspices of Constantinopolitan "high school" musicians and educators; these singers travelled to Kievan Rus's around the time of the Christianization of the Rus's community, and transmitted their art to their branch of the Orthodox Church (Gardner, 1980, p. 11). The ROC's use of Church Slavonic also ties it to the Bulgarian Orthodox Church, as any Western patriarchate would have viewed the decision *not* to use Greek or Latin as an abomination.

The earliest documentation of ROC music is found in the *Ostromirov Gospels* (ca. 1056–1057 CE), the second oldest documentation of East Slavic text after Christianization (the first being the *Norovgod Codex*, dated ca. 988–1030 CE). The *Ostromirov Gospels* feature ekphonetic neumes—mnemonic devices above the text of the hymns, used as guidelines for performance. Written music did not feature a staff at this time, and performance practice (similar to the aforementioned Byzantine rite) is remarkably vague. After the mid-11th century and once monasticism was established in Rus's (ca. 1057), extant manuscripts begin to surface, and the musical traditions of the ROC start to become more obvious.

As of the mid-11th century CE, two dominant styles of notation appear: *kondakarian* and *stolp* notation. Many surviving manuscripts were found in northern Russia, near Norovgod; this may be due to the 11th- and 12th-century destruction of Kiev in the south. The most developed centers for liturgical singing in the 11th century were Kiev (to the south), and Norovgod (to the north). Stolp notation evolved into what is known today as *znamenny* chant, an altogether separate chanting system practiced today by Russian "Old Believers"—members of the ROC who follow edicts and liturgical practices mandated by the ROC prior to the reforms of Patriarch Nikon (1652–1666). After the reforms of Patriarch Nikon, polyphonic "Western" singing was introduced into the Church (and later mandated by future Patriarchs of the ROC); these reforms are disregarded by the Old Believers, who continue to follow the musical traditions of monodic, melismatic cantillation.

ROC liturgical music can be divided into three principal categories: dialogue, psalmody, and hymnody. Dialogue comprises any responsorial chant that consists of a leader (in the case of a Great Litany, the celebrant), and the congregation responding to the petitions of the leader with "amen" or "Lord, have mercy" (Drillock, 2013).

Psalmody, extending back to the fourth century CE, can be further divided into four subcategories: direct, alternating, responsorial, and antiphonal. Direct psalmody involves the cantillation of the 150 psalms by a soloist, while the congregation listens; alternating chant involves two choirs (or a split congregation), alternating singing psalm verses. Responsorial psalmody reflects the natural antecedent and consequent phrasing of the psalms, the former sung by a soloist, and the latter sung by the congregation (Drillock, 2013). Antiphonal psalmody bridges a gap between responsorial and alternating psalmody practice: the congregation is divided into two halves, each singing in response to a psalm. Responses include *troparia* (small sacred hymns), short paraliturgical texts, an extrapolated section of a psalm verse, or an alleluia. Troparia are also regarded as short, expressive hymns that "depict the occasion of a feast or the life of a saint" (Archbishop Averky, 1976).

Hymnody, the third type of singing in the Orthodox Church, comprises all of the hymns and/or hymn fragments (which come from the New Testament) sung during a Church service. The most important genres of hymnody are the *kontakion*, the *kanon* and its odes, and *stichera*. The kontakion are metrical stanzas—18 to 30 on average—with a similar melodic and rhythmic structure (Drillock, 2013). The kontakia function quite similarly to troparia, as they depict the essence of the event (Archbishop Averky, 1976); however, in their chronological order within the service, the troparia precede the kontakia. The kanon is a collection of sacred hymns directly honoring a saint or feast day; these kanons, consisting of nine odes (each of which in turn consists of *irmosi* [connecting material for troparia] and more troparia), are performed at Matins—a canonical hour of monastic worship extending from late night (or early morning) into dawn. Stichera are small verses sung immediately after other psalm verses. Originally, stichera were metrically fixed, though this was lost from the Greek-to-Slavonic translation used in the ROC (Archbishop Averky, 1976).

The congregational and solo singing used in the ROC is an amalgamation of two types of Eastern rites (Drillock, 2013). The *typikon*, a liturgical book detailing the orders of the Eastern Orthodox Church and its daily hours, is a "mixed rite"—stemming from both the monastic *ordo* of the desert fathers, and the Cathedral Rite that developed out of the Constantinopolitan patriarchate, which included "extensive" use of soloists and congregational singing, most typically in refrain form (Drillock, 2013).

The ROC expanded to the West in the 17th and 18th centuries, establishing branches in America. Right before the separation of church and state in 1917, the ROC experienced a surge of interest, with many Russians attracted by the ROC's particular flavor of mysticism and theosophy (the belief of finding God through spiritual ecstasy or direct connection), both qualities regarded by many as primitive and, therefore, more honest. These aspects were subdued by the Soviet government until 1988, when the Church underwent several reforms and regained the religious freedom it once had. Today, the ROC exists both in and outside of Russia. It features several unique musical traditions, including the blend of Western polyphonic traditions introduced in the 17th and 18th centuries, and the continuation of the znamenny traditions, led by the interest of onlooking musicologists and Old Believers.

John Forrestal

See also: Classical Music, European; Gregorian Chant

Further Reading

Archbishop Averky. 1976. "Liturgics." http://www.holytrinitymission.org/books/english/liturgics_averky_e.htm#_Toc104768118.

Church of the Nativity. 2018. "What Is the Old Rite?" http://www.churchofthenativity.net/old-rite.

Drillock, David. 2013. "Orthodox Church." *Grove Music Online*. https://www.oxfordmusiconline.com.

Gardner, Johann von. 1980. *Russian Church Singing; Vol. 1: Orthodox Worship and Hymnography.* Crestwood, NY: St. Vladimir's Seminary Press.

Gardner, Johann von. 1980. *Russian Church Singing; Vol. 2: History from the Origins to the Mid-Seventeenth Century.* Crestwood, NY: St. Vladimir's Seminary Press.

Jeffreys, Elizabeth, John Haldon, and Robin Cormack, eds. 2008. *The Oxford Handbook of Byzantine Studies.* New York: Oxford University Press.

Krautheimer, Richard, Slobodan Ćurčić, and John Beckwith, eds. 1993. *Early Christian and Byzantine Art.* Hong Kong: Yale University Press.

Moss, Walter. 2002. *A History of Russia; Vol. 1: To 1917,* 2nd ed. London: Anthem Press.

Shevzov, Vera. 2004. *Russian Orthodoxy on the Eve of Revolution.* New York: Oxford University Press.

Steib, Murray, ed. 2013. *Music: History, Theory, Criticism.* New York: Fitzroy Dearborn/Routledge.

Wellesz, Egon. 1961. *A History of Byzantine Hymography,* 2nd ed. Oxford: Clarendon Press.

Whitehead, Kenneth D. 1995. "Four Marks of the Church." From "The Church of the Apostles," *This Rock.* https://www.ewtn.com/catholicism/teachings/four-marks-of-the-church-216.

S

Salsa

A musical form that mixes many traditions, *salsa* combines the traditions, rhythms, and sounds of multiple cultures. Born in the Caribbean but popular as a musical form and a dance in the United States and around the world, salsa has been described as "multicultural, multinational, multi-musical and multiracial" (Sommer, 2004). The name of the music, *salsa*, literally means "sauce" and refers to the spicy, flavorful, and delicious nature of the music and the dance that accompanies it.

When salsa music first became popular in Cuba and the Caribbean, it was not initially identified as a specific form. For the artists who developed salsa in the late 1940s and early 1950s, the form was simply traditional Cuban music with some new and innovative touches, seen by some artists as a gimmick (Rondón, 2008). The new sound, however, was extremely popular with audiences across the Caribbean and garnered huge sales numbers for the artists making and recording the music. Thus, while some traditional artists viewed salsa as an attack on the foundations of Cuban music, others rode the wave of success to fame and fortune.

Salsa, like mambo, is a fusion of traditional Cuban rhythms and melody with the input of Latino musicians living in the United States (Santoro, 1993). Salsa uses the traditional *clave* rhythm pattern of two bars of three-two or two-three beats that is traceable back to the mixed European and African roots of musicians on the island of Cuba. This beat and the music to accompany it underwent an evolution in Cuba from *son* to *charanga* in the 1920s and then to *rumba* and *mambo* in the 1930s (Santoro, 1993). In the 1940s and 1950s, mambo remained popular, and son and charanga saw a rebirth, mixed with American jazz and swing styles. Salsa was born of this mix of traditional and new musical forms. By the 1960s, the term "salsa" was being used to refer to the unique mixture of son vocals, jazz improvisations, the three-two clave beat and rock-chord sequences, and electronic instruments (Santoro, 1993). As the evolution of the sound progressed, other Latin nations added their particular musical traditions and influences to the form. It is therefore difficult to say with certainty whether salsa is a Cuban musical form, a Puerto Rican form, or an American form, as it is truly a combination of many different styles.

Although most researchers agree that Cuba remained the primary influence on the medium through the 1950s, during that decade the musical traditions and musicians of Venezuela and Puerto Rico began to offer new and different versions of the form (Rondón, 2008). In the 1980s, Cali, Colombia, emerged as an important new producer of salsa music, and musicians traveled from neighboring Venezuela to bring the sound to Colombia (Waxer, 2000).

Over time, salsa music lyrics have ranged from traditional party and love songs to works with political and social messages. Artists such as Celia Cruz performed

> ### *Salsa Dancing*
>
> Salsa is the most popular form of Latin American dance music in the United States. In addition to concert venues, the dance is taught in schools, clubs, and health clubs throughout the country. Salsa dance is also an excellent example of the synergy between music and dance. Salsa bands are typically outfitted with a cadre of percussion instruments, of which the conga, bongo, and bell players have prescribed patterns. The melodic players also have important roles in this music, but the bass guitar and *montuno* (often played by the piano) intertwine their rhythmic parts with the steps of the dances. Salsa dancing is based on eight-step counts and the musical parts often do not play on counts on which the dancers are to step. In this way, the dancer's steps fill in the space left by the musicians and vice versa.

music that spoke of unity and solidarity—music designed to not alienate a general public. Willie Colón and Ruben Blades, among others, used the vehicle of salsa to raise awareness about poverty and discrimination in Latin America and Latino communities of the United States (Abreu, 2007).

The boom in popularity and sales of salsa music across the Caribbean and in the United States came in the 1970s. During this period, the Fania All-Stars were one of the groups of greatest renown (Rondón, 2008). Members of the All-Stars over time are a "who's who" of important Latin artists, including the Cuban artist Celia Cruz, Panamanian Ruben Blades, Tito Puente, and the Dominican founder of the group, Johnny Pacheco (Fania, 2014). Joining the all-stars in all-time popularity are the Puerto Rican trombonist Willy Colón, Colombian bandleader Jairo Valera, and Puerto Rican singer Hector Lavoe.

Although salsa music saw a decline in popularity in the early 21st century, replaced in terms of popularity with young people by forms such as reggaetón, some artists began a revival of the form after 2010. The Puerto Rican artist Marc Anthony, in particular, has had great international success with salsa songs such as *"Vivir mi vida* (Live my life)" (Cobo, 2013).

Elizabeth Gackstetter Nichols and Timothy R. Robbins

See also: Reggaetón; Samba Instruments; Samba Music

Further Reading

Abreu, Christina. 2007. "Celebrity, 'Crossover,' and Cubanidad: Celia Cruz as 'La Reina de Salsa,' 1971–2003." *Latin American Music Review/Revista de Música Latinoamericana* 28(1), 94–124.

Cobo, Leila. 2013. "The Last Salsero." *Billboard* 125(26), 32.

Fania. 2014. "Fania All-Stars." http://www.fania.com/collections/fania-all-stars.

Rondón, César Miguel. 2008. *The Book of Salsa: A Chronicle of Urban Music from the Caribbean to New York City*, trans. Frances R. Aparicio and Jackie White. Chapel Hill: University of North Carolina Press.

Santoro, Gene. 1993. "Borrowed Beats." *Atlantic* 272(3), 96.

Sommer, Sally. 2004. "Some Like It Hot." *Dance Magazine* 78(6), 46–47.

Waxer, Lise. 2000. "*En Conga, Bonga y Campana*: The Rise of Colombian Salsa." *Latin American Music Review/Revista de Música Latinoamericana* 21(2), 118–168.

Samba Instruments

Samba, one of the most recognizable Brazilian musical expressions, flourished between the 1920s and the 1950s. Its genesis refers to slave music and dance traditions such as *batuque* (percussive ensembles) and *umbigada* (belly-bump dance). Over time, samba also came to incorporate European tonal harmonies and instruments, forming a diverse group of musical styles and repertoire.

In 2005, the traditional dance music performed in the northeastern region of Brazil called *samba de Roda* was declared a patrimony of humanity under oral and intangible cultural expressions by UNESCO. Samba de Roda appeared around the 19th century as an Afro-Brazilian dance performed as entertainment after informal *Candomblé* ceremonies (a region's main Afro-Brazilian religion), and incorporates clapping and chanting in a circle formation. Its main instruments are guitar, *atabaque, berimbau, chocalho, pandeiro*, and plate and knife (*prato-e-faca*). The presence of sounds stemming from corporeal (e.g., clapping, solo or choral chanting) and makeshift instruments (e.g., plate and knife, keychain, matchbox, wooden blocks, bottles, etc.) signal the creativity of many groups to fashion a musical laboratory out of the available resources. Many instruments have been manufactured from low-cost materials accessible to the communities involved. Moreover, unpitched instruments (e.g., shakers, whistles, bells, etc.) found in African-derived musics of the region are well regarded by performers.

After World War II (1939–1945), American jazz obtained a greater share of the Brazilian market, bringing with it the prominent use of brass instruments such as trombone and trumpet and resulting in "Brazilian-style" big bands. The carioca (Rio de Janeiro) influence of *choro* also affected samba by the insertion of flute and clarinet. The most common percussion instruments of samba are the pandeiro, *surdo*, and *tamborim*. These instruments generally mark the main pulse, while others add color (variety of timbres) and extra rhythmic layers. Another prominent instrument is the guitar (sometimes the seven- or eight-string guitar), whose rich harmonic and rhythmic versatility has been raised to the level of a "synthesis instrument" according to some scholars. The guitar (or sometimes a banjo or *cavaquinho*) provide an extensive melodic and harmonic range to the music. The cavaquinho (similar to a ukulele with different tuning), like the flute, may in fact take over the melody, acting as a substitute for the voice, and often accounts for a good portion of melodic improvisations. The piano has been another powerful instrument in terms of range in harmony, melody, and rhythm. Modern samba groups often make use of a standard "jazz band" combination: piano (keyboard or synthesizer), bass, drums, and vocals.

Samba groups range in size from duets (commonly voice and guitar) to symphonic ensembles. Samba as a music generally refers to a genre characterized by duple meter (2/4) or compound meter (6/8), overlaid with call-and-response singing, various unpitched percussive instruments, and complex syncopated rhythms which that additive rhythms and polyrhythms.

Brazil is a large country with a diverse population demographic, so given the variety of social settings in the country, many different styles of samba developed, with even more subgroups. The first is *Samba-Enredo*, a samba school's annual musical theme for Carnival. This type of samba requires a large ensemble, the *bateria*, a group of approximately 300 percussionists who accompany the singer and give rhythmic shape and sustenance to a large parade of dancers. The bateria is divided into smaller instrumental sections, usually in the following order: *cuícas* (a small cylindrical drum with a stick fastened to the internal center of the drumhead, whose pull and friction provides a high-pitched sound), *agogôs* (usually two iron bells connected through a curved stem), *pandeiro* (a flat, round tambourine made with a goatskin head mounted on a brass or a wood frame, whose adjustable bars often hold small metal shakers), *chocalhos* (a multiply lined shaker infused with tiny metal plates that produce a nice rattling sound), followed by a mixed group of *caixa* (a lightweight drum with nylon heads), *repique* (a middle-size drum) and *surdo* (a large drum).

Other samba styles include *Samba-Canção* (samba song) which is a more laid-back, sentimental, orchestrated type of samba promoted in the 1920s by musicians in the context of radio performances and recordings. Examples of Samba-Canção include *Samba-Exaltação*, which is a modality of samba that features extensive lyrics paying homage to the nation. This type of samba frequently makes use of orchestral resources, striving for grandeur and pomposity. The most famous example is "*Aquarela do Brasil* (Brazilian watercolors)" by Ari Barroso, recorded in 1939.

Samba de Gafieira is a fast-paced instrumental samba, created in the 1940s by saloon orchestras, that normally accompanies couples quickstep dancing. The *Pagode* originated in Rio in the 1970s and features a repetitive rhythm with percussion and electronic sounds. The Pagode adds the four-string banjo, *tantã*, and *repique-de-mão* to the general assortment of samba instruments (cavaquinho, guitar, and pandeiro). Famous Pagode groups include Fundo de Quintal, Só Pra Contrariar, Raça Negra, Katinguelê, Patrulha do Samba, Pique Novo, Travessos, and Arte Popular. In more recent years, many subgroups of samba fusion-styles have appeared, such as samba-reggae, samba-choro, samba-funk, samba-rock, samba-rap, and sambolero, among others.

Silvia M. Lazo

See also: Candomblé; Carnival, Music of; Samba Music

Further Reading

Döhring, Katharina. 2005. "*O Samba da Bahia: Tradição pouco conhecida* [The samba of Bahia: a lesser known tradition]." *Revista ICTUS*. https://www.academia.edu/4080791/Samba_de_Roda_uma_tradi%C3%A7%C3%A3o_pouco_conhecida_Revista_ICTUS_2005.

Murphy, John. 2006. *Music in Brazil*. New York: Oxford University Press.

Sandroni, Carlos. 2011. *Feitiço Decente: Transformação do samba no Rio de Janeiro (1917–1933)* [Under the spell: Transformation of samba in Rio de Janeiro (1917–1933)]. Rio de Janeiro: UFRJ.

Samba Music

As one of the principal urban popular music genres of Brazil, samba flourished between the 1920s and the 1950s. Its genesis refers to slave music and dance traditions such as *batuque* (percussive ensembles) and *umbigada* (belly-bump dance). The word "samba" is a derivative of *semba*, a term of Congo-Angolese origin that designates *umbigada*, choreography present in many Brazilian dances. Through time, the music also came to incorporate European harmonies and instruments, forming a wide and diverse group of styles and repertories that captivated Brazilians of all ages and social groups.

MUSICAL STYLES

Samba groups range from duets (commonly voice and guitar) to symphonic ensembles. Despite such variation, samba is generally a broad genre characterized by duple meter (2/4) or compound meter (6/8), overlaid with complex syncopated rhythms, call-and-response singing, and use of unpitched percussive instruments. Samba often combines music and dance learned through day-to-day interactions in bars, bakeries, cafes, parties, community activities, and larger events such as Carnival rehearsals.

Given the variety of social settings in which it appears, many different styles of samba developed, with many more subgroups. The first is *Samba-Enredo,* a samba school's annual musical theme for Carnival. The second is *Samba-Canção* (samba song), a more laid-back, sentimental, orchestrated type of samba promoted in the 1920s by musicians in the context of radio performances and recordings. Samba-Canção was commonly released at mid-year, outside of Carnival season. *Samba de Gafieira* is a fast-paced instrumental samba developed in the 1940s by saloon orchestras and used for couples quickstep dancing. *Pagode* originated in Rio in the 1970s and features a repetitive rhythm with percussion and electronic sounds.

Many subgroups of fusion styles have appeared, such as samba-reggae, samba-choro, samba-funk, samba-rock, samba-rap, and sambolero, to name a few. *Samba-Exaltação* has extensive lyrics paying homage to the nation. This type of samba frequently makes use of orchestral resources to enhance grandeur and pomposity. The most famous example is "Aquarela do Brasil" (Brazilian watercolors) by Ari Barroso (1939). After World War II (1939–1945), American jazz music obtained a greater share of the Brazilian market, bringing with it the prominent use of brass instruments such as trombone and trumpet and resulting in "Brazilian-style" big bands. The carioca influence of *choro* also added flute and clarinet to the range of samba instrumentation.

HISTORY AND DEVELOPMENT

The widespread popularity of samba today, both nationally and internationally, developed from a complicated history. Initially regarded as a "lowly" form of slave entertainment, a series of resolutions dating back to 1831 prohibited the "assemblage of slaves, *lundus*, vociferations, *batuques*, Black dances, uproars, and sambas." Further criticism and containment came from newspapers and police forces. After the abolition of slavery (1888), many Africans and Afro-Brazilians moved south toward the larger metropolitan capitals of Rio de Janeiro and São

Paulo. Settling in precarious huts in hillside areas (slums), African descendants revived rituals and dances that then blended with other immigrant traditions to form an greatly assorted collection of musical forms.

One of the main intellectual centers of samba music in Rio was Tia Ciata's house, where many professional musicians gathered to eat, drink, and play. Tia Ciata concurrently used her house as a center for *Candomblé* (the main Afro-Brazilian religion) ceremonies. Through such juxtapositions, samba's history became intricately connected to the world of Afro-Bahian religion. The musicians who frequented Tia Ciata's house included Donga (Ernesto Maria dos Santos, 1888–1974), João da Baiana (João Machado Guedes, 1887–1974), Heitor dos Prazeres (1898–1966), Pixinguinha (Alfredo da Rocha Viana Filho, 1897–1973), Sinhô (José Barbosa da Silva, 1888–1930), and Mauro de Almeida (1882–1956). Donga and Mauro de Almeida's composition "*Pelo Telefone* (Through the telephone)" (1916) is one of the earliest instances of successful samba recording in Rio de Janeiro. Its rhythmic basis bears a strong likeness to the *habanera* and the *maxixe*. The *ranchos*—semi-structured Carnivalesque groups that preceded *Escolas de Samba* (samba schools)—also exerted a strong aesthetic influence on the formation and dissemination of samba music, given that their samba style, based on percussion and metal instruments, was considered more humble, pure, and traditional.

Musicians whose expanding radio notoriety and record sales reached vast parts of the population represented a third group associated with "commercial" samba, more commonly performing the heavily orchestrated *Samba-Canção*. Noted musicians in this group include Ismael Silva (1905–1978, founder of *Deixa Falar,* Rio's first samba school), Brancura (Sílvio Fernandes, 1908–1935), Nilton Bastos (1899–1931), Noel Rosa (1910–1937), Silvio Caldas (1908–1998), Francisco Alves (1898–1952), Custódio Mesquita (1910–1945), and Cartola (Agenor de Oliveira, 1908–1980). These *sambistas* had close ties to the Estácio de Sá samba school, and thus defy strict categorization.

The mediums of radio and recording were frequently frowned upon, and became the subject of fierce debates wherein many cognoscenti divided samba into *Samba do Morro* (hillside samba) versus *Samba Desvirtuado* (distorted samba), the latter signifying samba produced for mass consumption. Two writers, Francisco Guimarães (nicknamed Vagalume) and Orestes Barbosa, especially symbolized this divide, each authoring news articles and books throughout the 1930s to the 1950s arguing the origins and definitions of the word "samba." Vagalume favored *Samba do morro*, whereas Barbosa made a case for samba as an authentically *carioca* tradition. The intellectual rift actually signaled a shift in Brazilian self-conception wherein samba (as an African-derived music) gained significant cultural status by meriting such discussions.

By the mid-1920s, during Brazil's Modernist movement, Brazilian intellectuals (including Gilberto Freyre, Mario de Andrade, and Heitor Villa-Lobos) promoted African and popular culture as authentic elements of national identity. Increasing acceptance and patronage of samba was also due in part to significant governmental backing during the dictatorship of President Getulio Vargas (1939–1945). As dictatorial governments attempt to mold a deferential citizenry, nationalist projects often appropriate cultural forms to create uniformity and social bonding. During the Vargas era, popular expressions such as capoeira, Carnival, and samba gained cultural status thanks to state-sponsored activities and propaganda vehicles like *Radio Nacional*. Samba schools received official recognition and financial subsidies, and Carnival was promoted as a major tourist attraction. Increasingly competitive, Carnival has become a large international festival boasting in excess of 6 million annual attendees; samba schools invest approximately $5 million *reais* (US $2.5 million) each annually in costumes, parade floats, and accoutrements.

SOCIOCULTURAL CONTEXT

Perhaps what best explains the prominence of samba, from a sociocultural standpoint, is its ability to promote irreverence and unity. The regularity of percussive samba rhythms—ranging from the rather subdued *Samba de Roda* (samba circle) to the frenetic *bateria* (Carnival ensemble of 300 drummers)—conveys a sense of contagious happiness and hypnotic frenzy. The interval between the first weaker beat and the second stronger beat of samba's double meter (in 2/4) permits complex rhythmic improvisations devised through singing, instruments, or dance moves. The balance between twirling (twisting) and flowing (elongated) corporeal movements constitutes a healthy interplay between mind and body for dancers and musicians alike. Some authors also describe the importance of *efeito-breque*, an abrupt melodic or lyrical interruption, which effectively breaks with auditory expectations and causes a sense of wonderment and renewal of the rhythm that follows. In *Samba de Breque*, these instrumental breaks also allow the singer to interject humorous commentary.

The vocals are straightforward, using unornamented speech-like patterns often running counter to the underlying meter, and thereby adding an additional layer of rhythmic effect (polyrhythm). Samba lyrics vary depending on the time, locale, and function. Carnival lyrics (*Samba Enredo*), for example, provide the main theme for the samba schools' parade, and are often drawn from Brazilian history, literature, folklore, and pop culture. Lyrics may address topics such as the founding of Brazil, pay tribute to native populations, or discuss contemporary issues such as the merits of test-tube babies.

Although difficult to generalize, standard sambas performed in small bars and cafes regularly deal with issues surrounding work, women, and money. Samba songs may speak about love and loss, conceived as complementary sides of the same coin, suggesting an affirmation of life regardless of its challenges or insecurities. Money is another common subject, featuring catchy lyrics confronting the dominant regime of unequal work and pay. A negative mindset about work all too often translates into "living-in the-moment" affirmations. Described by some scholars as the "politics of present time," lyrics argue for a state of enjoyment that defies hegemonic notions of modernity (too strict a work ethic, preoccupations with final rewards, the obsessive consumption of information due to a fear of social alienation, etc.). As such, samba functions as a sociocultural motto of creative will—the desire to make life anew, regardless of history.

Samba musicians and composers meet in Rio de Janeiro in 2009. Rooted in Brazil's African traditions, samba is one of the country's best known music and dance forms. (Ricardo Beliel/Brazil Photos/LightRocket via Getty Images)

Latin America in general, and Brazil in particular, has suffered an enduring stereotype of being a New World site of delayed development. The idea is not new, and many Brazilian musicians wrote about an archetypal cultural figure, the *malandro*, caricatured as a hustler whose poor working habits leave him constantly on the brink of financial ruin, and having to resort to all sorts of scams and trickeries. The malandro's bohemian personality also extended his moral economy to relationships with women. Despite being clearly a byproduct of Brazil's pre-industrial era, allusions to the malandro merit critical reassessment, as many songs also spoke of the unfeasibility of *malandragem* as a way of life.

SAMBA TODAY

Samba is a contemporary urban musical expression, encompassing persons of all social classes and ages, providing a respite from solitude and melancholy, encouraging social bonding, and creating a dynamic space for creativity. Over time, samba has become part of the Brazilian imagination and a main touchpoint of Brazilian national identity both nationally and abroad. The National Day of Samba, December 2, is commemorated annually. *Samba de Roda*, a traditional dance music performed in the northeastern region of Brazil, was declared a patrimony of humanity under oral and intangible cultural expressions by UNESCO in 2005. Samba de

Roda appeared in Bahia around the 19th century as an Afro-Brazilian dance performed as entertainment after informal *Candomblé* (religious) ceremonies, and incorporates clapping and chanting in a circle formation. Dancers take the "stage" at the center kindled by the ensemble: guitar, *atabaque, berimbau, chocalho,* and *pandeiro*.

Contemporary samba musicians (1970s–1980s) include Paulinho da Viola, Jorge Aragão, João Nogueira, Beth Carvalho, Elza Soares, Dona Ivone Lara, Clementina de Jesus, Chico Buarque, João Bosco, and Aldir Blanc. Other important names of an earlier generation include Pixinguinha, Ataulfo Alves, Carmen Miranda (a success in both Brazil and the United States), Elton Medeiros, Nelson Cavaquinho, Lupicínio Rodrigues, Aracy de Almeida, Demônios da Garoa, Isaura Garcia, Candeia, Elis Regina, Nelson Sargento, Wilson Moreira, Elizeth Cardoso, Jacob do Bandolim, Lamartine Babo, and Clara Nunes. Nunes was a famous Brazilian singer who mixed and promoted Candomblé and Umbanda's religious elements (her faith tradition) as a musical signature in many of her songs, such as "*Ê Baiana*," "*Tributo aos Orixás*," and "*Morena do Mar*."

Samba is a projection of Brazilian national identity. It has developed from a marginalized Afro-Brazilian musical expression to a musical form that in the early 20th century gradually conquered various sections of Brazilian society with its contagious rhythms and exquisite harmonies.

Silvia M. Lazo

See also: Candomblé; Carnival, Music of; Samba Instruments

Further Reading

Barcelos, Tânia Maia. 2009. "*Subjetividade e Samba: Na Roda com Paulinho da Viola* [Subjectivity and samba: on the wheel with Paulinho da Viola]." *Fractal Revista de Psicologia* 21(1) (January/April), 57–68.

Fernandes, Dmitri. 2011. "'*E fez-se o samba*': *Condicionantes intelectuais da música popular no Brasil* ["And they made samba": Intellectual creators of popular music in Brazil]." *Latin American Music Review* 32(1) (Spring/Summer), 39–58.

Murphy, John. 2006. *Music in Brazil.* New York: Oxford Press.

Napolitano, Marcos, and Maria Clara Wasserman. 2000. "*Desde que o samba é samba: a questão das origens no debate historiográfico sobre a música popular brasileira* [When samba is samba: The question of origins in the historiographical debate about Brazilian popular music]." *Revista Brasileira de História* 20(39), 167–189.

Oliven, Ruben George. 2011. "The Imaginary of Brazilian Popular Music." *Vibrant* [online] 8(1), 170–207. http://www.scielo.br/scielo.php?script=sci_arttext&pid=S1809-43412011000100007&lng=en&tlng=en.

Sanjo

Sanjo is a genre of Korean folk music performed on a solo melody instrument with *changgo* (*janggu*) (hourglass drum) accompaniment. A sanjo composition consists of three to six movements, each with a different rhythmic pattern. The movements are played consecutively, progressing from slower to faster tempos; one piece can last from 20 to 60 minutes. Sanjo has been composed for various instruments such as different zithers, a transverse flute, and a two-stringed spiked fiddle. Virtuoso performing techniques are required to convey its dramatic, expressive melodies. Recognized in 1967 as an Intangible Cultural Property by the South Korean government, sanjo contributes to a sense of national pride and identity. It is preserved and promoted by the National Gugak Center, taught in traditional music departments at Korean universities, and performed internationally.

The accepted explanation for the appearance of sanjo is that master musician Kim Chang-jo (1856–1919) first codified the form for the *kayagŭm* (*gaygeum*) (12-string zither) in the late 19th century. Music scholars in Korea are re-examining the attribution of sanjo to a single individual, since it is clear that other musicians were also borrowing and reworking musical materials from existing traditional vocal and instrumental genres (Provine, 2010, p. 2). In aristocratic circles, plucked zithers were used to perform and enjoy courtly music of a serene and elegant character, in contrast to the exciting rhythmic and musical effects of sanjo. Scorning such dramatic expression and sophisticated, technical skill, aristocrats called the instrumental solo scattered (*san*) melodies (*jo*).

Scholars agree that sanjo has a musical precedent in wind ensemble music, called *sinawi*, that accompanied shamanist dances. This improvisatory music progresses from slower to faster tempos and has roots in Korea's southern provinces, where particular 12-beat rhythmic patterns and melodies of a melancholy character predominate. The development of chamber music forms for aristocratic audiences of sinawi and *p'ansori* (a solo vocal music drama with drum accompaniment) contributed to the rise of sanjo. After the mid-19th century, performers began to prefer fixed rather than improvisatory melodies, and sanjo music has since reflected that change (Lee, 2009, p. 8). Although Kim Chang-jo may not have invented sanjo, he is influential for teaching his music to a number of pupils who became masters and transmitted their knowledge to the next generation, and for enabling the development of the genre for other Korean instruments.

Both government-appointed and independent master musicians teach and preserve sanjo. A traditional apprenticeship requires that the student both learn the master's melodies by rote, and study aristocratic and folk music. When the student is proficient in the master's sanjo, he can begin to revise musical material, add new melodies, and gradually evolve his own variant of the piece. Eventually, the composition bears the name of the newer master. In the 1960s, when sanjo compositions were first written down for teaching and study in traditional music departments of Korean universities, the term *ryu* ("school" in Japanese) was added to the newer master's composition to distinguish it as his personal variant in the lineage of his teacher (Killick, 2013, pp. 33–34).

Melanie T. Pinkert

See also: Janggu; Pansori

Further Reading

Howard, Keith. 2006. *Preserving Korean Music: Intangible Cultural Properties as Icons of Identity.* Aldershot, UK: Ashgate.

Howard, Keith, Chaesuk Lee, and Nicholas Casswell. 2008. *Korean Kayagŭm Sanjo: A Traditional Instrumental Genre.* Aldershot, UK: Ashgate.

Killick, Andrew. 2013. *Hwang Byungki: Traditional Music and the Contemporary Composer in the Republic of Korea.* Surrey, UK: Ashgate.

Lee, Bo-hyung. 2009. "Social History of Sanjo." In Yong-Shik Lee (ed.), *Sanjo*, 3–12. Seoul: National Center for Korean Traditional Performing Arts.

Lee, Yong-Shik. 2009. *Sanjo.* Seoul: National Center for Korean Traditional Performing Arts.

Provine, Robert C. 2010. "An Introduction to Sanjo: Background and Musical Structure." *Perspectives on Korean Music* 1.

Schlager

Schlager (German for "hit") emerged in Vienna, Austria, in the late 19th-century and is a relatively young musical phenomenon. The origin of the term is unclear; some argue that it first appeared in the Viennese *National-Zeitung* in 1881 to describe a musical melody, chorus, or song with rapidly growing popularity, regardless of its genre. Others point out that the term had already been applied to the premiere of Richard Strauss's waltz "*An der schönen blauen Donau* (On the beautiful blue Danube)" in 1867. The popular songs termed schlager were often originally drawn from operas or operettas, chansons, waltzes, polkas, or marches with lyrics and became popular beyond their original contexts. The roots of schlager lie in 19th-century entertainment music, comical songs, and soubrette albums. Nowadays, the term describes a large portion of popular music not characterized as Anglo-American pop or rock, regardless of its success. As a form of popular song, schlager is directly related to the production and distribution of music as a commodity.

Once the popular songs from Vienna had reached Berlin in the early 20th century, composers started to write complete evening entertainment programs in a way that invited the extraction of single songs as schlager. During the ensuing period, original songs labeled as schlager were circulated widely. As such, schlager is both closely connected to the emergence of urban culture and a typical product of industrialized society: the production of schlager is based on a division of labor among composer, lyricist, producer, and performer, followed by marketing and distribution. The short lifespan of most schlager songs reinforces their status as a commodity.

With the emergence of the recording industry at the beginning of the 20th century, schlager developed from single hit songs into a general musical genre. At the end of World War I, Berlin became the center for schlager production, with the establishment of revues and cabarets as popular stage entertainment. The parallel development of mass media broadened the reach of schlager and its audience, helping ensure its success. During and after World War II, schlager was used to entertain the population and troops, but also as propaganda (Wicke, 1998, p. 1068). Songs about endurance, home(land), and longing for loved ones resonated strongly with audiences. Besides jazz, rock, and pop, schlager became the most widespread musical phenomenon of the 20th century in Europe.

Musically, schlager generally employs 4/4 time and orchestral or pop arrangements; it usually avoids African American musical characteristics like syncopation and blue notes. It is based on standardized structures, catchy melodies, easy harmonies, and prominent danceable rhythms. Its general form is bound to eight-bar phrase building and the verse-chorus principle; however, these elements may vary. Schlager is often limited in its gamut and compound intervals are rare. Compositions are often limited to the basic functions of tonic, subdominant, and dominant, while arrangement (fashionable sounds and rhythms) and studio production techniques such as echo effects are crucial. It is hard to pinpoint exactly what differentiates schlager from other popular music genres, because it constantly adapts to and adopts recent musical trends in adjusted forms: cabaret-schlager, jazz-schlager, tango-schlager, rock-and-roll-schlager, and so on. Its aesthetic form is always related to its cultural and historical context, as schlager aims at broad commercial success and is oriented to suit its audience's familiar, everyday experiences. Hence, schlager form has to carefully balance a general recognizability in form and content with elements of innovation to promote success. Schlager songs usually contain lyrics in their respective national languages (and at times local dialects), often addressing issues such as (straight) love, *Heimat* (homeland), wanderlust, desire, and nostalgia, but also everyday happiness or friendship. Schlager refers to the zeitgeist and sometimes tentatively addresses socio-political issues—though never offensively—and objectionable themes are avoided. Generally, schlager represents stereotypical views of love and gender relations, and is dominated by a traditional worldview. As such, schlager has often been associated with escapism and superficial entertainment music. Central to the success of schlager is the performer, who is often not the originator of the song, but who personifies its emotions and lyrical content. Songs are often written for the performer's persona and to reinforce the performer's celebrity status. Popular schlager succeeds in offering a source of identification for its listeners, and thus the songs resonate with the needs and desires of the majority.

With the rise of rock and roll after World War II and the age-specific differentiation of musical cultures, the term "schlager" became associated with music that was particularly popular with a parent generation, and less identified as youth music. At least since the success of the Beatles in the 1960s, younger generations make negative associations with the genre as being unsophisticated, traditional, conservative, and reactionary; however, its popularity and commercial success exceed that of most other popular music genres. Schlager is widely popular all over Europe, not least due to the international success of the Eurovision Song Contest, which started as a schlager festival. Most countries developed their localized versions of the genre: in Finland, it goes under the name *iskelmä*, in the Netherlands and Flanders *levenslied*, and *šlager* or *uspješnica* in countries of the former Yugoslavia. However, countries such as Poland, Hungary, Switzerland, Turkey, Scandinavia, and the Baltic States, as well as (to a lesser extent) France, have adopted the German term to describe similar musical phenomena.

Melanie Schiller

See also: Eurovision Song Contest; Fiddle; Norwegian Folk Music; Nyckelharpa; Yodeling

Further Reading

Adorno, Theodor W. 1929. "Schlageranalysen." *Anbruch. Monatszeitschrift für moderne Musik* [Dawn. monthly magazine for modern music] (3), 108–114.

Bohlman, Phillip. 1996. *Central European Folk Music. An Annotated Bibliography of Sources in German.* New York: Garland.

Currid, Brian. 2000. "'A Song Goes Round the World': The German Schlager, as an Organ of Experience." *Popular Music* 19(2) (April), 147–180.

Larkey, Edward. 2000. "Just for Fun? Language Choice in German Popular Music." *Popular Music and Society* 24(3), 1–20.

Linke, Norbert. 1987. *Musik erobert die Welt oder Wie die Wiener Familie Strauß die "Unterhaltungsmusik" revolutionierte* [Music conquers the world like the Viennese Strauss family's revolutionary "Light Music"]. Vienna: Herold.

Lücke, Martin. 2010. "Schlager." In Anette Kreutzinger-Herr and Melanie Unseld (eds.), *Lexikon Musik und Gender* [Music lexicon and gender], 231–232. Stuttgart: Bärenreiter and Metzler.

Wicke, Peter. 1998. "Schlager." In Friedrich Blume (ed.), *Die Musik in Geschichte und Gegenwart. Allgemeine Enzyklopädie der Musik* [Music of the past and present. General encyclopedia of music], 1063–1070. Kassel: Bärenreiter.

Schottische

Also called the "Scottish" in the 19th century, the *schottische* is a duple-meter social dance for couples that includes energetic leaps and smooth hops, depending on the specific type. It is one of the oldest of all dances, with a simple fundamental step, and is traditionally performed at roughly 78 beats per minute (though slightly faster in pre-Civil War America). It was popular in England and on the European continent in the 1840s and 1850s, making it contemporaneous with the polka and galop. The French call it the *écossaise*, but English and Scottish dance experts consider the ecossaise to be a simpler country dance (also in duple time).

Douglas Kennedy, the Director of the English Folk Dance and Song Society, alleged that the schottische was "created by the Polish dancing master Markowski roughly one hundred years after the appearance of the écossaise, by combining the rhythm of the strathspey," but no documentary evidence currently supports this claim. The schottische was already danced in Sweden in the first decade of the 19th century, and contemporary references to it in Scandinavia specify two figures (floor patterns), consisting of several hopping steps forward in open formation, followed by the second movement in closed form.

The polka, based in part on a schottische step, appeared in Germany in the 1830s, and due to this similarity was called "die Schottische." By 1844, the actual schottische (in round dance form) was called the *Rheinländer* (in Bavaria), and the Bavarian Polka (in Rhenish countries). In the 1860s, music for the schottische could also include polkas played at half-speed. The schottische was first danced in England around 1848; the Highland Schottische was introduced to Scotland in 1855 and known as the "Balmoral Schottische." The waltz also employs a modified schottische step, which resulted from the incorporation of waltz-like turns into the écossaise. It resembles a waltz in 2/4 meter, with the left foot skipping forward while the right foot in extended in front, concluding on the second pulse with the feet coming together.

The social position of dancing masters declined dramatically throughout the 19th century, and middle-class dancers were admonished not to display extreme agility, lest they look too much like a dancing master. Manuals published in the 1840s and 1850s concentrated less on elaborate steps and correct methods for handling dance cards, and instead began to resemble etiquette manuals. New York dancing master Thomas Hill advised the reader not to "amuse yourself by hacking the woodwork or in any way mar the furniture," and to avoid "loud conversation, profanity, stamping the feet, writing on the wall, smoking tobacco, spitting or throwing anything on the floor" while performing the schottische and galop.

Different combinations employing the schottische step were danced in the United States from at least 1857, and most mid-century Americans knew how to waltz, polka, galop, and dance quadrilles. Charles Durang's *The Fashionable Dancer's Casket* (1856) described opportunities in most pre-Civil War urban centers to go to weekly soirées and balls. He mentions that the *schottische valse* was a particular favorite of American ballrooms and stated that the schottische was "as universally danced as the polka," although its hopping step led to "inevitable collisions" of couples on crowded dance floors. American author Mark Twain (Samuel Clemens) reported in a letter to his elder brother Orion (March 18, 1861) that his mother considered the dance to be scandalous. After the Civil War, etiquette books almost completely replaced dancing manuals, and ballroom dancing preferred round dances performed in closed position (by couples). The most popular urban dances included the waltz, the galop, cotillions, and quadrilles (including brief schottische steps), whereas rural settings preferred English country dancing, the schottische, the polka, and the parlor game known as the German. Dress was formal in the cities, with men usually in white tie and tails and women in gowns with long trains, supported by bustles, hoops, and corsets.

At the same time in Argentina, whites began to adopt black forms of dance, such as the *candombe* (*candomblé*). Throughout the last three decades of the 19th century, younger Afro-Argentines began abandoning the candombe in favor of imported European dance forms such as the schottische and habanera.

Continental dancers before 1890 preferred to face each other, but they later adapted the open position. Reaching the height of its popularity in England by 1880 (as the "Military" schottische) and as a continental social dance in the 1890s, the schottische fell out of fashion, and was then revived just before the Vernon Castle period in the United States under the name of "Barn Dance" (1905–1910) and again as the "Big Apple" and jitterbug of the Jazz Age. It survived during the heyday of "animal dances," the foxtrot, the Charleston, and early swing dance forms. The Trianon Ballroom in Chicago—one of the Midwest's grandest dance establishments of the 1920s–1940s—featured the schottische, foxtrot, and waltz in its evening programs until World War II.

Modern American folk varieties of the schottische exist, including the Danish schottische; the Mexican Schottis (for couples, danced on the U.S. West Coast since the beginning of the folk dance movement in the 1930s); and La Burrita (the Little Donkey), introduced to the West Coast by Carlos Rosas of Mexico City. Other European couples forms are present in Portugal and Naples, Italy (the *Fado Blanquita* and Neapolitan tarantella, which combined the schottische step with a buzz turn);

in Ireland (the *Siamsa Berite* and the *Staicin Eornan* (stack of barley), both introduced by Una O'Farrell of Dublin to the United States by adapting the schottische step to a hornpipe meter); and in Appenzell, Switzerland (*Der Gsatzlig*, invented by Jane Hinrich; and the *Chilbitanz*, brought to the United States by Millie von Konsky in 1954). The most thorough discussion of different combinations and patterns for the mid–20th-century traditional American schottische can be found in Lloyd Shaw's *The Round Dance Book* (1948).

Folk dances with related patterns include those danced in an open circle from Serbia (the Sarajeva *kolo*, the Rumunjsko kolo with an added rocking step, and the Milanovo kovo, in which the circle pulls in to the center), and Israel (*Kuma echa*, adapted by Rivkah Sturman for public dance in Israel and the Jewish diaspora before the creation of the Jewish state in 1946). Other folk variants adapt the pattern to a single line, as in Israel (*Ken Yovdu*, influenced by the Arab *debka* step) and Scotland (Ship o' Grace, a strathspey with an internal schottische section, composed in the 1950s by Jean McAdam of Glasgow)m and for trios of dancers (The Shepherd's Crook from Scotland, danced in a figure eight and incorporating several Highland fling steps). There is also a modern country-western dance called the "Sweetheart Schottische," which is danced in sweetheart (shadow) position.

STEPS

The schottische step takes two forms: the more traditional "step, close, step, hop" pattern; and the "run, run, run, hop" pattern, which is similar to the American "barn dance" or "modern" schottische. This dance requires a 4/4 meter, and each step is given one beat. It is danced in a modified running style, accenting the first step of each measure. On the hop, the free foot should be lifted only slightly off the floor, keeping the foot directly under the body and very close to the ankle of the supporting foot. This type of lift is also found in the Swiss schottische, in the Swedish turning schottische, and in the Serbian kolo, although Serbian forms include a characteristic faster tempo for the step-hop pattern. In the American schottische, however, the free leg swings easily forward and slightly across the supporting leg. The free foot is never kicked up behind or to the side.

The direction of the schottische is not always forward, so the step pattern may have to be adjusted accordingly. When dancers progress sideways or on a diagonal, the second and third steps cross in front or behind. Couples usually stand next to each other, in "open position," with the lead dancer's right arm around the waist of the partner, and the right dancer's left hand resting on the leader's right shoulder. English dancers usually change partners frequently and begin with the outside foot (thus, the couple's feet do not match). A typical 19th-century schottische pattern combines two schottische steps and four step-hops, moving counterclockwise around the room. During the four step-hops, dancers of the mid-19th century would make a half-round turn in place.

Laura Stanfield Prichard

See also: Austro-German Dances; Scotch Snap; Yodeling

Further Reading

Lidster, Miriam. 1965. *Folk Dance Progressions*. Belmont, CA: Wadsworth.

Richardson, Philip. 1960. *The Social Dances of the Nineteenth Century in England*. London: Herbert Jenkins.

Shaw, Lloyd. 1948. *The Round Dance Book: A Century of Waltzing*. Caldwell, ID: Caxton Press.

Wharton, Kendra Ann. 2011. "Schottisches and Scars." Master of Music thesis, Rice University (Houston, TX).

Schrammelmusik

Schrammelmusik is an umbrella term for various kinds of folkloristic music in Vienna, Austria, which are played in a special chamber setting. The name derives from the brothers Johann (1850–1893) and Josef (1852–1895) Schrammel, who studied violin at the Vienna conservatory, and who, with the guitarist Anton Strohmayer, beginning in 1878, formed a terzet (*Nussdorfer Terzett*) and, with the clarinetist Georg Dänzer, in 1884, the *Schrammel-Quartett* (*D' Schrammeln*). The guitar used is a Spanish guitar with (now) nylon strings, and three to nine additional bass strings on a second unfretted neck. This typical Viennese instrument is named *Kontra-Gitarre* or *Schrammel-Gitarre*. In 1891, Dänzer left the ensemble, and the high-G clarinet, which had played the melody parallel to the first violin, was replaced by an accordion.

The ensemble played native folkloristic music from Vienna, composed folkloristic music (still very famous today is Johann Schrammel's march *Wien bleibt Wien* (Vienna remains Vienna), 1886), and generated the term "Schrammelmusik." The quartet gave concerts until 1893, made folkloristic Viennese music socially acceptable, and was very popular in all walks of life. Their music was for listening, not for dancing. They published editions of their music (e.g., the three-volume *Alte oesterreichische Volksmelodien* (Old Austrian folk melodies), edited by Johann Schrammel, 1888/89) and also gave concerts abroad. Beside the *Schrammel-Quartett*, other ensembles, such as *D' Grinzinger* and the *Gebrüder Butschetty*, were also popular and toured abroad.

Many ensembles picked up folkloristic Viennese music and played Schrammelmusik. The basic instrumentation consisted mainly of two violins and a contra-guitar. During the first half of the 20th century, two violins, accordion (which for the Schrammel quartet was only a compromise), and a contra-guitar was the most common instrumentation. Even in the late 19th century, the ensembles (mostly male musicians) played at *Heurigen* pubs in the Vienna suburbs (the term "Heuriger," plural *Heurige(n)*, means both the young wine that is served, and the establishment itself), in traditional inns and at private gatherings. *Heurigenmusik*, with its melodic and rhythmic basis in the Austrian *Ländler*, is an umbrella term for Schrammelmusik and Viennese songs, including songs sung by the *Fiakersänger*, who drove cabs (the term *Fiaker* means the cab and the driver, today an attraction for tourists). During the 1880s, Schrammelmusik ensembles included a singer (also a yodeler or a whistler), who sang Viennese songs (the text dealt with Vienna, sung in the Viennese dialect). The songs supported a homelike atmosphere in the Heurigen, and helped patrons to forget their hard daily lives.

After the death of the Schrammel brothers, the musicians and the name of the ensemble changed several times. A "Schrammel-cult" started in the 1920s (mostly quartets with two violins, accordion, and contra-guitar, with a singer; or trios with one violin). The most important ensemble after World War II (1939–1945) was the *Faltl-Kemmeter-Schrammeln*, with the violinist Hans Faltl, a member of the *Wiener Philharmoniker* (Vienna Philharmonic). During the 1960s, a renaissance of Schrammelmusik started with the *Spilar Schrammeln*, who enlarged the repertoire with dance music of the Schrammel brothers. In 1963 and 1972, Louis Böck rediscovered manuscripts of the Schrammel brothers and performed them with his *Klassisches Wiener Schrammelquartett* (active until 1979) in the traditional setting with two violins, contra-guitar, and clarinet (or flute).

Today, duos (contra-guitar and accordion) and trios (violin, contra-guitar, and accordion) are common in Schrammelmusik. In Vienna, more than 30 Schrammel quartets are active. The *Schrammel.Klang.Festival* takes place in Litschau (where the Schrammel brothers' father was born, 100 miles northwest of Vienna) each year.

Jörg Jewanski

See also: Austro-German Dances; Ländler

Further Reading

Flotzinger, Rudolf, ed. 2002–2006. Various articles in *Oesterreichisches Musiklexikon*, 5 vols. Vienna: Verlag der Österreichischen Akademie der Wissenschaften.

Fritz, Elisabeth Th., and Helmut Kretschmer, eds. 2006. *Wien. Musikgeschichte. Teil 1: Volksmusik und Wienerlied* [Music history. Part 1: Folk music and Viennese song]. Vienna: Lit.

Montgomery, David. 2003. *Franz Schubert's Music in Performance: Compositional Ideals, Notational Intent, Historical Realities, Pedagogical Foundations*. London: Pendragon Press.

Pressler, Gertraud. 2002. "*Fiakersänger.*" In *Oesterreichisches Musiklexikon*, vol. 1, 440. Vienna: Publisher of the Austrian Academy of Sciences.

Suppan, Wolfgang. 1977. "Research on Folk Music in Austria Since 1800." *Yearbook of the International Folk Music Council* 8, 117–129.

Scotch Snap

The Scotch snap is a syncopated rhythmic figure in which a short, accented note is followed by a longer, unaccented note. The short note comes on the beat, rather than before it. It often appears together with a long-short syncopation. The Scotch snap often appears as a 16th note followed by and barred with a dotted eighth note. It is most often associated with Scottish music, from which it derives its name. It also appears in vocal and instrumental music from other Celtic and Anglophone traditions, as well as in Baroque music. The Scotch snap is also known as the "Scots catch" and the "Lombard rhythm."

The Scotch snap is a distinguishing feature of the strathspey, a type of Scottish country dance tune in 4/4 time that is slower and statelier than a reel or a hornpipe.

The Scotch snap gives the strathspey tune its rhythmic drive and helps the dancers find the correct lift and character for their steps. The fiddlers Niel Gow (1727–1807), William Marshall (1748–1833) and James Scott Skinner (1843–1927, known as "the Strathspey King") were among the musicians most closely associated with performing, composing, and notating fiddle strathspeys. Marshall is credited with the invention of the slow strathspey, in which the snap is a prominent feature. Scotch snaps are common in bagpipe tunes as well.

The Scotch snap also appears in Scottish and English vocal music. For example, the Scottish song "The Bonnie Banks o' Loch Lomond" features Scotch snaps in the first line of the chorus: "Oh, ye'll tak' *the high* road, and I'll tak' *the low* road." Similarly, "Heart of Oak," the official march of the Royal Navy of the United Kingdom, features Scotch snaps in the second line of the chorus: "We always are *ready*: *Steady*, boys, *steady*!" Snaps also appear in many traditional Irish songs in Gaelic.

Some musicians and linguists believe that the presence of the Scotch snap in Scottish, Irish, and English music reflects the high number of accented first syllables in the Gaelic, Scots, and English languages. These scholars also point to the prevalence of snaps in Gaelic work songs from the Hebrides, as well as the Scottish tradition of *puirt-a-beul*, sometimes called "mouth music," or vocal dance music, as evidence of the particularly Scottish nature of the Scotch snap. The Scotch snap corresponds to the metrical foot called the trochée. The poetry of Robert Burns (1759–1796), Scotland's national poet, is written in the Lowland Scots dialect, and often uses trochaic meters.

In the Americas, the Scotch snap appears in several folk music traditions influenced by working-class Scottish immigrants to the New World. Snaps appear in Cape Breton, Appalachian, and Texas-style fiddle tunes. Combined with similar rhythmic features of West African musical styles, they appear in African American musical styles such as spirituals, jazz, gospel, and soul. They also appear in music designed to evoke images of cowboys and the Wild West.

Under the alternate name "Lombard rhythm," which derives from particular folk music traditions of Lombardy in northern Italy in which snaps are also found, the Scotch snap has appeared in several works in the Western classical tradition. It was a common feature in Italian operas of the Baroque period, and composers such as J. S. Bach, Henry Purcell, Felix Mendelssohn, and Antonín Dvořák all made use of Lombard rhythms in their compositions. The Hungarian composer Béla Bartók is also known for his use of Lombard rhythms, which stands to reason because, like English, Scots, and Gaelic, Hungarian is a language that relies heavily on short-long rhythmic patterns.

Rachel Adelstein

See also: Bartók, Béla; Celtic Music; Fiddle

Further Reading

Collinson, Francis M. 1966. *The Traditional and National Music of Scotland*. London: Routledge.

Emmerson, George S. 1971. *Rantin' Pipe and Tremblin' String: A History of Scottish Dance Music*. London: Dent.

Hunter, James. 1988. *The Fiddle Music of Scotland*. Edinburgh: The Hardie Press.

Johnson, David. 1972. *Music and Society in Lowland Scotland in the Eighteenth Century*. London: Oxford University Press.

Purser, John. 2007. *Scotland's Music: A History of the Traditional and Classical Music of Scotland from Earliest Times to the Present Day*, 2nd ed. Edinburgh: Mainstream Publishing.

Skinner, James Scott. 1984. *A Guide to Bowing: Strathspeys, Reels, Pastoral Melodies, Hornpipes, etc.* (reprint of 1900 original). Edinburgh: The Hardie Press.

Skinner, James Scott. 2002. *The Strathspey King: Original Recordings of the Great Scottish Fiddle Maestro 1905–1922* [CD]. Shillinghill, Scotland: Temple Records.

Tagg, Philip. 2011. *Scotch Snaps: The Big Picture* [online video documentary]. https://vimeo.com/175910173.

Seeger, Peter (1919–2014)

Peter "Pete" Seeger was an American folk musician and activist who championed folk song as vital cultural heritage and as a tool for social change. His career included singing at labor and anti-war rallies, spearheading the 1950s folk revival movement, and advocating for various political and environmental issues. Seeger authored and recorded a number of significant folk songs, including "Where Have All the Flowers Gone," "If I Had a Hammer," and "Turn, Turn, Turn." His rendition of "We Shall Overcome" served as a rallying song for the American civil rights movement of the 1960s. The motto etched into his banjo, "This machine surrounds hate and forces it to surrender" embodied his belief in the power of music to effect change.

Music played a prominent role in the Seeger family household. Pete's father, Charles Seeger, was a musicologist, conductor, and professor of music at the University of California at Berkeley. His mother, Constance Seeger, was a violinist who taught at the Juilliard School in New York. The couple soon divorced and Charles remarried Ruth Crawford Seeger, a leading modernist composer and American folk music specialist. They introduced Pete to American folk

American folk musician, songwriter, and political activist Pete Seeger, ca. 1970. (Michael Ochs Archives/Getty Images)

songs, instruments, and dances and took him to various music festivals. While attending the Folk Song and Dance Festival in Asheville, North Carolina, Pete discovered the banjo, an instrument that would play a prominent role in his political and social activism. Pete would complete two years of an undergraduate degree in sociology at Harvard University before dropping out to pursue his political and musical interests. He worked alongside ethnomusicologist Alan Lomax cataloging and transcribing music at the Archive of American Folk Song at the Library of Congress. His respect for folk musician Woody Guthrie led him to travel the country collecting American folk music and expanding his performance repertoire. In 1943, Seeger married Toshi-Aline Ota, who shared and supported Seeger's passion for music and politics. They raised three children in a log cabin that Seeger built on a large plot of land overlooking the Hudson River in Beacon, NY.

MUSICIAN AND ACTIVIST

As a young man, Pete Seeger believed fully in the power of folk song to unify people and to engender social change. At Harvard, he joined the American Student Union, a leftist coalition concerned with the rise of fascism in Europe. His support of various causes, including desegregation and labor unions, led him to join the Young Communist League. There he discovered his talent as song leader: bringing his banjo to meetings and marches, he inspired his audiences to sing along. Seeger quickly achieved great popularity as a musician and social activist. In 1941, he joined Millard Lampell and Lee Hays in founding the Almanac Singers, a loosely organized musical collective devoted to the creation of a singing labor movement. With the start of World War II, the group performed patriotic antiwar songs, which earned them a spot on prime-time national radio. Although the Almanac Singers disbanded shortly after the war, Seeger remained in the spotlight for his role in the presidential campaign of Henry Wallace, supporting Wallace's promise for a peaceful resolution to the Cold War. Seeger then joined Lee Hays, Ronnie Gilbert, and Fred Hellerman to form a new band known as the Weavers. This group achieved significant fame, securing engagements at major nightclubs and a contract with Decca Records through which they sold an estimated 4 million albums and singles. Their best-known songs included "If I Had a Hammer," "Wimoweh," "Goodnight Irene," and "Kisses Sweeter Than Wine."

By the 1950s, Pete Seeger had become one of the most controversial musicians in American history. Demonstrators protested his concerts regularly, decrying his leftist politics and his early associations with the Communist Party. The most disturbing demonstration took place in Peekskill, NY, in 1949, when actor and singer Paul Robeson invited Seeger to join him in concert. As Seeger and his family drove away from the performance, protesters chanted slogans and threw rocks, smashing the windows of the Seeger family car. A prolonged and invasive FBI investigation, which questioned the political views and the patriotism of Seeger and his fellow musicians, led the Weavers to disband. In 1955, Seeger was called to testify in front of the House Un-American Activities Committee, where he famously resisted answering the leading questions of the interrogation committee. His conviction and sentence to one year in prison were later dismissed as being based on a faulty indictment.

Seeger later disassociated himself from any political party and focused instead on supporting various social and environmental causes. He became especially active in advocating for the removal of pollution from the Hudson River and for the closing of the Indian Point Nuclear Plant in upstate New York. In 2010, he released *Tomorrow's Children*, an album dedicated to environmental awareness that he had recorded with the Rivertown Kids, a group of students from a local middle school. Together, they won a 2011 Grammy Award for best musical album for children.

RECOGNITION

By the 1990s, Pete Seeger had transcended the complex intermingling of his politics and his music, and he received a number of prestigious awards and honors. These included a Grammy Lifetime Achievement Award in 1993, the National Medal of the Arts and the Kennedy Center Award in 1994, the Harvard Arts Medal and induction into the Rock and Roll Hall of Fame in 1996, and a 1997 Grammy Award for Best Traditional Folk Album of 1996 for his recording "Pete." In April 2000, Seeger was named one of America's Living Legends by the Library of Congress. In 2008, he performed "This Land Is Your Land" at the inauguration of President Barack Obama. Still steadfast in his demand for social equality, Seeger insisted on singing the version of the song (penned by Woody Guthrie) that included lyrics about economic inequality. His legacy includes inspiring a number of folk singers who adapted his style of revisiting older songs and applying them to current issues. He was especially influential for Bob Dylan, Don McLean, Bernice Johnson Reagen, and Bruce Springsteen. Springsteen drew from Seeger's repertoire for his 2006 album "We Shall Overcome: The Seeger Sessions" and shared the stage at the inauguration of President Barack Obama.

PUBLICATION

Pete Seeger left a rich legacy of both published and unpublished writings. *Where Have All the Flowers Gone: A Singalong Memoir* (1993) is an accessible musical autobiography about the musician and his beloved folk songs. His political songbooks include *Hard Hitting Songs for Hard-Hit People* (1967), compiled with Alan Lomax and Woody Guthrie; *Songs for Peace* (1966); and *Carry It On: The Story of America's Working People in Story and Song* (1985), coauthored with Bob Rieser. *The Incompleat Folksinger* (1972) is a collection of his writings on civil rights, the history of folk songs, and various folk musicians. His instructional manuals include *Henscratches and Flyspecks: How to Read Melodies from Songbooks in Twelve Confusing Lessons* (1973) and *How to Play the 5-String Banjo* (1948), the latter a book that he revised many times. Seeger was especially fond of his songbooks for children, such as *Foolish Frog* (1973) and *Pete Seeger's Storytelling Book* (2000). Concerned with the quality of cultural education disseminated on television, Seeger created *Rainbow Quest*, an educational show for children. A powerful film tribute, titled *Pete Seeger: The Power of Song*, was released by Jim Brown Productions in 2007.

Yona Stamatis

See also: Banjo; Folkways Records; Guthrie, Woody; Lomax, Alan and John

Further Reading

Dunaway, David King. 1981/2008. *How Can I Keep from Singing? The Ballad of Pete Seeger.* New York: Villard Books.

Rosenthal, Rob, and Sam Rosenthal. 2012. *Pete Seeger: In His Own Words.* Boulder, CO: Paradigm.

Seeger, Pete. 1993/2009. *Where Have All the Flowers Gone: The Songs of Pete Seeger.* New York: W. W. Norton.

Wilkinson, Alec. 2009. *The Protest Singer: An Intimate Portrait of Pete Seeger.* New York: Random House.

Winkler, Alan M. 2009. *"To Everything There Is a Season": Pete Seeger and the Power of Song.* New York: Oxford.

Sephardic Music

One of the early Jewish ethnomusicologists, Abraham Zvi Idelsohn (1882–1938), opens a chapter on Sephardic folk songs by asserting and then asking: "A folk song must spring from a nation. But are the Jewish people a nation?" Their dispersal (from Israel) for 2,000 years, he argues, would deny such a claim. Yet, "Jews have never been divorced from the land where they developed from nomadic tribes to a nation" (Idelsohn, 1967, p. 357). Sephardim had a shorter temporal association with their *adopted* lands, but those connections likewise endure. They contributed beyond their numbers to Jewish liturgy, intermingled with the larger folk culture, and contributed words and melodies that sometimes, today, constitute "world music" (e.g., Gregorian chant may have evolved from Middle Eastern Jewish and Christian sources).

Sephardic is nevertheless a debated term. The proper noun refers to the distinctly Jewish language and cultures of the Iberian peninsula, abbreviated as Spain and including Portugal. However, "Sephardic" has come to mean more. Some count "Mizrachi" or (Middle) "Eastern" Jews in this group; others view "Sephardic" as shorthand for non-Ashkenazic Jews in whatever country. Perhaps the largest group views the term broadly and inclusively.

Jews entered Spain during the sixth century CE when it was held by the recently converted Christian Visigoths. North African/Muslim forces conquered it in 711. Generally allowed to live and work freely under the Moors, Jews and Christians benefited from a society that valued learning, with "private foundations dispensing grants for artistic or scientific work" (Rubin and Baron, 2006, p. 84). The Caliphate likewise appreciated music, underwriting ensembles and performances.

This period of *convivienca* (harmony among the three major religions) foundered during the 14th century and ended abruptly in 1492 when the Christian monarchs Ferdinand and Isabella ordered the Edict of Expulsion (Alhambra Decree): Jews were forced to leave the country within four months. The resulting refugee population, numbering between 100,000 and 200,000, fled most notably to Morocco, North Africa, and European destinations both northward and eastward. At around the same time, another Muslim empire, the Ottoman Turks, began their broad conquest of Asia Minor, the Arabian peninsula, the Balkans, and beyond.

Two language groups, Judeo-Spanish (more commonly known as Ladino or Judezmo) and Judeo-Arabic, overlapped with the movement caused by the Expulsion and near-in-time Ottoman conquest. A third, related population/linguistic group also deserves mention. When the 12th-century traveler and ethnographer Benjamin of Tudela disembarked in Baghdad, he estimated that 40,000 Jews were resident there. Middle Eastern communities—Syrian, Persian, Iraqi, Yemenite—often predated Sephardic and Ottoman influences. Yemenite settlements, as one example, were geographically isolated and retained their Hebrew/Aramaic language infused with Arabic.

All told, the common factor for these former Spanish, Ottoman Turkish, and Middle Eastern communities are Judaic-Arabic confluences. The story of Sephardic music begins, however, with an older, more universal practice: chanting sacred texts in public venues, or "Torah by word of mouth." *Piyyutim* are poems put to music. Evolving from the Hebrew tradition of psalms, they contained both direct and allegorical references to God, survival, morals, and peoplehood that could be put to use in personal penitential prayer (*slichot*) or more communal song (*z'mirot*). Although Ashkenazim (European Jews characterized by an evolving Germanic language and culture) contributed to the genre, Sephardic piyyutim are among the best remembered. Solomon ibn Gabirol was a poet who created *Adon Olam*, repeated in Jewish services across the globe today. The same can be said of Mesullam ben Kalonymos's *Ein Kamocha* and Shlomo ha-Levi Alkabetz's *L'cha Dodi*. Similarly, *haggadot* (written guides for home-based Passover *seders*) are replete with memorable Sephardic piyyuttim such as *Chad Gadya* and *Echad Mi Yodeah*. Rubin and Baron (2006, p. 90) emphasize the disproportionate Sephardim contributions to Jewish liturgy: "Other lyrics for Chanukah, Purim, circumcision and wedding feasts, etc., were created by *paytanim* (poets) over the centuries. Many of them are still in use today. But in no time or place since the ancient world were there the number of fine poets writing outstanding religious songs as were found in the medieval Arab world."

Vocals were essential to piyyutim because religious practice forbade, as work, the playing of instruments on Sabbath and holidays. While numerous piyyutim grace Jewish services, the melodies vary. Medieval Sephardic tradition advanced this sort of diversity—and accessibility. First, the poets themselves adopted local tunes or styles for their words. Second, traveling cantors purposefully selected melodies that would be familiar to and quickly accepted in their host communities. Some scholars and rabbis of the era argued against what they deemed a sort of self-indulgent interfering with ritual (Idelsohn, 1967, pp. 125–127). They also at times sought isolation against outside religious practices which they found offensive ("dancing girls," for example). Whatever the case, performers composed *diwanim*, or songbooks, to recall their works. The most exemplary was a second edition published by Israel Najara in 1600, containing nearly 350 songs.

Looking back several hundred years, it may be difficult to ascertain the exact (Judaic or Arabic) origin of certain melodies. Yet, the cantorial role certainly has been evolving. From the mid-17th century, male choirs chanted the *maftirin* (Torah and related texts) on Saturday afternoons (Ben-Naeh, 2017). Such participation, though now not gender-restricted, has been solicited largely by Reform congregations since the mid-20th century. Meanwhile, Ashkenazic cantors enjoyed their roles as soloists; their well-trained voices reverberated throughout sanctuaries, and congregants listened. If a bit of a generalization, the Sephardim were closer to "song leaders." One increasingly popular (or revived) version of *Ein Keloheinu* fuses the traditional Hebrew refrain with Ladino verses.

In addition to piyyutim and clearly religious music, Kligman (2003, pp. 231–232) notes "faithfully transmitted" Judeo-Spanish folk genres: *romancero* ballads, often narrating women's experiences in love, child-bearing, parenting, and homemaking; dirges and tragic remembrances known as *endechas*; and short holiday and celebratory songs (*komplas*). (Ethnomusicologist Judith R. Cohen (2010) refers to this triumvirate as "romances, life cycle, and calendar.") The words and music hold appeal, yet test the performer. As John Griffiths writes about reviving and presenting this music to Australian audiences today: "With La Romanesca [his band] we tried to take as much of a reconstructionalist approach as possible. The idea was to take the Spanish ballad melodies in the way that they had been preserved by the Sephardic Jews, and attempt to reconstruct and reinterpret them in ways that arguably may have been the practice in 15th-century Spain, whether by Christians or Jews. One of the things that was so exciting about this was more than just the beauty of the songs and their texts, but the challenge that came from the head-on encounter of artistic intuition and scholarly knowledge" (Griffiths, 2012, pp. 5–6).

Scholarly knowledge has in fact been growing since the late 19th century, with social sciences (anthropology and psychology, for example) methodically demonstrating typologies and variation. A host of scholars—Susana Weich-Shahak, Israel J. Katz, Edwin Seroussi, Miguel Sanchez, and others—conducted and published fieldwork and recorded that music, attracting broader audiences for romanceros.

Sephardic music also echoed political changes. Jewish communities in Arab lands felt increasingly threatened during the various Middle Eastern tensions of the 20th century. Their response was immigration, usually to Israel, the United States, or Europe. The movement toward unity of Ashkenazic and Sephardic cultures resulted in *Musika Yam Tikhonit Yisraelit* (Israeli Mediterranean music). Israel also has hosted, since 2003, an annual FestiLadino. Meanwhile, in the historic capital of Sephardic culture, the death of Spain's General Francisco Franco (1975) and the reinstatement of political parties had a liberating effect; King Juan Carlos commemorated the quincentenary of the Expulsion Edict and Columbus's voyage to America with a public apology—and outreach—to its long-departed residents. Spain's re-engagement in Sephardic music certainly exceeds its current Jewish population. Performers also come from a variety of countries to rediscover their historic connection: France, Portugal, Greece, Turkey, Holland, England, and others. The established recording industry in the United States definitely reveals Sephardic inclusion.

All told, appreciation for this genre is pan-ethnic, reaching any nation with supportive educational resources and multimedia venues open to "world music." Women are often taking the lead in spreading the romancero music that once described their daily roles and existence. The (late) popular Israeli artist, Ofra Haza, recorded in Western languages; Yasmin Levy today tours internationally. Zohar Argov, Daklon, Ben Most, and Haim Moshe, too, have blended various instruments and styles. News about Sephardic music tends to be outdated quickly these days: Seattle Rabbi Simon Benzaquen presently raps with the hip-hop band, Los Serenos Sefarad.

Lynn C. Kronzek

See also: Arab Classical Music; Ashkenazi Jews, Music of; Ottoman Classical Music; Oud; Rap/Hip-Hop in Africa and the Middle East

Further Reading

Ben-Naeh, Yaron. 2017. "Urban Sephardic Culture in the Ottoman Empire." *Tablet*, September 18. http://www.tabletmag.com/jewish-arts-and-culture/218923/urban-sephardic-cultureottoman-empire.

Cohen, Judith R. 2010. "Judeo-Spanish Song: A Mediterranean-Wide Interactive Tradition." *Sociedad de Etnomusicologia*. http://www.sibetrans.com/trans/articulo/18/judeo-spanish-song-a-meditgerranean-wide-interactive-tradition.

Griffiths, John. 2012. Lecture presented at the "Seminar Amor y Odio: The Jews in Spain and Beyond." Melbourne: University of Melbourne, November 22.

Heskes, Irene. 1994. *Passport to Jewish Music: Its History, Traditions, and Culture*. Westport, CT: Greenwood Press.

Idelsohn, A. Z. 1967. *Jewish Music in Its Historical Development*. New York: Schocken Books.

Kligman, Mark. 2003. "Music." In Reeva Spector Simon, Michael Menachem Laskier, and Sara Reguer (eds.), *The Jews of the Middle East and North Africa in Modern Times*, 224–234. New York: Columbia University Press.

La Rondinella. 1993. Liner notes to *Songs of the Sephardim: Traditional Music of the Spanish Jews*. Troy, NY: Dorian Discovery.

Levin, Neil W. n.d. "A Garden Eastward: Sephardi and Near Eastern Inspiration." *Milken Archive of Jewish Music*, Introduction to Volume 2. www.milkenarchive.org/articles/view/introduction-to-volume-2/ A GARDEN EASTWARD: SEPHARDI AND NEAR EASTERN.

Rubin, Emanuel, and John H. Baron. 2006. *Music in Jewish History and Culture*. Sterling Heights, MI: Harmonie Park Press.

Shajarian, Mohammed-Reza (1940–)

Born September 23, 1940, in the northeastern city of Mashhad, Iran, Mohammed-Reza Shajarian is an internationally renowned singer, composer, and master of Persian traditional music. He started singing at the age of five in the Qu'ranic tradition under the mentorship of his father. At age 12, he began to study the *radif*, the tradition of Persian classical music, despite the disapproval of his father, who claimed that the music was *haram* (forbidden) in Islam. Shajarian began his career as a singer in 1959 at Radio Khorasan, and quickly rose to popularity in the 1960s.

Shajarian was taught by several well-known master musicians in Iran, including Ahmad Ebadi, Esmaeil Mehrtash, Nour-Ali Boroumand, and Abdollah Davami (1891–1980), the latter of whom was highly influential in Shajarian's interpretation of the radif. Shajarian was also highly influenced by the vocal styles of singers such as Reza Gholi Mirza Zelli, Qamar ol-Molouk Vaziri, Eghbal Azar, and Taj Isfahani. In 1971, he began taking *santur* lessons with master musician Faramarz Payvar (1933–2009). From Payvar, Shajarian also learned the vocal radif repertoire, as it had been passed down from legendary musician Abolhasan Saba (1902–1957). Above all, Shajarian has cited respected *tar* master Jalil Shahnaz (1921–2013) as the most influential in his musical development, and claims that he has tried to integrate Shahnaz's musical style with his own style of singing.

Although he has mostly performed as a solo singer during his career, Shajarian has also collaborated with many other musicians, including Hossein Alizadeh, composers and santur masters Parviz Meskatian and Faramarz Payvar, and tar and *setar* master Mohammad Reza Lotfi. He has toured with groups such as the Masters of Persian Music ensemble and Ava Ensemble. Shajarian has also taught and mentored many classical musicians both privately and at Tehran University's Department of Fine Arts, including his son, Homayoun, and his daughter, Mojgan, as well as prominent musicians Ali Jahandar, Shahram Nazeri, and Mozaffar Shafiei. In addition, Shajarian has contributed to the invention of new Iranian classical instruments, including the *kereshmeh*, the *saboo*, the *saghar*, the *sorahi*, and the *tondar*. In recognition of his musical achievement and contributions, Shajarian has been the recipient of several international awards, including the UNESCO Golden Picasso Medal in 1999,, and the Mozart Medal in 2006. He was also nominated for the Grammy Award in the Best World Music category in 2004 and 2006.

Shajarian's songs have become renowned by Iranians all over the world. During the Muslim holy month of Ramadan, a recording of *Rabana* ("Our Lord," a prayer sung to Persian melodies) is often played at sundown just before breaking the daily fast. Typically, his lyrics are taken from the words of revered Persian poets such as Rumi and Hafez. Today, these lyrics take on new meanings with Iranian audiences that reflect the current social and political situation in Iran. Shajarian's songs are now considered by many to be expressions of protest, giving expression to the people of Iran oppressed since the 1979 revolution. For example, at almost every concert he performs ends with the famous song, "*Morghe Sahar* (Bird of dawning)," a song written by Morteza Neydavoud in the early 1920s, which asks for the night of oppression to end so that the day of liberation may begin.

Following the June 12, 2009, Iranian presidential election, Shajarian expressed support for the oppositional Green Movement, which had lost the election to the conservative incumbent Mahmoud Ahmadinejad. When Ahmadinejad referred to postelection protesters in a speech as "dust and dirt," Shajarian reacted by declaring that he was proud to be the "voice of dust and dirt and . . . will always remain the voice of dust and dirt." He asked the Islamic Republic of Iran Broadcasting (IRIB) to stop broadcasting his songs following the election, as he did not want them to be used as political propaganda. In September 2009, Shajarian released his song "Language of Fire," which is thought to be directed at Iran's *basij*, or moral police, who violently reacted against protesters following the election results. It is often thought that because of Shajarian's position as a respected international figure, the Iranian government has been reluctant to arrest or punish him severely for his political opinions, although they have limited his concert performances within Iran. Since 2009, Shajarian tours around the world, but rarely in Iran.

Theresa Steward

See also: Dastgah; Iranian Classical Music; Kamancheh; Tar

Further Reading

Inskeep, Steve. 2010. "Mohammad Reza Shajarian: Protest through Poetry." National Public Radio (NPR), September 27. http://www.npr.org/2010/09/27/130047062/mohammad-reza-shajarian-protest-through-poetry.

Mostaghim, Ramin, and Borzou Daragahi. 2009. "Iran: Famous Singer Shajarian Decries 'Language of Fire.'" *Los Angeles Times*, September 6. http://latimesblogs.latimes.com/babylonbeyond/2009/09/iran-famous-singer-shajarian-decries-language-of-fire.html.

Simms, Rob, and Amir Koushkani. 2012. *Mohammad Reza Shajarian's Avaz in Iran and Beyond, 1976–2010*. Plymouth, UK: Lexington Books.

Shakuhachi

The *shakuhachi* is an end-blown flute that has a history in Japan since at least the early eighth century. The instrument was transmitted from China and used in Japanese court music (*gagaku*), as part of an orchestra comprised of various wind, string, and percussion instruments. The shakuhachi was eventually omitted from gagaku, although a slightly different version of the instrument emerged several centuries later, and by the 17th century it was this type of shakuhachi that became firmly established as an instrument of the *Fuke-shū* (a subset of Rinzai Zen Buddhism). Toward the end of the 19th century, the Fuke-shū lost control of the instrument and new schools of performance soon emerged, marking a period of new performers, contexts, and music. In the 20th century, several experimental forms of shakuhachi were developed, and the post-World War II era witnessed the dissemination and adoption of shakuhachi performance in many other countries. Today, the shakuhachi maintains its distinct cultural roots in Japan, yet has received much interest from players all over the world who hold shakuhachi festivals, workshops, and performances.

TYPES

In its usual traditional form, the shakuhachi is made of a bamboo tube and is played with the instrument held at about a 45-degree angle toward the ground. The upper surface of the tube has four finger holes, and a single thumb hole is on the lower surface. At the time the instrument was transmitted to Japan, it had five finger holes and one thumb hole. Several such instruments survive in the Shōsōin repository in Nara and the temple Hōryū-ji.

Japanese musician Kifu Mitsuhashi playing the *shakuhachi*, an end-blown bamboo flute used in traditional Japanese and Chinese music. (Jack Vartoogian/Getty Images)

In comparison to the shakuhachi, a number of similar and related instruments are found, though most of these are relatively rare. These include the *miyogiri*, which has three nodes in the bamboo; *hitoyogiri shakuhachi*, which has a single node and was slenderer than the shakuhachi; and *tenpuku*, which has three nodes and was used mainly in the former Satsuma province. More recent innovations in instrument design have seen wooden shakuhachi, plastic shakuhachi, electric shakuhachi, and cyber shakuhachi. Such changes have also included shakuhachi with more finger holes, including seven- and nine-hole instruments. In the 1930s, Ōkura Kishichirō (1882–1963) devised a shakuhachi with a Boehm key system (as on the transverse Western flute), and nowadays several adapters are made that take the form of the blowing edge of the shakuhachi, but are actually head joints that fit over a transverse flute in order to turn it into a vertical flute.

The type of shakuhachi most used today has its roots in the instrument as used by the Fuke-shū players. This instrument, known as *Fuke shakuhachi*, is characterized by its use of bamboo that often has the lower end showing clearly where the roots were cut off. The instrument is also often slightly curved, which helps define its more usual shape. The instrument is sometimes referred to as *komusō shakuhachi*, a term that adds the name of the shakuhachi's Fuke-shū performers. The Fuke shakuhachi has seven nodes: there is one very close to the blowing edge, three within the central part of the bamboo tube, and three tightly grouped at the sound hole at the other end of the instrument. In the Edo period (1600–1868), shakuhachi players were known to have made their own instruments. Given such an individualized process, along with the natural shape of the bamboo and the location of the finger holes, instruments were usually slightly different in terms of their tuning and timbre. In the 20th century, a construction method was developed that began to add paste in the instrument's bore, which could be smoothed and varied as a way of helping to tune the instrument. Instruments without this paste are referred to as *ji-nashi*, and those with paste are called *ji-ari* (some instruments may have just a small amount of paste in certain places).

MANUFACTURE

Gagaku shakuhachi were made of bamboo, jade, stone, or ivory, whereas later instruments were made of bamboo. Nowadays, cheaper instruments are made of wood or plastic. The length of a shakuhachi is traditionally 54.5 cm. Using Japanese measurements, this equates to 1 *shaku* 8 *sun*, and it is this system of measurement that gives the shakuhachi its name: *shaku* (i.e., 1 shaku) *hachi* (i.e., 8 *sun*). In practice, shakuhachi are also made in a number of other sizes based on instrument length, from about 1 shaku 1 sun (33.3 cm) to about 2 shaku 8 sun (84.8 cm), although longer instruments are known.

Traditionally, shakuhachi were made of a single bamboo tube, although nowadays shorter instruments are sometimes divided into two parts that are joined together to play the instrument. The bamboo tube that is used to make the shakuhachi has a blowing edge (*utaguchi*), which is cut at a slight angle across the top of the tube and shaped with a small amount of inlay. This inlay is made in several shapes, with three designs being typical of three main performance traditions (*ryū*): *Myōan-ryū* (*ōgigata*: fan shape), *Tozan-ryū* (*mikazukigata*: crescent shape), and *Kinko-ryū* (*bachigata*: plectrum shape). Some shakuhachi have rattan binding placed around the tube. The rattan might be placed over blemishes or cracks in the bamboo, but it also gives the instrument a distinct visual design. On instruments that have paste lining the bore, the paste is added at strategic places to help tune the instrument and give it a distinct timbre. Lacquer is often applied to the bore and the rims of the finger holes.

As well as the finest detail given to the making of shakuhachi, the instrument also has several accessories that are needed to help maintain its condition. A cleaning cloth is used for the inside of the bore to remove condensation after playing, and the blowing edge usually has a cap to be placed over it when the instrument is not in use in order to help protect this fragile and important part of the instrument. The instrument might typically be placed in a cloth or hard case to further protect it from damage.

PERFORMANCE TRADITIONS

The use of the shakuhachi in the Japanese imperial court was known from around the eighth century, when it was found not only in the gagaku orchestral context, but also as a solo instrument, as mentioned in the 11th-century novel *Genji monogatari* by Murasaki Shikibu. From around the 12th century, little is known about the shakuhachi, but by the 17th century a new form of shakuhachi was firmly established within the Fuke-shū Buddhist sect and used by performers known as *komusō* (priest of emptiness). The komusō were itinerant priests characterized by their wicker basket hats (*tengai*) that entirely covered the head and face. Komusō had their headquarters at the temple Myōan-ji in Kyoto, and there were branch temples around much of Japan. For the komusō, the shakuhachi was a religious object (*hōki*) used in religious practice (*suizen*; "blowing Zen") and in receiving alms (*takuhatsu*) as itinerant performers.

With political reforms in the 19th century, the Fuke-shū was abolished by the government in 1871. After that time a number of new performance traditions emerged, some of which were short-lived and some that continue to flourish. As a komusō, Kurosawa Kinko (1710–1771) is seen as the founder of the Kinko-ryū performance tradition, which nowadays has many different branch schools. One of the most influential new traditions that emerged after 1871 was the Tozan-ryū, established by Nakao Tozan (1876–1956). Nowadays, this tradition also has several branches and subtraditions, and its music is seen as progressive, whereas that of the Kinko-ryū usually focuses on the solo repertory that was transmitted by komusō. Numerous other performance traditions continue to this day, including Seien-ryū, Myōan Shinpō-ryū, Nezasa-ha Kinpū-ryū, Myōan-ryū Taizan-ha, Sōetsu-ryū, Chikuho-ryū, Chikushin-kai, and Ueda-ryū. Most performance traditions are based around the performance practices of an influential teacher and performer, and while originally focused in one region, contemporary social flows have meant that most performance traditions have been disseminated widely. The most popular context of shakuhachi performance is to accompany folk song (*min'yō*), which became widespread in the 20th century.

Traditional teaching practices usually involve one-on-one learning with a teacher, but there are many other new learning contexts that include class teaching. With contemporary transcultural flows, there are also many non-Japanese shakuhachi players all around the world. Such travel has allowed the instrument to be recontextualized in diverse ways, including its use in a range of music styles and crossover genres, as well as in "New Age" healing practices.

MUSIC

The basic scale that a standard shakuhachi (1 shaku 8 sun) can produce is roughly equivalent to the notes D-F-G-A-C. Because the tube is slightly different for each instrument, the notes on every instrument will vary slightly, and the player must use slight variations in performance practice such as blowing and fingering techniques to adjust the pitches.

Traditional shakuhachi music is full of ornamental techniques, which are produced by changes either to blowing or to fingerings. There are many such techniques, with some typical ones being: *uchi* (hit), *suri* (slide), *meri* (moving the head to produce a lower tone), and *kari* (moving the head to produce a higher tone). As an end-blown flute, the shakuhachi permits one technique called *muraiki* (uneven breath) that produces a very sudden and dynamic blowing sound across the blowing edge. The sound of this technique is sometimes more about the sound of the breath rather than the actual note produced.

Many different types of notation are used by shakuhachi players. These are usually determined according to specific performance traditions. While some players use Western staff notation, most traditional notations take the form of showing fingerings for the notes. Such notations would typically include symbols for some ornamental techniques and some rhythms, although it is not uncommon for much performance practice to be learned from one's teacher without corresponding symbols in the notation.

The solo shakuhachi music of komusō was called *honkyoku* (main pieces), which has been transmitted to the present day through a number of performance traditions. There are also many new honkyoku that have been composed in more recent traditions such as the Tozan-ryū. As well as honkyoku, there are *gaikyoku* (outside pieces), a term used to refer to non-honkyoku pieces, which are typically pieces derived from the *koto* (zither) and/or *shamisen* (lute) repertory. There are also many new pieces of shakuhachi music known as *shinkyoku*, which include a range of 20th-century and more recent pieces.

Henry Johnson

See also: Koto; Shamisen

Further Reading

Blasdel, Christopher Yohmei, and Kamisangō Yūkō. 1988. *The Shakuhachi: A Manual for Learning*, trans Christopher Yohmei Blasdel. Tokyo: Ongaku no Tomo-sha.

Casano, Steven. 2005. "From *Fuke Shuu* to *Uduboo*: The Transnational Flow of the *Shakuhachi* to the West." *The World of Music* 47(3), 17–53.

de Ferranti, Hugh. 2000. *Japanese Musical Instruments*. New York: Oxford University Press.

Gutzwiller, Andreas B., and Gerald Bennett. 1991. "The World of a Single Sound: Basic Structure of the Music of the Japanese Flute Shakuhachi." *Musica Asiatica* 6, 36–59.

Johnson, Henry. 2014. *The Shakuhachi: Roots and Routes*. Leiden: Brill.

Keister, Jay. 2004. "The Shakuhachi as Spiritual Tool: A Japanese Buddhist Instrument in the West." *Asian Music* 35(2), 99–131.

Lee, Riley K. 1993. "Yearning for the Bell: A Study of Transmission in the Shakuhachi Honkyoku Tradition." PhD diss., University of Sydney.

Linder, Gunnar Jinmei. 2012. *Deconstructing Tradition in Japanese Music: A Study of Shakuhachi, Historical Authenticity and Transmission of Tradition*. Stockholm: Department of Oriental Languages, Stockholm University.

Malm, William P. 1959/2000. *Traditional Japanese Music and Musical Instruments*, new ed. Tokyo: Kodansha International.

Mayers, Dan E., ed. 1985. *The Annals of The International Shakuhachi Society*, vol. 1. Wadhurst, UK: The International Shakuhachi Society.

Mayers, Dan E., ed. 2005. *The Annals of The International Shakuhachi Society*, vol. 2. n.p.: The International Shakuhachi Society.

Seyama, Toru. 1998. "The Re-contextualisation of the *Shakuhachi* (*Syakuhati*) and Its Music from Traditional/Classical into Modern/Popular." *The World of Music* 40(2), 104–117.

Wade, Bonnie C. 2005. *Music in Japan: Experiencing Music, Expressing Culture*. Oxford: Oxford University Press.

Shamanic Music in Mongolia and Inner Asia

Shamanic music covers a broad range of instrumental and vocal practices used by shamans throughout the world during ceremonies and rituals. Very little is known about shamanic music, largely due to the lack of field recordings. Shamanic ceremonies can comprise music, dance, recitation, and drama, including ventriloquism. Although there are similarities from continent to continent, ceremonies in Mongolia and Central Asia have some idiosyncratic qualities.

Shamanism is an ancient belief system practiced in Asia, the Americas, parts of Australasia, Africa, and (more recently) parts of Europe. It is difficult to determine when shamanism began, although there is some evidence from rock paintings and ancient burial sites that it could have existed as much as 12,000 years ago. It is more accurate to think of shamanism as a system of belief rather than a religion, given the absence of a deity, a specific place of worship, or a holy text.

Shamans, who can be male or female, access the spirit world through states of spiritual ecstasy or trances to provide services for their communities. These services include giving blessings, offering advice, telling fortunes, bringing about favorable weather conditions, or healing (usually by means of expelling negative spirits from the sufferer). Shamans have a calling to become a shaman rather than it being a lifestyle or professional choice. This calling is recognized when a person in the teens or early twenties starts to have visions or suffers a physical or mental illness that triggers a rite of passage into the spirit world. When it is possible within a community, the young shaman will be trained as an apprentice by an elder shaman. Shamans traditionally live as regular members of their community and perform ceremonies when required, although some modern-day shamans practice shamanism as a full-time business.

The shamanic ceremony is at the heart of a shaman's work, during which they reach a trance-like state through using musical instruments and vocal performance, and sometimes aided by taking hallucinogens, drinking alcohol, or smoking tobacco. During the ceremony, in addition to music and dance, the shaman may also gaze into a mirror or water, or throw objects such as a drum beater in order to answer questions. Such ceremonies may allow other members of the community to participate in or observe the shaman's communication with the spirit world, but they are not intended to be public performances for entertainment. Furthermore, shamans do not generally consider their use of musical instruments or voices as music, but rather an integral part of their ceremonies.

There is no set repertoire during ceremonies: shamans usually improvise vocals, drumming, and sometimes on other instruments according to the nature of the communication with the spirits and the intensity of the trance. Each shaman's instrumental and vocal performances will differ from those of other shamans, and even individual shamans' performances will differ from one ceremony to another. Shamans have extensive knowledge of the folklore and culture of their communities, which is necessary for them to execute their role successfully, and they are generally respected within their communities as people who are extremely knowledgeable in practical, metaphysical, and spiritual matters.

In Asia, shamanism is most prominent in Mongolia; Siberia, including the Republics of Tuva and Buryatia; Korea; northern China, namely Inner Mongolia and Manchuria; and Japan, where it has links with Shintō. Among the Turkic peoples of Mongolia and Central Asia, shamanism is connected to Tengerism, the ancient "religion" of the eternal blue sky; and animism, the belief that all living entities have spirits. Central Asian shamanism is also closely linked to animals due to nomadism and hunting. Animals are held in great respect within nomadic communities. They are killed only for meat and clothing, and the spirit of the animal is always thanked. In Mongolia, a fundamental concept within shamanism is that of *khii-mori* (literally, "wind-horse"), energy or power that resides within a person's chest and can change according to how it is used.

Shamanism was the principal system of belief in Mongolia and surrounding areas until the 16th century, when Tibetan Buddhism became widespread and lamas gained political power. Despite some suppression of shamanism by Buddhist leaders, the two systems of belief coincided relatively peacefully until the early 20th century, when communist regimes in China and the Soviet Union and its satellite states, including Mongolia, outlawed religious and spiritual practices. It has seen something of a revival since 1991, although many shamans now charge for their services or cater to tourists.

The most important musical instrument for shamans is the drum, called a *khese khengereg* in Mongolian or the *dungur* in Tuvan. The shaman's drum is a large round drum with a wooden crosspiece frame and an animal-hide skin, which produces a deep, resonant sound. Which animal skin a shaman chooses is a conscious decision, since it evokes the spirit of a particular animal (for example, a gazelle or a mountain goat), rather than the skin being chosen on the grounds of which animal hides were available locally when the drum was made. The drum is played with a special beater and, particularly in Siberia, shamans often hang metal keys or bells inside the drum to create additional sounds.

From the start of a person's life as a shaman, the drum is very important; it is used during the initiation ceremony that symbolizes his or her journey into the spirit world. The drum itself also goes through an initiation to allow it to receive spirits. Given the animistic nature of shamanism and shamans' belief that nonhuman entities also have spirits, the spirit world accessed via the drum is not too far removed from the physical world. During subsequent ceremonies, beating the drum is one of the best ways for the shaman to go into a trance, although the beating is not always steady like a metronome. The tempo and rhythms can often fluctuate to reflect the shaman's state of mind at any given point during the ceremony.

Shamans—*böö* in Mongolian—often hold their drums close to their faces or over their heads to feel it resonate throughout their bodies and to sing or speak into it. This can add to the spectacle of the ceremony, of which movement and gesture are integral parts. Some shamans, particularly in Mongolia, heat their drums over a fire at the start of a ceremony. This alters the sound of the drum and is also symbolic of fire, one of the four essences of shamanism (the other three being earth, air, and water). Some shamans pour vodka or fermented mare's milk, called *airag* in Mongolian, over the drum as an offering and also to modify the sound.

In addition to the drum, the shaman's voice is an essential part of ceremonies. Vocal performance during a ceremony can include singing self-composed or improvised songs, singing intermittent melodic fragments, overtone singing, reciting incantations, speaking in tongues, grunting, laughing, and imitating animal sounds. The vocal component of the ceremony is not necessarily meant to be comprehensible, and it is not seen as problematic if onlookers cannot understand the text or hear the sounds and melodies clearly. Often, shamans will end a ceremony by singing praise songs to the spirits that have assisted them. They can also use their voices in an aggressive-sounding manner while expelling negative spirits from an ill person. Almost all vocalizing is improvised, and the shaman sings or recites whatever comes to him or her during the trance.

Some shamans, particularly in Mongolia and Tuva, use overtone singing, also known as throat singing, during their ceremonies. Known as *khöömii* in Mongolia and *khöömei* in Tuva, overtone singing can help induce a trance due to its drone-like sound and the resonance the singers feel in their heads when producing overtones. Some shamans in Mongolia do not sing khöömii themselves during the ceremony so they can concentrate on drumming and other vocalizing, instead inviting other singers to perform the khöömii for them. These additional singers may sing khöömii at the start of the ceremony while the shaman gets dressed in his or her ceremonial attire. They may also improvise at a later point in the ceremony to follow the vocal sounds the shaman produces, and they do not normally sing set pieces.

Totem animals within Mongolian shamanism include the tiger, snow leopard, bear, eagle, cuckoo, swan, turtle, and raven, and shamans imitate the sounds of these animals within their ceremonies. They may also imitate the sounds of other animals relevant to a particular ceremony (for example, the sounds of prey animals during blessing ceremonies to bring good luck for a hunting expedition). Furthermore, shamans often wear animal skins or headdresses to evoke the spirit of a particular animal, and they may imitate the sounds of these animals during a ceremony, too.

Although the drum and voice are integral parts of a shamanic ceremony, other instruments may also be used on certain occasions or according to the preference of individual shamans. They use instruments to invoke spirits and to stimulate energy points in their bodies. The second most important musical instrument for many shamans in Mongolia and Central Asia is the jaw harp, also known as the Jew's harp. It is called the *aman khuur* in Mongolia, the *khomus* in Siberia, and the *komuz* in other parts of Central Asia such as Kyrgyzstan. The instrument can be made from metal or wood and has been popular for centuries among Central Asian herders. In a similar manner to overtone singing, the drone-like quality of the jaw harp is believed to help shamans reach a trance-like state, along with the beating of the drum.

Other instruments sometimes used during shamanic ceremonies in Mongolia include the horse-head fiddle (*morin khuur*), although, as with overtone singing, it is not usually the shaman who plays it. Certain shamans have horse-head fiddles with three heads, as opposed to the usual one, to symbolize past, present, and future. If a shaman requires a horse-head fiddle for a particular ceremony, he or she will invite a horse-head fiddle player to participate, and that player is expected to imitate the sounds the shaman produces.

In Western Mongolia, some shamans use the *tsüdger gedest khuur*, a Kazakh bowed stringed instrument with a bowl-like body and either two or three strings. Shamans may also use musical instruments more usually associated with Tibetan Buddhism, such as the *ganling*, a flute made from a virgin girl's thigh bone; or the *damaru*, a two-sided drum, which can sometimes be made from the skulls of virgin girls. (There has been some speculation in Mongolia as to whether the virgin girls in question died of natural causes, although shamans contest this is always the case.) Use of additional instruments is optional and always at the behest of the individual shaman; some shamans will never use instruments other than the drum and their own voices.

In addition to instruments, shamans often use a variety of paraphernalia during their ceremonies, including rattles, mirrors, pipes, feathers, swords, and sheep's ankle bones, known in Mongolia as *shagai*. Shamans usually decorate their homes with the musical instruments and other objects they use in their ceremonies. In nomadic communities in Central Asia, people live in round felt tents known as yurts (*ger* in Mongolian). A shaman's ger often has horse-head fiddles, shamanic robes, swords, and the ritual blue scarf called a *khadag* hanging from the walls.

Despite the revival of shamanism in Central Asia following the fall of the Soviet Union and the communist regime in China, this system of belief is on the decline in comparison to its popularity before the 20th century. This is partly due to Western medicine reducing the demand for shamans' healing abilities, organized religion providing for people's spiritual needs, and views that shamanism is outdated or inordinately superstitious. Furthermore, when shamans die, they may not be replaced, either due to the aforementioned reasons or because their apprentices have not been sufficiently trained to continue serving the community. Nonetheless, shamanism and its associated instrumental and vocal practices remain an under-researched and fascinating topic.

Lucy M. Rees

See also: Morin Khuur; Tuvan Popular Bands; Tuvan Throat Singing

Further Reading

Rees, Lucy M. 2015. *Mongolian Film Music: Tradition, Revolution and Propaganda*. Farnham, UK: Ashgate.

Teng, Liu Gui. 1991. *Shaman Music Culture in China: The Case of Northeast Altai*. Beijing: Central Conservatory of Music.

Van Deusen, Kira. 2004. *Singing Story, Healing Drum: Shamans and Storytellers of Turkic Siberia*. Seattle: University of Washington Press.

Shamisen

The *shamisen* is a Japanese lute. In its traditional form, it has three strings and is plucked by a single spatula-shaped plectrum. The earliest known version of the shamisen in Japan is thought to have been brought there from China, via Japan's southwestern islands, around the middle of the 16th century. Thereafter, the instrument was Japanized and disseminated widely around Japan into an array of performance styles. More recently, the instrument has gained in popularity as a result of much interest given to a virtuosic style of performance known as *Tsugaru shamisen*.

The term "shamisen" means literally "three, tastes, lines," and the instrument is known by several other slightly different names, such as *samisen* (especially in the Kansai region). When the instrument is played in ensemble with *koto* (zither)

and *shakuhachi* (end-blown flute), it is referred to as *sangen* (three strings). The shamisen is a long-necked spike lute, which is defined by the neck passing through the instrument's four-sided wooden body. The two larger sides of the body are covered with dog or cat skin, with the upper side acting as a sound table.

The shamisen is made in several sizes, with three broad categories: *hosozao* (thin neck); *chūzao* (medium neck), and *futozao* (thick neck). While these sizes are based on the thickness of the neck, the instrument's body is made to a corresponding size. The shamisen is a fretless instrument; its three strings run along the long neck and are tied to corresponding tuning pegs. The strings are usually made in three different sizes, with the thickest used for the lowest string and the thinnest for the highest string. A small movable bridge is placed on the sound table to raise the strings and allow them to sound. When playing the instrument, in some performance styles the plectrum hits a string and then strikes the sound table, thus making a percussive sound almost simultaneously with the sounding of the string. In the style of performance called Tsugaru shamisen, this percussive effect is predominant.

A version of the instrument that is known in southern Japan is called *sanshin*. This instrument, which resembles the Chinese *sanxian*, is defined by its smaller-size body as compared to the modern-day shamisen, with its two larger sides covered with snakeskin (a synthetic material is often used today). Another type of instrument that is a type of shamisen is the *gottan*, which is made entirely of wood, including the two larger sides of the sound box that are normally covered with skin.

When the shamisen was first transmitted to Japan, it was played by blind male players, most of whom also played instruments such as the *biwa* (lute) and *koto*. These biwa players used a large spatula-shaped plectrum to pluck the strings, which differed from other plucking styles used for the sanshin. Shamisen performance styles are often divided into lyrical and narrative genres. The instrument is also used to accompany folk song. The theatrical style of performance known as *kabuki* is a context where many different lyrical and narrative styles of shamisen performance can be heard, and a setting that helped popularize many of these styles in the Edo period (1600–1868). Some well-known lyrical styles are *jiuta*, *nagauta*, and *hauta*; some well-known narrative styles are *gidayū-bushi*, *tokiwazu-bushi*, and *kiyomoto-bushi*. The different performance traditions usually adhere to a certain size shamisen (based on the size of the neck), as well as size of plectrum and type of notation. Puppet theater (*bunraku*) is another setting in which the shamisen can be heard, in this case as accompaniment to the narrative style of performance. The sanshin is used in folk and popular music in Okinawa and the Amami islands.

The shamisen's three strings are often tuned in fourths and/or fifths. The basic tuning is called *honchōshi*, with the middle string tuned a fourth above the lowest, and the highest string a fifth above the middle string. The basic playing technique is to pluck a string with the plectrum in a downward movement. As a way of adding more sounds to shamisen music, players have developed many ornamental playing techniques, such as upward plucking, striking more than one string at the same time, sliding a finger along a string, hammer-ons, and pull-offs.

A number of different types of notation developed for shamisen music, mainly as a result of the instrument being used in such diverse performance styles.

Notation is generally a tablature that indicates finger positions on the strings. There are both vertical notations, which are shown in columns moving from the right of the page to the left; and horizontal notations, which are shown in rows that progress down the page.

In the 21st century, the shamisen continues to flourish in folk, lyrical, and narrative styles. As well as the sanshin being recontextualized in some styles of popular music from Okinawan and Amami, the shamisen has also been popularized in Tsugaru shamisen performance, especially with the dynamic performance styles of players such as the Yoshida Brothers and Agatsuma. In this context, shamisen performers show their virtuosic playing skills, sometimes in a contemporary performance setting that includes instruments more often associated with popular music.

Henry Johnson

See also: Japan, Music of; Koto; Shakuhachi

Further Reading

de Ferranti, Hugh. 2000. *Japanese Musical Instruments*. New York: Oxford University Press.

Johnson, Henry. 2006. "*Tsugaru shamisen*: From region to nation (and beyond) and back again." *Asian Music* 37(1), 75–100.

Johnson, Henry. 2010. *The Shamisen: Tradition and Diversity*. Leiden, Germany: Brill.

Keister, Jay. 2004. *Shaped by Japanese Music: Kikuoka Hiroaki and Nagauta Shamisen in Tokyo*. New York: Routledge.

Malm, William P. 1963. *Nagauta: The Heart of Kabuki Music*. Rutland, UK: Charles E. Tuttle.

Malm, William P. 1959/2000. *Traditional Japanese Music and Musical Instruments,* New ed. Tokyo: Kodansha International.

Tokita, Alison McQueen, and David W. Hughes, eds. 2008. *The Ashgate Companion to Japanese Music*. Aldershot, UK: Ashgate.

Wade, Bonnie C. 2005. *Music in Japan: Experiencing Music, Expressing Culture*. Oxford: Oxford University Press.

Shankar, Ravi (1920–2012)

Ravi Shankar was an Indian sitarist, composer, and educator who remains "the only South Asian musician to have become a household name in the West" (Farrell, 1997, p. 564). His global concertizing drew attention to the sitar, Hindustani music, and Indian culture more generally. His performances and recordings have educated generations and spread Indian classical music around the world.

Born in Varanasi in 1920, Shankar lived through numerous political and social upheavals, including Mahatma Gandhi's policy of passive resistance to English colonization, the collapse of imperial British rule, Indian independence, India's partition and ongoing conflicts with neighboring Pakistan, and the country's emergence as a global economic leader. Throughout these changes, Shankar remained steadfast in his commitment to Indian culture and its parity with other world traditions, doing more than perhaps any other single person to propagate North Indian music around the globe.

Shankar traveled extensively in his youth, and his later educational efforts benefited from his early cosmopolitanism and exposure to Western culture. In 1930, at the age of 10, Shankar went to Paris with his older brother Uday's dance company. Shankar performed on sitar, *esraj*, flute, and drums and also danced in the troupe. Through exposure to Paris's cultural scene and several world tours (until 1938), Shankar absorbed Western music, forming "experiences which would help him to bridge cultural gaps between India and other nations in his adult years" (Slawek, 1993).

In 1935, Uday invited *Baba* Allauddin Khan to tour with the company as a featured soloist. Khan was a prominent figure in the Maihar *gharana* (tradition) and chief court musician in the state of Maihar (now Madhya Pradesh). After running away from home in his youth to pursue musical studies, Khan studied voice, violin, *tabla*, and *sarod* for several years with a variety of gurus, eventually becoming the pupil of *bin* player Ustad Wazir Khan. These varied musical experiences meant that Allauddin Khan was conversant with numerous genres and styles of both instrumental and vocal music. Because of this wide-ranging fluency, Shankar credits Khan for "enlarging the scope and range of possibilities open to an instrumentalist" and leading musicians "away from the confines of narrow specialization" that characterized Hindustani music through the first quarter of the 20th century (Shankar, 1968/2007, p. 62).

While touring with the dance troupe, Khan gave lessons to Shankar, providing him with his first formal training in Indian classical music. In 1938, Shankar returned to India to begin formal study with Khan, entering into the traditional teacher-disciple relationship (*guru-shishya parampara*). Over seven and a half years of intense study in Maihar, Shankar learned sitar and *sūrbahār* as well as the characteristic forms of the *dhrupad* vocal genre. Khan was a demanding teacher and difficult man who insisted that Shankar master his instrument's physical technique as well as making a thorough study of both voice and tabla.

Shankar began his concertizing career in 1939 and quickly established a reputation as an innovator. He blended approaches from numerous genres and styles from both North and South Indian classical musics, all performed with a new technique on a modified instrument. After leaving Maihar for Bombay in 1944, Shankar struggled financially and artistically for several years. He relied on income earned from his recitals before music circles (private groups of connoisseurs that sponsored concerts). He also earned money performing privately for wealthy citizens and worked hard to elevate the music above its traditional role as background entertainment.

Hungry for creative outlets, Shankar joined the Indian People's Theatre Association as musical director. During his brief association with this group, he composed a ballet score, film scores, and ballet-opera (*The Discovery of India*, a retelling of the whole scope of Indian history that premiered during the Independence year of 1947). After the state-sponsored All-India Radio offered him a dual position as director of music and as conductor-composer of its newly formed instrumental ensemble, Shankar moved to New Delhi in 1949. His compositions from this period followed three principal patterns: fully notated performances of *ragas* played in an improvised fashion by the whole ensemble, new melodies written in "light" ragas that featured complex rhythms across the ensemble, or folk-inspired tunes.

Indian sitarist Ravi Shankar performing in 1973. Shankar helped popularize the Hindustani music of India around the world. (Tony Russell/Redferns)

As a result of his growing reputation and government connections, Shankar was selected as a representative for India's first cultural delegation, which traveled to the USSR in 1954. He continued his cultural outreach at home, performing concerts for growing numbers in numerous music circles in New Delhi. The success he had with these experiences encouraged him to leave his position with All-India Radio in 1956 and travel to the West to continue performing and educating new audiences. Shankar gave numerous concerts in Europe and the United States. His performances at London's Royal Festival Hall (1958) and New York's Carnegie Hall (1961) are considered important moments in the history of Indian music's reception in the West. He also remained busy as a composer, writing the score for Satyajit Ray's *Apu* trilogy (1955–1959).

The early 1960s were a time of intense concertizing in the West. Many Westerners came to know Shankar through his association with Beatle George Harrison, who studied sitar briefly with Shankar and incorporated the instrument on several recordings. Shankar's association with the Beatles was helpful in broadening his audiences. Shankar and tabla player Allah Rakah performed at the Monterey Pop (1967) and Woodstock (1969) festivals. During this time, Shankar also performed extensively with sarodist Ali Akbar Khan, most publicly at George Harrison's Concert for Bangladesh in 1971, a performance that demonstrated Shankar's oftentimes uphill battle to win acceptance with Western audiences. After asking the audience to be quiet, patient, and refrain from smoking during the performance, he and Khan paused to retune their instruments. The audience, unfamiliar with Hindustani music, broke out in applause, causing Shankar to quip, "If you appreciate the tuning so much, I hope you will enjoy the playing more."

Shankar's desire to teach others encouraged his Kinnara project, a school for Indian music he founded in Mumbai in 1967 that remained operational for only a few years. He valued his role as a teacher of Indian music, beginning each concert with explanations of the ragas (melodic structures) and *talas* (rhythmic frameworks) he was about to perform. During performances, he expected quiet and decorum from his audiences, linking Hindustani music with the values and social expectations of Western music and presenting the former as an explicitly "classical" music. He was critical of popular connections between the music and psychedelic counterculture, stressing sobriety as a necessary prerequisite for understanding and delighting in the music's melodic and rhythmic complexity and beauty.

His typical concert structure became a paradigm through which Westerners came to know Hindustani musical conventions, one which has affected later artists performing in the West. Shankar customarily began with an *alap–jor–jhala* of a shorter length than would be usual for a performance in India. He followed this with a medium-tempo composition (*gat*), departing from the traditional practice of including slow and fast gats. The second item on the program was often a slow gat in a different raga, concluding with a fast gat and fast, virtuosic jhala section. Following intermission and dependent on time, audience, and mood, he included a third raga with an extended alap–jor–jhala and medium-tempo gat or a brief alap followed by a gat. Shankar concluded with a semi-classical composition (possibly in multiple ragas) followed by a fast gat interspersed with tabla solos and concluding with a *saval-javab* (a call and response between soloist and tabla player).

In later years, Shankar slaked his thirst for experimentation through recordings with conductor-violinist André Previn (1971) and minimalist composer Philip Glass (1990), as well as projects featuring electronic music (*Tana Mana*, 1987) and conventional instruments (the film score for *Gandhi*, 1982). In addition to his musical pursuits, he also served in the *Rajya Sabba*, India's upper parliamentary chamber, from 1986–1992. In 1997, he established the Ravi Shankar Foundation, which funded the Ravi Shankar Institute for Music and Performing Arts in New Delhi. He received numerous accolades during his life, including the *Padma Vibhusan*, the greatest award the Government of India bestows on artists, as well as honorary doctorates and several titles from other countries. His daughters Anoushka Shankar and Norah Jones have had successful musical careers in their own rights. Despite failing health and increasing frailty, he continued performing, composing, and teaching until several weeks before his death.

Shankar exerted remarkable influence on 20th-century musical life. He not only spread Indian music to an international audience, he broadened his instrument's range and scope. His incorporation of a second resonating gourd at the top of the instrument's neck and an additional playing string, as well as his modified tuning system, helped the instrument achieve prominence as a concert instrument and expanded its expressive low register by a full octave, affording him greater options for exploring the bass register during introductory alap sections. His collaborations with sarodist Ali Akbar Khan helped popularize the *jugalbandi* duet form. Shankar also combined northern and southern musical elements in his performances. He enthusiastically invented new ragas (such as Ahīr Lalit and Bairāgī) and played in unusual talas (such as *cārtāl kī savārī*, an 11-beat tala divided 4+4+3 or *upa tāl jhampak*, an eight-and-a-half-beat tala divided 2+3+2+1.5). Continuing a process started by his guru, Shankar allowed his tabla players to play several improvisational segments while he marked time. This practice, which has become the new standard for performances, marks a departure from the drummer's traditional status as an accompaniment to the soloist and affords the tabla player a prominent role during performances.

Shankar's performances and recordings had a profound impact on many important 20th-century musicians, including jazz musicians John Coltrane and Miles Davis; rock improviser Jerry Garcia; Western classical composers Henry Cowell, Alan Hovhaness, and Philip Glass; and Western classical performers Yehudi Menuhin and Daniel Hope. Many of Shankar's compositions combined sitar with Western instruments (such as his concertos for sitar and orchestra), with jazz and popular music, or with other Asian musical traditions. His worldwide tours paved the way for other Indian soloists who sustain concertizing careers around the world. Similar interest has encouraged other musicians and scholars to specialize in Indian music, which is perhaps Shankar's richest legacy as an educator and devoted proponent of the beauty of Hindustani music.

John Hausmann

See also: Dhrupad; Khayal; Raga; Sitar; Tala

Further Reading
Farrell, Gerry. 1997. *Indian Music and the West*. Oxford: Oxford University Press.
Lavezzoli, Peter. 2006. *The Dawn of Indian Music in the West*. New York: Continuum.
Shankar, Ravi. 1964. *Portrait of a Genius*. Liberty LBS 83 079.
Shankar, Ravi. 1964. *Ravi Shankar in London*. Angel Records 07243 5 67024 2 4.
Shankar, Ravi. 1968. *Ravi Shankar in New York*. Angel Records B00004U92S.
Shankar, Ravi. 1968/2007. *My Music, My Life*. Delhi: Vikas Publications, 1968. Reprinted with a new foreword, 2007. San Rafael, CA: Mandala Publishing.
Shankar, Ravi. 2001. *Raga Mala: The Autobiography of Ravi Shankar*. New York: Welcome Rain.
Shankar, Ravi. 2005. *The Essential Ravi Shankar*. Sony BMG 82876 71610 2.
Slawek, Stephen. 1993. "Ravi Shankar as Mediator Between Traditional Music and Modernity." In Stephen Blum, Phillip V. Bohlman, and Daniel M. Neuman (eds.), *Ethnomusicology and Modern Music History*, 161–180. Chicago: University of Illinois Press.

Shape-Note Singing

Shape-note singing is a style of American folk hymnody. It is also known as "Sacred Harp singing" after the most popular of the shape-note hymnals, the *Sacred Harp*. Shape-note hymns represent a popular and democratic approach to sacred music and were among the first compositions by American composers. The name derives from the note-heads, which are printed in shapes to assist singers who have little musical training. Each shape is associated with a syllable, such as *fa* (triangle), *sol* (circle), *la* (square), and *mi* (diamond) in the four-shape system, or *do, re, mi, fa, sol, la,* and *si* (various shapes) in seven-shape systems. Because these syllables are sung along with the text, the music is sometimes also called "fasola" singing. Shape-note singing represents one of the oldest compositional styles in the United States, and it is also one of a minority of folk musical traditions to be associated with a written form.

HISTORY

Shape-note singing began in New England in the 18th century in response to a belief that the quality of congregational psalm singing was declining. Local singing masters such as William Billings of Boston, Massachusetts (1746–1800), Justin Morgan of Vermont (1747–1798), and Supply Belcher of Maine (1751–1836) composed books of three- and four-part hymn settings, frequently selecting the poetry of English theologians such as Charles Wesley (1707–1788) and Isaac Watts (1674–1748) for their texts. The singing masters traveled from town to town, holding short singing schools, at which they taught students to sing in harmony using shaped notes as a guide to intervals. The first book to be printed in shaped notes was *The Easy Instructor*, by William Little and William Smith, published in 1801.

The singing schools became popular in the South and along the Midwestern frontier, especially because the tunes were intended to be sung without instrumental accompaniment, an attractive feature to communities that did not have an organ or a piano to guide congregational singing. As the number of shape-note hymnals grew, publishers included both original compositions and arrangements of familiar folk and popular songs of the day. The shape-note style of hymnody died out in New England in the middle of the 19th century after music educator Lowell Mason (1792–1872) launched the "better music movement," an effort to educate schoolchildren in the principles of European-style harmony. Rural communities in the South and along the Mississippi River retained the older style of American hymnody.

During the 19th century, some rural Southern composers began to adapt the appealing, populist style of shape-note singing, rewriting the harmony to conform more closely to European standards, drawing on newer religious poetry for texts, and allowing for instrumental accompaniment. This style eventually became the basis of Southern gospel hymns. Some of the early gospel hymnals were printed in shaped notes, according to a seven-shape system, although the parts were condensed onto the grand staff (treble and bass clefs joined) used for piano notation, and the books were printed in an upright format rather than the oblong format used by true shape-note hymnals.

In the early years of the 20th century, rural Southern shape-note singers became an object of fascination for historians and musicologists, including George Pullen Jackson (1874–1953) and Alan Lomax (1915–2002). Lomax's recordings of the 1959 United Sacred Harp Convention are included in his recording anthology *Southern*

Journey. In the middle of the 20th century, the number of singers dwindled until the style was in danger of dying out. During the late 1960s and early 1970s, following on the heels of the folk revival, urban folk singers in the northern and upper Midwest began to rediscover shape-note music. They traveled to Georgia and Alabama to learn the art from Southern singers and established their own regular singings and annual conventions.

During the 19th century, many shape-note hymnals circulated in different areas of the country. These included the *Southern Harmony*, the *Missouri Harmony*, the *Kentucky Harmony*, the *Columbian Harmony*, and the *Sacred Harp*, all of which were printed with four-shape notation. The most popular hymnals printed in seven shapes were the *Harmonia Sacra*, the *Christian Harmony*, and the *New Harp of Columbia*. In 1844, following a publishing dispute, the *Sacred Harp* was split into two rival editions. One, edited by Benjamin Franklin White (1800–1879) and Elisha King (1821–1844), is commonly called the "Cooper Book," after Wilson Marion Cooper (1850–1916), who revised it in 1902. It was popular in Florida, southern Alabama, and Texas. The other edition is called the "Denson Book," after the brothers Seaborn (1854–1936) and Thomas Denson (1863–1935), and Thomas's son Paine Denson (1882–1955), who revised their edition in 1936.

The most popular shape-note hymnal in use today is the 1991 revision of the Denson edition of the *Sacred Harp*. Other four-shape hymnals in regular use include the Cooper edition of the *Sacred Harp* (latest revision 2012), the 2005 edition of the *Missouri Harmony*, the *Northern Harmony* (latest revision 2012), the *Norumbega Harmony* (2004), and the *Shenandoah Harmony* (2013).

STYLE AND NOTATION

Shape-note hymnals are primarily oblong, and the music is printed with each part on a separate staff. Most of the tunes are written for three or four voices, although there are some tunes written for two voices. Following Renaissance practice, the tenor line carries the melody. The remaining parts are called bass, treble, and alto. Many tunes in the *Sacred Harp* were originally written in three parts, and alto lines were added for the 1911 revision. The bass line is traditionally sung by men, and the alto line is traditionally sung by women. The tenor and the treble lines are sung by both men and women, giving the sound the illusion of a six-voice texture.

Shape-note tunes may be plainsongs, fuging (fuguing) tunes, or anthems. A *plainsong* is a tune in which all the parts move together, creating chordal harmony. In a fuging tune, the first half of the tune is often in plainsong, while the second half features the parts entering sequentially (the fugue) and moving in a polyphonic, or rhythmically independent, style before coming together at the end. An *anthem* is a setting of prose text rather than metered poetry. Most anthems are longer and more structurally complex than plainsongs or fuging tunes and may contain passages in both plainsong and fuging style.

Harmonically, shape-note tunes are similar to, but not the same as, common-practice Western harmony. Shape-note harmony admits dyads (two-note chords) and parallel octaves and fifths. The interval of the fourth is considered to be a consonance rather than a dissonance. The four voice parts may cross, and dissonances are often unprepared and unresolved. This produces a sound that some listeners perceive as rougher and rawer than common-practice harmony. Shape-note tunes are written primarily in the major (Ionian) and natural minor (Aeolian) modes. However, in practice, many songs written in the minor mode are sung in the Dorian mode, which is achieved by raising the sixth scale degree by one half-step. Many older tunes are also written using pentatonic, or gapped, scales.

The solfége syllables derive from the system of 11th-century monk Guido of Arezzo, who developed a musical scale using the syllables *ut, re, mi, fa, sol,* and *la*. The four-tone variation on this scale, using only *fa, sol, la,* and *mi*, arose in England in the 17th century, and came to America in the 18th century with English colonists. The syllables are arranged in the order fa-sol-la-fa-sol-la-mi-fa for the major scale, providing the singer with a quick visual reference to the intervals to be sung. To derive the notes of the minor scale, the major scale is shifted back by two syllables, resulting in the order la-mi-fa-sol-la-fa-sol-la. There are multiple seven-shape systems, each featuring a slightly different set of shapes attached to the syllables do, re, mi, fa, sol, la, and *si*. Many music educators who devised these systems took out patents on them, and shaped notes are sometimes called "patent notes" because of this.

CURRENT PRACTICE

Shape-note singing is an entirely participatory art, and there is no designated audience at a singing, although some attendees may choose to listen rather than sing. Singers sit in an arrangement called a "hollow square," with altos facing tenors and basses facing trebles. A leader will select a tune and stand in the middle of the hollow square, leading the singing by beating time, most commonly in duple or triple meter. As shape-note singing is entirely *a cappella* (unaccompanied), a "keyer" selects a starting pitch that is most comfortable for the particular group, often called the "key of convenience." The group will first sing through the tune using the solfége syllables indicated by the note-heads, a practice called "singing the shapes," and then sing through as many stanzas of the hymn as the leader requests.

The current practice of shape-note singing derives from the format of the early singing schools, and singers retain much of the singing-school terminology. A group of singers is called a "class," and any individual tune is called a "lesson." Shape-note practice is highly democratic, with all interested singers taking a turn in the hollow square to select and lead a lesson. At a small local or house singing, singers may simply stand in turn. At a larger state or national convention, an officer called an "arranger" will call singers to the square individually. A local singing may last only a few hours, whereas a larger regional event may last one, two, or even three days.

For a day-long "all-day singing" or a multiple-day convention, a chairperson is elected to oversee the process, and a chaplain opens and closes the singing with prayer. Local singers will provide a midday meal known as "dinner on the grounds." There may also be a moment set aside during the singing to remember sick, shut-in, and deceased singers. This moment is called the "memorial lesson." A typical memorial lesson will consist of a short speech, a reading of a list of names of people to be remembered, and a tune sung in their honor.

There are local shape-note groups in 42 states in the United States, as well as the District of Columbia. More recently, the practice has begun to spread outside the United States. Today, one may find shape-note singers in Poland, Germany, Ireland, Canada, Australia, and the United Kingdom. Each year, the Sacred Harp Musical Heritage Association (SHMHA) publishes the *Minutes and Directory of Sacred Harp Singings*, recording the attendance and tunes sung at singings in the past year, and providing a schedule of singings for the upcoming year. SHMHA also sponsors Camp Fasola, a large annual residential singing school held at a campsite in Alabama. Camp Fasola consists of two sessions of five days each, with one session intended for adults and one for youth.

Rachel Adelstein

See also: Amish Hymns; Gospel Music; Lomax, Alan and John

Further Reading

Bealle, John. 1997. *Public Worship, Private Faith: Sacred Harp and American Folksong.* Athens: University of Georgia Press.

Clawson, Laura. 2011. *I Belong to This Band, Hallelujah!: Community, Spirituality, and Tradition among Sacred Harp Singers.* Chicago: University of Chicago Press.

Cobb, Buell. 2004. *The Sacred Harp: A Tradition and Its Music.* Athens: University of Georgia Press.

Hinton, Matt, and Erica Hinton. 2006. *Awake, My Soul: The Story of the Sacred Harp* [DVD]. 75 minutes. Atlanta, GA: Awake Productions.

Jackson, George Pullen. 1933. *White Spirituals in the Southern Uplands: The Story of the Fasola Folk, Their Songs, Singings, and "Buckwheat Notes."* Chapel Hill: University of North Carolina Press.

Miller, Kiri. 2008. *Traveling Home: Sacred Harp Singing and American Pluralism.* Urbana: University of Illinois Press.

Sacred Harp Musical Heritage Association. 1995–2011. "fasola.org—Sacred Harp and Shape Note Singing." http://fasola.org.

Steele, David Warren, and Richard H. Hulan. 2010. *The Makers of the Sacred Harp.* Urbana: University of Illinois Press.

Webb, Chloe. 2010. *Legacy of the Sacred Harp.* Fort Worth: Texas Christian University Press.

Shômyô

Shômyô, a style of Buddhist vocal chant, has been practiced in Japan for at least 1,400 years. Buddhism came to Japan from China via the Korean peninsula starting in the sixth century CE, and by the eighth century CE, Buddhist chant was flourishing. It was first called *bonbai* (*bombai*) or "pure chanting," based on Chinese usage of the time (Sawada, 2001, p. 611). Buddhist chant can be traced back to the practice of *śabda-vidyā* (linguistic study of Sanskrit), one of the five fields of academic study mastered by the Brahmans of ancient India. The term "shômyô," which is a translation of *śabda-vidyā*, is written with Chinese characters meaning "voice-clear," but was not commonly used until the 12th century CE (Nelson, 2008a, p. 37). Today, shômyô generally refers to all traditional vocal practices in ritual Buddhist contexts. The style ranges from highly melismatic (extended single syllables sung over several pitches) singing style with free-form rhythm to syllabic (single syllables sung per beat) recitation style with fixed meter and form.

Today, two main forms of shômyô survive: the Tendai sect and the Shingon sect. These represent two distinct repertories that were introduced during the Heian Period (794–1192 CE) and consequently influenced other forms. The two sects further delineate chants into subsets and also by the texts' language. The original Sanskrit text is the oldest performed, followed by those translated into Chinese and Japanese. It is generally accepted that although shômyô is still performed in Sanskrit, these chants came to Japan via China and probably were transmitted with Chinese language and musical inflections. Shômyô, like *gagaku*, developed to become the contemporary musics in the Heian imperial court and Buddhist temples, and today shômyô remains an important component in Buddhist ceremonies.

These chants are monophonic, containing a single line per chant with no harmony. There are two basic performance types: solo and unison. A single priest or several alternating priests perform solo shômyô when strung together in a ceremony. Unison pieces can be performed in two ways. First, a chant will begin with one priest and is joined by a chorus in unison. Second, the chant is sung alternatively between a soloist and the chorus (Sawada, 2001, p. 615). Shômyô is mostly unaccompanied, but there are a handful of instruments that can be used to indicate religious meaning, to signal ritual timing, or to accompany the chants in certain contexts. Wooden clappers, metal gongs, and bells are common and vary in function. Additionally, a frame drum is used for accompaniment, and a trumpet made from a conch shell, known as a *hora*, is still commonly used. Though associated with the Huke sect of Zen Buddhism, the *shakuhachi* (end-blown notch flute) is not used with shômyô practices.

Performers use written notations that use a graphic mnemonic system to represent the vocal melodies. This notation is quite complex and can be difficult to understand, especially between sects, since each has its own version of representation. In general, these mnemonic representations are approximate to the melodic lines. No indication as to exact pitch or rhythm is supplied; rather, these notations, like other notations found in Japan, are used as reference material.

Justin R. Hunter

See also: Gagaku; Japan, Music of; Tibetan Buddhist Chant

Further Reading

Malm, William P. 2000. *Traditional Japanese Music and Musical Instruments (The New Edition)*. Tokyo: Kodansha International.

Nelson, Steven G. 2008a. "Court and Religious Music (1): History of Gagaku and Shōmyō." In Alison McQueen Tokita and David W. Hughes (eds.), *The Ashgate Research Companion to Japanese Music*, 35–48. Surrey, UK: Ashgate.

Nelson, Steven G. 2008b. "Court and Religious Music (2): Music of Gagaku and Shōmyō." In Alison McQueen Tokita and David W. Hughes (eds.), *The Ashgate Research Companion to Japanese Music*, 49–76. Surrey, UK: Ashgate.

Sawada, Atuko. 2001. "Buddhist Music in Japan." In Robert Provine, Yosihiko Yokumaru, and J. Lawrence Witzleben (eds.), *Garland Encyclopedia of World Music; Vol. 7: China, Japan, and Korea*, 611–618. New York: Routledge.

Singspiel

Singspiel or *singspiele* (song-play) is an opera-like musical drama that is performed in German. Originating in the 18th century, it features arias and ensemble pieces separated by spoken dialogue. Continuity of music and style is not necessary; plots are typically lighthearted and involve moralistic, magical, and comical themes. Notable composers of singspiel include Czech Georg Benda (1722–1795); Germans Johann Adam Hiller (1728–1804), Johann Friedrich Reichardt (1752–1814), Johann Rudolf Zumsteeg (1760–1802), Friedrich Heinrich Himmel (1765–1814), and E. T. A. Hoffmann (1776–1822); and Austrians Joseph Haydn (1732–1809), Carl Ditters von Dittersdorf (1739–1799), Wolfgang Amadeus Mozart (1756–1791), and Wenzel Müller (1767–1835). The singspiel is still performed today on a global scale.

Singspiel is inspired by the German miracle play genre of the early 17th century, created circa 1700 in Vienna at the Kärntnertor Theater, where it was produced by the Hanswurst company. Singspiel was also performed by wandering troupes, notably the Koberwein, Koch, and Döbbelin, Anton Seyler's group at Weimar and Gotha, and, beginning in the late 1770s, one directed by G. F. W. Grossmann.

In northern Germany, the main inspirations for singspiel were the 18th-century French *opéra comique* (a satirical genre featuring well-known songs and spoken French) and the English ballad opera (an opera using spoken dialogue and songs in the vernacular language). Some popular ballad operas and opéras comiques were translated into singspiel; for example, *The Devil to Pay* (1731) by Irish playwright Charles Coffey (d. 1745) was translated into German by Caspar Wilhelm von Borck as *Der Teufel ist los* (1743). Traditional opera was not as popular as singspiel in Hamburg, Leipzig, and Lübeck, the main production cities of singspiel. Unlike the audience of traditional and aristocratic opera, the audience of singspiel mostly came from the lower and middle classes.

In the 1760s and 1770s, Hiller and librettist C. F. Weisse (1726–1804) produced numerous singspiele in Leipzig including their own *Der Teufel ist los oder Die verwandelten Weiber* (The devil to pay, or The wives metamorphos'd) (1766). These two men were called the fathers of the German singspiel. Hiller elevated the singspiel from a lower form of popular entertainment to a higher quality musical genre. His style was melodic and simple, akin to the folksong, and sometimes marches or recruiting songs were used, indicative of Germany's involvement in the recent Seven Years' War (1756–1763). Benda composed singspiels for northern German venues, but he (unlike his contemporaries of the singspiel in Germany) also achieved production success in Vienna. His *Romeo und Julie* (1776) reflects a more serious plot for the genre.

Singspiel in Vienna is different from the German genre in that the Viennese works combine French, Italian, and German characteristics. Also, the singing roles are more vocally demanding and require a singer who can act rather than an actor who can sing. Lastly, the music, as a whole, resembles traditional opera more than its German counterpart.

Because Italian and French opera dominated the musical scene in Vienna, Emperor Joseph II, who ruled during the Age of Enlightenment, sought a nationalist focus when he created the German National-Singspiel in 1778 at the Burgtheater. This initiative was meant to bring more native-tongued opera to the area, but a good number of singspiele were simply translations of French or English works. Viennese composer and violist Ignaz Umlauf (1746–1796) composed the first singspiel of the initiative, the one-act work *Die Bergknappen* (The miners) (1778). Mozart's *Die Entführung aus dem Serail* (The abduction from the seraglio) (1782) was the most successful singspiel of this program, and had 40 performances at the Burgtheater. Singspiele by Ordonez, Ulbrich, and Benda also had successful runs. Joseph II helped recruit well-trained singers for this venture, including Therese Teyber, Caterina Cavalieri, Aloysia Lange, Wilhelmine Stierle, Joseph Ruprecht, Ludwig Fischer, and Valentin Adamberger. Mozart created roles in his singspiele for Teyber, Cavalieri, Lange, and Fischer.

Even though the singspiel program stopped operating on March 4, 1783, the genre experienced a revival at the Kärntnertor Theater from the autumn of 1785 until early February 1788. Some of the successful performances of this period included Dittersdorf's *Der Apotheker und der Doktor* (The pharmacist and the doctor) (1786) to a libretto by Gottlieb Stephanie (1741–1800), who was also a stage manager of the National-Singspiel. Stephanie published his collected singspiel texts in 1792. Works by Dittersdorf were popular with the audience because they were not too complicated or musically ornamented. Dittersdorf, along with Mozart, represented the most praised composers of the Viennese singspiel.

The director of the Leopoldstadt theater, Viennese actor and playwright Karl Marinelli (1745–1803), brought together a group of musicians who produced singspiele successfully for about 200 performances. Müller, one of the main composers of the theater, wrote music that highlighted the solo song and musical simplicity.

The singspiel genre was also moved to outlying theaters such as the Freihaus-Theater auf der Wieden. Emanuel Schikaneder (1751–1812), the manager of this venue just outside of Vienna, was a competitor of Marinelli's. In 1801, Schikaneder moved his productions to the Theater an der Wien. Before that, he produced Mozart's *Die Zauberflöte* (The magic flute) (1791) at the Freihaus-Theater for a total of 223 performances at this theater alone. The audience was a mixture of classes and cultures, and Mozart conducted the orchestra for the first performance. Subtitled by the composer and librettist as "*eine grosse Oper*" (a grand opera), this singspiel is one of the most commonly performed operas, internationally speaking, in the standard repertory. For example, productions in 2014 were given in multiple countries, including Australia, Bulgaria, Mongolia, Mexico, Russia, and Norway. *Die Zauberflöte* has arias that are more demanding than those of the standard singspiel. "*Der Hölle Rache kocht in meinem Herzen* (Hell's vengeance boils in my heart)" is said to be one of the most difficult arias for coloratura soprano (a female voice with great agility and the ability to be high-pitched and light). Sung by the Queen of the Night, this song features intense ornamentation and wide vocal range which the queen uses to express her desire for power and Sarastro's blood.

Die Zauberflöte is also referred to as a *zauberoper* (magic opera), a singspiel that features stage machinery, great spectacle, and magical themes. In Act 1, Tamino, an Egyptian prince, and the bird-catcher Papageno are on a mission to find Pamina, the daughter of the Queen of the Night. Pamina was taken by the high Priest of Isis and Osiris, Sarastro, but only for her own well-being because her mother is a force of evil. The magic flute and magic bells help Tamino and Papageno find Pamina; however, in the second act, the two men must go through an initiation in which they may not speak to any women. Because Tamino cannot speak to Pamina, she misunderstands his actions and her feelings are hurt. Papageno does not follow the rules and thus almost loses his lady friend, Papagena. However, there is a happy ending for both couples because they are brought together at last thanks to the powers of the magic flute and bells.

Singspiel did not have much lasting power by the turn of the 19th century, given the reality that it had a hard time competing with French and Italian operatic genres. However, there were some notable contributions from this period to the Viennese singspiel genre, including Johann Schenk's *Der Dorfbarbier* (The village barber) (1796) and Joseph Weigl's *Die Schweizerfamilie* (The Swiss family) (1809).

Emily A. Bell

See also: Classical Music, European; Opera

Further Reading

Batley, E. M. 1966. "The Inception of 'Singspiel' in Eighteenth-Century Southern Germany." *German Life and Letters* 19 (April), 167–177.

Bauman, Thomas. 1985. *North German Opera in the Age of Goethe*. Cambridge: Cambridge University Press.

Internet Archive, Community Video. "Wolfgang Amadeus Mozart—Der Hölle Rache." https://archive.org/details/MozartDerHlleRacheMozartDieZauberflIte.

Manning, Elizabeth. 1993. "The Politics of Culture: Joseph II's German Opera." *History Today* 43 (January), 15–21.

Neumann, Alfred R. 1963. "The Changing Concept of the Singspiel in the Eighteenth Century." In Carl Hammer (ed.), *Studies in German Literature*, 63–71. Baton Rouge: Louisiana State University Press.

Sitar

The *sitar* is a long-necked, fretted string instrument associated with Hindustani (North Indian) classical music. Described as "India's most famous contribution to world music culture" (Miner, 2000, p. 334), Ravi Shankar's performances spread the instrument and its music throughout the Western world over the course of the 20th century, and the sitar has become known globally as a symbol of India.

Formally classified as a type of lute, the sitar is the ancestor of the *bin*, a stick zither. The sitar is also related to *setar*, a small, three-stringed Persian lute. While legend holds that the instrument was invented by court musician and poet Amir Khusrau in the 14th century, evidence suggests the instrument was brought from Kashmir to Delhi by Khusrau Khan sometime in the early 18th century.

The wooden instrument's body consists of a hollowed-out gourd and a long, hollow neck. Both are similar to that of the *tambura* or *tanpura*, a four-stringed instrument plucked to provide the drone that supports soloists. The major difference between the two instruments is that a sitar is fretted, typically with 20 arching metal frets. These frets are tied around the back of the neck and are movable. Sitarists adjust them to raise and lower certain notes according to the *raga* they are performing. The frets are raised off the fingerboard, allowing a performer to play *mind* (bends) up to a fifth above the starting note.

Sitars have two sets of strings run over two separate bridges. One set consists of 13 sympathetic strings made of thin metal wire. The strings are tuned according to whatever raga the sitarist performs. These resonating strings drone, vibrating in sympathy with notes played on the main strings and creating the instrument's distinctive timbre. The second set is a group of six or seven main strings made from metal wire of various sizes. The highest of these strings (*chikari*) are used for rhythmic accents. Performers primarily play on one or two main strings. The left index finger is primarily used for fretting notes, which helps maintain a smooth, voice-like connection between pitches. The left middle finger (and occasionally the ring finger) is used to support bends, for playing ornaments, or for reaching a phrase's top pitch. The strings are struck with a wire pick (*mizrab*) worn on the right index finger. The performer sits cross-legged on the ground, holding the instrument across the left side of the body and resting the lower gourd on the bare sole of the foot.

Two styles of concert sitar dominate modern instrument-making. The Vilayat Khan style instrument is a smaller, minimally ornamented sitar with six main strings and one resonating gourd. The Ravi Shankar style instrument features intricate carving and inlays, a second resonating gourd behind the top of the neck, and seven main strings, including a lower string that extends the instrument's bass register. The Khan-style instrument shows the influence of vocal music and the *khyal* genre, whereas the latter shows the influence of the bin and the *dhrupad* genre (Miner, 2000).

A revival of interest in the bin encouraged sitarist Ghulam Muhammad to invent the bass sitar, or *surbahar*, in about 1820. The surbahar (the name translates literally as "springtime of notes") is a bigger instrument with a darker timbre. It is tuned a fourth or fifth lower than the sitar and played with a similar technique, but is capable of larger bends.

Many different styles of sitar playing have developed around certain schools or lineages (*gharānā*). The Jaipur gharānā, the oldest of these, drew from traditions of bin playing indebted to the sustained patronage of the Jaipur Maharajas. Artists from this school, such as Devabrata (Debu) Chaudhuri and Mustaq Ali Khan, value elaborate compositions that form the centerpiece of larger concerts.

The *Imdādkhāni* or *Etawah gharānā*, named after Imdad Khan, is the only gharānā in which the sitar has been played for five generations. This tradition stresses playing in *gayaki ang* (singing style), and its performers strive to achieve vocal qualities of fluidity and melodic beauty. Vilayat Khan is one of the tradition's most famous performers and one of the best-known sitarists of the 20th century. While notorious for his refusal to accept several national awards and his purported feud with contemporary Ravi Shankar, Khan is most famous for his redesign of the sitar, his avoidance of the tambura drone and subsequent use of the chikari strings (especially during his masterful *alaps*), and his interpretations of fundamental ragas such as Todi and Yaman. One current representative of this gharānā is the female sitarist Anupama Bhagwat, who has experimented with playing meditative alap-style lines over a *tala* framework and has achieved an international reputation for her melodic beauty, control, and virtuosity.

The *Maihar gharānā*, which has had a profound influence on 20th-century instrumental playing, is the gharānā most known to Westerners. While being particularly indebted to the dhrupad vocal style developed in Mughal courts, this style has also absorbed influences from numerous other sources. The school was formed by Allauddin Khan, the chief court musician of the Hindu state of Maihar. Khan sought to spread Hindustani music to a large audience and found success through the international concertizing careers of several pupils. In addition to teaching such well-known figures as Ali Akbar Khan (*sarod*) and Hariprasad Chaurasia (bamboo flute), Allauddin Khan was guru to two of the most significant sitarists of the 20th century, Ravi Shankar and Nikhil Banerjee.

Banerjee (1931–1986) has been described as "one of India's greatest exponents of the sitar" (Slawek, 2000, p. 204). His talent was manifest from an early age, and Banerjee won the All-Bengal Sitar Competition when he was nine years old. In addition to a globe-spanning concert and recording career, he held a number of professorships and won numerous awards, demonstrating great potential ultimately unrealized due to his premature death from a heart attack, a loss made greater by a lack of trained disciples carrying on his tradition.

Banerjee's performance of the afternoon raga *Multānī* in Rotterdam (May 17, 1970) illustrates his distinctive approach. The six sections of his alap systematically and sequentially introduce the raga's pitches while expanding in register. The second section explores the instrument's low register. Although Banerjee's sitar lacks the additional bass string customary on Shankar-style sitars, his lengthy passages in this low register display one of the distinctive hallmarks of the Maihar gharānā. The alap's third and fourth sections move higher, arriving on the upper octave in the fifth section before concluding with a final portion featuring the descending *glissandi* and large leaps that are characteristic of Banerjee's playing. The following composition (*gat*) begins on beat 10 of a 16-beat cycle and includes a series of *tans* (rapid passages) showcasing Banerjee's technique. He concludes his performance with a fast gat, creatively intertwining this music with a theme employing a *todā* technique (attacking a note twice within its normal subdivision), and concluding with a fast *jhala* section and a rapid *saval-javab* (question-answer) exchange with tabla player Kanai Dutta.

Recognized for his distinctive sound as well as his speed, precision, and expressiveness, Banerjee was widely regarded as the equal of his contemporaries Vilayat Khan and Ravi Shankar. It was Shankar, however, who popularized the sitar in the West. Shankar briefly taught George Harrison, who provided many listeners with their initial encounter with the instrument on Beatles songs such as "Norwegian Wood" and "Within You, Without You." A "raga rock" fad in contemporary popular music encouraged groups such as Traffic, the Yardbirds, the Rolling Stones, the Byrds, and the Incredible String Band to experiment with the instrument or with sitar-like timbres, but this fad was short-lived and ultimately overshadowed by Shankar's performances at rock festivals such as Monterey Pop, Woodstock, and the Concert for Bangladesh. Shankar's tireless concertizing and educational efforts introduced many Westerners to the instrument's use in classical traditions. His extensive recorded discography includes his concerts at London's Royal Festival Hall (1958) and New York's Carnegie Hall (1961), important albums in the reception history of the instrument and musical traditions Shankar worked to spread in the West.

John Hausmann

See also: Dhrupad; Khayal; Raga; Shankar, Ravi; Tala

Further Reading

Arnold, Alison, ed. 1999. *Garland Encyclopedia of World Music; Vol. 5: South Asia: The Indian Subcontinent.* New York: Routledge.

Banerjee, Nikhil. 1990[1970]. *Afternoon Ragas Rotterdam 1970.* Raga Records Raga-211.

Banerjee, Nikhil. 1990[1982]. *Live Berkeley 1982: Rag Misra Kafi.* Raga Records Raga-204.

Bor, Joep. 2002. *The Raga Guide: A Survey of 74 Hindustani Ragas.* Monmouth, UK: Wyastone Estate.

Khan, Vilayat. 1968. *The Supreme Genius of Ustad Vilayat Khan.* His Master's Voice—EASD 1332.

Khan, Vilayat. 1972. *Raga Yaman.* His Master's Voice—EASD 1350.

Miner, Allyn. 2000. "Musical Instruments: Northern Area." In Alison Arnold (ed.), *The Garland Encyclopedia of World Music; Vol. 5: South Asia,* 331–349. New York: Garland.

Slawek, Stephen. 2000. "Hindustani Instrumental Music." In Alison Arnold, ed., *The Garland Encyclopedia of World Music; Vol. 5: South Asia,* 188–208. New York: Garland.

Ska

Ska is a style of popular dance music that emerged in Jamaica in the late 1950s and early 1960s. It is the direct precursor to reggae music, with which it shares musical features. Many older reggae musicians began their careers performing ska music. The emergence of ska music coincided with Jamaica's independence movement, and at the time this new dance music was closely identified with the nation's new identity. Jamaican ska has inspired revivals of the form in various time periods and locations, including the British ska bands associated with the label 2 Tone Records, and "third-wave" ska bands in North America and the United Kingdom.

The creators of ska were various record producers and professional musicians, who responded to the tastes of local audiences for the jump blues and R & B emerging from the United States in the 1950s. At the time, working-class entertainment centered around open-air dances hosted by various sound systems (mobile DJs) that competed for the best new records from the United States. The most influential sound system operators were Arthur "Duke" Reid, who ran the Trojan sound system and later founded Treasure Isle records; and Clement "Sir Coxsone" Dodd, whose Downbeat sound system built the foundation for his label Studio One

Records. Other entrepreneurs who were influential in the development of ska included Vincent "Randy" Chin and Chris Blackwell, both of whom moved abroad and founded VP Records and Island Records respectively. Edward Seaga, who eventually became Jamaica's fifth prime minister, was an enthusiastic researcher and supporter of Jamaican music, and released a number of recordings on his label West India Records Limited (WIRL). Seaga later sold this label to bandleader Byron Lee, who renamed it Dynamic Records.

Although the ska sound has links to the jump blues and R & B of artists such as Louis Jordan, Fats Domino, Little Richard, and Professor Longhair, its distinctiveness was created in the studio by various professional musicians active at the time. The "upbeat" or "afterbeat" that is the hallmark of ska has been attributed to the rhythm section of Clue J & His Blues Blasters, which included bassist Cluett "Clue J" Johnson, guitarist Ernest Ranglin, and pianist Theophilus Beckford. Allegedly, the term "ska" comes from a description of the sound that Ranglin produced on his guitar, making the rhythm go "ska, ska, ska." Members of Johnson's band went on to form the Skatalites, which eventually became the house band for Studio One.

Early ska recordings include both instrumentals (typically incorporating a 12-bar blues progression with various members of the band soloing) and vocals (featuring singers who were influenced by artists such as Sam Cooke and Jackie Wilson). The most popular recordings of the period 1956–1960 include "Easy Snappin," which Theo Beckford released as a solo artist; "Boogie in My Bones," featuring vocalist Laurel Aiken; and "Oh Carolina," recorded by The Folkes Brothers.

By 1962, ska had achieved mainstream popularity in Jamaica, and was widely promoted as one of Jamaica's unique cultural contributions to the world. Established dance bands such as Byron Lee and the Dragonaires developed a more refined and polished ska sound that appealed to middle- and upper-class audiences. This period coincided with Jamaican independence, as well as the rise of local radio stations whose mandate was to support local music. In 1964, the Jamaican government sponsored a music festival at the World's Fair in New York City that included Byron Lee and his band, as well singers Prince Buster, Desmond Dekker, and the teenaged singing sensation Jimmy Cliff. The biggest ska hit of the time was "My Boy Lollipop." Recorded by Millie Small in the UK in 1964 and arranged and produced by Ernest Ranglin, the single sold 7 million copies worldwide. Other significant ska recordings of the period 1962–1966 include Jimmy Cliff's "Miss Jamaica," "Jamaican Ska" by Byron Lee and the Dragonaires, "Bam Bam" by Toots and the Maytals, and "Simmer Down" by the Wailers, led by a 19-year-old Bob Marley. The Skatalites were also influential, with recordings such as "Guns of Navarone" and "Man in the Street."

In London, ska recordings were popular with West Indian immigrants, who had established a lively nightclub culture in their working-class neighborhoods. Eventually, ska came to the attention of the mod subculture, and soon white teenagers who identified as mods began to frequent West Indian nightclubs and purchase recordings by the Skatalites and Prince Buster. Spurred by the success of the single "My Boy Lollipop," Chris Blackwell relocated his label Island Records to the

United Kingdom., which further increased the distribution of ska (and later reggae) in the British music scene.

By 1966, Jamaican audiences began to lose interest in ska and the frenetic pace of its musical arrangements. By 1968, ska had been eclipsed by the slower-paced musical styles rocksteady and reggae, both of which featured aspects of Rastafarian and other neo-African elements of Jamaican culture in both musical arrangements and lyrics. The worldwide success of Bob Marley and the Wailers, and Jimmy Cliff, further moved tastes away from what was by then considered an old-fashioned style of music.

Ska music did not really go away, however, and renewed interest in ska came about in the United Kingdom. as British youth of both European and West Indian heritage became involved with the punk rock movement. A number of bands emerged that interpreted old ska tunes and eventually wrote new material influenced by ska and reggae. The 2 Tone Record label, founded by Jerry Dammers in 1979, was instrumental in promoting this sound, and released recordings by Dammers's band the Specials as well as the Selecter (fronted by singer Pauline Black), the Bodysnatchers, Madness, and the Beat (known in North America as the English Beat). The association of ska with the rebelliousness of punk rock, and the socially conscious topics of then-current reggae songs, resulted in lyrics that critiqued various social and political problems in the United Kingdom at that time. Significant songs of this "second wave" ska period of 1979–1983 include "A Message to You Rudy" and "Concrete Jungle" by the Specials; "Too Much Pressure" and "Three Minute Hero" by the Selecter; "The Prince" by Madness; and "Ranking Full Stop" by the (English) Beat. The popularity of these bands led to a resurgence of interest in ska's "first wave"; the Skatalites, for example, reformed and have toured in various incarnations for the past three decades.

In the late 1980s and early 1990s, a third wave of ska emerged in the United States, representing a renewed interest in both 1970s punk and ska. Bands that have recorded songs in this style include Let's Go Bowling, No Doubt, Sublime, Rancid, and the Mighty Mighty Bosstones. This has inspired ska bands to form in various countries: these include Tokyo Ska Paradise Orchestra, France's La Ruda, Mexico's Maldita Vencindad, Kortatu from the Basque region of Spain, and Argentina's Los Fabulosos Cadillacs. It is likely that both the musical energy of ska and its history as a vehicle for social commentary contribute to its ongoing popularity among young people worldwide.

Hope Munro

See also: Calypso; Mento; Reggae; Soca; Steelpan

Further Reading

Augustyn, Heather. 2010. *Ska: An Oral History.* Jefferson, NC: McFarland.

Augustyn, Heather. 2013. *Ska: The Rhythm of Liberation.* Plymouth, UK: Scarecrow Press.

Bilby, Kenneth. 2016. *Words of Our Mouth, Meditation of Our Heart: Pioneering Musicians of Ska, Rocksteady, Reggae, and Dancehall.* Middletown, CT: Wesleyan University Press.

Katz, David. 2003. *Solid Foundation: An Oral History of Reggae.* New York: Bloomsbury.

Stolzoff, Norman C. 2000. *Wake the Town and Tell the People*. Durham, NC: Duke University Press.

Smith, Bessie (1894–1937)

Bessie Smith was an American blues, jazz, and vaudeville singer. Known as the "Empress of the Blues" for her forceful vocal delivery, Bessie Smith was an American blues, jazz, and vaudeville singer. Born in Chattanooga, Tennessee, on April 15, 1894, she grew up in poverty in Chattanooga's Blue Goose Hollow. Orphaned at age nine and raised by her sister Viola, Smith's singing career commenced on the street corners of Chattanooga, where she sang (often accompanied on the guitar by her brother Andrew) for spare change, and debuted more formally in 1912 when she appeared in the chorus of the Moses Stokes Minstrel Troupe with "Mother of the Blues" Ma Rainey. Smith eventually graduated from the chorus to performing duets with well-known singer Hazel Green. Building on this success, Smith subsequently performed in various traveling minstrel shows and cabarets as a solo artist (who incorporated comedy into her performances), and eventually became the leading artist on the Theatre Owners Booking Association (TOBA) circuit as well as at the 81 Theatre in Atlanta.

Smith had a large voice and demonstrated a wonderful talent for interpreting lyrics in a deeply personal style. She would perform any given song by reshaping it to her own special vocal style and to her own feelings about the text. Smith infused the melodic line by embellishment—melodic and rhythmic changes with a special type of word emphasis. Through her unique style of singing, Smith not only became known as the "Empress of the Blues," but also served as a model for the blues and jazz singers who followed. Recruited by jazz pianist Clarence Williams, Smith's initial recordings for OKeh and Columbia in 1921 were abandoned because producers believed her voice was "too rough" and would not be salable. Smith revised her musical style, becoming the champion of "city blues," with a refinement and sophistication in lyrics that focused upon mature observations of love constructed to fit rhythm and meter that held audiences and played on their feelings. Bessie Smith was particularly talented in this regard. Performers such as Ella Fitzgerald

---

Bessie Smith and Race Records

Throughout her relatively short life (1894–1937), Bessie Smith was widely regarded as one of the most important and influential singers of the first part of the 20th century. The iconic Smith is credited with connecting Southern blues culture with urban city culture in urban areas through the United States—especially Northern cities such as New York. Perhaps the most famous "race record" artist of the day, Smith recorded well over 100 releases for Columbia Records and numerous other records for various recording companies. Smith was a champion of the working class, which was a common theme in her music, and she was a well-known feminist. In addition to her recording work, Smith worked in radio, theater, and film, and by the early 1930s was the highest-paid (male or female) black performer in the entertainment industry.

American blues singer Bessie Smith in 1936. Smith was one of the most famous and influential blues singers of the early 20th century, earning her the moniker "Empress of the Blues." (Carl Van Vechten Photographs Collection, Library of Congress)

and Sarah Vaughan drew inspiration from Smith's musical legacy. With new management at Columbia, her inaugural recording of "Downhearted Blues" (and "Gulf Coast Blues" on the B-side) in February 1923—made at the behest of Frank Walker of Columbia Records' race records division—cemented her reputation as the most successful female black performing artist of the generation: it sold 780,000 copies in six months. By 1927, she had sold 4 million recordings. Smith recorded 160 songs and literally saved Columbia Records from bankruptcy at that time. Using the newfound popularity of recordings as a promotional tool and receiving no royalties for her efforts, Smith entered into an exclusive, $20,000-per-year contract with Columbia, enabling her to record and tour extensively before large crowds and drawing a salary of up to $2,500 for personal appearances until 1928.

Smith's national prominence and celebrity led to other opportunities as well as challenges. Her first film appearance occurred in 1929 in *St. Louis Blues*—quite a breakthrough for the time. Unfortunately, alcoholism and the poor economic climate of the Great Depression severely damaged her career. By 1930, public interest in her began to wane, likely due to her unwillingness to adjust to or perform more modern song material. Smith was always selective in choosing her accompanying musicians. Among them were Clarence Williams, Fletcher Henderson, Louis Armstrong, and Bennie Goodman. Columbia renegotiated her contract in 1930, reducing the guaranteed fee per record side by nearly 50 percent. In 1931, Columbia dropped her from its ranks altogether.

The next several years were challenging for Smith, both personally and professionally. She left her first husband and moved in with a wealthy former bootlegger while dreaming of regaining her status and career. Smith's last recordings embraced the newer swing style of jazz and featured talented back-up musicians, including trombonist Jack Teagarden and clarinetist Benny Goodman. Smith's last recording session was arranged in 1933 by the critic John Hammond and was targeted to the increasing European jazz audience. These recordings featured Teagarden and Goodman on OKeh Records ("Give Me a Pigfoot"). By 1936, Smith's career had resurrected itself and she was once again performing in shows and clubs. However, late in the evening of September 26, 1937, Smith died in a car accident following a performance in Memphis. At the time of her death, approximately 10 million of her records had been sold. The somewhat obscure circumstances of her death formed the subject of Edward Albee's play "The Death of Bessie Smith" (1959).

Bessie Smith's great gift of communication set the standard for all future singing of the blues. She was without doubt the greatest of the female vaudeville blues singers, packing the emotional intensity, personal insight, and expression of blues singing into mainstream jazz repertoire through her unparalleled vocal artistry. Her duet recordings for Columbia with Louis Armstrong—"St. Louis Blues" and "J. C. Holmes Blues" (both 1925)—along with recordings for Columbia with Joe Smith—including "Baby Doll" (1926), "After You've Gone" (1927), and "Nobody Knows You When You're Down and Out" (1929), with Ed Allen on the cornet—illustrate her capacity for sensitive interpretation of popular songs. Smith also recorded versions of jazz standards, notably for Columbia, including "Cake Walking Babies (from Home)" (1925) and "Alexander's Ragtime Band" (1927), both made with members of Fletcher Henderson's orchestra. Likely her best and most well-known recording was "Back Water Blues" (1927), with James P. Johnson on piano.

Eldonna L. May

See also: Blues; Jazz; Race Records; Vaudeville

Further Reading

Albertson, C. 2005. *Bessie* (rev. and expanded ed.). New Haven, CT: Yale University Press.

Albertson, C., and G. Schuller. 1975. *Bessie: Empress of the Blues.* New York: Schirmer Books.

Brooks, Edward. 1982. *The Bessie Smith Companion: A Critical and Detailed Appreciation of the Recordings.* Wheathampstead, UK: Cavendish.

Harris, S. 1981. *Blues Who's Who: A Biographical Dictionary of Blues Singers.* New Rochelle, NY: Da Capo Press.

Oliver, P. 1959/1978. "Bessie Smith." Repr. in S. Green (ed.), *Kings of Jazz*, 305–36. South Brunswick, NJ: Barnes.

Soca

Soca is a fast-tempo popular music originating in Trinidad and Tobago, though held in high regard throughout the global Caribbean diaspora. While today's soca is easily recognized by its aggressive, rhythmically driven sound, soca's early history is less apparent. The earliest movement toward a recognizable soca aesthetic came with the advent of Panorama, Trinidad and Tobago's national steel orchestra competition, in 1963. To win the prize money and prestige that went along with a first-place finish, steel orchestras gravitated toward increasingly complex and exciting arrangements that quickly fed back into calypso, which began featuring faster tempos, foregrounded bass lines, and driving 16th-note rhythms with accented upbeats. Calypsonian Mighty Sparrow (Slinger Francisco) produced many calypsos in the 1960s that exemplify this trend.

North American funk and soul additionally contributed to the development of soca, as is evident in the work of calypsonian King Wellington (Hawthorne Quashie). Wellington's "More Woman" is typical of his music from this period. Despite this early movement toward a new kind of calypso, the invention of the word "soca" and the music style it implies is widely credited to calypsonian Lord Shorty (Garfield Blackman). Born in the predominantly Indian-Trinidadian area of Barrackpore in south Trinidad, Shorty (later known as Ras Shorty I) set out to revive young people's interest in calypso and "to unite Indian and African peoples" through music. Shorty hoped to combat animosity between Trinidad and Tobago's two largest ethnic majorities by creating a harmonious fusion of Indian- and African-derived musical elements in a new style he called "sokah." As Shorty explained, "The 'so' comes from calypso. And the 'kah' . . . represents the first letter of the [Hindi] alphabet" (Rommen, 2007, p. 113). Though later iterations would invariably be spelled "soca," Shorty's original rendering of the term is telling of his aim of musical and aesthetic synthesis.

Shorty's early experiments culminated in a set of songs in the early 1970s including "Indrani," a song often regarded as the first soca hit. Each verse of "Indrani," with texts detailing the narrator's growing frustration with not comprehending a Hindi-language song sung by an "old Indian chick," follows typical calypso form in terms of lyrical and harmonic structure. However, the refrain—which references the song this Indian woman sings—is set with Hindi text to Bollywood-inspired melodic contours and instrumental timbres. Even in the verses, however, Shorty fuses Indian-derived elements with traditional calypso features. Most importantly, the Indian-Trinidadian drum *dholak* is used as a rhythmic foundation throughout, not only contributing a unique timbre but also lending its rhythmic groove to the drum set and electric bass. In the end, Shorty creates a soundscape in which African- and Indian-Trinidadian musical references are inextricably fused within the rhythmic, timbral, and melodic layers of "Indrani."

Shorty continued to produce hits highlighting this Indian-African fusion throughout the 1970s, the most popular of which was "Om, Shanti, Om," the catchy chorus of which is drawn from a common Hindu mantra. Though intended as a message of unity, Indian-Trinidadian leaders were offended by Shorty's use of a sacred text in Carnival-oriented music. Nonetheless, "Om, Shanti, Om" represents Shorty's mature soca style—one which recalls elements of Mighty Sparrow and King Wellington's post-Panorama music of the previous decade. Its percussive groove is characterized by strong bass drum strokes on every downbeat, the snare drum playing an uneven syncopation between the downbeats, and the hi-hats emphasizing every upbeat. This rhythmic play between the strong foundation in the bass drum and the syncopation in higher-pitched instruments still remains an important part of soca today.

After Lord Shorty's success, "soca" became a household word, and by the mid-1970s, numerous calypsonians were actively using the new soca groove. Calypso Rose (McCartha Lewis) was one of soca's biggest stars in this period. Her music mixed calypso's bawdiness and social commentary with soca's up-tempo groove and celebratory mood. "Come Leh We Jam," for example, is a rollicking tune featuring lyrics infused with calls to dance and party, yet using the word "jam" as an

Calypso Rose performing during the Trinidad Carnival in 2017. Calypso Rose is one of the first prominent female calypso and *soca* artists. (Sean Drakes/LatinContent via Getty Images)

all-purpose metaphor for musical, cultural, and sexual mixing. Although this kind of metaphorical language is typical of calypso, nearly all other aspects signal a soca aesthetic. Immediately apparent are the repetitive lyrics—a five-line verse contrasts with a refrain three times as long—indicating the importance of rhythm and groove rather than calypso's lyricism. The upbeat is highly stressed, while hi-hats and "iron" (as in the steelband engine room) pound out a 16th-note pattern over the foundation laid down by the steady bass drum.

Lord Kitchener's "Sugar Bum Bum," released the same year as "Come Leh We Jam," represents soca in a slightly different vein. Like "Come Leh We Jam," Kitchener's tune features repetitive lyrics and a typical soca groove. Yet, the tempo is relatively slow with a lot of musical space between repetitions of the verse-chorus cycle. Although this structure highlights the instrumental groove, there remains some sense of calypso-like narrative, however elementary it may be (with each verse, we learn more about the narrator's relationship with a woman in possession of a flattering backside). Because of its laid-back mix of soca's danceable groove and calypso's stress on lyrics and melody, Kitchener's "Sugar Bum Bum" was a huge hit and has remained popular, having been covered by countless calypsonians, steelbands, and soca artists over more than three decades.

The popularity of soca skyrocketed around the Caribbean in the 1980s and reached international fame with the pan-Caribbean hit "Hot, Hot, Hot" written and first recorded by Monserratian calypsonian Arrow (Alphonsus Cassell). Regarded by some as the most successful soca tune of all time, "Hot, Hot, Hot" also encapsulates the broad reach of the soca phenomenon, having been composed by a non-Trinidadian and covered by a host of diverse musicians, most notably in 1987 by North American protopunk lounge singer Buster Poindexter. Soca's international success in the 1980s coincided with the popularization of *zouk*, an up-tempo French Antillean pop genre closely associated with the band Kassav, whose music referenced traditional dance genres such as *gwo ka* and *belé* but also embraced contemporary pan-Caribbean fusion styles like *cadence-lypso* as well as new music technologies including drum machines and MIDI keyboards. By the end of the decade, soca had absorbed a great deal from zouk, including some rhythmic characteristics and the use of electronic timbres.

Meanwhile, soca's success abroad influenced its massive popularity back home in Trinidad and Tobago. One of the most important developments in this decade was the emergence of a variety of soca fusion styles, foremost among them *chutney soca*, a genre blending soca with chutney, an Indian-Trinidadian pop genre comprising a mix of Indian folk and classical elements. The breakaway success of Drupatee Ramgoonai's 1987 album *Chatnee Soca* signaled the viability of this new style, though her achievement was tinged with controversy. Some found her status as a woman an unwelcome intrusion into the Carnival music scene that still today remains largely the domain of African-Trinidadian men, while conservative forces in the Indian-Trinidadian community criticized Drupatee's frankly sexual lyrics as too sensual for a respectable Indian-Trinidadian female performer.

With the growing popularity of soca and its increasing divergence from calypso, entrepreneur William Munro inaugurated a new Carnival-time soca contest in 1993, today referred to as the International Soca Monarch Competition and comprising two broad categories, power soca and groovy soca. The former denotes the kind of fast, loud, and boisterous music descended from the likes of Calypso Rose's "Leh We Jam"; the latter blends R & B-style vocal melodies with a laid-back groove more closely related to Kitchener's "Sugar Bum Bum." The most successful Soca Monarch is Superblue (Austin Lyons), who first rose to prominence while dominating the Calypso Road March competition, capturing the crown nine times since 1980. His experience performing danceable songs for Carnival parades (i.e., the "road march") helped him establish a new identity as a soca artist in the early 1990s. Supterblue's success was instrumental in the institutionalization of the soca competition (he has won Power Soca Monarch seven times to date), and his high-energy performances quickly became the model which others would follow and by which they would be judged.

Competition transformed both musical and performative aspects of soca, which have moved toward increased speed, vocal dexterity, and audience interaction. This is typified by Superblue's "Bounce," his 1996 winning competition entry that features a highly abbreviated habanera rhythm in the bass (stressing two eighth notes on beat two in duple meter); fast, syncopated drum-set rhythms; electronic keyboard accentuating the upbeat; and a horn section reminiscent of older calypso style (that frequently quotes the signature horn riffs of Arrow's "Hot, Hot, Hot"). In Superblue's memorable competition performance of "Bounce," the repetitive rhythm, harmony, and melody allowed for vast improvisation on stage. At the midpoint of the song, the band began to vamp, allowing Superblue to direct the audience in an impromptu call-and-response, urging them to scream, dance, and wave their flags. Such a malleable and participatory musical structure recalls the late 19th-century *lavway* style of calypso, which was predicated upon call-and-response between leader and chorus.

Soca's emphasis on revelry rather than social commentary (as in calypso) has long been a sticking point for its most vocal critics. On the one hand, soca—like calypso and steelpan—is a uniquely Trinidadian creation that has garnered international appreciation. On the other hand, soca's detractors argue that the music has little to offer in terms of sociocultural uplift. In response to such criticism, the Groovy Soca category was added to the International Soca Monarch Competition in 2005, thereby promoting a middle ground that allowed for a variety of lyrical content while maintaining the musical vigor that soca audiences enjoy. One result is that female performers, who have largely been excluded from the elite ranks of the more aggressive (and indeed more socially transgressive) power soca contest, have been able to make inroads into the world of soca as groovy soca specialists. Only one woman has won the power soca crown: Fayann Lyons-Alvarez—daughter of Superblue and calypsonian Lady Gypsy—whose winning 2009 performance of "Meet Super Blue," a tribute to her father, included an appearance of the soca legend on stage. In the same year, Lyons-Alvarez also won the groovy soca crown with "Heavy T Bumper," a song that evokes the image of Trinidadian women's sensual beauty as a metaphor for female empowerment. Other prominent female soca artists who have gained a wide following throughout the Caribbean include Denise Belfon, Destra Garcia, and Alison Hinds, among others.

Changing attitudes about Carnival-time music have also allowed non-African-Trinidadians soca success as well. Rikki Jai (Samraj Jaimungal) first rose to prominence as a chutney soca artist in the late 1980s, but has produced numerous straight soca hits throughout his career. Though it uses some Indian-derived instrumental timbres and features a few words in Hindi, Jai's seminal self-produced hit "Sumintra" confirms soca as a cross-cultural phenomenon. In the chorus of the song, the narrator's love interest memorably scolds, "Hold the Lata Mangeshkar / give me soca!" Jai and other prominent Indian-Trinidadian chutney soca stars frequently collaborate with their African-Trinidadian soca counterparts. Drupatee and Machel Montano joined forces on "Real Unity," whose message of social harmony is reflected in the musical texture. Drupatee weaves a popular Bollywood film song ("*Aap Jaise Koi*") sung in Hindi around Montano's rapid-fire lyrics about dancing together at Carnival.

Another recent innovation is the increasing popularity of soca bands, reflecting conventions of North American popular music but bucking the long-held tradition of promoting individual performers as calypso and soca celebrities. Among the top Trinidadian soca bands are Xtatic and Kes the Band. Xtatic's popularity has benefited from the high profile of Montano, its lead singer. By contrast, Kes the Band was founded in 2005 and rose to prominence outside the mainstream, only later entering soca competition under lead singer Kees Dieffenthaller's name. Kes the

Band's 2011 groovy soca-winning tune, "Wotless," exemplifies the contemporary ensemble-driven soca aesthetic that expertly borrows from pop and rock styles while maintaining a distinctly Caribbean soca flavor.

Christopher L. Ballengee

See also: Calypso; Chutney Soca; Steelpan

Further Reading

Chutney Soca. 2000. JMC Music Group JMC 1228.

Guilbault, Jocelyne. 2007. *Governing Sound: The Cultural Politics of Trinidad's Carnival Musics.* Chicago: University of Chicago Press.

Her Majesty Calypso Rose. 1978. CLO Records CLO-444.

Manuel, Peter. 2000. *Tān-singing, Chutney, and the Making of Indo-Caribbean Culture.* Philadelphia: Temple University Press.

Rommen, Timothy. 2007. *"Mek Some Noise": Gospel Music and the Ethics of Style in Trinidad.* Berkeley: University of California Press.

Shorty's Gone, Gone. 1973. Island Series FP-1006.

Soca Explosion. 1978. Charlie's Records S.C.R. 1004.

Thompson, Dave. 2002. *Reggae & Caribbean Music.* San Francisco: Backbeat Books.

Soul

Soul is a genre of African American popular music that combines elements of rhythm and blues (R & B) and gospel music, but with an emphasis on complex, expressive vocal performance and feeling. Unlike R & B, a style of upbeat popular music made by African Americans and marketed primarily to African American audiences beginning in the 1940s, and gospel, a form of African American church music that focused on spiritual subjects and themes, soul music established itself in the 1960s as a commercially viable music that could be both widely appealing and artistically complex. Though it reached full prominence in the late 1960s through the recordings made by various African American singers and a combination of African American and white musicians, producers, and businesspeople at independent studios and labels located primarily in the American South, soul music reached beyond its regional origins to become a rich, nuanced genre with lasting musical and cultural significance.

The beginning of soul can be traced to the music of Ray Charles (1930–2004). Charles, born in Albany, Georgia, blind from the age of seven, was the first musician to successfully combine R & B music with gospel singing in an original way. His use of melisma (a vocal ornamentation in which the singer takes one syllable of a word and sings it in a string of several different notes), call-and-response vocal patterns, and the way his music blurred boundaries by imparting nonreligious themes with religious overtones marked Charles as both a musical innovator and a controversial figure. On his 1954 recording, "I Got a Woman," Charles transposed the melody and lyrics of a gospel song, "It Must Be Jesus," into an R & B arrangement in which he sang about his female lover with the kind of passionate expression that was traditionally reserved for nonsexual, spiritual love. Though subsequent recordings, such as "This Little Girl of Mine" (1955) and "Hallelujah, I Love Her

So" (1956), were created in a similar mode, Charles went on to make music in a variety of styles and genres throughout his career, to varying degrees of artistic and commercial success. Charles died in 2004 of liver disease.

Charles's contemporary, Sam Cooke (1931–1964), had brief, yet tremendous success as a singer, as his music better exemplified the popular appeal and commercial viability of soul music while embodying its key musical elements. Cooke, born in Clarksdale, Mississippi, was raised in Chicago, Illinois, where he spent most of his early years in the church, and started singing gospel music at the age of nine. In his twenties, Cooke recorded music with a gospel group called The Soul Stirrers. However, his distinct singing style, good looks, and consummate professionalism made him stand out, and Cooke soon began making records as a solo artist. His 1957 record, a slow ballad titled "You Send Me," was a no. 1 hit on both R & B and pop music charts, making Cooke one of the first soul singers to become popular among both African American and white audiences. "You Send Me" illustrated Cooke's singing talent, which combined smooth intonation and phrasing with the melisma he learned as a gospel singer, and made it very appealing in a pop context. Cooke's numerous recordings, particularly the live albums *Sam Cooke at the Copa* (1964) and *Live at the Harlem Square Club, 1963* (1985), captured the extent of his vocal flair and ability to entertain audiences. Cooke's career ended tragically when he was shot and killed in 1964.

Though soul music was being produced and released throughout the 1960s by record labels such as Atlantic Records in New York City, and Motown Records in Detroit, Michigan, independent studios located in the American South played a more significant role in developing the distinct sound and style of soul music. The most prominent of these was Stax Records, formed in Memphis, Tennessee, by businessman Jim Stewart and his sister Estelle Axon. Stax originally began as a record label named Satellite in 1958, under which Stewart released several records by aspiring local musicians. Satellite changed its name to Stax in 1960 when Stewart and Axon acquired and converted an unused former movie theater into a recording studio to accommodate an expanding roster of singers and musicians. Stax had its first national breakthrough in 1961 with a record titled "Gee Whiz," by young singer Carla Thomas, which was a hit on both the R & B and pop music charts. More early success followed with records by groups such as the studio-based band called the Mar-Keys, whose instrumental, titled "Last Night" (1961), was another national hit; William Bell's "You Don't Miss Your Water (Till Your Well Runs Dry)" (1961); and another instrumental, titled "Green Onions" (1962), by Booker T. and the MG's. The success of these early recordings demonstrated that Stax had much creative and commercial potential, and in 1961, Jerry Wexler, of the New York City-based record label, Atlantic Records, negotiated a distribution deal with Stax, in which Atlantic agreed to promote Stax products to larger markets across the country in exchange for a portion of the profits. This arrangement allowed Stax to focus on the studio production and creative aspects of the music. With its profile of both African American and white in-house studio musicians, as well as its integrated production staff and welcoming neighborhood atmosphere, Stax developed a reputation for creating a natural, lean sound on its records that distinguished it from other recording studios. Throughout the 1960s, the label was responsible for producing a number of successful soul artists, including the duo Sam and Dave, and singers Wilson Pickett and Otis Redding.

Otis Redding (1941–1967) was the most prominent soul artist associated with Stax Records. Redding grew up in Macon, Georgia, where he started to develop his soul singing style—vulnerable and impassioned, yet well controlled—by performing regularly in local clubs and on the television talent show *The Teenage Party*. Determined to make a career as a singer, Redding formed a professional and creative partnership with Phil Walden, whose business connections led to Redding's first Stax recording session for the song "These Arms of Mine" in 1962. Redding went on to have remarkable success as a live performer, booking regional package tours with other performers at notable venues such as the Apollo Theatre in New York, as well as international tours through Europe. His creative talent, which encompassed an ability to write his own songs and contribute to the studio production of his own recordings, earned him the respect of his musical peers. His best-known songs include "Respect" (1965), "I've Been Loving You Too Long (To Stop Now)" (1965), "Fa-Fa-Fa-Fa-Fa (Sad Song)" (1966), "Try a Little Tenderness" (1966), "Knock on Wood" (with Carla Thomas) (1967), and "(Sittin' On) The Dock of the Bay" (1968). Redding reached the pinnacle of his career in 1967, when he participated in two major musical events. In the spring, Redding was the headline performer in the largely successful Stax-Volt Revue tour of Europe, along with label mates Sam and Dave, the Mar-Keys, Booker T. and the MG's, Eddie Floyd, Arthur Conley, and Carla Thomas. Then, in June, Redding performed at the Monterey International Pop Music Festival in Monterey, California, marking his artistic crossover to a predominantly white audience. Redding's expanding success as a soul singer was ended, however, on December 9, 1967, when he and a group of several other Stax-affiliated musicians were killed in a plane crash while traveling to Madison, Wisconsin, for a club engagement.

The northwest area of Alabama known as Muscle Shoals was home to a small number of recording studios and labels that also produced soul music in the 1960s. Fame Music was founded in 1959 by Tom Stafford, who, with the help of songwriters Rick Hall and Billy Sherrill, constructed a recording studio in the space above the drugstore owned by Stafford's family. Fame (an acronym for Florence Alabama Music Enterprises) soon became the center of the Muscle Shoals music scene, attracting a multitude of aspiring singers and musicians, including singer-songwriter Dan Penn, keyboardist Spooner Oldham, and songwriter Donnie Fritts. Rick Hall produced various records for Fame, including "You Better Move On" (1962), by Arthur Alexander; and "Steal Away" (1964), by Jimmy Hughes. Singer Percy Sledge's 1966 hit record, "When a Man Loves a Woman," recorded at Quinvy Studio, was the most famous example of soul music to come out of the Muscle Shoals area.

The New York City-based Atlantic Records was not only instrumental in producing various soul artists who recorded at Stax and Muscle Shoals in the 1960s, but was also responsible for developing Aretha Franklin, the most prominent female soul singer of this period. Franklin was born in Memphis, Tennessee, in 1942, the daughter of a well-known reverend, and grew up in Detroit, Michigan. She began singing in her father's church, New Bethel, at the age of eight, and recorded a full gospel album at age 14. After recording several pop-oriented albums for the

Columbia label, she was signed to Atlantic by its vice-president, Jerry Wexler, in 1967. Franklin's first Atlantic album, 1967's *I Never Loved a Man The Way I Loved You*, recorded partially at Muscle Shoals' Fame Music, was a breakthrough artistic and commercial success for the singer. The album featured songs co-written by Franklin and new versions of songs written and recorded previously by soul singers such as Sam Cooke and Otis Redding. Franklin's version of Redding's song, "Respect," became a no. 1 pop hit. "Respect" captured Franklin's immense vocal talent, mixing gospel style with impassioned demands for her lover's respect, and the record went on to become a popular anthem for female dignity, grace, and confidence. Through the 1970s, Franklin recorded many more albums for Atlantic, and her successful music career earned her the title "Queen of Soul." Franklin's influence as a soul artist in the 1960s was both musical and social, as she publicly supported the civil rights movement and maintained a friendship with leader Martin Luther King, Jr. before his death.

James Brown (1933–2006) was a singer, musician, dancer, bandleader, producer, and businessman whose all-encompassing career influenced the development of soul music in a way that distinguished him from other soul artists. Brown grew up in Augusta, Georgia, and became noticed at a young age for his ability to entertain audiences with his singing and athletic dancing in local talent shows. In his twenties, Brown sang with a gospel group called the Gospel Starlighters. Under his leadership, they eventually switched to R & B music and changed their name to James Brown and the Famous Flames, to attract a bigger audience. In the mid-1950s, Brown and his backing band developed a following throughout areas of the South for their intense and flamboyant performances, as well as Brown's textured singing voice. The group's first hit record, a gospel-influenced song co-written by Brown called, "Please, Please, Please," was released in 1956, and went on to become a signature part of their live act. During performances, Brown and his band would draw out the song until Brown collapsed to his knees on stage. Appearing too exhausted to continue, a member of the band would drape Brown with a towel and start to lead him off the stage. At the last moment, Brown would drop the towel and finally finish the song in a fit of passion. The 1963 album, *Live at the Apollo*, financed by Brown himself, captured the ferocity and drama of Brown's stage show and became one of his most commercially successful recordings. Though it combined elements of gospel and R & B, Brown's music—much more so than that of any other soul artists—made innovative use of rhythm and percussion. The singles "Out of Sight" (1964), "Papa's Got a Brand New Bag" (1965), and "I Got You (I Feel Good)" (1965) are among Brown's most noteworthy records and illustrate the importance of rhythm in his music. As Brown's career as a soul artist extended beyond the 1960s, his music continued to develop and became critical in the formation of the musical genre known as funk. His reputation for being a tireless entertainer and businessman throughout his life cast Brown as a symbol of African American pride and self-respect, earning him popular titles such as "The Hardest Working Man in Show Business," "Soul Brother No. 1," and "The Godfather of Soul." Brown died of heart failure in 2006.

Luis Sanchez

See also: Blues; Funk; Gospel Music

Further Reading

Cohn, Nick. 1969. "Soul." In *Rock From the Beginning*, 127–146. New York: Stein and Day.

Gillett, Charlie. 1970. "Are We Together? Soul Music." In *The Sound of the City: The Rise of Rock and Roll*, 261–288. New York: Outerbridge & Dienstfrey.

Guralnick, Peter. 2012. *Sweet Soul Music: Rhythm and Blues and the Southern Dream of Freedom*. New York: Back Bay.

Steel Guitar

Developed in Hawaii during the late 19th and early 20th centuries, the term "steel guitar" can refer to the method of playing a slide guitar using a steel or to a specialized instrument built for playing with the steel guitar method: either the lap steel guitar, an electric console steel guitar, or an electric pedal steel guitar. Most generally, the steel guitar is played horizontally, with the strings plucked with one hand, while the other hand changes the pitch with a metal bar (or slide) called a steel. The instrument/style is prevalent within traditional Hawaiian music and country ("honky-tonk") music of the 1940s and early 1950s, as well as bluegrass. Some modern musicians have also used the instrument within rock, jazz, and blues techniques. The *Concerto for Pedal Steel Guitar and Orchestra*, written by American composer Michael A. Levine and premiered in 2005 by the Nashville Chamber Orchestra (with Gary Morse as soloist), has further expanded the style and audience of the instrument.

In typical steel guitar technique, the instrument is held horizontally with the bass strings situated toward the player. The lap steel guitar usually has six strings, tuned either to standard guitar tuning or (more commonly) an open chord. This classification actually encompasses a few different styles, such as the lap slide guitar or resonator guitar (acoustic instruments, often containing pickups for amplification) or the electric lap steel guitar (a solid body electric guitar). According to a common—but dubious—story, the Hawaiian lap steel guitar was invented in 1889 by Joseph Kekuku as a modification of the contemporary Spanish guitar (by raising the bridge and head nut to generate a higher action). Some modern lap slide guitars have two necks, each with six strings apiece. With the increased height of the strings above the surface of the neck, guitar frets are not used in lap steel guitar technique, and are often eliminated from the instrument in favor of markers alone.

The console (or table) steel guitar is an electric instrument with multiple necks (up to four) and additional strings (up to eight). Lacking pedals, the number of tunings on the console steel guitar is limited to the number of necks on the instrument. The most common instrumental configuration in contemporary Hawaiian music is two necks and eight strings per neck, although other arrangements also exist. The pedal steel guitar typically expands the number of strings per neck (up to 14), with two or three necks and pedals and knee levers (up to eight of each) to enable multiple tunings of different strings. The instrument also includes legs or a stand. While these expansions increase the versatility of the instrument, they also create a greater instrumental complexity and corresponding difficulty of performance, making skilled performers often hard to come by.

As the story goes, at the age of 11, Kekuku was walking along a railroad track (in Hawaii), picked up a metal bolt, slid the bolt along the strings of his guitar, and thus created the steel guitar, later developing the sound through the use of a knife blade along the strings. While this story may or may not have any actual basis in reality, and while other musicians have also been credited for the discovery around the same time (including Indian sailor Gabriel Davion and Portuguese-Hawaiian James Hoa), and regardless of actual instrumental nascence, by the 1920s and 1930s, the lap steel guitar had become popular not only in Hawaii, but also (through variety-show performances by Hawaiian musicians) throughout the mainstream United States. Following the introduction of the instrumental style by Hawaiian groups at the Panama-Pacific International Exposition in San Francisco in 1915, the sound spread throughout the country, with methods and songs further distributed by the major music publishers. In 1932, the first electric steel guitar was produced, known as the Rickenbacker Electro A22 "Frying Pan" (due to its round body and long neck) lap steel.

In 1940, Gibson Guitar Corporation added pedals to the steel guitar to facilitate the tuning of the instrument, thus creating the "Electra-harp" (its name indicating a close relationship to the standard pedal-based tuning system of the harp), the first commercially produced pedal steel guitar. Throughout the 1940s and 1950s, a number of other companies—including Epiphone, the Harlin Brothers, and Fender, as well as Paul Bigsby and Zane Beck—contributed to the practical evolution of the pedal steel guitar. In 1955, Nashville-based steel guitar players Harold "Shot" Johnson and Buddy Emmons teamed up to form the popular "Sho-Bud" manufacturing of pedal steel guitars. Although the pedals of the steel guitar were initially used simply to change the tunings of the instrument, later players (starting with musicians such as Bud Isaacs in the 1950s) began to use the pedals in combination with the slide to create moving-chord harmonies and expressive forms of ornamentation.

Following the introduction of the Hawaiian steel guitar onto the mainland of the United States, the style started to be transformed and incorporated into other genres. Blues musicians in the Southern United States used open-chord guitar tunings and a glass bottleneck, knife, or piece of pipe along the strings. Bluegrass musicians began to use a resonator guitar (generally known now as a Dobro) invented by brothers John and Emil Dopyera of the Dobra Manufacturing Company, consisting of a wood body and single cone resonator designed to increase the volume of the instrument. In 1935, Bob Dunn played the "Frying Pan" electric lap steel on a Western swing recording with Milton Brown and His Musical Brownies, producing the first commercial recording of an electric stringed instrument. The steel guitar quickly became an important part of Western swing and early country music, as demonstrated by Leon McAuliffe's performance in the recording of "Steel Guitar Rag" by Bob Wills and His Texas Playboys from 1936.

In 1953, Bud Isaacs played the pedal steel guitar on "Slowly" by honky-tonk star Webb Pierce, creating the first pedal guitar sound on a hit recording. In addition to its common use in country music, the steel guitar has been included on a number of recordings by modern pop and rock musicians, such as Dire Straits, Sting, Megadeth, and Barbara Streisand, among others. Despite a general reduction in the use of the steel guitar during the last decades of the 20th century, the sound has seen a recent resurgence, with established Nashville player Russ Pahl contributing to albums by Luke Bryan, Jason Aldean, and Lana del Ray, among others.

A cautionary note: the steel guitar—in its many forms—should not be confused with the steel-strung guitar, which is a standard acoustic guitar using steel strings rather than nylon (or other) strings. Nor does the term refer to the actual body of the instrument. The word "steel" indicates only the type of slide used, not the strings or body of the instrument. Also, though the term "Hawaiian guitar" is often used outside of Hawaii to refer to the steel guitar, that name actually (within the Hawaiian musical community) indicates a steel-strung acoustic guitar played with a characteristic method of slack-key (open) tuning.

Erin E. Bauer

See also: Bluegrass; Blues; Country Music; Hawaii, Music of; Jazz; Rock and Roll

Further Reading

Hood, Mantle. 1983. "Musical Ornamentation as History: The Hawaiian Steel Guitar." *Yearbook for Traditional Music* 15, 141–148.

Ruymer, Lorene, ed. 1996. *The Hawaiian Steel Guitar and Its Great Hawaiian Musicians.* Anaheim, CA: Centerstream Publications.

Stone, Robert L. 2010. *Sacred Steel: Inside an African American Steel Guitar Tradition.* Champaign: University of Illinois Press.

Volk, Andy. 2003. *Lap Steel Guitar.* Anaheim, CA: Centerstream Publications.

Steelpan

The *steelpan* (commonly called "steel drum" outside the Caribbean region) is an idiophonic percussion instrument native to Trinidad and Tobago, where it has been closely linked with Carnival celebrations since the instrument's emergence in the late 1930s. Though high-pitched steelpans are frequently played as solo instruments, steelpans are most often played in orchestras ranging from a few players to groups of 50 or more. Trinidad and Tobago remains the epicenter of steelpan activity—where it was named the country's national instrument in 1992—though capable orchestras have been organized throughout the Caribbean region and around the world, especially in North America, Europe, and Japan.

Many of the early pioneers of steelpan were young, unemployed Afro-Trinidadian men, some of whom had notorious reputations as hustlers and ruffians. Therefore, the respectable classes of colonial Trinidad generally looked down upon pannists and the instruments they played. Therefore, steelpan was largely ignored by academics and historians until the 1960s, and the exact history of steelpan is somewhat murky and often contradictory.

Steelpan's history begins with the confluence of European and African streams of music and culture in late 19th-century Trinidad. African-Trinidadians had essentially assumed creative control over Carnival celebrations by the 1860s. With this came distinctly African-derived music and dance traditions to accompany

> ### *Why Trinidad? Why Steelpan?*
>
> In the 1920s and 1930s, Trinidadians used bottles, biscuit tins, pots, pans, and other spare bits of metal to create rhythm-based musical instruments. In early 1941, however, Nazi U-boat sightings off the shores of Trinidad increased at an alarming rate as the German forces attempted to disrupt American and British shipping interests in the Caribbean Sea. The proximity of these U-boats to the Panama Canal greatly concerned the U.S. military, which began increasing its presence in Trinidad, first with the U.S. Army post at Ford Read (1941), and later Waller Field within Fort Read (also 1941) in central Trinidad and then the Chaguaramas base in 1942. Discarded oil drums were abundant around these military bases, and intrepid Trinidadians utilized the barrels as prime material for making steelpans into a melodic family of instruments.

masquerade bands parading through the streets. This singing and dancing was at first accompanied by a multilayered drumming ensemble featuring a high-pitched lead drum, at least two lower-pitched supporting drums, and idiophonic percussion accompaniment. In an effort to curb what elites perceived as obnoxious revelry, colonial police banned the use of drums for Carnival in 1884. In the years that followed, some defied the ban and continued drumming. Others turned to alternative instruments, most importantly tamboo bamboo, an ensemble comprised of bamboo stamping tubes playing music characterized by interlocking rhythms that reflected the original drumming parts. For Carnival, tamboo bamboo accompanied *lavways*, songs sung by a leader and a responding chorus that gave rise to a style of calypso known as the "road march" that continued to be sung with tamboo bamboo accompaniment until the ensemble was itself outlawed by colonial authorities in 1937.

Even before this restriction, musicians were already supplementing tamboo bamboo with improvised instruments made of metal. The first important addition was a *boom* (low-pitched drum) made from a large metal tin turned upside down and played with one or two sticks. Players soon discovered the possibility of tuning two or three different notes into the playing surface of the instrument. This was done by pounding concave indentions into the tin's flat bottom, each at a different depth and size to create distinct pitches. These early experiments soon gave way to more refined tuning methods. In the 1940s, Winston "Spree" Simon prepared a convex playing surface by hammering out the bottom of a metal container. On this bubble-like surface, Simon tuned a handful of definite pitches. In stories of steelpan's origins, Simon is frequently—though perhaps incorrectly—cited as the "inventor" of steelpan. However, it is indeed likely that Simon was among the first pannists to play recognizable melodies on an instrument refined from the crude metal cans of the previous decade.

A *steelpan tuner* is one who builds a steelpan from scratch and has the skill to accurately adjust both pitch and timbre of each note. Tuners were indeed the early celebrities of the steelband movement and continue to be the most enduring figures in steelpan's history. Individuals first competed with one another in terms of tuning an increasing number of pitches onto the playing surface of a pan, but soon turned to refining the timbre, or sound quality, of the instruments as well. Ellie Mannette and Tony Williams are two pioneering tuners generally accepted as among the first to experiment with using 55-gallon oil drums as the raw material for pans, thereby helping to extend the range of the steelpan family of instruments and greatly influencing the collective timbre of the steel orchestra.

Many mid–20th-century pan builders, including Mannette and Williams, learned from Sonny Roach, a founding member of Sun Valley steel band and a pioneer tuner. One of Roach's important contributions was his vision of a fully voiced steel orchestra with instruments playing in the soprano, alto, tenor, and bass ranges. This sought-after goal spurred innovation, experimentation, and competition among steelpan tuners. Mannette is perhaps best known for developing steelpans with concave playing surfaces that allowed him to tune a wider pitch range on a given steelpan. Williams took full advantage of the 55-gallon oil drum to create new pans that extended the range of the orchestra. By the 1950s, Williams's designs for multiple-drum steelpans—including, for example, a bass voice comprised of three oil drums each tuned with only a handful of low pitches—were imitated by virtually every other pan tuner. However, Williams's most important contribution was the invention of the so-called "fourths-and-fifths" tenor steelpan, a lead melodic instrument whose layout of notes on the playing surface, arranged in pitch intervals of fourths and fifths, resembled a spider's web.

Many other tuners, too numerous to detail, worked alongside of and in competition with Mannette and Williams. The vibrancy and lush sound of the steel orchestra as we know it today is mostly thanks to the legacy of these tuners, as the improvements they introduced in turn allowed for increasingly complex repertoire and performance technique. By the 1960s, steel orchestras regularly performed arrangements of calypso, European and North American folk and popular tunes, and European classical music. The ability of steel orchestras to perform classical music in particular helped to modify the perception of steelpan among Trinidadians and international admirers alike. Just as often, however, classical music was arranged with a calypso groove. As Trinidad and Tobago transitioned from British control to independence in 1962, local politicians supported the development of steel orchestras (and Carnival arts in general) as a means of establishing a national identity, one based upon unique local traditions. The transitional government subsidized the development of steel orchestras and essentially nationalized the steelpan, lauding it as a quintessential aspect of the ingenuity and creativity of the people of Trinidad and Tobago.

The conception of steelpan as a national symbol brought about a variety of changes in steel orchestral practice. Whereas early steel orchestras often maintained bitter rivalries among one another, often to the point of prolonged gang-like violence, steel orchestras after World War II were largely focused on musical competition rather than physical altercations. The Trinidad and Tobago Steel Band Association (today known as Pan Trinbago), comprised of representatives from various orchestras, was organized in 1950 in part to address issues of violence among bands. The Steel Band Association became an important force advocating for the financial well-being of steel orchestra members, promoting the steel orchestral art form, and regulating formal competitions. In 1963, the Steel Band Association played an important role in establishing a national steel orchestra competition called Panorama that remains the most important annual event for steelpan performance.

International audiences have long been taken with the dynamism of the steelpan. A landmark in the internationalization of the steel orchestra occurred when the Trinidad All Steel Percussion Orchestra (TASPO), a band handpicked from the most talented pannists in Trinidad and Tobago, performed in London at the Festival of Britain in 1951. Their performances spurred interest in steelpan both at home and abroad and set an important precedent for the export of steelpan around the world. West Indian immigrants also brought steelpan with them as they migrated out of the Caribbean in the mid-20th century, establishing thriving communities in New York City, Toronto, and London, where annual Carnival celebrations feature capable steel orchestras comprised of players of mixed nationalities and ethnicities. A handful of steel orchestras were organized by non-Trinidadians as early as the 1950s. Of note is the U.S. Navy Steel Band formed by Rear Admiral Daniel V. Gallery in 1957 as an extension of the Navy band stationed in Puerto Rico (the band was originally named "Admiral Dan's Pandemoniacs"; it was disbanded in 1999).

After permanently moving to the United States, Ellie Mannette was instrumental in establishing steel orchestras in United States high schools and colleges in the 1960s, and in the 1990s established a steelpan workshop in Morgantown, West Virginia. Pannist and educator Dawn Batson joined the faculty of Florida Memorial College (FMC) in the 1990s, establishing a steel orchestra and undergraduate steelpan performance major there. Many of her students are recruited from the West Indies, and the FMC steel orchestra boasts a reputation as one of the best institutional steel orchestras in the United States. In 1985, noted tuner Clifford Alexis joined the faculty of Northern Illinois University, an institution that has since 1987 offered undergraduate degrees in steelpan, in which students learn not only to play the instruments but also to build them. Perhaps the most influential graduate of this program is Liam Teague, a Trinidad-born pannist who now codirects the Northern Illinois University steel orchestra. A virtuoso player, composer, and educator, Teague is among a new international vanguard of pannists, including Andy Narrel, Jonathan Scales, Victor Provost, Mia Gormandy, and others, who consistently explore the capabilities of the steelpan by commissioning, composing, and performing new solo and ensemble work for the instrument in a wide variety of genres.

Christopher L. Ballengee

See also: Calypso; Soca; Tamboo Bamboo; Tassa Drumming

Further Reading

Dudley, Shannon. 2008. *Music from Behind the Bridge: Steelband Spirit and Politics in Trinidad and Tobago.* New York: Oxford University Press.

Stuempfle, Stephen. 1995. *The Steelband Movement: The Forging of a National Art in Trinidad and Tobago.* Philadelphia: University of Pennsylvania Press.

Sufism, Music of

Sufism refers to the mystical orders of Islam of which large communities of practitioners, or Sufis, exist primarily in Turkey, Iran, and India, though also in Muslim communities across the Middle East, Africa, Eastern Europe and the Mediterranean, and the United States. It is mostly a male-dominated practice, with rituals handed down through male leaders, although some female orders exist in Egypt. Sufis are often known for their spiritual rituals involving music and dance practiced by specific Sufi orders, such as the Melevi of Turkey and the Chishti of the subcontinent. This practice has evolved into what is known as *Sama*, a ceremony in which participants, commonly known as *dervishes*, whirl into a trance as they seek to experience a greater awareness of their relationship with God.

HISTORY OF SUFISM AND MUSIC

Since the eighth century, Sufis have used music as a tool to achieve a closer, transcendent relationship with God. In the ninth century, Sufis introduced dance and Sama, or the ceremonial use of music, into their rituals. The role of music in Sufism gradually grew with the support of such scholars as Majd Al-Din Ahmad Al-Ghazali (d. 1126 CE) and Abu Hamid Muhammad Al-Ghazali (1058–1111). Around 1300, the Islamic scholar Kamal al-Din al-Adfuwi wrote a treatise on the varied interpretations of music practice: *Kitab al-imta bi-ahkam* (Guide to the application of the rules for listening to music), which broke down the appropriate uses for music within Islam, outlining those musical forms which were considered *halal*, or permitted, and those which were *haram*, or forbidden. But still other scholars warned against too much absorption in musical practice, believing that music encourages earthly desire that detracts from religious study and worship. Many scholars continue to rely on the *hadith*, a collection of proverbs of the Prophet Muhammad, for guidance, which shows that the Prophet listened to music while

---

Tuning Systems: Half-Tone Versus Quarter-Tone

When Johann Sebastian Bach wrote his *Well Tempered Clavier* (BWV 846–893, dated 1722), the composer sought to take advantage of the equal temperament of all 24 major and minor scales of the Western European tuning system. Musicians and composers had only recently settled on a standardized tuning of instruments that relied on chromatic half-tones to parcel octaves into 12 equal parts. Bach's work provided workable compositions in all keys and in doing so solidified the West's preference for scales divided with half-tones. In the Middle East, however, traditional music utilizes scales divided with quarter-tones, lending the musical styles there harmonic capabilities beyond those of Western music. Similar systems featuring quarter-tones (sometimes called micro-tones) are common throughout the world of music cultures. Still others rely on tuning systems that have fewer than 12 pitches (pentatonic and septatonic). However, the naturally occurring mathematical principle of the octave (the soundwave of a given pitch's octave will vibrate twice as fast or slow) governs all musical scales in all musical cultures across the globe.

simultaneously warning against its influence. The ambiguity of the hadith renders them highly interpretable and scholars often disagree on their exact meanings.

The continual disagreement about the role of music and dance in Islam has often contributed to the persecution of Sufis in the Islamic world. In the 16th century, music and dancing were forbidden in Shi'a Sufi orders, causing some to give it up entirely. Other orders continued to integrate music into their rituals, particularly in the Ottoman Empire. The Mevlevi, Rifa'i, and Qadiri orders cultivated their own music between the 15th and 17th centuries. In recent years, however, attacks on Sufi shrines and mosques have been prevalent throughout the Muslim world, including areas in India, Somalia, and Mali. Attacks on Sufi orders have often been conducted by militant and extremist Islamic groups, such as the Taliban, who have increasingly targeted Sufi shrines and centers in Pakistan and Afghanistan.

USE OF MUSIC IN SUFISM

Early Sufi music used a simple instrumentation of reed pipes, flutes, and drums, so as to avoid any secular music. The *daf*, or frame drum, for example, offers a basic rhythmic foundation and continues to be used on its own in rituals. Great emphasis has always been placed on the practice of *dhikr*, meaning "remembrance (of God)," which features the vocalization of the names of God and recitations from the Qur'an. *Sama* is the ceremonial ritual involving dhikr, music, and dance which is said to have been developed by the Persian poet, theologian, and Sufi master Jalal al-Din Rumi (1207–1273). It is often said that Rumi was inspired by the dhikr "la elaha ella'llah" (There is no god but Allah), that he heard rhythmically chanted by goldsmiths as they hammered their gold. Rumi felt so overcome with joy that he began spinning in a circle with his arms outstretched. This has become the basis for the Sama, which is practiced by various Sufi orders.

The incorporation of music fluctuates among Sufi orders. Ottoman orders include vocal solos or a chorus with free improvisation. The Dayfi and Shadhili orders in Algeria, as well as the Ammari in Morocco, often alternate song and dance, or even performers. There is also sometimes crossover between indigenous folk/art music and devotional Sufi music practices. For example, Arab-Andalusian traditions can be found in Tunisian Sufi repertory, and native Kashmir traditions are often incorporated in the rituals of local orders. The poetry of Sufi poets, especially Rumi, is also used in both Sufi repertory and Iranian and Turkish classical music.

On special occasions, such as the Prophet's birthday, *mawlid* (celebrations) mark the day with performances by a variety of Sufi orders. Mawlid begins with dhikr followed by songs that commemorate the different parts of the Prophet's life, with musical styles varying between orders. The Melevi order, for instance, performs the ritual entirely as a recitative limited in range, but with climactic accelerations and ascensions.

THE MELEVI ORDER

Perhaps the best-known Sufi order to integrate devotional music into religious rituals is the Melevi Order of Turkey (sometimes spelled Malawi). Since the

13th century, the Melevi order has made dance equally important as recitation and music, and dance movements are experienced as spontaneous expressions of divine enlightenment. Founded in 1273 following Rumi's death in Konya, Turkey, the order takes its name from Rumi's popular name in Turkey, "Mawlana." During the Ottoman Empire, the arts flourished, as many well-known poets, musicians, and celebrated composers were attached to the Melevi order. Vocalists and musicians, especially *ney* (flute) players, were highly valued and many composers wrote music specifically for the Melevi musical ceremony. Musical repertoire for the Sama, or *ayin*, dates back to the 16th century, and mid–16th-century compositions combined both Persian and Turkish traditions. The ayin became standardized, as we know it today, in the 19th century.

Under Ottoman rule, the Melevi order spread beyond Turkey to the Balkan region, as well as throughout Egypt, Syria, Lebanon, and Palestine. In 1925, however, the Melevi order was banned in Turkey by Atatürk, the leader of the new Turkish Republic, who sought to modernize the country by leaving many historic cultural traditions behind, seeing them as symbols of a "backward" nation. Since 1946, the Melevi order has been allowed to perform annually at the anniversary of Rumi's death. In 1954, the Melevi were also granted rights to perform Sama publicly as a tourist attraction for Turkey.

Today, the Melevis continue to survive as a nonpolitical organization. The Melevi center has remained in Konya. The Melevis also perform Sama in a *dergah*, or Melevi monastery, in the Beyoglu district of Istanbul, which is accessible to the public. Since the 1970s, the Melevis, known as "the Whirling Dervishes," have become a global tourist attraction and continue to perform public ceremonies in Konya and Istanbul as well as in cities throughout the world. In most cases, Melevi Sama performances have been designated as secular rituals for tourist consumption, with the length and structure adapted to conform to the requirements of public performance. In 2005, UNESCO declared the Mevlevi Sama ceremony to be a Masterpiece of the Oral and Intangible Heritage of Humanity.

THE MELEVI SAMA

One of the core practices of Islamic music is Sama (*Sema* in Turkish), meaning "listening," a complex ritual that involves the act of listening with the soul, or hearing actual sounds, as well as listening with the mind, in which the listener hears the glory of God in everything. To become a practitioner of Sama—a *semazen*—a Sufi must spend 1,001 days of training in a monastery, learning about prayer, religious music, poetry, and dance, as well as ethics and behavior. Sama is symbolic of the spiritual journey that man undergoes to reach enlightenment through closeness to God. This journey takes several stages: the Sufi must grow through divine love, abandon the ego, find truth, and arrive at the "Perfect." Once this is achieved, the Sufi is able to devote his love and attention to God and the whole of God's creation. After this training period, semazens continue to integrate their spiritual training with the rituals of daily life.

Sama is accompanied by small ensembles and dancers. Generally, group performances of Sama are led by a spiritual leader and can last several hours, with participants standing, sitting, or dancing. The ayin is played at Sama with contrasting rhythmic cycles and fluctuations in tempo and dynamics in correspondence with bodily movements. The ayin must not contain any reference to physical love, desire, vanity, or any sentiments that could lead to a superficially induced trance.

The Melevis were the first Sufi order to develop dance with fixed structure and rules for group performance. Qur'anic recitation and prayers precede and follow the ayin. Turkish art songs are performed with traditional instruments such as the ney, daf, and *kudum* (small kettledrums). Often the musical ensemble will include several ney and pairs of kudum, as well as additional instruments such as the *tanbur*, a long-necked lute; the *rebab*, a bowed fiddle; and *halile*, a pair of cymbals. The use of vocals is also permitted as long as it does not detract from the remembrance of God, which is the sole purpose of Sama.

Sama takes place in a ritual hall, or *samahane*. Semazens, or dervishes, typically fast for several hours prior to the ceremony. They wear white gowns, known as *tennure*, which symbolize death, which are initially covered by black cloaks known as *hurka*, which are symbolic of the grave. They also don a *kulah* or a *sikke*, which is a tall brown hat that symbolizes the tombstone. The dance consists of moving continuously in a circular motion. The semazens move in two circles around the central figure, the Sheikh. This movement is meant to represent the moon. The Sheikh, who represents the sun, spins around his own axis in the center of the group. All participants twirl on the left foot, using the right foot to drive the spinning motion. The right palm faces upward toward heaven while the left hand points downward to the earth. The semazens turn with their eyes open, the images before them becoming blurry as they enter a trance.

Sama is comprised of distinct parts that carry specific meanings. The introduction consists of three sections. The first, the *na'at*, addresses the Prophet. Then the flute takes over, with a nonmetric *taksim* which establishes the mode of the piece. This is followed by the *devr-i veled*, an instrumental part in four sections, with each section ending in a refrain, or *teslim*. At this point, the dervishes bow toward one another to acknowledge the Divine that is present in one another, as they file around the samahane. Then, they kneel and remove their black cloaks in preparation for the dance.

Once the dance, or whirling, begins, it is accompanied by four vocal compositions (the four *selams*), which are usually taken from Rumi texts. These texts are chosen according to the *maqam*, a musical system of melodies used in Turkish classical music which traditionally changes on a weekly basis. The selams represent the Sufi's spiritual journey. The first is free in meter and symbolizes the recognition of God. The second is slow and further symbolizes the recognition of the existence of God's unity. The third selam is the longest, comprised of several vocal and instrumental sections. It is during this selam that the semazen wholly surrenders to the height of ecstasy experienced. Finally, in the fourth selam, sometimes a repetition of the second, the Sheikh joins the dance, representing the peace created by Divine unity. An instrumental final section concludes the performance with a piece that is named after its meter. The Sama concludes with a recitation from the Qur'an and a prayer by the Sheikh.

Performance of *qawwali*, a type of Sufi devotional music, at the shrine of the Sufi saint Nizamuddin Auliya, Delhi, India. (IndiaPictures/Universal Images Group via Getty Images)

QAWWALI

The Chishti, a Sufi order most prevalent in Pakistan and Northern India, participates in rituals that also revolve around spiritual musical performance, known as *Qawwali*, which is said to have been established by Amir Khusraw (1244–1325 CE). Qawwali takes its name from the Arabic *qual*, (to speak), symbolizing the speech of the Prophet Muhammad. Qawwali is traditionally performed by professional male singers in a hypnotic, trance-like style. Usually a main singer leads the chorus as they call back and forth to one another. The vocalists are accompanied by musicians playing the harmonium (a small, hand-pumped organ) or the *sitar*, both of which support the melody; and percussive instruments such as the *tabla* or *dholak* (single- and double-headed drums) and hand-clapping, which accentuate the piece's rhythmic structure. Performances may last for several hours as the participants, known as *qawwals*, can decide how long or short a piece will be based on how the audience responds. Generally, songs begin in a slow tempo and gradually increase in speed as the qawwals enter an ecstatic trance.

The sung text of a Qawwali performance is often taken from poetry, most commonly in the form of *ghazal*, a poetic form composed of rhyming couplets. Ghazals are usually centered upon themes of love, but for the purposes of Qawwali, they are interpreted as representations of Divine love. Most Qawwali texts are sourced from ghazals by the Persian poets Rumi and Hafez. Qawwali usually begins with a *hamd*, a hymn praising Allah, followed by a *na'at*, another hymn praising the Prophet Muhammad. The songs that follow are usually a combination of ghazals expressing love; songs praising Imam Ali, Imam Hussein, or other Sufi saints; and devotional prayers thanking Allah.

Qawwali is most popular in the Punjab and Sindh regions of Pakistan, but also is practiced in many areas in India and Bangladesh. In addition to Arabic, local texts and languages, such as Farsi, Urdu, and Punjabi, are also integrated into Qawwali performance. In the mid-1970s, Qawwali was introduced to the United States by Pakistani brothers Haji Gholam Farid Sabri and Maqbool Sabri. Since the late 1980s, Qawwali has become a globally recognized form of music, as qawwals tour internationally and perform in secular settings for the general public.

Theresa Steward

See also: Arab Classical Music; Iranian Classical Music

Further Reading

Al-Faruqi, Lois Lamya. 1985. "Music, Musicians and Muslim Law." *Asian Music* 17(1), 3–36.

Chittick, William. 1983. *The Sufi Path of Love: The Spiritual Teachings of Rumi*. Albany, NY: SUNY Press.

Farmer, Henry G. 1995. *A History of Arabian Music to the XIIIth Century*. London: Luzac Oriental.

Hag, Sirajul. 1944. "Sama and Rags of the Darwishes." *Islamic Culture* 17, 111–30.

Lewis, Franklin. 2000. *Rumi Past and Present, East and West*. London: Oneworld Publications.

Qureshi, Regula. 2006. *Sufi Music of India and Pakistan: Sound, Context and Meaning in Qawwali*. London: Oxford University Press.

Shiloah, Amnon. 1995. *Music in the World of Islam: A Socio-Cultural Study*. Detroit, MI: Wayne State University Press.

Swing

The term *swing* has a dual connotation. It is the word applied to the era following boogie-woogie in the development of jazz, and it also embodies a musical quality inherent in the performance of jazz. Generally, swing refers to the music of large dance bands that performed written arrangements, occasionally incorporating improvised solos. Most noteworthy jazz encompasses a rhythmic drive or "swing." Yet, more than rhythmic activity is essential to swing: also necessary is the manipulation of musical components such as attack, vibrato, pitch and timbre, and tempo devices such as rubato, accelerando, and ritard. Interestingly, most popular music of the time did not swing; instead, it involved jazz musicians presenting jazz interpretations of Tin Pan Alley ballads. One unusual aspect of swing jazz is that the ensembles actually performed more ballads than anything else; however, what remains popular in the musical lexicon are up-tempo musical numbers such as Benny Goodman's "Sing, Sing, Sing." Regardless, the era of jazz in the 1930s and 1940s is commonly called the swing era.

Swing evolved as a jazz style and a related genre of popular music that originated around 1930 when New Orleans jazz was declining and the more sophisticated style known as Chicago-style Dixieland was prominent. Early swing

Swing (Bebop)

In the late 1930s, swing jazz—or *swing* as it is more commonly known—came the closest it has ever come to being America's popular music. This popularity would over time fade away and in the genre of jazz make way for bebop. Besides its obvious artistic merits, bebop was initially panned by important jazz artists of the day, including Tommy Dorsey, who claimed that bebop "set [jazz] music back 20 years," and the legendary Louis Armstrong, who claimed that bebop was full of "malice" with "no melody to remember and no beat to dance to." The latter were dire harbingers for the swing era, where the dance component was key to a music's success. Bebop, however, marked jazz music's transition away from dance music to a more passive-listening art music.

emphasized musical precision, used written arrangements ("charts"), emphasized well-rehearsed ensemble work, placed great weight on solo improvisation, featured a repertory based primarily upon Tin Pan Alley songs, and gave equal weight to the four beats of the bar (this is why swing is sometimes known as "four-beat jazz"). Fletcher Henderson, with his brother Horace and Don Redman, is credited with having created the structural plan for swing arrangements. This plan was tremendously successful and was adopted by many popular dance bands of the era. Henderson is also credited with establishing the independent use of trumpet, trombone, saxophone, and rhythm sections with the use of soloists. The personnel roster in Henderson's 1924 band included Louis Armstrong, Coleman Hawkins, and Don Redmond. Henderson, Redmond, and others adapted the parts that were typically conceived for one trumpet and harmonized them to be performed by three instrumentalists. Similar swing bands were led by virtuoso instrumentalists such as clarinetist Benny Goodman, drummer Gene Krupa, trombonists Glenn Miller and Tommy Dorsey, and clarinetist Artie Shaw. Duke Ellington's band, although influenced by swing, had such an impressive roster of virtuoso players that improvisation played a prominent role in his compositions.

The seismic change in jazz rhythm took place between 1930 and 1935 concurrently with the transformation of New Orleans-style Dixieland to Chicago style through changes in instrumentation and musical style. The string double bass replaced the tuba, providing a more lyrical, sophisticated bass line that outlined chord qualities and incorporated passing tones and "blue" notes (known as a "walking bass"); the rhythm guitar replaced the banjo; and the drum set was enhanced with hi-hat and ride cymbals that carried the rhythmic pulse more eloquently than the snare and bass drum. Swing's harmonic rhythm also was faster than in New Orleans jazz, sometimes changing as often as twice a bar, and soloists were expected to improvise melodies freely over these shifts. There was a notable increase in instrumental virtuosity among soloists in this period; some of the most prominent were Henry "Red" Allen, Roy Eldridge, Coleman Hawkins, Chu Berry, Benny Goodman, Johnny Hodges, and Lester Young. At the same time, instruments not previously regarded as suitable for solo work began to be given solo roles, including the drums (Gene Krupa and Chick Webb), double bass (Jimmy Blanton), vibraphone (Lionel Hampton and Red Norvo), and guitar (Django Reinhardt and

Charlie Christian). The development of swing coincided with the emergence by 1932 of the 13-piece dance band—the "big band"—which became the standard vehicle for this music. Such bands included those led by Duke Ellington, Fletcher Henderson, Count Basie, Jimmie Lunceford, Benny Goodman, Artie Shaw, and Earl Hines. The swing rhythm section became an important element in rhythm and blues and hence in early rock and roll, and was also used by some traditional jazz groups from the early 1940s. Although by the late 1940s the swing style had ceased to be the dominant movement in jazz, it continued to attract excellent young players and was still commercially viable into the 1990s.

The music that captured the public imagination was the rhythmically charged swing from bands that featured rosters including three trumpets, two trombones, three reeds (saxophone doubling on clarinet), and four in the rhythm section, resulting a more transparent sound. Arrangers for these bands discovered ways to translate the freedom and flexibility of improvising soloists into the musical fabric by incorporating antiphonal call-and-response patterns of African American spirituals, short repeated phrases (riffs) that could accompany solos or serve a primary melodic function, and lighter textures achieved by reducing doubled parts and streamlining harmonies. These elements provided flexibility and grace, along with infectious vibrant, energetic rhythmic patterns that became known among practitioners as "swing."

In the guise of swing, jazz became domesticated in the 1930s. Earlier, jazz had been associated with gin mills and smoky cabarets, illegal substances (alcohol and drugs), and illicit sex. Swing generally was considered more respectable, though some warned of the dangers it supposed posed to the morals of young people ("the sin in syncopation"). This exuberant, extroverted music, performed by well-dressed ensembles and their clean-cut leaders, entered middle-class households through everyday appliances such as the Victrola and the kitchen radio. It reached a wider audience as musicians transported it to small towns and rural areas. Traversing the country by bus, car, and train, big bands played single-night engagements in dance halls, ballrooms, theaters, hotels, nightclubs, country clubs, military bases, and outdoor pavilions. They attracted crowds of teenagers who came to hear the popular songs of the day and dance the Lindy hop and jitterbug.

By the late 1930s, there were signs that jazz was gaining respect as a musical tradition in both the United States and Europe. It began to be heard more often in Carnegie Hall, from Goodman's first concert there in 1938, to John Hammond's "Spirituals to Swing" events in 1938–1939, and Ellington's annual series of programs there starting in the mid-1940s. In Europe, such visiting American musicians as Armstrong, Ellington, and Hawkins gave jazz lovers in England and on the Continent first-hand opportunities to hear major artists whose careers they had been following on recordings.

The swing era reached its apogee in the early 1940s, with the bands of Ellington, Basie, Goodman, Shaw, Dorsey, Miller, and many others enjoying unprecedented popularity and commercial success. There were problems: wartime conscription thinned the ranks of big bands; record manufacturing was slowed by a shortage of shellac being otherwise used in the war effort; and the musicians' union called for a ban on commercial recording, which limited distribution of the music between 1942 and 1944. Generally, however, swing remained the popular music of choice throughout the years of World War II.

Eldonna L. May

See also: Bebop; Blues; Congo Square; Jazz

Further Reading

Chilton, John. 1985. *Who's Who of Jazz: Storyville to Swing Street.* New York: Da Capo Press.

Feather, Leonard. 1960. *The Encyclopedia of Jazz.* New York: Bonanza Books.

Hentoff, Nat, and Albert J. McCarthy, eds. 1975. *Jazz: New Perspectives on the History of Jazz by Twelve of the World's Foremost Jazz Critics and Scholars.* New York: Da Capo Press.

Porter, Louis. 1997. *Jazz: A Century of Change.* New York: Cengage.

Porter, Louis, Michael Ullman, and Edward Hazell. 1993. *Jazz: From Its Origins to the Present.* Englewood Cliffs, NJ: Prentice Hall.

Shapiro, Nat, and Nat Hentoff. 1955. *Hear Me Talkin' to Ya: The Story of Jazz as Told by the Men Who Made It.* New York: Peter Davies.

Symphonic Poem

The *symphonic poem* (also referred to as a *tone poem*) is a one-movement, orchestral and programmatic composition. This Western art music genre, which originated in the late 1840s, is often based on extramusical ideas from literature or other sources. The symphonic poem remained, for at least one-half of a century, one of the most popular types of program music. Numerous Western European, Eastern European, and American composers contributed to the orchestral genre. Although it lost momentum by the 1920s, the symphonic poem has found a permanent place in the orchestral repertory.

Composers of the Romantic era (1780–1910) were encouraged to draw from literature, art, and theater when creating their orchestral program music. The composers wrote a "program," an explanatory summary regarding the meaning of the music, as a preface within the musical score, or simply gave the piece a descriptive title as a way of communicating their program. Musical effects depicted nonmusical subjects; for instance, the flowing of a running stream was represented via rapidly and repeatedly played notes. The symphonic poem was influenced by the earlier concert overture, a single-movement, programmatic piece that was not part of an opera or play. Though it does not contain sung text, the symphonic poem takes imaginative insight from sung music. Further, the genre strives to be a vehicle of musical expression by providing deeper meaning to the musical experience. Like the mid–19th-century symphony, which usually contains four distinct movements, the symphonic poem has multiple continuously-played sections with different moods for each. Similar to the first movement of a symphony, the symphonic poem is written in forms such as sonata, rondo, and theme and variations, or it may be free of form altogether. The length of the genre varies: *Prélude à l'après-midi d'un faune* (Prelude to the afternoon of a faun) (1894) by French composer Claude Debussy (1862–1918) runs approximately 10 minutes in length, whereas

Eine Alpensinfonie (An alpine symphony) (1915) by German composer Richard Strauss (1864–1949) is approximately 50 minutes in length.

Hungarian composer and pianist Franz Liszt (1811–1886) is often credited as the creator of the symphonic poem. *Les préludes* (1848) is the best known of the 13 compositions he wrote in this genre. Some pieces focus on literary characters, such as *Hamlet* (1858) and *Orpheus* (1853–1854). Liszt wrote programs for his symphonic poems long after composing the music. These works greatly influenced others to write in the same genre.

Czech and Russian composers sometimes used the symphonic poem as a mode for expression of their national history and identity. Czech composer Bedřich Smetana (1824–1884) described the river's course in his program for "The Moldau" (1874), one of six symphonic poems from his orchestral cycle *Má Vlast* (My country) (1872–1879). Other Czechs contributed to the genre, including Antonín Dvořák (1841–1904), Zdeněk Fibich (1850–1900), Leoš Janáček (1854–1928), Vitězslav Novák (1870–1949), and Josef Suk (1874–1935). Russian symphonic poems include *Night on Bald Mountain* (1867) by Modest Mussorgsky (1839–1881), *Sadko* (1867) by Nikolai Rimsky-Korsakov (1844–1908), and *Tamara* (1867–1882) by Mily Balakirev (1837–1910) (the latter based on a poem by Lermontov and featuring references to the Orient, including the use of a gong). Other Russian contributors to the genre were Alexander Borodin (1833–1887), Pyotr Ilyich Tchaikovsky (1840–1893), Alexander Scriabin (1872–1915), Sergei Rachmaninoff (1873–1943), and Igor Stravinsky (1882–1971).

Strauss's symphonic poems utilized realism, an arts movement that depicted subjects in a brutally realistic manner. He applied the term "tone poem" to his symphonic poems so as to avoid association with the symphony form. Strauss sought to increase the overall expressive capacity of the genre via thematic transformation, complex orchestration and subject matter, and large orchestral forces. His tone poem *Also sprach Zarathustra* (Thus spoke Zarathustra) (1896), inspired by Friedrich Nietzsche's novel, has an opening section provided by the trumpets' three-note motif (C-G-C) that was later featured in Stanley Kubrick's 1968 film *2001: A Space Odyssey*. Another German example is a set of four tone poems by Max Reger (1873–1916), *Vier Tondichtungen nach Arnold Böcklin* (1913), of which one was attributed to the same painting that inspired Rachmaninoff to write his 1908 symphonic poem: Böcklin's *Isle of the Dead*.

The French symphonic poem placed more emphasis on illustrative music. Members of the Société Nationale de Musique were drawn to and supported the genre, including César Franck (1822–1890), Henri Duparc (1848–1933), Ernest Chausson (1855–1899), Claude Debussy, and Maurice Ravel (1875–1937). *Danse macabre* (Dance of death) (1874) by Camille Saint-Saëns (1835–1921) was based on Henri Cazalis's poem about an old French superstition in which Death appears at midnight every Halloween. The augmented fourth interval (E-flat to A), created by the top notes of each chord performed by a violin, known as a tritone (sometimes called the "Devil's interval"), is meant to represent Death playing his fiddle to make the dead dance.

The symphonic poem's scope reached other European countries and the United States. Examples are the nationalistic *Finlandia* (1899) by Finnish composer Jean

Sibelius (1865–1957) and *Fontane di Roma* (Fountains of Rome) (1916) and *Pini di Roma* (Pines of Rome) (1924) by Italian composer Ottorino Respighi (1879–1936). *On Hearing the First Cuckoo in Spring* (1912) by English composer Frederick Delius (1862–1934) features a cuckoo-call theme played by an oboe and strings. American symphonic poems include the jazz-infused *An American in Paris* (1928) by George Gershwin (1898–1937) and *The Pleasure Dome of Kubla Khan* (1912) by Charles Griffiths (1884–1920).

At times, contemporary audiences and musicians performing the symphonic poem struggled with the genre's complex nature. The inherent problem that music cannot precisely express extramusical ideas was an ongoing obstacle for the genre. Although a written program may distract the listener from the music, it can also provide context for a direct interpretation. The later decline of the genre's output occurred in tandem with the fading interest in musical Romanticism, especially by the mid-20th century when abstract music was favored over descriptive music. A good number of these works have endured over time, and the importance of the symphonic poem within the context of late-Romantic ideals has secured its place in the orchestral repertoire.

Emily A. Bell

See also: Classical Music, European; Symphony

Further Reading

Mendl, R. W. S. 1932. "The Art of the Symphonic Poem." *The Musical Quarterly* 18(3) (July), 443–462.

Moore, Earl V., and Theodore E. Heger. 1974. *The Symphony and the Symphonic Poem: Analytical and Descriptive Charts of the Standard Symphonic Repertory,* 6th ed., rev. Ann Arbor, MI: Ulrich's Books.

Symphony

The *symphony* is a composition for orchestra, established in the 17th century as an introductory piece for operas, oratorios, or cantatas; it became an independent work in the following century. In Western classical music, the symphony is one of the most important genres for large ensembles. The noun comes from the Greek συμφωνία (*symphonia:* agreement, concord of voices or sounds) and in Greek musical theory it is ascribable to the concept of consonance. In the Middle Ages the term was used as an antonym of *diaphonia,* dissonance. Its Latin variant *symphonia* could also refer to musical instruments capable of producing more than one sound simultaneously.

ORIGINS

Starting in the 16th century, the term stood for musical collections, as the madrigals featured in *Symphonia angelica di diversi eccellentissimi musici* (Angelic symphonies of diverse excellent musicians) (Antwerp, 1585) suggest. Later, further examples denote a similar approach, including *Cantus sacrae symphoniae* (Singing sacred music) (Venice, 1597), a set of compositions by Giovanni Gabrieli, and *Sacrae symphoniae diversorum excellentissimorum auctorum* (Excellent sacred music of various composers) (Nuremberg, 1603). As the introduction of a longer vocal piece, the purpose of the symphony was to prepare the audience's mood for the composition it was going to hear.

In the 17th century the symphony manifested itself in two different types: the Italian *sinfonia* and the French *ouverture*. The former was divided into three sections (fast-slow-fast) and had the founder of the Neapolitan school, Alessandro Scarlatti (1660–1725), as its main exponent. The latter was the prototype of Jean-Baptiste Lully (1632–1687), who inverted the movements, yielding a slow-fast-slow form. These two formal principles each evolved separately and had their own successors: Giovanni Paisiello and Niccolò Piccinni were affiliated with Scarlatti's Neapolitan school; Françoise-André Philidor and André-Ernest-Modest Grétry can be reckoned Lully's heirs. In the following century, the Bavarian composer Christoph Willibald Ritter von Gluck (1714–1787) achieved an important reform of musical theater (decisive for the history of opera), in which the fruition of the sinfonia played a crucial role.

18TH CENTURY

During the 18th century, the symphony assumed an increasingly prominent position for both composers and society. Symphonies by Franz Joseph Haydn (1732–1809), in contrast to their role in the previous century, frequently introduced the second half of a concert, which meant they enjoyed more attention from the audience. Symphonies were played mostly for private performances, in palaces or monasteries, and were mainly considered background music to complement further entertainment. Nonetheless, public performances in coffee houses or other communal spaces were not uncommon.

The term "symphony" was not yet universally accepted; consequently, several different nouns were used to describe this type of composition: overture, prelude, *sonata*, and *divertimento*, among others. The earliest symphonic corpus is mainly scored for four-part string orchestra only, with the aid of a harpsichord and other instruments playing the *basso continuo* part (bass line). Nonetheless, from the 1730s onward composers began to write six-part symphonies (strings plus horns or oboes) and later a more standardized eight-part composition, with strings and two pairs of horns and oboes. The full symphonic classical orchestra around the 1750s was composed of pairs of flutes, oboes, clarinets, bassoons, horns, and trumpets; timpani; strings; and often harpsichord.

Ninety percent of the symphonies from the 18th century are in major tonalities, with generally no more than three accidentals, and most follow the Italian structure of the sinfonia (fast-slow-fast). This cannot be considered the only precursor of the symphony, though; other genres were involved, such as Vivaldi's *concerto ripieno*, which was orchestral music for the *ripieno* section (strings and basso continuo) only. Around the middle of the century, a slow introduction was added to the first movement, which is most often shaped in sonata form—a form that continued to characterize sonata first movements in the centuries thereafter.

The Milanese Giovanni Battista Sammartini (ca. 1700–1775) is considered the most important Italian symphonist of the early 18th century, and a leading figure in the development of the early classical style. Most of his symphonies are in three movements, and he demonstrated great interest in binary and sonata forms. Starting in 1740, Sammartini expanded the range of instruments used in symphonies, making use of wind instruments such as horns, trumpets, and oboes. At that stage, strings and winds tended to work as two separate sections, each one providing harmonic background for the other.

In the German-speaking lands, Johann Stamitz (1717–1757) epitomized the birth of the Mannheimer school around the 1740s. This school achieved unprecedented fame, not solely because it was composed of a large group of instrumentalists (48 in its early years, 90 in the last period), but also because it featured several famous virtuosi who brought an outstanding level of precision to the performances. In the 1750s, only Sammartini could boast of 60 elements in his orchestra. Although Mannheim maintained a peculiar and undisputed brilliance, around the 18th century the Vienna area started to attract numerous exceptional musicians, as it could offer possibilities for patronage like no other place in Europe.

Franz Joseph Haydn (1732–1809), who worked most of his life for the Esterházy family, is often considered "father of the symphony" because of his considerable contribution to this repertoire. He mostly focused on working through his own procedures rather than developing styles and compositional processes taken from others. He was quite prolific; in fact, he composed more than 100 symphonies. In his early years Haydn's symphonies mostly consisted of three movements, derived from the Italian sinfonia. Later he adopted the four-movement skeleton allegro-andante moderato-minuet and trio-presto, of which no. 3 (1762) is a clear example. The works he wrote in the period 1768–1774 have been associated with the literary movement *Sturm und Drang* (ca. 1760–ca. 1780), as they shared with it a deeply emotional character; among those is Haydn's *Farewell* symphony no. 45 (1772).

In his six Parisian symphonies (1785), and especially in the London symphonies (1791–1795), Haydn exploited humoristic and intellectual ploys, audacious harmonies, orchestral brightness, and extraordinary thematic ideas. Excellent examples of these are the *Surprise* no. 94 and the *Miracle* no. 96 (both 1791), the *Clock* no. 101 and the *Military* no. 100 (both 1793).

Haydn's great friend Wolfgang Amadeus Mozart (1756–1791) embraced styles and techniques taken from composers outside the Austrian borders, mostly Italy and Mannheim. He wrote his first symphony at the age of eight, in 1764, and continued composing in this genre sporadically for the rest of his life. In his earliest works he adopted the classic structure of three movements, the first of them being in binary-sonata form. The last years of the 1760s witnessed a turn in favor of the four-movement model and a mixture of Italian and German styles. A return to the three-movement symphony can be attributed to Mozart's trips to Italy in the early 1770s. In 1773 he developed a neater and more mature style, progressively increasing the length of the movements. The Symphony no. 12 (1771) is an example of Mozart's growing musical confidence, making use of uneven phrases, prominent melodies in the woodwinds, and bright fanfares. In contrast, symphonies from

1773 and 1774 are more influenced by his experiences in Mannheim and Paris. Later ones, commencing from 1781 when he permanently moved to Vienna, are among the masterpieces of the genre, such as the well-known *Jupiter* no. 41.

19TH CENTURY

Purged of many of the simultaneous and conflicting currents active during the classical period, the 19th-century symphony enjoyed a relative formal stability. Usually in four movements, the first consisted of a full sonata form, possibly announced by a slow introduction; the second movement might be again in sonata form but with a slower pulse and solemn in character; a ternary dance-style third movement could swap with the previous one; a faster finale closed the composition. Thanks to modern technical improvements, the instrumental spectrum of the orchestra grew considerably over this century, especially expanding the wind section (piccolo, English horn, and trombone) and percussions (cymbals, snare and bass drums, triangle, and tambourine). With Ludwig van Beethoven (1770–1827), the symphony established itself as primary among all orchestral genres, thus overturning the hegemony of the concerto for soloist and orchestra. Whereas in the previous century the symphony was merely appreciated as entertainment, in the 19th century it was seen as a means to deliver moral, political, or philosophical ideas. In particular, Beethoven enormously expanded the meaning of this repertoire. Beethoven's *Symphony* no. 5 (1808) is by far the best-known symphony in the world, with its unique opening five notes.

His Symphony No. 9 marked the history of this genre as no one else ever has, either before or after. Written when he was completely deaf, it was the first work in its genre to treat vocal parts on an equal level with the instrumental parts, setting to music Friedrich Schiller's *lied "An die Freude."* After that extraordinary work, during the first decades of the 19th century, composers thought it would be impossible to write anything superior to Beethoven's Ninth.

Despite this, the French composer Hector Berlioz (1803–1869) achieved tasks Beethoven never attempted. He developed the use of key themes in Beethoven's Third and Fifth Symphonies, building the concept of *idée fixe*, a recurrent musical phrase associated with a concept or a person, such as his heroine in the revolutionary masterpiece *Symphonie fantastique* (1830). Berlioz's *idée fixe* is not only crucial for understanding of the Wagnerian *leitmotiv* (leading motif), it also paved the way for a new approach to music. The *Symphonie fantastique* attempted to musically render an extramusical plot, providing program notes for the audience. To this extent, it represents the birth of "program music." Such an aesthetic created frictions with the classical and conservative approach to "absolute" music, which had no particular narrative reference.

In the 19th-century, symphonic music had in Johannes Brahms (1833–1897) its main exponent. In 1876, at the age of 43, Brahms wrote his first symphony. Such a work was strongly influenced by Beethoven's legacy; the impact of the *Eroica* is clearly identifiable. Berlioz's philosophy particularly influenced the Hungarian Franz Liszt (1811–1886). Liszt's *Faust Symphony* (1857), which consists of three movements named after the main characters of the story (Faust, Gretchen, and

Mephistopheles), is one of the most representative works of its genre. Following this example, the Czech composer Bedřich Smetana (1824–1884) wrote *Má Vlast* (My country) (1874–1879), depicting some aspects of Bohemian history and landscapes.

Anton Bruckner (1824–1896) occupies a curious position in the polemic that contrasted absolute and program music. Although he never indicated any programmatic intent for any of his 11 symphonies, composed between 1863 and 1896, a clear Wagnerian style is evident in the vast size of the orchestra and the length of the compositions themselves, as well as the extended harmonic language. Although Wagner tubas are used in his last three symphonies, Bruckner's symphonies are nevertheless remarkably independent in their generic conception. Building on the traditional four-movement design, they combine lyricism with an inherently polyphonic structure.

Like Bruckner's, the symphonies by Gustav Mahler (1860–1911) are long, complex, and monumentally orchestrated. The eighth symphony (1906–1907) is known as *Symphony of a Thousand*, as such is the number of players it requires. His abilities as orchestrator are undisputed; he was capable of ranging from the gentlest to the most overpowering sound. The use of the grotesque is also noticeably representative of his style: the use of the tune of "Frère Jacques" changed to the minor modality in the third movement of the first symphony (1888) is just one of the earliest examples.

Although the 19th-century symphony can be considered a particular form of German supremacy, the rise of European nationalisms and political ferments characterized the activity of composers from peripheral areas of the main European empires. The Bohemian Antonín Dvořák (1841–1904) mostly borrowed from Czech popular-music tunes and dance rhythms. However, he was inspired by Native Americans' traditional melodies in his last symphony *From the New World* (no. 9, 1893), the result of various tours in the United States.

Although Mahler can be considered the last symphonist, closing the long list of the German tradition that goes from Haydn, through Mozart and Beethoven, Richard Strauss (1846–1949) played a decisive role in shaping the characteristics of programmatic music, a distinctive current of late romanticism, following the tracks of Berlioz and Liszt. Although he wrote two traditional symphonies (1880 and 1884), he never returned to that style. *Also sprach Zarathustra* (1896) and the *Alpensinfonie* (1915) both feature philosophical and descriptive programs and stand among the masterpieces of the repertoire of symphonic poems.

20TH CENTURY

The 20th century saw the rise of non-German composers. The Danish Carl Nielsen experimented with the use of harmony, which often fluctuates between more than one single tonic in such a way that a single tonality is not always perceivable. The Finnish Jean Sibelius owes much to the classical Beethovenian style but borrows also from Brahms and Bruckner. He made use of modes and kept harmonies static or ambiguous over long segments. His symphonies also feature repeated bass lines and sustained pedals. In the work for chamber orchestra

Kammersymphonie op. 9 (1906), the Austrian composer Arnold Schönberg (1874–1951) rejects any late or post-romantic gigantism, scoring the piece for just 15 soloists. Through this work, Schönberg subverted the borders of tonality as it was traditionally used.

Twentieth-century Russia saw the rise of great symphonists, among them Sergei Prokofiev (1891–1953) and Dmitry Shostakovich (1906–1975). Prokofiev's style was characterized by unexpected and frequent modulations, which nonetheless do not alter the neatness of the music. The return to the main tonality is always an aggressive passage colored with interesting and intense timbral choices. Shostakovich was probably one of the most prolific symphonic composers of his own century, with 15 works in this compositional output. The fifth symphony (1937) was acclaimed with great emotion and enthusiasm. He also dealt with programmatic music in his *Leningrad* symphony (no. 7, 1941), glorifying the valiant defense of St. Petersburg against Nazi armies.

In the first half of the 20th century, Paul Hindemith wrote *Mathis der Maler* (1934), which is now considered one of his most famous compositions. It reworks melodies from the composer's homonymous opera. Later, the *Symphony in B-flat for Band* (1951) featured strong contrapuntal lines and now represents a milestone for band music. At the end of World War II, Aaron Copland (1900–1990) composed a symphony (no. 3, 1946) that embodies the fusion of tradition and a peculiarly American touch.

Jacopo Mazzeo

See also: Classical Music, European; Concerto; Symphonic Poem

Further Reading

Ballantine, Christopher John. 1983. *Twentieth Century Symphony.* London: D. Dobson.

Bonds, Mark Evan. 1996. *After Beethoven: Imperatives of Originality in the Symphony.* Cambridge, MA: Harvard University Press.

Brook, Barry S. 1986. *The Symphony, 1720–1840.* New York: Garland.

Brown, Maurice J. E. 1971. *Schubert Symphonies.* Seattle: University of Washington Press.

Carse, Adam. 1951. *18th Century Symphonies.* London: Augener.

Cuyler, Louise Elvira. 1973. *The Symphony.* New York: Harcourt Brace Jovanovich.

Heartz, Daniel. 1995. *Haydn, Mozart, and the Viennese School, 1740–1780.* New York: W. W. Norton.

Holoman, D. Kern. 1997. *The Nineteenth-Century Symphony.* New York: Schirmer Books.

Horton, John. 1969. *Brahms Orchestral Music.* Seattle: University of Washington Press.

Horton, Julian. 2013. *The Cambridge Companion to the Symphony.* Cambridge: Cambridge University Press.

Landon, H. C. Robbins. 1961. *The Symphonies of Joseph Haydn: Supplement.* London: Barrie and Rockliff.

Lang, Paul Henry. 1969. *The Symphony, 1800–1900: A Norton Music Anthology.* New York: W. W. Norton.

Lawrence, Gilman. 2013. *Stories of Symphonic Music: A Guide to the Meaning of Important Symphonies, Overtures, and Tone-Poems.* [n.p.]: HardPress Ltd.

Layton, Robert. 1993. *A Companion to the Symphony.* London: Simon & Schuster.

Locke, Ralph P. 1997. *The French Symphony: David, Gounod, and Bizet to Saint-Saëns, Franck, and their Followers.* [n.p.]: R. P. Locke.

Macdonald, Hugh. 1969. *Berlioz Orchestral Music.* Seattle: University of Washington Press.

Rosen, Charles. 1980. *Sonata Forms.* New York: W. W. Norton.

Sammartini, Giovanni Battista Churgin Bathia. 1968. *The Symphonies of G. B. Sammartini.* Cambridge, MA: Harvard University Press.

Steinberg, Michael. 1995. *The Symphony: A Listener's Guide.* New York: Oxford University Press.

Ulrich, Homer. 1952. *Symphonic Music: Its Evolution Since the Renaissance.* New York: Columbia University Press.

Zaslaw, Neal. 1989. *Mozart's Symphonies: Context, Performance Practice, Reception.* Oxford: Clarendon Press.

T

Tabla

Tabla is the most popular percussion instrument of South Asia, in particular North India. Tabla consists of a pair of hand drums that are played by the fingers and palm of the hand. It is typical of North Indian Hindustani music, but it is also common in Pakistan, Bangladesh, Nepal, and Sri Lanka. The tabla is also used in Indonesia for the *dangdut* genre. The tabla described here is separate from the Egyptian drum tabla, which is a goblet-shaped drum. The name "tabla" is closely related to many drum names in the Middle East; however, those instrument shapes are quite different from that of the Indian tabla.

The term "tabla" (or *dayan*) can refer to the right-hand drum (from the player's perspective) alone, or to the pair of drums. Dayan, the right-hand drum, is a cylinder that is slightly flared near the base and has a tight skin that makes a high sound. *Bayan* (also called *duggi*, *dugga*, or *botu*), the left-hand drum, is bowl-shaped, larger, and less tight, to produce a lower sound. Together they produce a fine texture with their contrasting timbres and pitch.

Tabla are made out of wood from the neem, jackfruit, tamarind, mango, or sandalwood tree. Three-fourths of the dayan is hollow and one quarter is solid. The top of the dayan is covered with goat skin. The leather used for covering dayan and bayan is called *pudi*. At the edge of the pudi there is an additional ring of leather called *chanti* or *kinar*. At the center of the skin, there is a black spot called *gab* (also called *siyahi*), which is made out of a combination some of the following: iron filings, coal dust, copper sulfate, rice powder, fine wheat flour, and glue; the recipe varies with each drum maker. The gab produces a clear pitch and high level of resonance. The place in between chanti and siyahi is called *luv*.

The drumhead is secured with tight leather laces. At the edge of the drumhead there is a ring called *pagri* and on the bottom of the drum is another leather ring. The pagri has 16 holes, and leather laces (*daal* or *chot*) threaded into those holes are used to tighten the drumhead. Between the double layer of skin at the pagri and the single layer of skin is the *sur* (or luv). The performer strokes the sur while tuning the tabla. There are eight small cylindrical wooden blocks that go under the *daal* laces or ropes, called *gutta*: by moving the gutta up and down, the pitch is made higher or lower. If the diameter of the head of the tabla is larger, it produces a lower sound; if it is small, the resulting pitch is higher. A hammer is used to fine-tune the dayan. Padded cloth rings (*bida*) sit under the bayan and dayan to keep the tabla stable.

Some newer tabla dayan have 16 metal rods secured with bolts that allow the drumhead to be tightened with a nut. On a scale-changer tabla, a knob underneath the tabla allows adjustment of the pitch of the entire drumhead much faster than

Musician playing the *tabla*, a pair of hand drums used in Hindustani music and a number of other Indian musical styles. (Icaffeine/Dreamstime.com)

adjusting 16 bolts. Although these advances sacrifice a bit of sound quality, performers can easily change the drumhead without the need for a drum maker; the pitch also holds steadier with the metal rods added. The bayan (or dugga) is made of brass, copper, or clay and covered with goatskin. Clay is breakable, so metal is more popular nowadays. The sound of a traditional clay bayan is the most resonant. In performance practice, the tabla is nearly always played while sitting on the floor. Playing with the tips of the fingers allows a high level of intricacy and virtuosity.

Sounds of tabla created by the dayan include: (1) ta or na; (2) ti or tin; (3) tun; (4) te; and (5) re or te. Sounds created by the bayan are: (6) ghe, ge, ghi, or ga; and (7) kat. All of these sounds are combined to create a rhythmic cycle called *tala*. Tabla is played to express musical rhythm, which is the nucleus of Indian tala.

There are many theories and legends about the origins of tabla. Some scholars and musicians cite a link to the ancient drums called *puskara*; pictorial evidence from the sixth and seventh centuries in the temple carvings at Muktesvara and Bhuvanesvara show a pair of hand drums used in ancient India. The most popular legend holds that the Turkish Sufi poet and musician Amir Khusrau (1253–1325 CE) invented the tabla as well as the lute *sitar*. He divided the barrel drum into two parts to invent the tabla. The contention is that musical instruments came into India from the Middle East along with Islam and developed further in South Asia.

Despite the popularity of the claim that Amir Khusrau invented the tabla, research into the history of tabla shows that the instrument appeared much later, most likely emerging in the middle 18th century.

There are six major schools or *gharana* in tabla. The term "gharana" is derived from a Persian word *ghar* meaning home, house, family, or room. Therefore, gharana means a tradition of a certain house or family. Most are named after the locality where the founder lived. The most highly regarded performers are exponents of one of these gharanas. The six major gharanas are Delhi Gharana, Ajrada Gharana, Lucknow Gharana, Farrukabad Gharana, Banaras Gharana, and Punjab Gharana.

Tabla players have traditionally had a low status in the societies in which they emerged. Performers were primarily low-status Muslim hereditary minstrels. The earliest use of tabla was as accompaniment for dance. Later it was used for accompaniment of *kayal* vocal forms, then it became popular for solo instrumental styles such as sitar and *sarod*. Because of the increasing popularity of the instrument, high-caste Hindus have become successful performers, raising the reputation of the instrument.

Tabla has two roles: accompaniment and solo. Most importantly, it is used in accompaniment of vocal and instrumental music, *kathak* dance and fusion. An accompanist might simply keep the rhythm. This is known as *sath sangat*. Skillful *sangat*, however, is the art of accompaniment: the tabla player interacts with the soloist in a highly sensitive and responsive way. In the past century, tabla has developed as a solo instrument. It is much less common for tabla to play solo, but a virtuosic tabla solo is very exciting. A tabla solo recital is usually performed with a melodic accompaniment provided on a bowed lute *sarangi*, or harmonium. The sarangi accompaniment repeats a melody called *nagma* throughout the tabla solo.

Abdur Rahman

See also: Bol; Dhrupad; Harmonium; Rakha, Alla; Sitar

Further Reading

Fox Strangways, A. H. 1914. *The Music of Hindostan.* Oxford: Clarendon Press.

Gottlieb, Robert S. 1993. *Solo Tabla Drumming of North India.* Delhi: Motilal Banarsidass Publishers.

Kippen, James. 1988. *The Tabla of Lucknow: A Cultural Analysis of a Musical Tradition.* Cambridge: Cambridge University Press.

Neuman, Daniel M. 1980. *The Life of Music in North India: The Organization of an Artistic Tradition.* New Delhi: Manhohar.

Shankar, Ravi. 1969. *My Music, My Life.* London: Jonathan Cape.

Wade, Bonnie. 1979. *Music in India.* Englewood Cliffs, NJ: Prentice-Hall.

Tagore, Rabindranath (1861–1941)

The first Asian Nobel Laureate, Rabindranath Tagore is considered the greatest creative artist of modern India and one of the most prolific, diverse, and outstanding writers of the world. He is noted for his extraordinary achievements in literature, music, and art. A multiply talented literary genius, mystic, and visionary, Tagore was a prolific Bengali poet, lyricist and song writer, novelist, short-story writer, and creator of modern fables and humorous pieces, as well as a playwright, essayist, travel diarist, painter, musician, and composer who also excelled in prose, autobiographical works, letters, original works in English, and his English translations of his own works. Tagore was an innovative educator, entrepreneur, philosopher, reformist thinker, artist, nationalist, social reformer and activist, and a radical crusader fighting for the social uplift of the downtrodden masses, especially women and the socio-economically marginalized classes.

A major voice in 19th-century Bengal, as well as in the Indian Renaissance and the nationalist movement, Rabindranath Tagore remains a major presence and a great intellectual force in both Indian and world literature even today. In his universal appeal, incredible versatility, and varied genius, Tagore crosses all constraints of time and space. The immense and diverse corpus of his works in literature, education, culture, society, politics, and countless other fields challenges any essentialist reading of him simply as an artist, or an aesthetician, a philosopher, or a litterateur.

Rabindranath Tagore (pronounced Rabindranath Ṭhakur in Bengali, his mother tongue and the language in which he wrote), was born on May 7, 1861, in Calcutta (now Kolkata), India, to the illustrious Ṭhakur family in Jorasanko; he was the youngest child of the religious reformer Maharshi Debendranath Ṭhakur and his wife, Sarada Sundari Devi. Tagore's home, the Jorasanko Ṭhakur Bari, situated in the northern part of the city of Calcutta, functioned as a cultural hub during the 19th and early 20th centuries and was a formative influence in nurturing Tagore's inherent creativity. Tagore was educated at home, as he felt constrained by the regulations of formal schooling.

A child prodigy, Tagore started composing poems and plays in his early teens, and published his first work, a poem titled "Abhilash," anonymously in the *Tattvabodhini Patrika* in 1874. In 1883, Tagore married Mrinalini Devi (1873–1902); Rabindranath and Mrinalini had two sons and three daughters, all of whom died young. In 1901, Tagore founded an experimental school blending the Eastern and Western traditions of thought at a place called *Santiniketan* (Abode of Peace) in rural Bengal (now West Bengal) that later became Viśva-Bhārati University in 1921. Tagore was knighted by the British King George V in 1915, but in 1919 he resigned the honor as a protest against the atrocities perpetrated by the British rulers of India.

In addition to his varied literary and creative activities, Tagore managed the family estates, basing himself in Selaidaha by the river Padma. He also participated actively in the Indian nationalist movement, especially during the movement against the division of Bengal in 1905 when, in order to maintain communal harmony among the Hindus and the Muslims, Tagore composed patriotic songs and organized a *Raksha Bandhan* ceremony, in which people tied auspicious strings on each other's wrists with a pledge to protect each other. Tagore travelled the world, lecturing and reading from his works and spreading the knowledge of Indian culture around the world in Europe, the Americas, and East Asia. He died on August 7, 1941, in Calcutta.

Rabindranath Tagore was awarded the Nobel Prize for Literature in 1913 for his mystical collection of songs *Gitanjali* (Song offerings) (1912), containing the English prose versions of Tagore's religious poems from several of his Bengali verse collections, which he had translated himself. Primarily a poet and a songwriter, Tagore produced more than 50 volumes of poetry and 2,000 songs that are included in his compendium of songs, *Gitabitan* (A garden of songs). A skilled and versatile musician noted for his variety and innovation, Tagore is famous for *Rabindra Sangeet* (songs written and composed by him), in which he freed Indian music from its stereotyped patterns of the purely abstract Indian classical tradition by associating it with traditional Indian religious and folk music, and sometimes with Western classical and folk musical sources as well, and blending it inextricably with the poetry of his words, thus giving rise to a novel, and popular, idiom in Indian music. Tagore also created original rhythms (*talas*) to be used with his songs. Tagore's songs are regarded as cultural treasures and have been adopted as the national anthems of two countries, India and Bangladesh.

Sutapa Chaudhuri

See also: Harmonium; Khayal; Tabla; Thumri

Further Reading

Alam, Fakrul, and Radha Chakravarty. 2011. *The Essential Tagore*. Cambridge, MA: Belknap Press.

Kripalani, Krishna. 1980. *Rabindranath Tagore: A Biography*. New Delhi: UBS Publishers Distributors.

Lago, Mary M. 1976. *Rabindranath Tagore*. Boston: Twayne Publishers.

Robinson, Andrew, and Krishna Dutta. 1995. *Rabindranath Tagore: The Myriad-Minded Man*. New York: St. Martin's Press.

Som, Reba. 2009. *Rabindranath Tagore: The Singer and His Song*. New York: Penguin Global.

Taiko

Taiko (literally, "great/big drum") refers both to traditional Japanese drums and the playing of those traditional Japanese drums. Beginning in the seventh or eighth century, taiko was used in Japanese court music (*gagaku*), Buddhist rituals, Shintō festivals, and also for various nonceremonial performances. Also, taiko became essential to traditional festivals (*matsuri*) of all kinds. Many various forms of taiko drums exist, small to large, and many different performing traditions have developed. Over the centuries, taiko playing has become a part of most traditional theater and/or ensemble performing traditions. Particularly within the past 60 years, the playing of taiko has expanded beyond the realms of traditional Japanese music to include *kumi-daiko* (group/ensemble taiko), in which a taiko ensemble plays in a style that incorporates jazz/Western rhythms and synchronized choreography as well as other traditional instruments into the performance.

Many types of taiko have been built and used over the centuries. Drums are handmade in a manufacturing process that has been handed down by family ancestors (as is often the case with Japanese artistry); an example is of Asano Taiko, a 400-year-old family business in Japan that makes drums for all types of traditional and contemporary taiko functions. A complete listing of all taiko varieties would

> ### San Jose Taiko
>
> Modern *taiko* drumming in the West owes a big debt to third-generation Japanese Americans looking to reconnect with their heritage. This was the case when several musicians in San Jose, California, formed in San Jose Taiko in 1973. The troupe looked to historical Japanese taiko drumming for inspiration and instruments; however, they also look to musical traditions of other cultures from across the world to supplement and broaden the development of their unique take on taiko drumming. The result was a new style of taiko drumming rooted in the Japanese tradition but also including African, Brazilian, Filipino, Latin, and jazz influences. San Jose Taiko also incorporated a significant choreography component in their taiko art form; this new style of taiko has since become popular in the West and adopted by many other taiko drumming troupes across the globe. In this way, San Jose Taiko has remade taiko drumming into a new tradition, yet one with strong connections to past traditions.

be vast; however, certain taiko are representative of specific traditional Japanese art forms and deserve particular mention.

Taiko drums come in three different types. The first type is the drum most often associated with the word "taiko": *nagado daiko* typically resemble the shape of a wine or whiskey barrel (varieties range from relatively small to very large) with skins that are fastened with large tacks (*byou*). The second type, *tsuzumi* drums, have hourglass-shaped bodies with skins held by ropes on the sides. The third type are a myriad of cylindrical drums the heads of which are also tightened by ropes pulled and wrapped around the sides. These cylindrical drums can be flat and squat or long and thin, but they typically do not curve like a barrel (although there is no known standard).

Taiko used for gagaku (ancient Imperial Court music) are most closely akin to ancient mainland drums (Chinese, Korean, Indian). Several traditions of gagaku exist and details recorded in writings are unfortunately incomplete; therefore, various aspects of the taiko terminology and usage detailed here will either overlap or suffer ambiguity. The *yōko/koshi-tsuzumi/san-no-tsuzumi* are double-headed, hourglass-shaped drums that lie horizontally on the lap of a kneeling player. The *kaiko* is a circular, short, double-faced drum played by a drummer kneeling on one knee. The drum is supported on the elevated knee and struck by one hand. The *kakko* is a small, horizontal drum with two skinheads bound by cords and placed on a pedestal. The kakko is played with two sticks (*bachi*). The *tsuri-daiko* is a squat, cylindrical drum that is suspended vertically in a circular frame. The drum is played with two sticks. The *ninaidaiko*, a large cylindrical drum, hangs from a horizontal, ornate support structure that can act as a suspension system for transport. The *happu* is similar to the tsuri-daiko but is filled with rice powder. The *dadaiko* is a very large, cylindrical drum that is often housed in a teardrop-shaped structure and elevated on a platform. This drum is played with two, large lacquered beaters.

The playing of the larger drums in gagaku performance follows the ancient Chinese philosophical principles of *yin* and *yang*. The yin/female/*mebachi* is held in

Members of the Japanese taiko drumming company KODO performing in 2016. Taiko drums are typically large and loud. (Yasuyoshi Chiba/AFP/Getty Images)

the left hand and tends to strike the drum first. The yang/male/*obachi* is held in the right hand and tends to strike the drum second.

The two drums developed in the *nō* tradition, which are still used in several other traditions today (such as *kabuki*), are the *ōtsuzumi* and the *kotsuzumi*. Both drums are in the hour-glass shaped family of drums. The kotsuzumi is often placed on the shoulder of the player and then struck on one side only with the hand. The ōtsuzumi is a larger version of the kotsuzumi. Usually resting on the right hip, this drum is struck with the right hand. To achieve the exceedingly dry timbre desired for this type of percussion playing, the skin heads are heated before each performance. An *ōdaiko* is also typically used for nō performances. This barrel drum is about twice as large as the average *nagado daiko* drum. The *utadaiko/gezadaiko/shime* is a relatively small cylindrical drum with very tightly bound skins that extend just beyond the body of the drum and are bound to the other drum head by ropes. This drum is played on one side only with two bachi and usually rests in a small stand.

Many varieties of taiko are used in kabuki performance. The *okedo* is a medium-sized cylindrical drum; the drum heads extend beyond the edges of the drum and the ropes are bound around the center of the drum in order to adjust the tension. This drum is typically played by two thin sticks and often fastened with a long, looped rope that can be placed over the shoulder for easy transport. This drum is often played on both sides. The *daibyoshi* is a smaller version of the okedo. The *gaku-daiko* is a small, squat, and relatively rounded (barrel-like) drum played with two thin bachi. The *uchiwa-daiko* is a very thin-skinned, handheld drum often referred to as a fan drum (of the Japanese variety), but to Americans looks more like a handheld cosmetic mirror. The instrument is played with a single thin stick.

In Japan, taiko drums are most visibly used in traditional Japanese festivals (matsuri), such as the Buddhist summer ōbon festival of the ancestors. The ostinato rhythms of the drums are typically accompanied by dancing (*odori*), chanting, or recorded singing (*min'yō*). These drums are of the barrel variety, commonly known as *nagado daiko* (long-bodied drums). Nagado daiko have skins/heads that are fastened with heavy tacks to the body of the drum. These drums come in three different varieties: *kodaiko, chūdaiko,* and *ōdaiko*. Kodaiko (literally, small drum) are usually less than 12 inches in diameter; chūdaiko (literally, medium drum) are the most common size and often placed on a small stand. Ōdaiko (literally, large drum) are the largest of this type, usually 30 inches or more in diameter, placed on a tall stand, and often played by two drummers on each end. Out of this matsuri tradition grew many regionally specific styles of taiko drumming. For example, the styles of Hachijo and Miyake taiko drumming come from islands off the Southeastern coast of Japan called Hachijo and Miyake, respectively.

Currently more famous than gagaku- or matsuri-style taiko playing is the contemporary practice of kumi-daiko (group drumming), which incorporates more instruments than just nagado daiko. Various sizes of *hira daiko* (literally, flat drum) such as shime are used, as well as *katsugi*, okedo, gongs, *chappa* (small handheld cymbals), *chanchiki* (a small brass gong played by striking with a small mallet), and even *fue* or *shinobue* (wooden flutes). These instrumental accessories have come to kumi-daiko via other traditional Japanese arts such as gagaku, Buddhist and Shintō performance, nō drama, kabuki, and *bunraku* puppetry.

The kumi-daiko movement started with ensembles such as Sukeroku Daiko, who played summertime ōbon festivals and matsuri in the Tokyo *shitamachi* (literally, old town) area. Another such group, Osuwa Daiko, was led by Oguchi Daihachi, a jazz drummer who incorporated many modern rhythms into his ensemble's routines. These groups began to hold contests and in that process began to elaborate and expand on the technique of taiko performance. Additionally, due to Oguchi's influence and the fact that the ensembles in the shitamachi were also in the most urban/cosmopolitan area of Japan, they began to incorporate modern, complex rhythms and choreography into their performances. Soon, these taiko groups were asked to perform in venues other than festivals, essentially taking the art form of out its traditional context. A group called Ondekoza formed on Sado Island, off the western coast of central Japan, to revitalize folk traditions in a new style focused on taiko performance. Their mission also included taking this talent around the world to raise money for the ultimate goal of creating an artisan community. The group currently in residence for this artisan community on Sado Island is called Kodo. Due to the national and international exposure of these two primary ensembles and many others, kumi-daiko has become a musical phenomenon. Within the past 20 years, taiko groups have begun to form in America, Europe, Australia, and many other countries. Some of these groups are professional ensembles and other groups are instructional/recreational in nature. Today, the training of a taiko player typically starts either within the context of a family tradition or in an educational class atmosphere.

Even before a taiko player can approach the drum, the correct bachi (drumsticks) must be chosen for performance. Many different lengths, widths, and types of wood can be used for taiko playing depending upon the drum being played and the player's preference. The heavy/hard woods that are typically used for bachi are oak and maple. The light/soft woods used are often magnolia, hinoki, and paulownia. On average, the harder/heavier woods will produce a louder sound on the drum and the lighter/softer woods will produce a quieter sound. The bachi come in various widths and/or diameters, from very thin to very thick. Typically, if one plays a smaller drum at close range, a thin stick will be more useful. Often the thinner sticks will be tapered for even more precise and clear playing. For larger drums that require great strength, players find that thicker bachi are most useful to create a full sound.

When training for taiko, various warm-up or practice exercises are employed. Many taiko groups engage in a physical warm-up (*taisō*). Then, a series of rhythmic exercises (*renshū*) will be conducted both to prepare the body for taiko playing and to practice one's *kata* (form). The concept of kata is very important in Japanese traditional arts. The way (*dō*) in which an artist performs the art is as important as the art itself. For example, in Japanese tea ceremony known as *chadō* (literally, the way of tea), the way in which one holds a tea cup or pours the tea is as important as the taste of the tea. The concept of kata originated from the martial arts (karate, judo, aikido, kendo) as a way of approaching combat from a logical, systematic perspective rather than a haphazard one. Practicing the kata develops instinctual reactions that can be perfected over time, making them more effective in combat. In taiko, the rehearsal of kata applies to drum strokes and choreographed movements. Some kata are standardized, particularly in ceremonial taiko playing; however, various taiko groups in modern times have developed (and continue to create) their own choreographies and kata, which can vary widely. The ultimate goal in kumi-daiko is a synchronous ensemble movement. Whether the movement is fast or slow, the kata should stay consistent. The overall effect is likened to a marching band or dance troupe whose steps and movement are so synchronized that it creates a sense of awe in the spectator. Some groups treat kata with the utmost importance, with strict adherence to movement, whereas others allow and/or encourage more spontaneity within the performance.

In most ensemble taiko performances, a general rhythmic pattern or ostinato is maintained throughout a large section of the piece, creating rhythmic vitality. This rhythmic *ji*, or *jiuchi*, literally means earth or ground. This ostinato is the rhythmic grounding for the piece as a whole and is typically played on a shime drum, which emits a high and bright timbre so that it can be heard above the cacophony of lower drums. The theoretical opposite of ji would be *ma* or space. In Japanese philosophical aesthetics, empty space (ma) elicits as much interest as filled space. For example, the open spaces in a Japanese flower arrangement (*ikebana*) are a very important aspect of the work as a whole because they remind the observer of the balance between matter and nothingness. In taiko, ma is used particularly in solo performances and evokes the nō music tradition. These sonic spaces allow for reflection on the balance between sound and silence as well as a chance to appreciate the overall aesthetic of the sound.

During a performance, in addition to hearing percussive rhythms, an audience member will notice that certain vocalisms are also present. *Kakegoe*, or "shout," comes from the kabuki tradition. During pauses in the action on the kabuki stage, audience members will shout encouragement to the performers. In taiko, a single player or the entire group might say a word or phrase together. These shouts are often at the beginnings and endings of pieces, but are also used to denote rhythmic spaces or transitions. Words or phrases may also be shouted spontaneously to add excitement and/or variety to the piece. A very similar concept, *ki-ai*, which means "yell," is a word or phrase shouted by one or more players for encouragement and/or to create a sense of excitement. The characters for the term "ki-ai" literally translate to "combining energy." Philosophically, then, ki-ai is a linking of energies between players and the drum, between players themselves, and also between the players and the audience.

Typically, kumi-daiko compositions are not notated, but are learned and/or transmitted orally. *Kuchishōga* (literally, mouth chant song) is a traditional Japanese technique for learning music orally (this technique is also used in the instruction of other traditional musical instruments, such as the *nōkan* flute). This method employs various syllables that designate the type of stroke to be played. Many kuchishōga are quite standard, but may differ between regions, groups, or composers. For example, "don-kon" might equate to one right-handed stroke followed by one left-handed stroke. "Do-ko" then would equate to right and left strokes that are half the value of "don-kon." "Tsu" could designate a rest. "Kara" might designate that one play should the sides or rim of the drum. "Chon" might designate that both sticks strike the drum simultaneously. With this oral method of transmission, a player can learn a song by hearing and repeating the kuchishōga, which then also acts as a mnemonic device. Of course, not every rhythmic nuance to a piece can be encapsulated within the kuchishōga vocabulary, and often one must hear the precise rhythm played in order to replicate the rhythm exactly. More importantly, no vocabulary or notation exists for the canonized choreographic elements that accompany many kumi-daiko performances; these elements can only be learned by observation and repetition.

Another significant aspect of many taiko and kumi-daiko performances is the costumes or outfits. In many traditional matsuri or festival performances the *fundoshi* is worn. *Fundoshi* are traditional undergarments, a cross between a loincloth and a thong. In fact, the idea to wear fundoshi for kumi-daiko performance was suggested by the French designer Pierre Cardin. The taiko groups Ondekoza and Kodo often appear in fundoshi during performance. Fundoshi are often accessorized by *happi* (loose-fitting, short cotton jackets with untapered sleeves). For many kumi-daiko groups (particularly outside of Japan where fundoshi are less common), happi are accompanied by *momohiki* (loose-fitting pants). Most players of taiko wear a headband called a *hachimaki*. The characters for hachimaki literally translate to "rolled crown" because the cloth for the headband is typically twisted and then placed around the crown of the head. Another popular garment worn for taiko playing is the *haragake*, which is an apron of sorts. The haragake has straps that go over the shoulders and behind the back, covering mainly the chest and belly (*hara*). Additionally, many taiko players wear *tabi*. This type of footwear is a descendent of tabi socks, which separate the big toe from the other toes so that socks can be worn with *zōri* (flat sandals) or *geta* (elevated sandals). Taiko tabi have separated toes (in the manner of tabi socks) and rubberized soles for increased stability and traction.

Many traditional Japanese art forms (such as kabuki) have for centuries excluded women from participation. Professional taiko had, until the 1970s, been predominantly an all-male endeavor; yet the inclusion of women in many American and Canadian taiko ensembles has recently led to more acceptance of professional female taiko players in Japan. In essence, female participation in taiko contributed to a transnational flow of gender equality and empowerment for women involved in taiko playing. The ability of taiko to facilitate a transmission of social markers can also be witnessed in the sense of national or racial identity that many Asian Americans experience when performing or watching taiko. In fact, the seeds of kumi-daiko's popularization in North America were planted in World War II internment camps, as a way to perpetuate a Japanese identity among Japanese individuals who were held there.

Today, in North America, at least 150 professional and/or educational kumi-daiko groups exist, and this number does not include the many collegiate groups that have become popular as student organizations. In Japan, kumi-daiko groups are quite ubiquitous; therefore, the worldwide number of ensembles is difficult to calculate. However, with the popularity of international tours, collegiate participation, regional conferences, and educational opportunities for students, kumi-daiko will likely continue to prosper for quite some time. Kumi-daiko's amalgamation of traditional instruments, costume, and aesthetics mixed with modern elements of jazz/Western rhythms and non-Japanese social influences has created an internationally unique musical and cultural phenomenon.

Bradley Fugate

See also: Bunraku; Gagaku; Japan, Music of; Kabuki; Nô Theater

Further Reading

Bender, Shawn. 2012. *Taiko Boom: Japanese Drumming in Place and Motion.* Berkeley: University of California Press.

Creighton, Millie. 2008. "*Taiko* Today: Performing Soundscapes, Landscapes and Identities." In Henry Johnson and Jerry C. Jaffe (eds.), *Performing Japan: Contemporary Expressions of Cultural Identity*, 34–67. Kent, UK: Global Oriental.

Piggot, Francis. 1971. *The Music and Musical Instruments of Japan.* New York: Da Capo Press.

Varian, Heidi. 2001. *The Way of Taiko.* Berkeley, CA: Stone Bridge Press.

Wong, Deborah. 2004. "Taiko in Asian America." In *Speak It Louder: Asian Americans Making Music*, 195–232. New York: Routledge.

Wong, Deborah. 2006. "*Taiko* and the Asian/American Body: Drums, *Rising Sun*, and the Question of Gender." In Jennifer C. Post (ed.), *Ethnomusicology: A Contemporary Reader*, 87–96. New York: Routledge.

Taiwanese Opera

Taiwanese opera usually refers to *gezaixi* (*kua-á-hi* in Taiwanese), which includes songs with spoken dialogues, stereotyped tunes and role types, and stylized movements. Taiwanese opera is one of the vernacular Chinese drama types, alone with Beijing opera, Kungqu opera, Cantonese opera, and so on. It is commonly considered to be the only native genre that was originated in Taiwan (Wang, 2001, p. 426), although it still shows influences from southern Fujian.

The name "gezaixi" includes two parts: song (*gezai*) and drama (*xi*). It is given the name "Taiwanese opera" probably for two main reasons. First, it is performed in Taiwanese, the language that is considered the mother language of the majority of Taiwanese people. Second, and maybe more importantly, it is an indigenous Taiwanese drama type. The language used is a combination of both literary (for serious characters, such as the *sheng* [male leads] and *dan* [female leads]) and colloquial (for comic characters, such as a *chou* [jester]) registers of Taiwanese.

The history of Taiwanese opera can be traced back to the 17th century, when many immigrants came to Taiwan from China. During their leisure time, amateur singers got together and sang folk songs that set poetry in Taiwanese, without a stage. Gradually they adopted a complete storyline, and the performance type of song singing became storytelling through songs. Later on, it developed into a sung drama with actions. One of the earliest performance formats was *Luo-di-sao* (literally, coming down to the ground and sweeping). This is a simple outdoor performance where four bamboo poles framed a space; performers would act and sing in this area. It was followed by *Ye-tai-xi* (literally, outdoor drama), which usually took place in front of a temple and entertained the general public instead of elites. During the colonialization by Japan (1895–1945), Taiwanese opera kept flourishing and many troupes were started, first in Yilan County in northern Taiwan and later in other cities. In the 1910s, some Chinese opera troupes came to Taiwan and won much success. Some of the actors and actresses stayed into the 1920s and joined local opera troupes, which enriched the elements in Taiwanese opera. In the 1920s, this form moved into theaters and remained popular. Around the same time, Taiwanese opera was performed in Fujian, China, and other countries in South Asia, such as Singapore, Malaysia, and the Philippines.

However, after the outbreak of the Pacific War, the Japanese government initiated the *kominka* movement, which tried to "Japanize" Taiwanese people, under which the performance of Taiwanese opera was prohibited (Wu, 2009, p. 149). It became a propaganda vehicle for promoting Japan, and the actors of the Taiwanese opera were forced to perform in Japanese kimonos and sing Japanese songs. Some of the actors would wear Taiwanese opera costumes under their kimonos, and as soon as the overseeing policemen left, they would take off their kimonos and perform Taiwanese opera (Chang, 1997, p. 115). Many troupes were disbanded, although some retreated to the countryside and performed in secrecy.

After the restoration of Taiwan to China in 1945, Taiwanese opera was revived and entered its golden age (Wu, 2009, p. 150). More than 500 troupes were registered in 1949 (Tsai, 1992, p. 35). In the 1950s, it was performed on the radio, and in 1955, a black-and-white movie of Taiwanese opera, *Xue Ping-Gui and Wang*

Bao-Chuan, became a huge success; the films of Taiwanese opera were continuously produced until the 1970s. In 1962, Taiwanese Television Company established and launched the broadcast of Taiwanese operas. Televised operas were similar to soap dramas and increased the popularity of Taiwanese operas. In the early 1980s, there were many popular Taiwanese opera television series, which also won huge acclaim. Its stars were known in every household. Many of them were cross-dressing performers, such as Lihua Yang and Qing Ye.

However, even during the golden period, Taiwanese opera still faced many challenges. First, the Kuomintang government advocated the Chinese identity, tried to work against the communist People's Republic of China, and suppressed all the dialects in Taiwan, including Taiwanese. Meanwhile, the government-sponsored Beijing opera was promoted as the national opera, much more than any other dramatic genre. The Taiwanese opera troupes needed to make a living by themselves. Although the production of radio and televised opera helped increase their popularity, live indoor performances were significantly curtailed.

The Taiwanese opera troupes in the late 20th century found ways other than television to promote themselves. One of the most notable troupes is Ming Hua Yuan, which was the first to appear on the stage of Sun Yat-Sen Memorial Hall, a national theater, in 1983, and also the first troupe other than Beijing opera companies to tour military bases. It also participated in the Art Festival of the Asian Games in Beijing in 1990. The storylines that they adopted stressed more romantic elements, rather than the traditional plots based on historical and heroic legends. One of its most popular dramas is *The Legend of the White Snake*, a typical story combining myth, religion, and romance.

The orchestra used for Taiwanese opera usually consists of two parts: lyrical and martial. The lyrical part uses melodic instruments, whereas the martial has only percussion. There are a couple of stereotypic tunes. One of the most popular is a "crying tune," which is used as a vehicle for singers to express their sadness and also reflect on their depression and anger under cultural suppression, either by the colony of Japan or the rule of the Kuomintang (after 1945 to the 1970s). Before television, the actions, stage sets, and scenery were very simple, and usually uses symbolic items: for example, a red flag represents fire, a blue flag represents water, and two flags sometimes indicate a carriage. These conventions are still used today for live productions.

Chloe Hsun Lin

See also: Jingju; Opera; Taiwanese Traditional and Popular Music

Further Reading

Chang, Huei-Yuan Belinda. 1997. "A Theatre of Taiwanese: Politics Ideologies, and Gezaixi." *TDR: The Drama Review* 41(2), 111–129.

Tsai, Tsung-Te. 1992. "Taiwanese Opera: A Theatre between Stability and Change." PhD diss., University of Maryland.

Wang, Ying-fen. 2001. "Music and Chinese Society: Contemporary Taiwan." In Robert Provine, Yosihiko Yokumaru, and J. Lawrence Witzleben (eds.), *Garland Encyclopedia of World Music; Vol. 7: China, Japan, and Korea*, 423–429. New York: Routledge.

Wu, Ming-Lun. 2009. "Return from Exile: On Min Hwa Yuan Gezaixi Company's Survival in the New Century." *Asian Theatre Journal* 26(1) (Spring), 148–158.

Taiwanese Traditional and Popular Music

Taiwan (Republic of China), located about a hundred miles off the southeastern coast of the People's Republic of China, is home to an ethnically and socioeconomically diverse population of more than 23 million. The island has been subject to numerous migrations and colonial projects over the past 400 years, giving rise to local hybrid musical cultures shaped by contact with various Han Chinese, Japanese, and Euro-American traditions, and by the practices of the island's indigenous communities. In tandem with the growth of its economy during the latter half of the 20th century, Taiwan became a major exporter of Mandarin popular (Mandopop) music. More recently, the island has developed an expansive independent and underground live music scene anchored by the contributions of folk, rock, metal, and hip-hop artists, as well as performers influenced by indigenous idioms.

HISTORICAL AND SOCIOPOLITICAL CONTEXTS

Musicological texts typically categorize the island's musics according to ethnicity, because Taiwan's complex and shifting demographics have influenced the languages, ritual contexts, lyrical themes, and sonic character of different types of performance. Austronesian language-speaking peoples began settling on the island around 5,000 years ago (Blust, 1999). Ethnic Hoklo and Hakka migrants from China began to surpass them in numbers during the latter half of the 17th century. A succession of different colonial powers governed Taiwan over the past 400 years, including the Netherlands (1624–1662) and Spain (1626–1642). The Dutch overtook the Spanish, but were in turn driven out by Ming dynasty loyalists who sought to establish Taiwan as a base of resistance against the Manchu-controlled Qing dynasty. The island fell to the Qing in 1683 and was made a separate province of China in 1885, following invasions by the British during the Opium War and the French during the Sino-French War. Taiwan's provincial standing was short-lived: the island was a Dependency of the Empire of Japan from 1895 to 1945, after which it was ceded to the Chinese Nationalist Party, at that time fighting a civil war against Chinese Communist forces. Following defeat by the Communists in 1949, Chiang Kai-shek (1887–1975) and approximately 2 million refugees fled to Taiwan to establish a new base for the Republic of China (ROC), a measure that further diversified the island's population to include peoples from numerous Chinese provinces.

Taiwan's political climate has determined the kinds of music made and valued at different times. During the latter part of the Japanese colonial period, authorities instituted a policy called *kōminka* (imperialization) to inculcate loyalty to the Japanese empire. As part of this program, they suppressed the use of Sinitic languages and the performance of local cultural traditions. The government of Chiang Kai-shek curbed the expressive autonomy of individuals and communities on the island through nearly four decades of martial law (1949–1987), to quell pro-Communist and pro-independence activities and bolster support for Nationalist claims to political legitimacy. Beginning in the 1960s, the Chinese cultural renaissance movement strenuously promoted art forms thought to embody Confucian values, especially Peking (Beijing) opera, Chinese painting, and the canonical works and styles of classical Chinese literature. Non-Mandarin cultural production and the public use of non-Mandarin languages were vigorously suppressed. Hoklo modes of performance such as *gezaixi* (literally, song-theater) and *budaixi* (glove puppetry; literally, cloth-bag theater) were targeted by both the Japanese and Nationalist regimes. Authorities also censored popular songs that violated current language policies or, during the period of martial law, fostered anti-Nationalist sentiments.

The question of what constitutes "Taiwanese" culture has pervaded public and political discourse in the years since the end of martial law, as the government transitioned to a multiparty democratic system and formally recognized Taiwanese multiculturalism. This period has seen a flowering of creativity on the island and many attempts to revive and promote previously suppressed cultural traditions. Taiwan's formal international political status is an ongoing source of contention, as the People's Republic of China continues to regard the island as a breakaway province. Many musicians have examined questions about Taiwanese sovereignty and the nature of Taiwanese identity in their creative works.

TRADITIONAL MUSIC

Indigenous Music

The Taiwan government currently recognizes 16 indigenous groups (Amis, Atayal, Bunun, Hla'alua, Kanakanavu, Kavalan, Paiwan, Puyuma, Rukai, Saisiyat, Tao, Thao, Tsou, Truku, Sakizaya, Sediq), the collective population of which totaled approximately 540,000 in 2014 (*Taiwan Yearbook*). Colonizing powers subjected these peoples to numerous assimilation campaigns, which resulted in the loss of some of their distinct languages and cultural traditions. Nevertheless, music remains a cornerstone of daily activities, ritual practice, and cultural memory, transmitted within and between generations primarily through oral/aural processes. There is considerable variation in musical practice, but the subjects of worship, farming and fishing, military, hunting, love, drinking and celebration, and narratives/epics are common across groups.

The vast majority of indigenous musics are vocal, and performances can be monophonic, biphonic, polyphonic, homophonic, and/or heterophonic in texture. Songs may be precomposed, improvised, or a combination of the two. Certain traditional practices that have gained greater visibility outside indigenous communities in part because of their prominence in musical scholarship include the distinctive homorhythmic chordal singing that characterizes the Bunun millet harvest song "Pasibutbut"; the mellifluous singing of Puyuma epic ballads and work songs; and the ornamented vocal lines and multiple call-and-response styles of the Amis. Amis and Puyuma singers are also distinguished by their frequent use of nonlexical syllables. Music and dance performed at annual festivals have become emblems of indigenous identity as well as centerpieces of tourism to indigenous areas. Group singing and circle dancing (*malikoda*) at the Amis Harvest Festival (*Kilomaan/Ilisin*) and the performance of song cycles at the Saisiyat Ritual to the Short People (*Pas-ta'ai*) attract large numbers of participants and spectators.

Instrumental music is less prominent than vocal music in indigenous life. Different instruments, like different singing practices, serve distinct social functions. Tuned to a pentatonic scale, pitched wooden pestles are employed in Bunun and Thao communities, especially in festival contexts. Musical bows, often used for entertainment purposes, take a variety of forms across indigenous communities, as do a wide range of Jew's harps, sometimes played in dance performances. Bamboo nose, transverse, and horizontal flutes are also widespread. Many groups—including but not limited to the Amis, Atayal, Bunun, Puyuma, Rukai, and Saisiyat—wear small leg and waist bells that jingle percussively in dance performances.

The island's indigenous and Han peoples alike were subject to Christianization campaigns by the Catholic and Presbyterian churches beginning in the 17th century. Missionaries from the Netherlands, Portugal, Spain, Canada, and England introduced European traditions of hymnody and praise-singing to the island. These practices took root particularly among indigenous peoples, many of whom identify as Christians.

Traditional indigenous music gained exposure outside of Taiwan when Michael Cretu, leader of the Romanian-German New Age music group Enigma, sampled the voices of Amis elders Difang Duana (1921–2002) and Igay Duana (1922–2002) in the 1993 hit song "Return to Innocence"—without asking the singers' permission, and without crediting or remunerating them. The Duanas eventually filed a lawsuit against Cretu, EMI/Capitol Records, Virgin Records, and others connected to the recording and its distribution. They settled out of court in 1999, having raised new awareness of the complex issues surrounding copyright and cultural ownership in indigenous communities.

Han Music

The Hoklo, Hakka, and those who came to Taiwan from various parts of China after the Nationalist retreat have all contributed to the development of the island's hybrid soundscape. Although popular singers command the lion's share of public attention, artists working in traditional genres are active in both rural and urban areas. Temple festivals, many of which merge practices from Buddhism, Daoism, Confucianism, and local folk religion, are common sites of encounter with traditional Han musics. Musicians at such events aspire to create a "hot and noisy" (*renao*) atmosphere, a sense of bracing movement, sonic intensity, and levity intended to please both deities and human participants in rituals of belief. To attain adequate levels of heat and noise, a temple festival might feature gezaixi, Western-style marching bands, *beiguan* (northern pipes) ensembles, and popular ballad singers riding on electrified, festooned parade floats. Traditional Han musics can also be heard at wedding and funerals, recitals in public parks, outdoor plazas, and concert halls.

The majority Hoklo ethnic group brought a number of traditions with them when they began migrating to Taiwan from southeastern China in the late 17th century. *Nanguan* (southern pipes) has roots in Fujian, but is now performed in Taiwan, Hong Kong, Malaysia, the Philippines, and Singapore. The core nanguan ensemble consists of four silk and bamboo instruments (*pipa, sanxian, xiao, erxian*), and a wooden clapper (*pai*) often played by a vocalist. Nanguan is transmitted through amateur clubs, which perform both for entertainment and also sometimes at temple festivals. Professional troupes such as Hantang Yuefu have also reimagined the music as part of multimodal performances that present historical stories from China in combination with Fujianese *liyuan* dance. The music is heterophonic, with the pipa and sanxian performing a core melodic line and the xiao, erxian, and vocalist performing the same line with elaborations. Where nanguan is slow, quiet, and delicate, the genre of beiguan, also originally from Fujian, is predominantly boisterous and strident. Closely associated with processions at funerals and temple festivals, the beiguan ensemble typically consists of gongs, drums, and multiple *suona*, a double-reed instrument. An expanded beiguan ensemble that includes silk and bamboo instruments, voice, and wooden clapper may be employed in gezaixi, budaixi, and the rarely performed *luantan* opera.

Gezaixi and budaixi are the most popular local theatrical genres on the island. Gezaixi is a relatively recent innovation, having emerged during the Japanese occupation in the early 1900s. There are today two main forms of live gezaixi, one performed outdoors in association with a temple, and the other performed indoors as a form of commercial theater. Although gezaixi was originally an all-male genre, casts have been female-dominated since at least the 1960s. Sung in the colloquial Hoklo language, the form is musically eclectic. Depending on the type of venue, performances might incorporate local and Fujianese folk tunes; Japanese *enka*; modern Chinese ensemble music; nanguan and beiguan musics; and local popular songs. Gezaixi also incorporates stories and techniques from various Chinese opera forms, including Peking opera. Minghuayuan, established in 1929, is perhaps the most famous gezaixi company, performing at both indoor and outdoor venues in Taiwan and embarking on international tours.

Traditional budaixi is performed using hand puppets before a small, intricately decorated theater. Like gezaixi, it has long been staged at temple festivals as a divine offering, and was historically accompanied by an array of live musics, including beiguan and nanguan. Troupes working today often use prerecorded music, especially newly composed or arranged modern Chinese ensemble music, and music from Hollywood and Hong Kong movies and television dramas. A more recently established form of budaixi, popularized by the Pili Company, uses larger puppets to tell new stories that blend martial arts, fantasy, and science fiction. Televised with elaborate digital effects, these productions feature a range of global and local sounds.

Beyond these theatrical traditions, Taiwan is home to a diverse array of Hoklo *shuochang* (speech-song) genres, including narrative ballad singing from the Hengchun peninsula region in southern Taiwan and *niange* (songs with narration, or song reading). Both are typically performed by a vocal soloist who accompanies himself or herself on a *yueqin* (moon-shaped lute), although in some cases a second musician may be present. Vocal melodies are frequently improvised and derived from a limited number of tune types, the contours of which bend to accommodate the tones of the Hoklo language. Lyrics may consist of folk tales, historical tales, and exhortations to quit drinking and gambling, among other topics.

The Hakka peoples in Taiwan maintain distinctive musical traditions, some of which have cross-pollinated with Hoklo musics, others of which have remained relatively autonomous. For example, the instrumental ensemble *bayin* (literally, "eight sounds," referring to the sounds of metal, stone, silk, bamboo, skin, earthenware, gourd, and wood instruments) sometimes performs beiguan repertoire, typically at weddings, birthdays, funerals, and temple festival celebrations. The folk songs known as *shange* (mountain songs) represent an important source and symbol of Hakka identity. So named because Hakka peoples traditionally settled near mountains and practiced agriculture, shange can be performed by a solo singer or a duo. Like Hengchun folk songs and nianbge, they draw on a tune matrix, which also forms the basis of the three-role Hakka tea-picking opera. Shange are often improvised, with lyrics on an array of topics reflecting the everyday lives and struggles of Hakka peoples.

Those who fled to Taiwan following the Nationalist retreat to the island brought with them additional styles of opera and narrative song. The government designated Peking opera Taiwan's national opera in the mid-1960s as part of cultural policies designed to foster an emotional connection to China. Military personnel also imported *bangzi* opera from Henan province and a variety of shuochang genres, including the comic dialogues of *xiangsheng* (cross-talk).

POPULAR MUSIC

Gezaixi and nanguan were among the first types of music captured by record companies in Taiwan during the Japanese colonial period, when the island's popular music industry first developed. The first Taiwanese popular song, however, was "Peach Blossom Weeps Blood" by lyricist Zhan Tianma and composer Wang Yunfeng, performed by singer Chun Chun in 1932. The song's use of a vocal line influenced by local folk music and jazz orchestral accompaniment was in step with developments in the urban popular music scenes of China and Japan, where genres such as *shidaiqu* and enka fused Eastern and Western musical idioms to great commercial success. Many songs from this period have become today's classics, including "Awaiting the Spring Breeze," by lyricist Li Linqiu and composer Deng Yuxian; and "Flower in the Rainy Night," by lyricist Zhou Tianwang and composer Deng Yuxian.

The Hoklo popular music business dwindled later in the decade when the Japanese colonial government began suppressing the use of Sinitic languages. A number of Hoklo songs were translated into Japanese and appropriated by colonial authorities for political propaganda. The 1950s saw a partial reversal of these circumstances, as Taiwanese musicians began adapting Japanese tunes and translating them into Hoklo and Mandarin for the local market.

The conclusion of World War II and the advent of Nationalist rule on the island gave rise to additional changes in Taiwan's popular music landscape. Chinese refugees who arrived at the end of the 1940s were partial to shidaiqu, Mandarin-language pop songs from 1920s Shanghai that merged the sensibilities of Chinese folk songs with the sounds of jazz and Hollywood musicals. The style's success in Taiwan was bolstered by a political environment that increasingly restricted non-Mandarin cultural expression. Although Taiwan produced a few notable home-grown shidaiqu artists, such as Tse Wei (Zi Wei) and Yao Surong, the style began to fall out of fashion toward the end of the 1960s. This coincided not only with the aging of the first-generation émigré population, but also with a deepening American pop cultural presence on the island and a persistent appetite for sounds from Hong Kong.

The market for Mandarin-language popular music grew in step with Taiwan's economic resurgence and rapid urbanization during the second half of the 20th century. Moreover, broadcast laws restricted the number of non-Mandarin songs on television and radio. Influenced by enka, shidaiqu, and Western pop styles, Deng Lijun (Teresa Teng) was Mandopop's leading light from 1970 until her tragic death from an asthma attack in 1995. Born in Taiwan to a military family, she rose to fame throughout East and Southeast Asia as a gifted singer of folk tunes and romantic ballads. Teng was revered for her power to reach audiences across deeply entrenched linguistic, cultural, and geopolitical divides, and she continues to inspire next-generation Mandopop performers such as Beijing-born Wang Fei (Faye Wong) and Taiwan-born Zhou Jielun (Jay Chou) today.

The 1970s also saw the birth of the grassroots Modern Folk Song Movement (*xiandai minge yundong*), which responded to a sense of encroaching American cultural imperialism, as well as a string of political crises that ultimately led to the Republic of China's diplomatic isolation from the international community. Artists such as Yang Xian, Li Shuangzi, and Ara Kimbo (Hu Defu) exhorted students to reject cultural imports from the West and Japan and to instead "sing our own songs" (*chang zijide ge*). The movement proceeded along two main pathways: some songs expressed nostalgia for life in China in a manner affirming Nationalist ideology, whereas others incorporated social realist themes that expressed their composers' affinity for Taiwan. The spirit of critique that characterized singer-songwriter Luo Dayou's works during the 1980s incorporated aspects of both strands as it built on and expanded the modern folksong ethos.

Despite government suppression, Hoklo popular songs maintained a significant audience through the 1970s and 1980s, particularly in rural and working-class communities. Artists such as Bai Bingbing and Kang Hui (Jiang Hui) built robust careers on the performance of deeply sorrowful romantic ballads influenced by Hoklo songs from the 1930s and enka.

The lifting of martial law in 1987 brought about the legalization of opposition political parties and the gradual repeal of policies that had suppressed Hoklo, Hakka, and indigenous culture. These changes triggered a burst of musical creativity known as the New Taiwanese song movement (*xin taiyuge yundong*). Eschewing the Mandarin language and romantic themes characteristic of Mandopop, and the lachrymose qualities of Hoklo popular songs and enka, artists such as Blacklist Workshop

(*Heimingdan Gongzuoshi*), Lim Giong (Lin Qiang), New Formosa Band (*Xin Baodao Kangledui*), and Jutoupi were inspired by local and global musical styles, from Hengchun folk singing to hip-hop. They also cultivated a critical acumen with regard to politics and history, writing lyrics that explicitly critiqued Nationalist policies.

Since the 1990s, the number of musicians working on smaller labels (sometimes independent, sometimes subsidiaries of major multinational labels) has grown, spanning a variety of genres including folk, rock, metal, and rap. Hakka musician Lin Sheng-xiang and the Labour Exchange Band (*Jiaogong Yuedui*) rose to prominence in 1999 with the release of the album *Let Us Sing Mountain Songs* (*Wo deng jiu lai chang shange*), which drew on the Hakka mountain song tradition to chronicle community opposition to a dam-building project in Meinong, a predominantly Hakka town. Extreme metal band Chthonic invokes traditional musical idioms and explores themes related to folk culture, history, and social justice. Beginning in the early 2000s, local labels such as Rock Records, Wonder Music, and Taiwan Colors Music began to showcase the talents of indigenous artists. Singers and songwriters Suming, Biung, Panai, Pau-dull, and Samingad perform newly composed music in Mandarin and indigenous languages, as well as traditional melodies.

Mandopop remains the dominant form of popular music in Taiwan, although revenues from album and song sales have declined in part because of piracy, illegal MP3 downloading, and competition from other regional music industries. Nevertheless, Mandopop stars such as Zhou Jielun, Wang Lee-hom, and A-mei (also known as Amit and Zhang Huimei) continue to draw massive audiences to concerts in Taiwan and abroad, and also profit significantly from commercial sponsorships.

Meredith Schweig

See also: Chinese Pop; Enka Music; Jingju

Further Reading

Chang, Huei-Yuan Belinda. 1997. "A Theatre of Taiwaneseness: Politics, Ideologies, and Gezaixi." *TDR: The Drama Review* 41(2), 111–129.

Guy, Nancy. 2005. *Peking Opera and Politics in Taiwan*. Urbana: University of Illinois Press.

Hsu, Pattie. 2009. "Expanding Practices and Performing Popular Songs in Taiwanese Opera." *Asian Musicology* 14, 45–83.

Lin, Sylvia Li-chun. 2003. "Toward a New Identity: Nativism and Popular Music in Taiwan." *China Information* 17(2), 83–107.

Lin, Tse-Hsiung. 2011. "Mountain Songs, Hakka Songs, Protest Songs: A Case Study of Two Hakka Singers from Taiwan." *Asian Music: Journal of the Society for Asian Music* 42(1), 85–122.

Moskowitz, Marc L. 2010. *Cries of Joy, Songs of Sorrow: Chinese Pop Music and Its Cultural Connotations*. Honolulu: University of Hawai'i Press.

Tan, Shzr Ee. 2012. *Beyond "Innocence": Amis Aboriginal Song in Taiwan as an Ecosystem*. Surrey, UK: Ashgate.

Wang, Ying-fen. 1992. "The 'Mosaic Structure' of Nanguan Songs: An Application of Semiotic Analysis." *Yearbook for Traditional Music* 24, 24–51.

Tala

A *tala* is "a cyclically repeating fixed time cycle" (Qureshi, Powers, and Widdess, 2015). Along with *raga* (the melodic structure), tala is a cornerstone of all Indian music. This metric framework underlies fixed compositions and improvisations and provides the framework for all creative thought and action.

The theoretical concept of tala can be found in ancient treatises dating back to 200 BCE. The cyclic nature of tala shows the influence of Indian philosophical and metaphysical thought, which conceives of time as circular rather than linear. The word's root comes from the Sanskrit word "tala" (flat surface, palm), indicating the concept's physical nature and its origins in ancient practices of using claps and other hand gestures to mark time.

As for the concept of ragas, there is a considerable body of older theories and texts surrounding tala, which are valuable sources of information for understanding the historical antecedents of modern tala practice. One of these, the early *mārga-tāla* system, used elaborate bodily gestures to visualize the time cycle. These were essentially binary and represented a duple division of time. The later *deśī-tāla* system, the basis for modern systems of tala, did away with these movements and accounted for additive time divisions (groupings of 5, 7, 9, etc.). Both systems were inspired by the rhythms and meters of classical poetry. While there is theoretically no limit to the number of tala, the number of tala in practical use is quite small. There are roughly 20 Hindustani tala and no more than 10 Carnatic (Karnatic) tala that are used frequently in actual practice (Qureshi, Powers, and Widdess, 2015).

Each tala arranges a number of beats (*mātrā*, "unit of measurement" in Hindustani music; *akṣara*, "syllable," in Carnatic) into a cycle (Hindustani *āvart*, Carnatic *āvartanam*). These cycles are defined by the stressed or accented beat that falls at the beginning of the cycle (*sam*, represented by an X). Certain pulses within this cycle are marked by a clap or by a noiseless hand wave marking a beat that is de-emphasized within the overall cycle (*khali*, "empty," represented by a 0). Nearly all tala cycles revolve around an internal *khali/bhari* (empty/full) duality. Khali sections are unaccented and bhari sections are accented. This duality is key to understanding *ṭhekā* (support, repeated accompanimental patterns) as well as the entire system of improvising within tala.

The word *lay* or *laya* can refer to general aspects of rhythm or to tempo. While many shadings are possible, musicians refer generally to three basic speeds: slow (*vilambit*), medium (*madhya*), and fast (*drut*). Many terms refer to smaller divisions within beats, which in Hindustani music are typically subdivided into two (*dugun laya*), three (*tigun*), four (*caugun*), or six (*chegun*). Instrumental musicians use other less common laya that divide each beat into asymmetrical divisions (five, seven, etc.). These are typically subdivided into two or four (*caturaśra*), three or six (*tiśra*), five (*khaṇḍa*), and seven (*miśra*) in Carnatic music of southern India.

The most frequently used Hindustani tala is called *tīntāl*, a 16-beat cycle grouped 4 + 4 + 4 + 4. Performers mark each grouping of four with a clap (*tālī*) except the third, which is indicated by an open-palmed hand wave (*khālī*). This explains tīntāl's name (which translates as "three-clap tala"). The tala can be conceived of in three large sections. The bhari portion begins on *sam* (beat 1). The khali portion begins on khālī (beat 9) and includes beats 9–12. Beats 1–8 and 13–16 are stressed and beats 9–12 are unstressed.

Carnatic music most commonly features talas and rhythmic groupings arranged around groups of four and three, and less commonly in groups of seven, five, or nine. These numbers structure rhythmic thought at the macro level by providing "building blocks out of which lengthy improvisations are structured" as well as at the micro levels providing different ways that beats may be subdivided (into fourths, thirds, etc.) (Viswanathan and Allen, 2004, p. 35). Tala are marked by hand gestures (audible claps, silent waves, and touching fingers to the palm or thumb). The most frequently used tala is *adi* tala, an eight-beat cycle called grouped 4 + 2 + 2.

In both traditions, performances start with a unmetered introduction (Hindustani *alap*, Carnatic *ālāpana*). In certain genres, such as the Hindustani *dhrupad* vocal genre, Hindustani instrumental performances, and Carnatic *rāgam-tānam-pallavī*, this section is extended to considerable length. Following this section, tala and laya are introduced. In Hindustani music, the tala and laya are first established by the instrumental or vocal soloist and then marked by a percussion instrument. The most popular of these instruments is the *tabla*, a pair of drums with both pitched and unpitched heads. The tabla player keeps time within a repeated pattern called a *thekā* (support), which outlines the tala and provides a rhythmic framework for the soloist's compositions and improvisations. Although these thekā are a rather recent innovation within Hindustani music, talas are often defined and identified by their thekā. Another important rhythmic pattern is called *tihai* (one-third). These are melodic and rhythmic patterns that are repeated three times, often to signal the conclusion of an improvised section. A tihai creates tension with the tala and resolves it by accenting the arrival on sam or at the beginning of a composition. A longer *chakradhar tihai* (constructed as a pattern made of three parts that repeats itself three times) is used for marking structural arrival points.

In Carnatic music, the most commonly used accompanimental drum is the *mridangam*, a two-headed drum with both pitched and unpitched heads. Because the tala is marked through hand gestures by musicians on stage (and by some audience members), the drummer does not need to establish and keep time, but instead plays a more flexible and elaborate role. A mridangam player has rhythmic freedom to respond to and interact with the soloist, as long as he or she maintains the integrity of the underlying tala.

There are several differences between the Hindustani and Carnatic systems. Performances in each tradition features different ways of marking or keeping the tala and showing the divisions within metric cycles. During Hindustani performances, these gestures are typically confined to the performers, whereas during Carnatic performances, most of the audience will engage in hand gestures that physically count the tala. A second difference is that the major sections of Hindustani performances are typically differentiated by an increase of the tempo at which the tala moves. Once the tala is introduced, early sections of a performance are typically slower, while subsequent sections increase the tempo. In Carnatic music, the tempo remains constant throughout. Another major difference between the two systems is that the Carnatic concepts of tala are "rigid and highly systematic," whereas the Hindustani concept is "unsystematic and nebulous" (Arnold, 1999, p. 116). Some scholars believe this is the case because the Hindustani system "arose organically through performance, not as the result of a theoretical scheme" like the Carnatic system (Arnold, 1999, p. 116).

John Hausmann

See also: Dhrupad; Karnatic Music; Khayal; Shankar, Ravi; Sitar

Further Reading

Arnold, Alison, ed. 1999. *Garland Encyclopedia of World Music; Vol. 5: South Asia: The Indian Subcontinent.* New York: Routledge.

Bor, Joep. 2002. *The Raga Guide: A Survey of 74 Hindustani Ragas.* Monmouth, UK: Wyastone Estate.

Qureshi, Regula, Harold S. Powers, and Richard Widdess. 2015. "India, §III: Theory and Practice of Classical Music." *Grove Music Online.* http://www.oxfordmusiconline.com.

Ruckert, George E. 2004. *Music in North India.* New York: Oxford University Press.

Viswanathan, T., and Matthew Harp Allen. 2004. *Music in South India: The Karnatak Concert Tradition and Beyond.* New York: Oxford University Press.

Tamboo Bamboo

Tamboo bamboo is a musical ensemble comprised of players of bamboo stamping tubes that originates in the Caribbean nation of Trinidad and Tobago. Percussion ensembles using bamboo stamping instruments are found in many places around the world. Most of these are characterized by one or more players pounding various lengths of bamboo on a hard surface (e.g., the ground or large stones) to produce indefinitely pitched, though recognizably differentiated sounds. Similar ensembles are common throughout much of west central Africa and likely served as a model for bamboo-based percussion ensembles in the Caribbean, with tamboo bamboo one of the most notable of these. Despite the ensemble's relatively quick decline in popularity with the advent of steel orchestras in the 1930s, tamboo bamboo has been revived in folkloric contexts in recent decades and is today a regular feature of old-time Carnival. The name "tamboo" derives from *tambour*, the French word for drum, thereby indicating tamboo bamboo's direct relationship to African drumming traditions.

After the abolition of slavery in 1838, Trinidadian colonial authorities looked to curtail the musical activities of Afro-Trinidadians, an act prompted by fears that music-making fostered a dangerous solidarity among the laboring class and threatened social order. As part of this strategy of control, colonial authorities banned skin drums for Carnival celebrations in 1884. Many Afro-Trinidadians, however, skirted the law by using improvised instruments—discarded boxes, bits of metal, and the like—to pound out drumming patterns. By the early 20th century, revelers commonly used various lengths of bamboo to stand in for each part of the now-illegal skin drumming ensemble.

Despite the fact that tamboo bamboo bands might perform for various events year round, the ensemble was primarily associated with Carnival in the late 19th and early 20th centuries, where it was primarily used to accompany *lavways*, call-and-response songs sung in Creole, English, or a combination of both that eventually gave rise to calypso. Lavways with tamboo bamboo accompaniment were mostly sung on the road for Carnival parades and during organized stick fights (known locally as *kalinda*) to encourage the combatants. Tamboo bamboo was itself banned in 1937, prompting revelers to once again turn to alternative materials, this time opting for more durable metal instruments, a trend that led, in part, to the advent of the steel orchestra. Today, tamboo bamboo is played infrequently by musicians interested in preserving old-time Carnival traditions.

The instrumentation of tamboo bamboo ensembles varies, with at least three distinct rhythmic layers played on at least three distinct instrument types. The *boom*, the longest and lowest-pitched instrument, is played by striking the tube on the ground with a slow and syncopated rhythmic motion. The *foulé* is the middle voice of the ensemble, though its exact structure may vary. In the past, some bands used two pieces of bamboo, each about one foot long, pounded end-to-end as a foulé. In today's bands, however, the foulé voice is most often played with a single stamping tube. Though only one foulé player is necessary, there are often two or more foulés playing interlocking patterns on differently pitched tubes. In these instances, players often differentiate between the two by referring to one as a *buller* or *boula*. In all cases, foulé features relatively faster rhythmic motion than the boom that together with the boom provides the distinctive rhythmic groove of the ensemble. The *cutter* is the highest-pitched instrument, and the only one also played by striking the side with a hardwood stick. In this way, the cutter provides a high-pitched rhythm that cuts through the musical texture of the ensemble. When the band is stationary, the cutter may also be stamped on the ground for extra emphasis. Often complementing these three voices are timekeeping instruments such as *chac-chac* (maraca-like shakers), bottle-and-spoon, irons (as in steel orchestras), or low-pitched "dud-up" steel pans that may double or stand in for the boom.

Christopher L. Ballengee

See also: Calypso; Soca; Steelpan, Tassa Drumming

Further Reading

Courlander, Harold. 1941. "Musical Instruments of Haiti." *The Musical Quarterly* 27(3), 379–380.

Dudley, Shannon. 2008. *Music from Behind the Bridge: Steelband Spirit and Politics in Trinidad and Tobago.* New York: Oxford University Press.

Stuempfle, Stephen. 1995. *The Steelband Movement: The Forging of a National Art in Trinidad and Tobago.* Philadelphia: University of Pennsylvania Press.

Tango

Both the tango dance and tango music are associated with the essence of Buenos Aires: its vibrant energy, sophistication, sensuality, passion, fashion, melodrama, and its mysterious qualities. Often referred to as "the Paris of South America," the capital city of Argentina, equally rich, lavish, tasteful, and colorful as its European counterpart, is imbued with tango. Tourists from as far away as Japan are eager to see the best tango performances in the la Boca district of Corrientes Avenue or in Caminito Street, lined with its mosaic of wooden houses. The "story" of tango in Argentina has been an evolving product, with its identity shaped by immigrants, poverty-stricken people, and social outcasts. Tango is a hybrid product expressed in song and dance, but it is defined by the world as "Argentine."

There was a significant slave trade in Buenos Aires at the start of the 19th century. The city was used as a stopping point before people were shipped to the north. The black population brought to Argentina was culturally varied: 71% of the slaves came from the Bantu area of Eastern Africa, while the others came from areas of Western Africa, Gambia, the Gold Coast, and Senegal where the Kimbundu language was spoken. In the Argentine War of Independence in 1810, the majority of the slaves fought for their owners, and many died for them. In 1810, there were 11,837 black people (29.3 percent of the total population) in Buenos Aires, and 77% of them were slaves. In 1822, there were 13,685 black people in the capital (24.7% of the total population), but only 6,611 (48.3%) of them were slaves. Juan Manuel de Rosas, the president of Argentina from 1829 to 1832 and a member of the Federal Party, was himself a slave owner. He tolerated the black population but did nothing to improve its conditions. The Unitarians (Rosas's opponents) wanted to exterminate any blacks or "gauchos" and any indigenous Indians left in the country. Two cholera epidemics in 1871 and 1873 wiped out many of the blacks who lived on the outskirts of Buenos Aires. Those who survived carried their traditional dances and music into their places of congregation, their visible cultural expression in a city of white people. They danced *candombe* (the generic term for all black dances that evoke the rituals of their race). The Bantu lexeme *Kandombe* derives from *kulomba* and means "to pray" or "to ask for a god's intervention." These slaves transported to Buenos Aires found themselves in a country where they were treated in a brutal way by the "civilized" white Argentinians and Spanish or English immigrants. The only way they could express their sorrow, nostalgia, and pain was by playing their drum tango. By extension, their dances were called "tangos." Black people lived in slums that were not accessible to the general population, where they celebrated their festivities preserving the memories from their homeland.

In the 1840s, Argentine President Domingo Sarmiento and a well-known writer, Juan Alberdi, initiated Argentina's integration with the most powerful nations of the world through the cultivation of European-ness and white-ness. Sarmiento's purpose was to create "a Europe in America," and he would not countenance the concept of "mixing" races. In his famous work *Facundo, civilización y barbarie* (Facundo, civilization and barbarism), he claimed that white immigrants from Europe, with their work ethic and modern lifestyles, were better equipped to build a new Argentina than the *mestizo* native population, whom he considered uncivilized, lazy, and close-minded. However, Sarmiento's efforts regarding Argentina's education system were unquestionably positive, as he invested in building public schools for boys and girls. At the same time, Argentinean *gauchos* (nomadic cattle-raising cowboys) who lived in Pampas began arriving in the port city of Buenos Aires, where society witnessed its transformation from a colonial village into an urban cosmopolitan city in a short time. Gauchos arrived in Buenos Aires looking for employment with their guitars, their milongas, their songs, and their knives (which were used either for cattle slaughter or in self-defense in the rural areas). They brought their traditions but not their horses into the urban spaces of Buenos

Aires. They played guitar pieces expressing their sorrow for the lost freedom formerly experienced in the vast Pampas.

At the beginning of the 19th century, massive waves of immigrants from Italy, Spain, and Eastern Europe came to Buenos Aires in search of better fortune than they had had in their homelands. These people were white but poor. Many of them were peasants from rural environments in their countries; others were from the fringes of society (prostitutes, pimps, knife fighters). Not welcomed in Argentina, these people together expressed their sadness and nostalgia for the "paradise lost" by performing their own dances: *polkas*, *mazurkas*, the *tanguillo* (a type of flamenco dance from southern Spain), Cuban *habanera*, and African *candombe*, and combining elements from of all these dances and performing them in their own unique way. In consequence they created a new dance, *tango*, while also creating a new identity for themselves in their new homeland. They danced in the urban spaces of the streets, dance halls, brothels, cabarets, and bars, the only public places available to them. These newcomers were forced to live on the "border" sites of Buenos Aires, where they began to create a new blend of trans-cultures through their traditions, values, languages, and religions.

Tango dance was disapproved of in the circles of the Argentina middle and upper classes of the first part of the 20th century. However, in the second decade of the 20th century, tango was introduced by professional dancers to the nightclubs of Buenos Aires where it took on a life on its own. New instruments were introduced—mandolins and accordions complementing flutes, violins, and harps. In the dance academies of Paris, tango was further transformed into a more "refined" art form, and between the two World Wars, it was enthusiastically accepted by all classes of society in Europe.

Eduardo Arolas, also known as "the Tiger of the Bandoneon," incorporated the bandoneon, an accordion-like German instrument, into playing tango music and created a deep melancholy sound that struck a chord with the sentimental sorrows of the immigrants (including unemployment, family dissolution, alcoholism, prostitution, and loneliness). As the main objective was to produce music for dancing, the style of playing was oral, in the sense that the musicians improvised all the time without performing real solos. Tango was born out of incurable sorrow. Enrique Santos Discépolo, the greatest composer of tangos, defined the tango as a melancholy thought that is danced.

Even though tango was created in Buenos Aires, only after it had achieved success in the main capitals of the world after 1914 did it gain full popularity in its birthplace. Argentinean dances were dependent on more "civilized" judgments. The acceptance of the tango in Europe positively influenced the class and moral identification of the tango in Buenos Aires. It also produced distinctions among men and women of the various social classes and new distinctions in the quality of the tango itself. Now, the "high-class" prostitutes were sought after by talented tango dancers, as they would dance in a softer and more refined way than the "lower-class" prostitutes who danced in smoky, dirty, uninviting bars and did not display the subtleties of their rivals. The European acceptance of the dance and music also caused a stir among, and influenced, the Argentinean elite that had so far enjoyed economic, political, and moral superiority. Foreign recognition gave tango a status as part of the national identity. The "high class" and social elite in Argentina conformed to "the mirror phenomenon" of the tango in Europe, as the controversy unleashed by the tango was one of the most remarkable issues ever discussed in worldly circles. It was spoken about in London, New York, Paris, Berlin, and Rome all at the same time. Monarchs proscribed the tango, priests disapproved of it, and the populace generally loved it; in the midst of censure, tea-tangos, tango suppers, and tango contests were organized everywhere. The tango debate, rampant among major world powers, was reflected in equally lively controversy among Argentinians. Enrique Rodriquez Larreta, Argentinean writer and foreign minister in Paris, and other intellectuals reflected on the humble and "trashy" origins of the tango dance in Argentina. They wanted to enlighten the "international elite," and especially "respectable ladies" about the pornographic spectacle that they were performing.

Tango became symbolic of the identity of an inferior class of Argentinians, and as it was twisted through the projection of the "popular" image of the national culture it became representative of an image that the Argentinean upper social class wanted to display. The "cultures" of the "inferior people" had become a source of enjoyment and pleasure for others. According to the Argentinean elite, the lower class of the people should appreciate, and be content with, being the source of "enjoyment" for the nobles of the civilized class. Internal struggles for national representation among the colonized also involved the Catholic Church, which voiced its strong opposition to tango, seeing it as the worst of modern dances. The sexual poses of the dancers were indecent in the eyes of Argentinean clergy. Only the identity of liberals was not threatened. They were frequent visitors to the brothels that often were protected by the patronage of affluent politicians. They also contributed to the promotion of the tango in Paris through frequent trips abroad.

In the 1920s, after the international fame of the tango had been well established, the Argentinean national elite finally came to terms with the existence of the popular class in Buenos Aires. Carlos Gardel and José Razzano had become the most popular duo on the Argentinean tango stage. Gardel was soon the most popular singer in Latin America, singing tangos in his velvety baritone. Tango also lent its name to many commercial products, from perfume to silk blouses and corsets. Paris was swept by a tango craze by 1923, where the popular *orquéstra típica*, including Francisco Canaro, Osvaldo Fresedo, and the Pizarro brothers, performed on stage in their national "gaucho costumes."

In the United States, the spectacle of tango was linked to the vision of the "Latin lover" played by Rudolph Valentino in *The Four Horsemen of the Apocalypse* (1921) and *Blood and Sand* (1923). Thanks to tango, the Argentinean lower classes ended up representing the nation in spite of the strong reaction from the elite. Marginalized people, through tango performances, became powerful enough to represent the nation. Tango, with its sensual primitiveness, passion, colors, and energy, became associated fully with Argentina's identity, and yet the uncivilized connotations had prevailed.

However, the tango could also be seen as the expression of male power, just like the power of the "superior" Argentinean "civilized" class. The tango dance is a silent performance; the interaction is limited to intense physical proximity. In the dance, silent listening, emotions, and nostalgia prevail. There is a certain vulnerability in dancing tango by "macho" men who begin to feel a great capacity to love and protect their partner, and who go back in time to their childhood ideals and childhood dreams. In tango, women also achieve a certain level of equality with their "vulnerable" partners on the dance floor. At times they are fragile, at times strong, but always searching for unrequited love. This perceived equality of partners on the dance floor mirrors the reluctant acceptance of the tango by the "superior" social class in Argentina, as the "inferior class" of poor, urban Argentinians was given some recognition.

The tango story was immortalized in film by Bernardo Bertolucci's *Last Tango in Paris* (1972) with Marlon Brando and Maria Schneider; and Patrice Leconte's *Tango* film (1993). *The Tango Lesson* (1997), by Sally Potter, an experimental British film director, explores the dynamics of power between man and woman on the dance floor. Tango also opened the door to serious musicians such as "avant-garde" composer Astor Piazzolla (1921–1992), who created new, distinctive music that does not have much in common with traditional tango, in style, rhyme, or rhythm. It is a blend of jazz and classical music based on the African and European roots of tango.

The story of tango is one of an exiled, disenfranchised people in search of an identity, recognition, and dignity. Today tango dance and music have reached the status of "global" music and "global" dance.

Anna Hamling

See also: Calypso; Carnival, Music of; Cumbia; Marimba; Merengue; Piazzolla, Astor

Further Reading

Castro, Donald S. 1990. "The Soul of the People: The Tango as a Source for Argentine Social History." *Studies in Latin American Popular Culture* 9, 279–295.

Cooper, Artemis, Maria Susana Azzi, Richard Martin, Simon Collier, and Ken Haas. 1997. *Tango! The Dance, the Song, the Story*. London: Thames & Hudson.

Ferrer, Horacio. 1996. *The Golden Age of Tango: An Illustrated Compendium of its History*. Buenos Aires: Argentina Department of Culture and the National Academy of Tango.

Salmon, R. O. 1977. "Tango: Its Origin and Meaning." *Journal of Popular Culture* 10, 859–866.

Taqsīm

The element of *taqsīm* (pl., *taqāsīm*) in Arab instrumental music (with *Mawwāl* the vocal equivalent) reflects the Arab aesthetic and illustrates essential differences between Eastern and Western compositional and performance practices, and even audience etiquette. In a concert of Western classical music, musicians perform one or more works that have been precomposed and notated on sheet music, which they follow without deviation during the concert. The audience, sitting silently, refrains from applause until the conclusion of the music. In contrast, musicians in the traditional conductor-less *takht* ensemble, comprised of stringed and percussive instruments along with the *nāy*, an indigenous wind instrument, may or may not use sheet music, having learned the classical and folk repertoire via oral transmission from master teachers in the Arab world and diaspora. An Arab audience—while listening as intently as a Western one—is primed for the highlight of the performance, the taqāsīm that one or more musicians will each play in turn as a soloist while the percussionist (usually playing a *riqq* [tambourine]) quietly maintains a rhythmic ostinato. The solo musician may embellish notes and melodies, repeat musical phrases, or even import whole sections of other compositions into the taqsīm. As each is concluded, members of the audience enthusiastically applaud and call out their approval with phrases such as "ya salam" or "Allah!"

Taqāsīm could be considered analogous to the improvisations of a jazz performance, in which the virtuosity of individual musicians is demonstrated. Indeed, A. J. Racy quotes the writings of early 20th-century Syrian composer Tawfīq al-Sabbāgh, who considered the taqsīm "the litmus test of performers' talent, a medium through which their ability and scope of imagination can be ascertained" (Racy, 2003, p. 95). In both jazz and Arab music, no two performances of a composition are ever the same, because audience reaction generates a variety of musician responses during improvisation. This dynamic—the circular process of mutual responsiveness between performer and audience—inspires the experience of *tarab* which occurs during the performance of Arab music. "Tarab" can be translated as "enchantment" or "ecstasy"; al-Sabbāgh refers to the "direct correlations between ecstatic feeling and improvisatory freedom" (Racy, 2003, p. 95). Despite this freedom, certain protocols are generally observed during taqāsīm, such as the technique of modulating out of and back into a *maqām* (mode) and ending the taqsīm with a final cadence, or *qaflah*, that is musically satisfying and not jarring to the ear. Habib Hassan Touma singles out Iraqi *'ūd* player Munir Bashir for the "mystical expressive content" of his taqāsīm, which would often exceed the customary 10-minute limit by half an hour or more (Touma, 1996, p. 147).

Hicham Chami

See also: Arab Classical Music; Bashir Brothers (Munir and Jamil)

Further Reading

Nettl, Bruno, and Roland Riddle. 1973. "Taqsīm Nahawand: A Study of Sixteen Performances by Jihad Racy." *Yearbook of the International Folk Music Council* 5, 11–50.

Racy, A. J. 2003. *Making Music in the Arab World: The Culture and Artistry of Tarab.* Cambridge: Cambridge University Press.

Touma, Habib Hassan. 1996. *The Music of the Arabs*, trans. Laurie Schwartz. Portland, OR: Amadeus Press.

Tar

The *tar* is a double-bowled, long-necked, plucked lute, originating in 18th-century Persia, and is shared by many countries near the Caucasus and central Asia, including Armenia, Afghanistan, Georgia, Azerbaijan, and Tajikistan. Its very name means "string" in Persian and it is perhaps the most widely used plucked instrument. Most commonly associated with the *radif*, or traditional practice of Iranian classical music, the tar has also been used in *motrebi*, a popular form of musical entertainment. It has a very similar range to the older *setar*, from which it is descended, but with a greater resonance and richer sound due to its larger chambers and doubled courses of melodic strings.

Originally carved of mulberry wood, the tar has a rounded, hollowed-out body with two interconnected parts in the shape of a figure eight, as well as a long neck and square peg box. Its belly, traditionally covered with stretched lambskin, is now typically covered with a parchment membrane. The tar used to have five strings, until a sixth was added by musician Darvish Khan in the late 19th century. Today, its six metal strings are doubled into three courses of octaves, which overall have a range of two octaves and a fifth: c/c'-g/g'-c/c'. The fingerboard consists of between 25 and 28 movable gut frets which divide each octave into 15 intervals. The tuning, however, is often changed according to the *dastgah*, or mode, that is being played. The first two courses of strings are made of steel and provide the main melody; the third is made of copper and provides an accompanying drone. The tar's strings are plucked with a wax-coated, brass plectrum, which allows for very rapid and smooth, virtuosic plucking.

Another form of the tar, known as the Caucasian, or the Azerbaijani, tar also exists. The Caucasian tar is usually smaller, with a shallower, less curved body and a thicker membrane. It also has a wider neck and bridge with 22 gut frets. The modern version has five or six strings which are tuned slightly differently than the Iranian tar (g'-c"-c-g-c'), and has fret intervals that differ as well. The strings are usually plucked with a plectrum made of a hard, synthetic material such as Bakelite, which contributes to the harder sound of the instrument. As the strings are plucked, the performer simultaneously shakes the tar up and down, creating a resonating, vibrato-like sound.

Famous performers Mirza Hossein Qoli (1854–1916) and Ali Akbar Shahnazi (1897–1985) made the instrument popular in the late 19th and early 20th centuries. Equally respected tar master musicians include Mirza Abdollah Farahani (1943–1918), Ali-Naqi Vazeri (1887–1979), and Morteza Neydavoud (1900–1990). Renowned contemporary musicians include Mohammad Reza Lotfi, Dariush Talai, and Dariush Pirniakan. Also revered are the great tar makers, such as Armenian tar master Hovanes Abkarian (1876–1932), also known as Yahya Khan, the most famous tar maker in Iran. Well-known contemporary tar makers today include Ostad Farahmand, Ostad Pourya, and Ramin Jazayeri.

Theresa Steward

See also: Dastgah; Iranian Classical Music

Further Reading

During, Jean, Zia Mirabdolbaghi, and Dariush Safvat. 1991. *The Art of Persian Music*. Waldorf, MD: Mage Publishers.

Miller, Lloyd. 1999. *Music and Song in Persia: The Art of Avaz*. Salt Lake City: University of Utah Press.

Tassa Drumming

Tassa is an Indo-Caribbean folk drumming style popular in Trinidad and Tobago, Guyana, and their diaspora in North America. Most often, the ensemble is simply called *tassa*, this referring both to the individual kettledrums that play the most striking rhythms in the repertoire and to the ensemble itself. In Trinidad and Tobago in particular, tassa is an important symbol of Indo-Trinidadian identity, invariably played to accompany Hindu weddings and the Shi'a Muslim Muharram observance. Despite tassa's association with religious ceremonies, neither the instruments themselves nor the music they play are necessarily sacred. Tassa is commonly played for many secular celebrations, as well as Trinidadian cultural and national events such as Carnival. (Though the information contained here provides general detail about tassa performance throughout the Caribbean, it is most pertinent to tassa in Trinidad and Tobago.)

The term "tassa" derives from the word *tasha*, the Indian name for the drum, which in turn derives from a Persian root word meaning "bowl" or "cup." In North India, tasha accompanied Muharram processions from at least the early 1800s, though its use history probably dates to earlier times. By the mid-19th century, contemporary reports confirm that tasha was played in an ensemble together with the double-headed membranophone *dhol* and hand cymbals *jhanjh*. The music of this so-called *dhol tasha* ensemble was martial in character, owing to its association with the military, and appropriate for accompanying a variety of sacred and secular events, especially those involving processions through the streets as is done during Indian weddings, the Muharram observance, and a variety of Hindu festivals.

From 1834 to 1921, laborers primarily from the northeastern Bhojpuri-speaking region of India were recruited to work in British, French, and Dutch colonies in the Caribbean, Africa, Asia, and Oceania. This system of contract labor resulted in the export of Bhojpuri culture, including dhol tasha, to many places across the world. In the West Indies, the most prominent dhol tasha tradition is tassa drumming in Trinidad and Tobago.

In Trinidad, dhol tasha developed into the present-day tassa ensemble while maintaining its function as an accompaniment for many Hindu and Muslim religious rites. In addition, there also developed an expectation for virtuosic performance that in turn influenced the emergence of new repertoire first drawn from other Indian and Indian-Caribbean rhythmic elements and later distilled from popular song genres such as calypso, soca, and chutney. Drummers generally recognize three categories of tassa repertoire: folk and classical hands, breakaway hands, and Hosay hands. In Indo-Caribbean drumming terminology, a *hand* is essentially a unique composite ostinato that identifies a particular composition. In performance, drummers usually play a suite of hands in succession, often following a relatively standardized progression from one to another according to the context of performance.

Folk and classical hands comprise a category of esoteric repertoire built from rhythmic elements of other Indian-derived musical styles. The folk hand *nagara* approximates typical rhythms played on the north Indian *nagara* drum pair. The classical tassa hand *chaubola* refers to a certain four-beat meter used in Indian *nautaki* theater, a genre once popular in Trinidad. The classical hand *thumri* is drawn from rhythms typically played on *dholak*, a small double-headed drum used to accompany a particular Indian-Caribbean genre of local classical singing also called thumri. In all cases—there are perhaps 15 or more commonly played hands in this category—folk and classical hands are regarded as old and recognized as borrowings from other genres. The function of folk and classical hands varies. Mostly, they are used as introductory hands in a drumming suite, for entertainment during tedious parts of a wedding ceremony, or (in increasingly rare instances) to accompany singing, as in the improvisatory *biraha* style usually accompanied by nagara hand.

In Trinidadian English, the term "breakaway" refers to vigorous dancing. Therefore, breakaway hands are those typically used to accompany an audience of dancers at specific points in the three-day Hindu wedding ceremony. Breakaway hands are also appropriate to play for parties or cultural celebrations. The most common breakaway hands are derived either from generic dholak patterns or from popular song genres. Tassa hands called *calypso* and *chutney*, for example, feature rhythmic patterns distilled from Trinidadian pop music genres by the same names. Some folk and classical hands can also be breakaway hands. For example, nagara and a few others are commonly played for dancing, thereby demonstrating the fluid boundaries between these two categories.

Folk, classical, and breakaway hands can be combined into a larger category of wedding-appropriate hands. By contrast, *Hosay* hands are inappropriate for weddings. As passed down from the Persian-influenced practice of Shi'a Islam in north India, "Hosay" in Trinidad is a time of mourning in remembrance of the martyrdom of Hussein and Hassan, the Prophet Mohammed's grandsons who were killed by political rivals who usurped power over the Islamic caliphate in the late 600s CE. Hosay hands range from slow and mournful to fast and frenetic as hands progress from one to another to accentuate points in the narrative of Hussein's death.

Tassa repertoire calls for four parts played on at least four instruments: one lead tassa called the *cutter*," one accompanying tassa called the *foulé*, one bass, and one *jhal*. In Hosay performances, there is always one cutter (though this role may be passed among a number of capable players), but there are usually many players on each of the other parts. For weddings, parties, competitions, and other contexts, the ensemble usually consists of only one player on each part.

The bass, jhal, and foulé work together to create a composite ostinato for each hand. The cutter is the musical leader of the ensemble, playing *taals*, specific patterns that signal the band to start, stop, or move between sections of music. Moreover, the cutter improvises a near-constant solo throughout the performance, generating musical interest through innovative, varied, and unexpected "cuts," or rhythmic improvisations.

The earliest tassas in Trinidad likely resembled the relatively flat, metal-shelled tashas of North India. By the early 20th century, Trinidadian tassa shifted toward deeper, more resonant shells fashioned from large clay pots covered with goatskin. Clay drums, however, have all but disappeared from regular use, as drummers regard them as heavy, fragile, and generally inconvenient to maintain compared to more recent designs. Today, pressurized gas canisters, especially Freon and propane tanks, are the most common materials for tassa shells. In performance, the tassa is suspended from the player's neck by a long piece of cloth, so the drum hangs about the groin, and played with a pair of thin and very flexible sticks called *chopes* that are traditionally made from supple cane or reed, but today are more commonly constructed from thin fiberglass rods.

Tassa drummers playing hands in Port of Spain, Trinidad and Tobago. Tassa drumming is rooted in the folk traditions of northern India. (Sean Drakes/LatinContent via Getty Images)

To play tassa, each chope strikes the head with a rimshot-style technique executed with a downward twisting wrist motion. Drummers can achieve tonal variation on tassa by placing their strokes closer to the edge of the drumhead for a thinner, slightly higher pitched tone and in the center for a fuller, slightly lower pitched tone. The sound most closely associated with tassa is the lightning-fast buzz roll played by allowing the tip of each chope to bounce multiple times on the drumhead per stroke.

The Trinidadian dhol, more commonly called "bass," is a double-headed cylindrical membranophone. Shells are made from dense woods such as mango or cedar that are preferred for their strength and resonance and covered with goatskin heads. In performance, the bass is strung around the player's neck with a strip of cloth connected to the drum at either end. Drummers position the bass at a diagonal to their bodies so that the lower-pitched "boom side," played with a stick called a *dankar*, drops lower than the higher pitched *tan* side, which is played with the other bare hand. The bass can vary greatly in diameter, though most are 15 or 16 inches with the diameter of both ends consistent throughout the length of the shell.

The cymbals of the jhal set are most often constructed from solid brass sheets, cut and hammered to shape and about one centimeter in thickness. Unlike the conical cymbals used for the Western-style drum set, jhal are flat, with only a small crown in the middle through which a hole is drilled for the addition of handles. The handles are made from cylindrical pieces of wood or plastic pipe a few inches in length and no more than one inch in diameter. They are attached to the cymbals by cloth or sinew wrapped around the handle, passed through the hole, and tied in a knot on the other side. The jhal are played by combining crash and sizzle techniques.

Tassa drumming has become an important symbol of identity for Indo-Trinidadians. With its roots in India and a Caribbean developmental trajectory, tassa reflects the multiple locality of the Indo-Trinidadian community that regards India as a place of origin and the Caribbean as home. Tassa bears a strong affinity with North Indian folk music styles, though it has been nurtured by a distinctly Indo-Caribbean musical system. Yet, this musical system is a flexible one, encouraging adaptations, innovations, and invention, evidenced by changes in instrument construction, increasingly virtuosic repertoire, and consequent modification of performance practice. Where conventional wisdom would suggest that tassa is a creolized music, one reliant on a fusion of African- and Indian-Trinidadian musical ideas, it is striking that tassa to the contrary is largely conceived along the lines of specific Indian-Trinidadian notions of musical aesthetics and that tassa performance is largely the domain of Indian-Trinidadian musicians and audiences.

Christopher L. Ballengee

See also: Calypso; Soca; Steelpan; Tamboo Bamboo

Further Reading

Ballengee, Christopher L. 2013. "From Indian to Indo-Creole: Tassa Drumming, Creolization, and Indo-Caribbean Nationalism in Trinidad and Tobago." PhD diss., University of Florida.

Korom, Frank. 2003. *Hosay Trinidad.* Philadelphia: University of Pennsylvania Press.

Manuel, Peter. 2015. *Tales, Tunes, and Tassa Drums: Retention and Invention in Indo-Caribbean Music.* Urbana: University of Illinois Press.

Tejano Music

Tejano music has its roots in European, Mexican, and Northern American musical influences. Spanish settlers, who made their homes in the area of the Rio Grande Valley (south Texas) during the 17th century, were influenced by the culture of the Mexicans living in the states of Tamalipas and Nuevo Leon in Mexico. In the mid-19th century, a wave of Czech, German, and Polish immigrants to both southern Texas and northern Mexico brought their own cultures with them, including their dances such as the polka and waltz. They also introduced a new musical instrument, the accordion.

During the Mexican Revolution (1910–1917), many Europeans left Mexico and settled in southern Texas, bringing with them their stories (which had been exposed to Mexican influences), legends, their own music, and other aspects of their native cultures that all merged with the local Tejano culture. New immigrants were well received by the existing agricultural communities whose vernacular music comprised of drums, guitars, and flutes.

One of the most popular musical traditions among the Mexicans and Mexican-Americans was the accordion-based ensemble known as *conjunto* and as *música norteña* (northern music) outside of Texas. It became popular in the 1920s among working-class Texas-Mexicans and North Mexicans, serving as a symbol of their own identity against other types of music. Narciso Martínez (1911–1992), a Mexican living in Texas who became known as the "father of conjunto music," defined its identity by the use of the accordion, drum, and the *bajo sexto*, a 12-string bass guitar from Spain. Tejano music retained musical traditions from the European polkas and waltzes, as well as the German tradition of circle dancing. In modern conjunto, the acoustic bass is replaced by an electric bass guitar.

Well-known conjunto performers in the 1920s and 1930s, the accordionists Pedro Ayala and Narciso Martínez were succeeded by Tony de la Rosa and Leonardo ("Flaco") Jiménez in conjunto's "golden age" of the late 1940s and early 1950s. In the 1930s, a second major style emerged in Tejano music: *banda* or *orquesta*, based around trumpet and saxophone. Tejano bands, such as La Orquesta de Beto Villa, incorporated Mexican folk music and conjunto traditions. By the mid-1950s, band leader and vocalist Isidro López had made folk music a staple of banda; however, his addition of the traditional bajo sexto and the accordion to the orchestral lineup was reversed by Oscar Martínez, whose band featured a brass-oriented instrumentation. His template for banda (two trumpets, alto and tenor saxophones, guitar, bass, and drums) remained very popular into the 1970s.

Tejano's third musical style, *grupo*, rejected the horns, saxophones, and the accordion even as it embraced a largely conjunto repertoire. Tejano grupo originated in the 1960s and featured keyboard instruments and synthesizers as its foundation.

During the 1960s, a new subgenre of Mexican American music, *la onda chicana* (the Chicano wave) combined a variety of musical styles, such as Mexican folk music, blues, rock and roll, and country, with many characteristics of conjunto music, including the accordion and lyrics in Spanish. La onda chicana was also part of the political and social movement known as the *Chicano* movement of the 1960s and 1970s. Young and well-educated Mexican Americans wanted to preserve the older Mexican traditions and also to take a more active role in fighting for the legal, economic, and political rights of Latinos in the United States.

Two musicians who best represent the biculturalism of the 1960s and 1970s were Sunny Ozuna and Joe Hernandez. Born into poverty, as were many of the post-World War II generation, they benefited from access to public education. Having listened to the idols of their parents' generation, such as Beto Villa, Isidro Lopez, and Valerio Longoria, they were also drawn to the emerging rock and roll. They were instrumental in creating the group Little Joe and the Latinaires, a band that drew on the older orquestra tradition of using many instruments and covering Mexican folk music and mainstream pop. In the 1970s, Roberto Pulido was instrumental in developing *progressive conjunto* by expanding the traditional four-piece, accordion-based conjunto ensemble to saxophones and other *pitos* (horns), and bringing more country and ballads into conjunto music, which reflected the growing Mexican American cultural pride in the last half of the 20th century. All three forms of traditional tejano have continued their popularity into the 21st century.

In the late 1970s and early 1980s, Brownsville native Joe Lopez y El Grupo Mazz introduced the keyboard sound to Tejano. This was influenced by the disco sound of the time period. The *grupos tejanos* formed in the 1980s were influenced by pop and rock and usually replaced the traditional accordion with the keyboard accordion and electric guitars. By the early 1980s, all these earlier influences—namely, orquestra, conjunto, la onda chicana, progressive conjunto, Chicano country and grupo tejano—gave rise to a new style called *Tejano*. Ruben Ramos or El Gato Negro (Black Cat), and Laura Canales were the pioneers of Tejano music. Tejano is the most difficult subgenre of *musica tejana* to define because it fuses so many different styles and includes a variety of different instruments, such as the electric guitar, bass, and drum sets.

The grupos tejanos incorporate pop, blues, jazz, and rock, together with other mainstream influences, and often include very complex dance routines and other stage effects as part of their performances. They also include the more traditional conjunto format such as polkas, country music, and accordions. These are the most popular among the working class of Mexican Americans as they try to preserve older Mexican cultural traditions.

Referred to as the "Queen of Tejano music," Mexican American singer Selena was one of the most successful Latin artists of the 1990s before her tragic death in 1995. (Arlene Richie/Media Sources/The LIFE Images Collection/Getty Images)

Perhaps the most famous grupo tejano performer, Selena, was an international celebrity before she was murdered in 1995. Selena (Selena Quintanilla) is a historic figure in the Tejano music industry. She paved the way for future tejano artists, using a mixture of the English and Spanish languages, hip-hop beats, and female fashion. Born in Texas in 1971, she began singing with her family band, the Dinos, and was taught and guided by her father, Abraham Quintanilla. With charismatic personality, strong stage presence, and a powerful voice, she quickly became famous by including mariachi, ballads, pop, and rock into her Tejano repertoire. She was comfortable balancing the Mexican and American parts of her identity and learned Spanish to reach her Spanish-speaking audience. Selena won Best Female Vocalist in 1987 at the Tejano Music Awards and a Grammy Award for her album *Selena Live* in 1992. Her 1994 CD *Amor Prohibido* (Forbidden love) was her first gold album, selling more than 500,000 copies. At the peak of her career, she was shot on March 31, 1995, by Yolanda Saldivar, the former president of her fan club, who had had a number of financial disagreements with her. After her death, Selena became known as the "Queen of Tejano music."

In the 21st century, tejano music continues to be diverse and dynamic. Artists such as Alejandro Escovedo, the Sisters Morales, Patricia Vonne, Rosie Flores, Joel Guzman, South Park Mexican, Grupo Fantasma, Vallejo, and many others cover a wide range of styles. Still rooted in an older, Mexican folk music, tejano music has absorbed a wide variety of other ethnic influences. Some critics consider it simply a cross between American country and mariachi music, others say it is a polka in Spanish, but the truth is that tejano sound is complex, reflecting influences of the ethnic melting pot of cultures that have lived in Texas, and the unique history of Texan Mexican society.

Anna Hamling

See also: Conjunto; Conjunto (Norteños); Mariachi; Mexican Regional Music

Further Reading

Paredes, Americo. 1995. *A Texas-Mexican Cancionero: Folksongs of the Lower Border.* Austin: University of Texas Press.

Pena, Manuel. 1985. *The Texas-Mexican Conjunto: History of a Working-Class Music.* Austin: University of Texas Press.

Vargas, D. 2002. "Bidi Bidi Bom Bom: Selena and Tejano Music in the Making of *Tejas*." In Michelle Habell-Pallan and Mary Romero (eds.), *Latino/a Popular Culture*, 117–126. New York: New York University Press.

Thumri

Thumri is a popular light classical form of traditional North Indian or Hindustani vocal music. Composed in dialects of Hindi (mainly Vraj Bhasha and Urdu), and associated with folk songs of Uttar Pradesh and Punjab, thumri songs are romantic and devotional in nature, characterized by lyrical and erotic word play dealing with the Radha-Krishna theme.

Famed for rendering *ragas* or melodic modes such as bhairavi, khamaj, kafi, and pilu, thumri compositions are usually set to *talas* or meters such as kaharva and dipchandi (among others). Thumri, as a highly expressive art form, gives primary importance to the text of the compositions. Concentrating on the emotional meaning conveyed by the words, thumri compositions are typically short, consisting of a *sthai* and one or more *antara* and usually sung in a slow tempo with short *alaps* (improvised melodic ornamentations). A thumri recital, usually consisting of a vocalist accompanied by a *sarangi*, a *tanpura*, and a harmonium, thus creates an immediate and personal impact on the audience, as it renders, in a leisurely manner, the sentiment expressed by the lyrics, meaningfully bringing out the nostalgic tenor of a song through musical embellishments.

Originated in ancient times in Purab, the region to the east of the Ganga and Yamuna Rivers in North India, the modern thumri is believed to have been patronized by Nawab Wajid Ali Shah of Oudh (1847–1856) and flourished in Uttar Pradesh, India. A form of refined, secular entertainment that blended the elements of both Hindu and Muslim cultures, thumri was originally performed by female courtesans for their aristocratic male patrons in the courts and elite gatherings.

Along with Benaras and Lucknow, Calcutta and Hyderabad also developed as important centers of the thumri genre. Sweet, light, and attractive, thumri is often considered to be a feminine form because it has traditionally been associated with female singers, and because its lyrics primarily express feminine emotions. Moreover, though most thumri compositions are penned by men (indeed, even the renowned teachers are mostly men), the narrator and the emotions expressed are typically female.

There are three main performing styles or *gharanas* of thumri: Benaras, Lucknow, and Patiala. Girija Devi, Qadar Piya, Ustaad Bade Ghulam Ali Khan, and Sobha Gurtu are some of the renowned singers of thumri.

Sutapa Chaudhuri

See also: Harmonium; Khayal; Tabla; Tagore, Rabindranath

Further Reading

Broughton, Simon, and Mark Ellingham. 2000. *World Music: Latin and North America, Caribbean, India, Asia and Pacific*, vol. 2. London: Rough Guides.

Kumar, Raj, ed. 2003. *Essays on Indian Music*. New Delhi: Discovery Publishing House.

Manuel, Peter Lamarche. 1989. *Thumri in Historical and Stylistic Perspectives*. New Delhi: Motilal Banarsidass.

Tibetan Buddhist Chant

Depending on the geographic location, institutional setting, and personal training, Tibetan chanting takes on a number of forms. The most basic of such practices involves the musical repetition of short *mantras* (sacred syllables or formulas), such as "Om Mani Padme Hum" or "Om Ah Um," which is done over and over again by many Tibetans during their daily activities. The proper chanting of more extensive recitations requires the study of Buddhist texts, chanting techniques, and liturgy. These experiences are typically acquired during arduous monastic training. Historically, and in the larger Tibetan monasteries, such a pursuit was undertaken by only a minority of Buddhist monks. In a few small colleges, advanced lamas devote themselves to a range of full-blown performance skills with definite aesthetic and spiritual rules. Chanting and many other aspects of Tibetan religious culture were interrupted or completely discontinued in Tibet itself as a consequence of the Chinese occupation of Tibet. The diaspora of Tibetans in 1959 has led to the establishment of new Tibetan Buddhist monasteries in India and the West and to the dissemination of Buddhist ideas and practices, including the chanting of Indo-Tibetan mantras.

The chanting of sacred texts and formulas in Buddhism is a means for monks to awaken or realize the presence of Buddhist deities in their bodies, speech, and minds. Ultimately, Buddhist chanting is considered to play a key role in attaining a level of being comparable to that of the historical Buddha, whose earthly, bodily existence is considered but a temporary shell of an eternal, universal existence. To use the Western term "music" to describe the vocal and instrumental sounds of the Tibetan liturgy may be misleading, as deriving purely sensual pleasure from listening to or making music is not the goal of Tibetan rituals.

Buddhist Beastie Boys

Though he came to Buddhism later in his life, musician and member of the rap band Beastie Boys Adam Yauch was a devout practitioner of the religion and integrated Tibetan chant and spiritualism into several of the band's albums. Perhaps the most notable example is the multi-platinum *Ill Communication* album from 1994, which featured the Buddhist-inspired tracks "Shambala" and "Bodhisattva Vow." The latter prominently features Tibetan chant throughout the song and is vastly different in character from the album's lead track, "Sabotage," which went on to be a song-of-the-year candidate for the year 1994. The album's success inspired Yauch to become more outspoken regarding his spirituality and saw the band promote many pro-Tibet causes during the 1990s.

Two aspects unite most chanting practices inside Tibet (as well as several ones outside Tibet, such as in Japan): one is the cultivation of a guttural voice quality; the other is the use of a very low pitch range. In this way, the spectrum of the human voice, which is always comprised of a fundamental pitch and many higher pitches called *overtones* (or *harmonics*), emphasizes the higher frequency components. It becomes brighter or harsher, sometimes to the point of sounding unlike a human voice. Different systems to classify Tibetan vocal sound mention such elements as the natural voice (*rang ke*) or guttural voice (*dzo ke*), speeded-up (*khan dön*) or slowed-down (*chölogpa*) recitations, a clear articulation (*ta*), or the deliberate transformation of syllables to hide the meaning from the uninitiated (*yang*) (Vandor, 1978, pp. 126–132). However, across the five main traditions within Tibetan Buddhism (Bon, Nyingma, Kagyu, Sakya, and Gelug), these terms may still indicate quite different ways of vocal production. When executed a cappella and in a more melodic way, voices tend to be in unison, that is, following the same pitch and tempo. During communal recitations monks produce a variety of loosely organized pitches simultaneously. The chant leader (*umze*), a function rotating among advanced practitioners, secures a tight structuring of the sequence and tempo of musical events.

Tibetan monks have developed a profound understanding of how the many muscles involved in creating vocal sound can be manipulated to change the voice quality. These modifications effect the perceived sound quality of vowels and pitches, which again influences the processes of the mind. Tibetan chanting thus constitutes an elaborate, practical science of controlling vocal muscles with the aim of gaining deeper insight into the human experience, somewhat parallel to the system of body postures called *yoga* in India. Throughout the centuries, musical techniques, body movements, and rules for ritual attire, dancing, and so on have become codified, partly in ritual books and partly in practices transmitted from master to apprentice.

An unusually homogenous, immersive vocal sound is produced by lamas from Gyütö, a college devoted to higher learning. They create a choral form of overtone singing, a technique in which the natural overtones of the voices are reinforced to such an extent that they can be heard as one or more separate voices. The perceived effect is that one hears a chord comprised of a major third (the fifth or tenth harmonic) even when all monks intone the same fundamental pitch. When heard live, the overtones seem to be floating in the air, independent of the human bodies that give rise to it. This technique of producing clear overtones is combined with a method to produce a rattling fundamental pitch one octave below an already low male voice, or what one could call "undertones" (*subfundamentals* is a term that scholars use). Though guttural pitches with a bright spectrum of overtones are common across the many schools of Tibetan Buddhism, as are very low, "normal" pitches, the lowered, rattling fundamental and clear overtones can rarely be heard.

The geographical origins of Tibetan Buddhist chant are the Tibetan Autonomous Republic and adjacent provinces within the People's Republic of China. Situated around the Earth's highest peaks, and extending to vast grasslands where nomads have been roaming with their flocks for centuries, Tibet came to absorb Buddhist influences from its southern neighbor, India, from the eighth century onward. Buddhism itself goes back to the teachings of the historical Buddha, the son of a Sakya king known by the name of Gautama who lived around the fifth century BCE.

For centuries after the death of the historical Buddha, chanting, reciting, and other oral transmissions of texts helped to preserve the teachings and events of his life. These formalized and ritualized vocal practices form the backbone of all Buddhist chant, and served as a mnemotechnical device. An immense corpus of texts, called *sutras*, preserves and codifies the Buddha's teachings according to the interpretations of early Buddhist teacher-scholars. Even though these sutras eventually were written down, the accompanying oral tradition of reciting or chanting them with specific vocal techniques, learned from an established master, continues today.

The events in Tibet during the 1950s marked a dramatic shift in all aspects of Tibetan culture. In 1959, many monks, including the spiritual leader of Tibet, fled the country and re-established monasteries in the homeland of the historical Buddha. During the Cultural Revolution in China (1966–1976), many monks were persecuted and monasteries were destroyed. Only several years after the cultural reforms were abolished did a formerly large monastery such as Drepung receive official permission to reintroduce chanting practices and train students, and even then only under strict rules (Goldstein, 1998, pp. 31–46). Nowadays, the largest concentrations of Tibetan monks pursuing the full scope of Buddhist performing and ritual activities reside in and around Dharamsala (northern India) and Mundgod (southern India). These relocated monasteries have in turn given rise to further establishments of Tibetan religious centers in the West. The new social and political situations that Tibetan monks find themselves in, whether in China, India, or the United States, profoundly affect their traditions, including its musical aspects. For example, live performances and audio and video recordings of Tibetan rituals produced for world music audiences abroad require adaptation, by cutting down the length of a ritual or by increasing the duration of parts that are more appealing to Western ears. Since the 1980s, successful projects have been launched by Western composers (e.g., Philip Glass) and popular music groups (e.g., the Beastie Boys) to join Buddhist practices with Western art and culture. The fact that both Philip Glass (1937–) and Beastie Boy Adam Yauch (1964–2012) have adopted Tibetan Buddhism as one of their spiritual practices is indicative of the role of music as a conveyor of spiritual ideas and experiences. Thousands of new adherents to Tibetan Buddhism have studied with lamas travelling between their Indian bases and foreign Buddhist centers. Though the emphasis lies on spreading Buddhist doctrine, students learn at least the basics of Buddhist recitation and mantra chanting. However, few if any of the non-Tibetan students to study Tibetan Buddhism have been exposed to the full, rigorous training program that makes every advanced lama a highly skilled vocal and instrumental performer.

Mark C. van Tongeren

See also: Shômyô; Tibetan Singing Bowls; Tuvan Throat Singing

Further Reading

Goldstein, Melvyn. 1998. "The Revival of Monastic Life in Drepung Monastery." In Melvyn Goldstein and Matthew Kapstein (eds.), *Buddhism in Contemporary Tibet: Religious Revival and Cultural Identity*, 15–52. Berkeley: University of California.

The Music of Tibetan Buddhism (Anthology of World Music Series) [3-CD set]. 1999. Commentary by Peter Crossley-Holland. Rounder Records CD 5129/30/31.

Sacred Tibetan Chants from the Great Prayer Festival [CD]. 1991. Performed by 10 Buddhist monks from the Drepung Loseling Monastery; commentary by Glenn H. Mullin and Damdul Namgyal. Music & Arts CD 735.

Smith, Huston, et al. 1967. "On an Unusual Mode of Singing of Certain Tibetan Lamas." *Journal of the Acoustical Society of America* 41, 1262–1264.

van Tongeren, Mark. 2004. *Overtone Singing: Physics and Metaphysics of Harmonics in East and West*. Amsterdam: Fusica.

Vandor, Ivan. 1978. *Die Musik des Tibetischen Buddhismus* [The music of the Tibetan Buddhists], trans. W. Sczepan. Wilhelmshaven, Germany: Heinrichhofen's Verlag.

Tibetan Singing Bowls

Singing bowls of the Himalayas have both ancient and modern traditions, both as music and as meditational tools. In Asia, use of sounding objects, or idiophones, is very ancient. Chinese rulers of the Shang dynasty owned stone chimes (11th–16th centuries BCE) and records describe "ringing stones" made of jade as early as 2000 BCE. Bronze began to be used to make different types of bells, gongs, and drums from around 1600 BCE through the Western Han period (206 BCE–22 CE). Formerly an emblem of royal power and agrarian rites, bronze drums tended to lose their role as aristocratic cultural objects as private ownership of land became the norm.

Archaeological finds in Thailand and Burma suggest that bronze was already in use at the same time, and metal "skull bowls" were known throughout Asia by 1100 BCE. These bowls are struck on the "forehead" by the nasal bone and the point of the "temple" on the edge of the bowl to produce two distinct tones (most commonly, the interval of a major third). Sung harmonics follow a similar pattern, with different overtones being reinforced through resonance created in different cavities in the head, mouth, and throat. Skull bowls are the oldest objects known as "singing bowls," and like Tibetan bowls, they are standing bells, sounding the first three notes of the harmonic series.

Tibetan and Indian Buddhist rituals also employ various forms of skull drums (*damaru*) to evoke the primordial sound. They are made by joining two human skull bones at the apexes in an hourglass shape. These are called *rnga-ch'ung* and *thod-rnga* in Tibet, and the drumheads are either human or snakeskin.

By the sixth century BCE, the Chinese were the most advanced in the creation of metal alloys. In the fifth century, "fountain bowls" with codified shapes and dimensions appear in several court documents; these were designed to be filled with specific amounts of water and to be set vibrating by rubbing the side handles with the hand. Black metal-alloy bowls are still used in Japan and Vietnam as standing temple bells (without clappers), and are used to mark the passage of time and to signal a change of activity.

A variety of metals were transported to Central Asia by shamans (south from China via Mongolia) and early Buddhists (crossing the Himalayas from India to the north). These two forces met in Tibet, where the local practices combined elements of shamanism and animism in the Bön religion. Singing bowls began to be used to signal the beginning and end of meditation.

Around 600 CE, King Namri Srong-tsen (g'Namri Srong-b Tsan) of Tibet married two Buddhist princesses: one, named Dringma Togo, of the Tsepong clan from Nepal, the other from China. Gradually, two new Tibetan movements developed: lamaism, which is essentially Buddhist with strong Bön influences; and the Bön religion, which is now a semi-shamanistic branch of Buddhism. Both branches make extensive use of sound in their rituals and meditations, but the traditional practice of using bowls as instruments has waned in the contemporary Himalayas. Metal bowls are more commonly cast in sand, rather than hand-hammered, and they are more frequently used to collect offerings and serve food than as Tibetan or Nepalese temple instruments.

The making of traditional singing bowls in Tibet and Nepal has been handed down through generations in India, Nepal, and Tibet through verbal teaching within a highly structured family clan or caste system. Today, craftsmen of the Shakyamuni clan in the Kathmandhu Valley of Nepal work to revive ancient techniques for making these bowls. These artisans and those in one village in West Bengal, India, still make healing bowls according to traditional methods, chanting mantras during the construction process.

Oral history tells us that singing bowls came to Tibet from India at the same time Buddhism was introduced to Tibet by the classical Indian guru Padmasambhava in the eighth century CE. In traditional Tibetan practice, Tibetan singing bowls are usually played along with the *tingsha* (two three-inch metal gongs connected by a leather strap), and both are usually replaced in temple services by the *dril bhu* bell and *dorje* (a metal scepter made from two pairs of small ornamental metal ovals, joined by a short shaft).

Tingshas, common in Buddhist, shamanist, and Naxi Dongling traditions, are also usually made of seven metals, but the iron is sometimes replaced by meteorite metal mined north of Shigatse, Tibet. This is the "celestial" metal which gives them a more pearly shine. It is roughly 90% iron, but can include nickel, cobalt, germanium, gallium, gold, silver, tin, and chromium. Tingshas are found among the Tibetan, Mongolian, Naxi, and Han people (and are called *jinang ling*, or small thunderbolt bell, in Chinese). Decorations on tingshas include dragons and the *Ashtamangalas*, or eight symbols of happiness.

Bells (in Sanskrit, *ghanta*; in Tibetan, *dril bhu*) are traditionally made of bronze, combined with precise amounts of silver to create specific sounds. The dorje, which

Tibetan singing bowls are traditionally associated with Buddhism, although they are also used more generally for meditation and relaxation. (Lightpoet/Dreamstime.com)

means "thunderbolt" in Tibetan, is a sacred symbol of wisdom, representing the masculine element; they are traditionally decorated with eight lotus leaves, representing the eight Bodhisattvas. The dril bhu is used to awaken participants in *pujas* (Buddhist prayer services) to the present moment, representing the feminine element, and both objects are used in *mudras* (Buddhist ritual gestures).

Traditional singing bowls are made of a special seven-metal alloy, hand-hammered by at least three people. One person holds the hot metal with blacksmith tongs while the others alternate hammering and chanting. Tibetan bowls are made with more silver and tin, giving them a dull, anthracite luster, whereas Nepalese bowls have a more golden color. Bowls originating in Nepal often have an inscription on the outside in the Devanagari script, indicating the name of the owner. Contemporary bowls range from three to 14 inches in diameter. Each metal represents, or is considered to be aligned with, one of seven heavenly bodies, one of the seven chakras of the body, and a particular tone. The Vedic and Himalayan chakra systems have evolved differently over time.

In the Vedic system, the correspondences are as follows: first chakra (root)—silver—moon—C; second chakra (sacral)—copper—Venus—D; third chakra (solar plexus)—iron—Mars—E; fourth chakra (heart)—gold—Sun—F; fifth chakra (throat)—mercury—Mercury—G; sixth chakra (third eye)—lead—Saturn—A; and seventh chakra (crown)—tin—Jupiter—B.

In the Himalayan system, the correspondences are as follows: first chakra (root)—lead—Saturn—F; second chakra (sacral)—tin—Jupiter—C; third chakra (solar plexus)—iron—Mars—G; fourth chakra (heart)—gold—Sun—D; fifth chakra (throat)—copper—Venus—A; sixth chakra (third eye)—mercury—Mercury—E; and seventh chakra (crown)—silver—moon—B. The Himalayan order of planets corresponds to how fast they appeared to move to an observer on Earth, with the moon as the fastest and Saturn as the slowest, with the sun in the middle. This is an ancient system used by astrologers and alchemists, omitting further planets that were unknown at the time.

Contemporary teachers of Tibetan singing bowl therapy set up multiple bowls in intervals of fifths, starting with F at the root chakra. This results in the series: F, C, G, D, A, E, B (moving from root to crown chakras, according to the Himalayan system). Generally, smaller bowls are used for meditation and larger ones for therapeutic healing. Bowls used primarily for healing are struck, rather than rubbed, as this produces a clearer fundamental tone. Leather, brocade, felt, or velvet mallets are preferred for this approach, and the bowl should be struck with a fluid, upward gesture, rather than tapped. Bowls used primarily for meditation are rubbed, with a wooden or leather stick being drawn in a slow, clockwise direction around the outer rim of the bowl. This brings out more of the natural harmonics of the bowl and is considered a "less clear," but more spiritual, tone.

The mathematical relationship of a perfect fifth (3:2) and the resulting overtones are believed by practitioners of this kind of therapy to "favorably influence the parasympathetic nervous system while modifying the listener's state of consciousness," according to Dr. Harold Moses, director of the Institute of Harmonic Science in Flagstaff, Arizona. However, if one asks a contemporary Tibetan lama holding a singing bowl whether it is true that they are used for psychic, psychological, and physical purposes, most will smile and reply, "Perhaps."

Tibetan musical aesthetics describe temple instrument sounds such as singing (bowls), rustling (conch-shell trumpet), beating (hand drums), thumping (mallet-struck drums), clanging (tingsha), tinkling (dril bhu bell), groaning (shawm), blaring (large upturned *gchang* bells in the Bön religion), thunderclapping (rnga-ch'ung skull drums), complaining, and praying.

Laura Stanfield Prichard

See also: Karnatic Music; Tibetan Buddhist Chant; Tuvan Throat Singing; Wayang Kulit

Further Reading

Jansen, Eva Rudy. 2001. *Singing Bowls: A Practical Handbook of Instruction and Use*. Havelte, Holland: Binkey Kok.

Kaufmann, Walter. 1975. *Tibetan Buddhist Chant*. Bloomington: Indiana University Press.

Shrestha, Surn. 2009. *How to Heal with Singing Bowls: Traditional Tibetan Healing Methods* [with CD]. Boulder, CO: Sentient Publications.

Tin Pan Alley

Tin Pan Alley is a name that became a synonym for the American popular music industry from the late 19th century to the early 20th century; it is also a term used for the style of songs of the period, notable for their memorable melodies, fresh and witty lyrics, and accessibility to the audience. The term originally referred to the area of West 28th Street between Fifth and Sixth Avenues in Manhattan, New

Tin Pan Alley

Beyond its namesake as the music publishing industry in New York from 1880 to approximately 1950, "Tin Pan Alley" is also associated with a specific type of American popular music song form. The Tin Pan Alley form has many semantic names, including song form, AABA form, and 32-bar form. This type of song form is for singing American popular music songs: i.e., those that are intended to be sung along with rather than danced to. In Tin Pan Alley song form, the composition is structured around repetitions of verses, choruses, and a bridge, with each section typically lasting eight measures of four beats each. Scholars estimate that at least 30% of American popular music songs recorded in the past 100 years utilize or are based on Tin Pan Alley song form, making it one of the foundations of American popular song writing.

Tin Pan Alley Song Form:

Verse 1 = **A**
Verse 2 = **A**
Bridge = **B**
Verse 3 = **A**

York City, where many of the publishers, songwriters, and arrangers were based. The origins of the name may refer to the sound made by many cheap pianos played by poorly paid songwriters.

The main target for the market of Tin Pan Alley was the urban, white audience, although ragtime and cakewalk are two of the most important music styles in the first generation. Although it largely adopted the African American music style, few African American composers found jobs there. Nonetheless, Scott Joplin (1867/8–1917), titled "The King of Ragtime," is an exceptional example, and his "Maple Leaf Rag," one of his early hits, became ragtime's first and most influential piece: the first instrumental piece to sell more than 1 million copies. The "Maple Leaf Rag" has been recognized as the archetypal rag, with the right hand playing syncopated rhythms while the left hand provides steady eight-note patterns.

The music of Tin Pan Alley was largely created by musicians of the second generation of U.S. immigrants, especially from Eastern Europe; many of them are Jewish Americans, including Irving Berlin, Ira and George Gershwin, Jerome Kern, Richard Rodgers, Lorenz Hart, and Al Jolson. In fact, more than 50% of the lyricists and composers from the heyday of Tin Pan Alley were Jewish, and about 70% of the songs in this style were created by them (Pessen, 1985, p. 84). Cole Porter is probably the only well-known composer who is not a second-generation immigrants.

The origin of the name of Tin Pan Alley is obscure, but some suggest that it derived from an interchange between a columnist (and part-time composer) Monroe H. Rosenfeld and a music publisher. In 1899, the *New York Herald* hired Rosenfeld to write a series of articles on the booming music business in New York. He visited Harry von Tilzer's office and noticed the tinny sound of the overworked, cheap upright pianos played by song pluggers in publishers' salerooms in the area of West 28th Street between Fifth and Sixth Avenues. He commented, "It sounds like a tin pan," to which von Tilzer responded, "Yes, I guess this is tin pan alley" (Calta, 1976, p. 18). Later Rosenfeld reported, "As prominent as Tin Pan Alley became in the first half of the twentieth century, it was still aborning in the very late nineteenth century and beginning of the twentieth century" (Tawa, 1990, p. x). Gradually, the term "Tin Pan Alley" was widely applied to all of these early publishers who were printing and distributing sheet music in the late 19th and early 20th centuries. Their publications included not only popular music, but also church music, music instruction books, etudes, and classical pieces for use at home and school.

"Song pluggers," or "song demonstrators," are vocalists or piano players who are employed by music stores and song publishers to promote and help sell new sheet music, which is how songs were advertised before quality recordings were widely available. Frank Harding, a Tin Pan Alley music publisher who was active between 1880s and 1920s, was credited with the innovation of this method of selling music. He paid singers to sing his published songs in shops and beer halls to get the songs known and attract customers. Most of the music stores had song pluggers on staff; George Gershwin was one of them for a while. One of the oldest and leading publishers during this era was Marcus Witmark & Sons. The firm of M. Witmark & Sons was established in New York City in 1886 and published works of leading composers at that time, such as Victor Herbert, Sigmund Romberg, and George M. Cohan. In 1898 they started a rental library. In 1925, the Witmark Music Library and the Arthur W. Tams Music Library merged and became the Tams-Witmark Music Library. In 1929, Warner Brothers purchased M. Witmark & Sons and ended this family publishing business (Gomery, 2005, p. 122).

The way the Tin Pan Alley system worked was usually that songwriters came to demonstrate their tunes before publishers. When a tune by an unknown composer was purchased, the publisher would often add the name of a famous established one as co-composer to help promote the song—and also keep a higher percentage of royalties within the firm. Sometimes all rights to the song, including the right to put someone else's name on the sheet music as composer, were purchased outright for a flat fee. Some of the notable Tin Pan Alley songs include "After the Ball" by Charles K. Harris (1892); "Mister Johnson, Turn Me Loose" by Ben Harney (1896); "A Bird in a Gilded Cage" by Harry Von Tilzer (1900); "In the Good Old Summer Time" by Ren Shields and George Evans (1902); "Give My Regards to Broadway" by George M. Cohan (1904); "Let Me Call You Sweetheart" by Beth Slater Whitson and Leo Friedman (1910); "Alexander's Ragtime Band" (1911), "God Bless America" (1918), and "All Alone" (1924) by Irving Berlin; and, of course, "Swanee" by George Gershwin (1919).

A three-act play named *Tin Pan Alley*, written by Hugh Stanislaus Stange and produced by Harry Lang and Henry B. Forbes, was published in 1928. There are a couple films named *Tin Pan Alley*, the most famous of which is probably the 1940 musical film that starred Alice Faye and Betty Grable as vaudeville singers and sisters and John Payne and Jack Oakie as songwriters in the years before World War I. Alfred Newman, the composer for the movie, received the 1940 Best Music

Academy Award. There are also television episodes that introduce works from the actual Tin Pan Alley, Tin Pan Alley today, or draw on its history.

Tin Pan Alley Rag (2009) is an off-Broadway musical based on an imaginary encounter between Irving Berlin and Scott Joplin, two important Tin Pan Alley composers, who probably never had a chance to meet each other in reality. The play is set in New York City in 1915, the golden era of Tin Pan Alley. This imaginary encounter happens when Joplin tries to sell his opera, *Treemonisha*, to Berlin and his partner Snyder. Written by Mark Saltzman, directed by Stafford Arima, and produced by The Roundabout Theatre Company, the play adapts songs of Joplin and Berlin, which creates an interesting combination of these two major composers of the era. Material used includes Berlin's "I Love a Piano," "Play a Simple Melody," and "Alexander's Ragtime Band" and Joplin's "Maple Leaf Rag," "The Entertainer," and more.

Chloe Hsun Lin

See also: Cohan, George M.; Joplin, Scott; Musicals

Further Reading

Calta, Louis. 1976. "Tin Pan Alley (Remember?) Is Celebrated." *New York Times*, July 27, p. 18.

Gomery, Douglas. 2005. *The Coming of Sound*. New York: Routledge.

Kantor, Michael, dir. 2004. *Broadway: The American Musical* [DVD]. Hollywood, CA: PBS Home Video.

Pessen, Edward. 1985. "The Great Songwriters of Tin Pan Alley's Golden Age: A Social, Occupational, and Aesthetic Inquiry." *American Music* 3(2) (Summer), 180–197.

Tawa, Nicholas E. 1990. *The Way to Tin Pan Alley: American Popular Song, 1866–1910*. New York: Schirmer Reference.

Tin/Pennywhistle

The tin whistle, also called the Scottish penny whistle, Irish whistle, flageolet, and *feadóg stáin*, is a simple, six-holed duct flute, usually of brass, tin, or plastic. It is a modern version of the Baroque flageolet, itself a simple variant of the recorder. It has been widely used in street music since the late 19th century and remains common in pubs today, especially in Ireland.

Vincent Megaw first applied the term "penny whistle" to all of the duct flutes of antiquity, irrespective of size or the number of finger holes. In the third through 12th centuries, Britons and Norman were playing bone flutes, and Irish Brehon law mentions flutes (although only harpists had noble standing). The 17th-century French flageolet was a whistle with a fipple headpiece (common to the modern penny whistle), and such instruments are linked to the development of later recorders and whistles.

The widely dispersed 19th-century "Clarke Flageolet" was a modern factory-made whistle of tin or brass with a six-hole diatonic system. It was produced from 1840 to 1882 in Manchester and New Moston, England. Robert Clarke's first whistle, the Meg, was pitched in high A and was later made in other keys suitable for Victorian parlor music. Clarke's whistles sold for a penny for more than thirty years, possibly inspiring the nickname "penny whistle." By the late 19th century, some flute manufacturers, such as Barnett Samuel and Joseph Wallis, also sold whistles. These had a cylindrical brass tube (contrasting with Clarke's slightly flattened tube), and a fipple plug made of lead.

Although whistles have most often been produced in higher pitches, Boston's Museum of Fine Arts owns a 19th-century low whistle from the famous Galpin collection. During the 1960s revival of traditional Irish music, the low whistle was "recreated" by Bernard Overton. The most common whistles today are made of brass tubing (sometimes plated with nickel) with a plastic fipple mouthpiece. The next most common form is the conical sheet metal whistle with a wooden stop in the wide end to form the fipple (including the modern Clarke whistles). The tone of a tin whistle is largely determined by its manufacturing. Clarke-style rolled metal whistles tend to have an airy, "impure" sound, whereas Generation-style cylindrical instruments tend to have clear or "pure" whistle sounds. Playability can be improved by placing a piece of tape over one edge of the fipple slot (just below the mouthpiece) to narrow the fipple.

Gaining popularity as a folk instrument in the early 19th century through Celtic music revivals, penny whistles now play an integral part of several folk traditions. Whistles are a prevalent starting instrument in English, Scottish, and Irish traditional music, and the fingerings are nearly identical to those on the traditional six-holed flute (Irish flute, baroque flute) and similar to that of the *uilleann* pipes, which have similar finger technique, range of notes, and repertoire.

The whistle is tuned diatonically, which allows it to be used to easily play music in two major keys and their corresponding minor keys and modes. The whistle is identified by its lowest note, which is the tonic of the lowest major key. D whistles (playing in the keys of D and G) are the most common tuning, followed by C whistles (playing in the keys of C and F). The standard range of the whistle is two octaves. For a D whistle, this includes notes from the second D above middle C to the fourth D above middle C.

It is possible to play additional notes by half-holing (flatting by partially covering the highest open finger hole) or by cross-fingering (covering lower holes). The most common use of cross-fingering produces a flattened form of the seventh note (C natural instead of C sharp on a D whistle, making a G major scale available on a D whistle). Some whistle designs allow a single fipple, or mouthpiece, to be used on differently keyed bodies.

Traditional Irish whistle playing uses a variety of small embellishments to articulate within legato melodies (rather than tonguing many notes separately). Cuts involve very briefly lifting a finger above the note being sounded without interrupting airflow into the whistle. For example, a player playing a low D on a D whistle can cut the note by very briefly lifting the first finger of the lower hand. This causes the pitch to briefly shift upward. The cut can be performed either at the very start of the note or after the note has begun to sound; some people call the latter a "double cut" or a "mid-note cut." Strikes/taps are similar to cuts except that a finger below the sounded note is briefly lowered to the whistle.

Combinations of these elements include the "long roll" (three slurred notes of equal pitch and duration, the second sounded with a cut, and the third sounded with a strike) and the "short roll" (two slurred notes of equal pitch and duration, the first sounded with a cut and the second sounded with a strike). *Cranns* (or *crans*) are ornaments borrowed from the uilleann piping tradition, and are used for notes where a roll is impossible (only cuts are used). Vibrato can be achieved on most notes by opening and closing an open hole (usually two holes from the holes being covered) or by variation of breath pressure (less common).

Traditional music from Ireland and Scotland is by far the music most commonly played on the tin whistle, and comprises the vast majority of published scores suitable for whistle players. Kwela music from South Africa features the tin whistle as a leading melodic instrument. This jazz-influenced genre thrived in 1950s apartheid-era townships and accounted for the sale of more than 1 million tin whistles (mostly Hohner brand instruments). Kwela sheet music is rare, but the recording *African Jazz 'N Jive* (Rhino, 2000) is a good source for reissued recordings from the 1950s.

European tin whistle music collections are notated in standard musical notation (not transposed), "tonic sol-fa" (especially in Irish and Welsh schools), and Abc notation (using English letter names for each note, A-G). Most tutorial books show graphical representations for fingerings (sometimes called whistle tablature), with holes to be covered for a given note shown filled in, and a plus sign (+) at the top for notes in the second octave.

During the 1960s, Tommy Makem brought the tin whistle to prominence as a member of The Clancy Brothers. American folk revival groups also adopted the instrument; contemporary masters include Paddy Maloney of The Chieftains, Sean Potts, Spider Stacey of The Pogues, Bob Hallet of the Canadian folk rock group Great Blue Sea, and Bridget Regan of the punk band Flogging Molly. American Celtic and Irish punk bands featuring the instrument include The Tossers, Dropkick Murphys, and The Cranberries. Howard Shore featured a D whistle in his scores for *The Lord of the Rings* film trilogy to symbolize the Shire and nostalgic themes. The tin whistle is heard in the 1997 film *Titanic* (most notably during the introduction and in the song "My Heart Will Go On") and to represent the main character (Hiccup) in *How to Train Your Dragon* (2010).

Laura Stanfield Prichard

See also: Bagpipes; Bones (Britain and Ireland); Irish Dance Music

Further Reading

African Jazz 'N Jive: An Authentic Selection of South African Township Swing Classics from the 50s & 60s [CD]. 2000. Rhino.

Megaw, J. V. S. 1960. "Penny Whistles and Prehistory." *Antiquity* 34(133), 6–13.

Vallely, Fintan. 1999. *The Companion to Irish Traditional Music*. New York: New York University Press.

Tombak

Also known as *zarb*, the *tombak* (also spelled *tonbak*) is a goblet-shaped drum originating in Qajar-period Persia (1794–1925 CE). It is the primary percussion instrument associated with Iranian classical music. It is also played in other regions of Asia, as well as Eastern Europe and Africa.

The tombak is a single-headed drum carved from a single block of wood, traditionally a solid piece of mulberry, and sometimes walnut wood. Sometimes the design includes ornate geometric patterns around the sides. The drum's base is narrower than its head, and is open on the bottom. The drumhead is traditionally covered with a goatskin, but sometimes sheepskin, cowskin, or camelskin membranes are used as well. The large width of the head allows for a greater range in sound, from a deep bass tone to higher treble tones. The tuning of the tombak is usually fixed, as its membrane is glued or tacked into place. However, the membrane may be slightly manipulated by cooling, warming, or dampening it, to change the drum's pitch. Normally, two or three contrasting timbres can be clearly achieved through applying varying amounts of finger pressure as the player taps the drum. Tombaks can differ in size as well, which changes their fundamental pitch.

The tombak is held either perpendicular to, or diagonally across, the torso so that the head of the drum tilts slightly downward. The player uses all fingers, either individually or in combination, as well as the palm of the hand, to hit the drumhead. Hitting closer to the rim of the head produces a higher, more resonant timbre. Sometimes metal rings are worn on the fingers to accentuating the rapid "clicking" tones, which are created by tapping closer to the narrow edge of the drumhead. Sounds produced in the center of the drumhead have a deeper, bass timbre. The bass tones are known as the *tom* while the higher tones are the *bak*, or rim-stroke. The tom is struck with the four fingertips, whereas the bak is usually produced by the ring or middle finger. These represent the two main strokes of tombak playing. Other strokes include *meyaneh*, or "middle" stroke (also produced by the ring finger), and *pelang*, or "the snap," a stroke that involves striking the drumhead with the ring finger held against the thumb. Ornamental flourishes are provided by strokes known as *riz*, or "the roll," which involves a smooth roll of the fingers in sequence, one after another, to create a seamless purring sound, as well as *eshareh*, or "allusion," which is inserted in between main strokes, as a kind of grace note, or pick-up note.

The tombak initially gained recognition as an accompanying percussion instrument, until virtuoso tombak musician Hossein Tehrani (1912–1974) popularized the tombak as a solo instrument in the 1950s. Other master players, such as Nasser Farhangfar and Hossein Kohandani, are well known for innovative techniques used in performance. Today, it is the drum most commonly heard in Iranian classical music, and is often heard in solo performance with fast, complex rhythmic passages in a variety of tones. Well-known tombak makers today include Helmi, based in Tehran, Iran, who creates instruments with ornately carved patterns and *khatamkari*, a Persian art technique of creating intricately inlaid patterns with contrasting thin pieces of wood.

Theresa Steward

See also: Dastgah; Iranian Classical Music

Further Reading

During, Jean, Zia Mirabdolbaghi, and Dariush Safvat. 1991. *The Art of Persian Music.* Waldorf, MD: Mage Publishers.

Nasehpour, Peyman. 2001. "Styles of Tonbak Playing in Classical Music of Persia." Tombak Network. http://www.tombak.co.uk.

Touré, Ali Farka (1939–2006)

Born Ali Ibrahim Touré, on October 31, 1939, in Village Kanau in the northwestern area of Mali near Tombuctou, Ali Farka Touré is considered the father of desert blues. The music of Touré is characterized by a distinct fusion of Malian traditional music with the North American genre of blues, specifically that of the Mississippi Delta. In his music, the sounds of traditional Malian instruments such as the *njarka*, a single-stringed violin; the *djerkel*, a single-stringed guitar; and the *kora*, a 21-stringed harp, are replicated on the more contemporary six-stringed guitar. As a guitarist, Touré has received such recognition as a ranking of 76th on *Rolling Stone*'s "The 100 Greatest Guitarists of All Time" and 37th on *Spin Magazine*'s "100 Greatest Guitarists of All Time." Ali Farka Touré has also received three Grammy Awards for his *Talking Timbuktu* album (1994) with Ry Cooder (1947–), *In the Heart of the Moon* (2005), and *Ali and Toumani* (2010). Following his death, Touré was a recipient of the prestigious *Commandeur de l'Ordre National du Mali*, the highest honor of the Malian government, along with a state funeral. His work has inspired the next generation of artists, such as Habib Koité, Salif Keita, Amadou & Mariam, and his son Vieux Farka Touré to strive for international success (Black, 2017).

Ali Farka Touré, though not born into a musical caste, was descended from a noble Malian family which could trace its lineage from Spanish Moors. Touré, the 10th and only son of his mother to survive infancy, had his name changed from Ali Ibrahim to Ali Farka as was the tradition if a family had suffered deaths of infant children (Duran, Gold, and McGuire, 2009). Following his father's death, Ali's mother moved the family to Niafunké, a village with a population of more than 20,000.

It was in Niafunké that the young Touré would find his musical inspiration, in both religion and a spirituality inspired by the mythology of the Niger River. Ali Farka Touré, a devout Muslim, developed a special connection to the *Ghimbala*, an underwater world populated by *djinn* in the Niger River. Those with a strong connection with this world were referred to as "Children of the River," and it is known that Touré's grandmother, Kounandi Samba, was considered a priestess of the *Ghimbala*

Guitarist Ali Farka Touré merged the traditional music of Mali—his home country—with the blues. (Frans Schellekens/Redferns)

(Duran, Gold, and McGuire, 2009). It was during this time that Ali Farka Touré was plagued by episodes thought to be a result of the spirits of the river. These episodes caused him to be sent away to a nearby village for treatment. However, upon his return a year later he was considered a "Child of the River" and was thought to have a special power to communicate with this spiritual world. As a devout Muslim, he did not wholly embrace these powers; however, he carried its influence with him, as evidenced by his constant travel companions, a *njarka* violin and recordings of the river's spiritual music (Duran, Gold, and McGuire, 2009).

In Touré's early career, music was discouraged by his family in favor of more practical training as a farmer and as the apprentice to a tailor. It was following a 1956 encounter with the director of Guinea's National Ballet, Keita Fodeba, that he made the decision to take up the guitar seriously. Along with the guitar and the traditional instruments of his youth, Touré took up an interest in percussion and made his own drum set. He learned to incorporate the *Sonraï, Peul,* and *Tamascheq* traditional styles on the guitar, which became the foundation of his distinct musical sound. In 1968, at the introduction of a friend, Touré first encountered the records of such artists as James Brown, Otis Redding, Wilson Pickett, Jimmy Smith, and the especially influential John Lee Hooker, whose music Touré found to be exceedingly similar to his own, as evidenced by his eventual nickname, "the African John Lee Hooker" (Cartwright, 2007). After Mali's independence, Touré's directorship of the Niafunké artistic troupe from 1962 until 1971 gave the artist the opportunity to travel, and he gave his European debut in 1968 at an international festival in Sofiya (Barz, 2016). After this debut, he began to gain popularity as a solo artist, both in his home country and abroad.

Following Touré's increased popularity and recordings in France during the 1970s, he began a return to his roots in the 1980s, and an era of collaboration in the 1990s with such artists as Taj Mahal on *The Source* and Ry Cooder on *Talking Timbuktu*. In 1986, one of his Radio Mali albums caused a stir with London's radio DJs such as Andy Kershaw and Charlie Gillet and ultimately *Folk Roots* magazine who were mystified by this African blues musician left unnamed on the record jacket. Thus began a search initiated by Anne Hunt of the World Circuit record label for Touré's name. With the help of Radio Mali and Toumani Diabate (1965–), a radio appeal was put out for Touré to present himself (Duran 2009). This led to both Touré's first performances in the UK and his partnership with World Circuit. Following his arrival on the musical scene in London in 1992, he first met his eventual collaborator, Ry Cooder (Obrect, 2011). It was this partnership with Cooder as producer and guitarist that led Touré to his first Grammy Award for *Talking Timbuktu* (on the Rykodisc label).

Following this first Grammy Award, Touré retreated to his homeland in favor of working on his farm, to the dismay of his record label, World Circuit. An executive of the label, Nick Gold, eager to record another album with Touré, brought a recording studio to Niafunké to pursue this goal (Duran, Gold, and McGuire, 2009). Between stints tending his crops, Touré recorded what became the album *Niafunké*. Upon the release of this album, Touré once again became a recluse, until 2005, when he started work on the first album of a trilogy recorded at Bamako's Hotel Mandé. The first album of the trilogy, *In the Heart of the Moon* (2005), and the second, *Ali and Toumani* (2010), both recorded as duets with Toumani Diabete, won the artist his second and third Grammy Awards.

Touré would never see the release of the final album of the trilogy, *Savane*, due to his death in 2006 caused by bone cancer. In 2004, prior to his death, Touré was elected mayor of Niafunké. He used his record earnings and personal finances to support infrastructure efforts in Niafunké, such as irrigation projects, road grading, installation of sewer canals, and fueling the generator that gave the town electricity. Following his death, Ali Farka Touré has been consistently honored and recognized for both his music and his philanthropy.

Phillip Alexander Ducreay

Further Reading

Barz, Gregory F. 2016. "Touré, Ali Farka." *Grove Music Online.* http://www.oxfordmusiconline.com.

Black, Elspeth. 2017. "Desert Blues: The Legacy of Ali Farka Touré." Culture Trip. https://theculturetrip.com/africa/mali/articles/desert-blues-the-legacy-of-ali-farka-tour.

Cartwright, Garth. 2007. "Ali Farka Touré (Mali)." BBC.http://www.bbc.co.uk/radio3/worldmusic/a4wm2007/2007_ali_farka_toure.shtml.

Duran, Lucy, Nick Gold, and Dave McGuire. 2009. "Biography." World Circuit. http://www.worldcircuit.co.uk/#Ali_Farka_Toure::Biography.

Obrect, Jas. 2011. "Ry Cooder: The Complete Ali Farka Touré Interview." http://jasobrecht.com/ry-cooder-ali-farka-toure-interview.

Touré, Ali Farka. 2006. In Colin Larkin (ed.), *Encyclopedia of Popular Music*, 4th ed. Oxford Music Online. http://www.oxfordmusiconline.com.

Turbo-Folk

Turbo-folk is a subgenre of popular music that originated in Serbia during the early 1990s. Although closely associated with Serbian musicians, the turbo-folk subgenre is widely popular in the entire Balkan region, in Turkey, and in Romania. This style uses folk music elements and combines them into an ultramodern pop music setting. The term "turbo-folk" is a neologism coined during the late 1980s by Rambo Amadeus, a Montenegrin singer and songwriter. It originally combines two contradictory concepts: on the one hand, the concept of "turbo," a way of injecting a fuel-air mixture into the modern engine, and on the other hand the concept "folk," a symbol of the local traditions.

Figuratively, "turbo" also refers to participation in fashionable and luxurious trends. As a musical movement, the turbo-folk style that emerged in 1990s Serbia might be seen as a development of the popular songs composed in the style of traditional music from Šumadija or Bosnia during the 1950s, turned into a modern entertainment product during the 1980s with the incorporation of electronic instruments and models from pop productions. The early 1990s, however, witnessed a visible change in this music, which relied heavily on hip-hop, techno, and dance music as its sources (Baker, 2007).

In the 1990s, Serbian popular music was dominated by three musical subgenres: newly composed folk music, dance music, and turbo-folk (Kronja, 2004). Newly composed folk music combined the influence of traditional Serbian melodies with modern musical influences, transforming the sound into a fusion of the folk musical and rap, hip-hop, dance, and techno music. Dance music had its roots in pop-dance, disco, techno, commercial rap, and hip-hop. Turbo-folk combined dance with techno rhythms and with a way of singing that originated from the newly composed folk music. Additionally, the media promotion, iconography, and values system of turbo-folk music are substantial elements of this powerful subgenre in the fashionable Balkan culture and lifestyle during the 1990s.

During the 1980s, the former Federal Republic of Yugoslavia experienced a growth in consumerism as part of a capitalist lifestyle, in a process of social transformation in which mass media, and in particular television, was the key factor. However, this social transformation turned into a civil war at the beginning of the 1990s. The several different parties involved used media propaganda and the monopolization of media space to spread nationalistic values. Turbo-folk then became the dominant political and social pattern in the region, shaping the national patriotic culture and folk entertainment cultivated by local and populist television stations that specialized in music videos.

The success of turbo-folk and dance music was achieved in a situation of social disintegration of the former Yugoslavian society, which encouraged the flourishing of youth subcultures. Turbo-folk, which represented a perfect combination of nationalist ideas and aggressive attitudes in its visual and musical presentation, incorporated lyrics and images into the ideological and populistic messages of the political propaganda. This subgenre, mainly promoted through music videos on TV, included provocative female stars and encouraging luxurious images.

The dance that accompanies turbo-folk music also reveals the mixture of nationalist-populistic and contemporary character of this subgenre. Female and male singers combined movements from all sorts of styles (techno and hip-hop to belly dancing), the main intention being to seduce the audience, stressing the erotic qualities of the dance in a provocative way. The values messages contained in the lyrics of turbo-folk music promote the idea that the end justifies the means, and stress the importance of money and appearance for establishing social status. The texts express masochism, jealousy, and murderous moods. The "Warrior Chic" style incorporated into turbo-folk music implies that a woman is to be considered an object and represents a potential status symbol, while the man portrays a dangerous, robust image of the macho guy.

This musical subgenre embodied a solution to the identity crisis of Balkan society during the war, by combining different influences, ideologies, dances, and videos in a hybrid musical experience that preserved some traditional Serbian national characteristics, while adding outside influences. After the fall of Slobodan Milošević's (1941–2006) regime on October 5, 2000, turbo-folk entered a transitional phase in which many performers responded by incorporating more pop elements into their songs.

Antonella Di Giulio

See also: Ganga Singing

Further Reading

Baker, Catherine. 2007. "The Concept of Turbo-folk in Croatia: Inclusion/Exclusion in the Construction of National Musical Identity." In Catherine Baker, Christopher J. Gerry, Barbara Madaj, Liz Mellish and Jana Nahodilová (eds.), *Nation In formation: Inclusion and Exclusion in Central and Eastern Europe*. London: SSEES Publications. https://eprints.soton.ac.uk/66293/1/Baker_-_turbofolk_2007.pdf.

Grujić, Marija. 2006. "Inclusiveness of the 'Turbo Folk' Music Scene in Post-Socialist Serbia: Transgression of Cultural Boundaries or a New Model of Cultural Exclusions?" 7th International Postgraduate Conference on Central and Eastern Europe UCL-SSEES Inclusion/Exclusion, London, February 16–18, 2006.

Kronja, Ivana. 2004. "Turbo Folk and Dance Music in 1990s Serbia: Media, Ideology and the Production of Spectacle." *Anthropology of East Europe Review* 22, 103–114.

Tuvan Popular Bands

Tuvan music has attracted the attention of music lovers in the Western world since the mid-1990s, in particular the Tuvan bands Huun-Huur-Tu and Yat-Kha. Situated in South Siberia on the Mongolian border, Tuva was formerly an autonomous republic of the Soviet Union and has been a constituent member of the Russian Federation since 1992. Tuva achieved international prominence among philatelists in the 1920s and 1930s when it issued unusually shaped illustrated postage stamps. Nobel Prize-winning physicist Richard Feynman further helped raise awareness of Tuva in his decade-long and ultimately unsuccessful attempt to visit the region in the late 1970s and 1980s. Tuva has cultural and musical traditions similar to those of neighboring Mongolia, but has its own language (Tuvan) and some idiosyncratic musical instruments and vocal styles.

The sound most readily associated with Tuvan music is overtone singing, also known as throat singing, which plays an intrinsic role in the overall sound of both Huun-Huur-Tu and Yat-Kha. Overtone singers are able to produce more than one pitch simultaneously by singing a note (the fundamental) and amplifying the overtones or undertones in the head or chest. The most well-known and broadest categories are *khöömei*, a term also used to describe all Tuvan overtone singing; *sygyt* (literally, whistling), the high-pitched variant; and *kargyraa*, the low style. All members of Huun-Huur-Tu, past and present, sing and they showcase a variety of khöömei styles. Albert Kuvezin, guitarist, lead vocalist, and linchpin of Yat-Kha, sings a variant of kargyraa that musicologists and journalists have called *kanzat kargyraa*, although he has developed it into his own style that he describes as "rock kargyraa." Other members of Yat-Kha sing styles other than kargyraa, sometimes in octaves or harmonies with Kuvezin's voice.

The traditional instruments used by Huun-Huur-Tu and Yat-Kha include the *khomus* (jaw harp); a two-stringed bowed spike fiddle called the *igil*; a two-stringed plucked lute called the *doshpuluur*; the Mongolian *morin khuur* (horse-head fiddle); a variety of frame drums such as *kengirge* and *dungur*; an end-blown flute called the *shoor*; and the *yat-kha*, a long zither similar to the Mongolian *yatga* or Chinese *guzheng*, from which the band gets its name. Huun-Huur-Tu use a broad variety of traditional instruments and have incorporated more non-Tuvan instruments, such as acoustic guitars and accordions, into their lineup over the years. Yat-Kha use the electric guitar, bass guitar, and drum kit in addition to traditional instruments, and they also experiment with instruments from various other countries, including the Turkish *jumbush*, the Balkanese *bazuki*, and Chinese gongs. Both bands perform arrangements of traditional Tuvan songs, with lyrics mostly about the natural beauty of Tuva and horses, which are of great cultural significance in the region as well as an integral part of nomadic life.

Huun-Huur-Tu, which means "sunbeams," is the more traditionally Tuvan of the two bands. Members wear national costume during performances and their song arrangements are generally less experimental than those of Yat-Kha. The band was formed in 1992 by Kaigal-Ool Khovalyg and Sayan Bapa (the two remaining original members), Alexander Bapa, and Albert Kuvezin, who left in 1993 after founding Yat-Kha. Their first album, *Sixty Horses in My Herd*, was released in 1993 by the American independent label Shanachie, which also produced their subsequent three studio albums.

The album includes some classic Tuvan folk songs, a traditional igil solo and two khöömei solos. Other tracks provide clues as to the influence the Soviet Union had on Tuvan folk music before 1991. Throughout the Soviet Union and its satellite states, government-led initiatives brought about dramatic changes to folk music, including standardization of instrumental tunings and harmonization of melodies that previously would have been performed solo or with voice and instrument in unison. The processes by which these changes were made were complex, and the reasons why equally complex, although homogeneity and the destabilization of ethnic communities were part of the governmental agenda. In *Sixty Horses in My Herd*, songs such as "Bayan Dugai," featuring a solo vocal line doubled by the igil, are more representative of Tuvan folk music of the pre-Soviet era, whereas the track "Kongurei," with a vocal melody harmonized by chords on plucked stringed instruments, is closer to the newly composed folk music that would have been commonplace during the Soviet era.

Huun-Huur-Tu's second album, *Orphan's Lament* (1994), features a broader spectrum of Tuvan musical traditions, both ancient and modern, as well as non-Tuvan instruments such as the acoustic guitar, making it more accessible to a wider audience. Anatoli Kuuler joined the band following Kuvezin's departure, and remained a band member for the following two studio albums, *If I'd Been Born an Eagle* (1997) and *Where Young Grass Grows* (1999). The lineup for these two albums was completed by Alexei Saryglar, who replaced Alexander Bapa in 1995, on vocals and percussion.

The band released live albums in 2001, 2003, and 2008 before their next studio album, *Ancestors Call*, was released on the World Village label, an imprint of Harmonia Mundi, in 2010. This album features the multi-instrumental and vocal talents of Radik Tulush, a former member of Yat-Kha and director of the Tuvan National Orchestra, who joined the band in 2006 to replace the relatively short-term member Andrei Mongush.

All of Huun-Huur-Tu's solo studio and live albums showcase traditional music, but it is in their numerous collaborations with other artists that the more experimental side of the band is showcased. Notable collaborations include the albums

Fly Fly My Sadness (1996), with The Bulgarian Voices; *Early Music* (1997), with the Kronos Quartet; *Spirits from Tuva* (2003), a collection of remixes by Russian techno-trance act Malerija; *Altai Sayan Tandy-Uula* (2004) with the Russian producer Alexei Samsonov; *The White Dragon* (2008), with English Cretan lyra player Ross Daly; and *Eternal* (2009), with American electronica producer and DJ Carmen Rizzo.

Albert Kuvezin began experimenting with blending traditional Tuvan music with rock in the 1980s, while studying music in the Tuvan capital, Kyzyl. At the time, Western rock music was all but banned in the Soviet Union, although he managed to access records by the likes of Led Zeppelin and Deep Purple. Kuvezin released *The Spectre of Coming Disaster* on cassette in 1989, which won him the Brian Eno Special Prize at the Voice of Asia competition in Kazakhstan in 1990. His distinctive vocals are largely responsible for Yat-Kha's trademark sound.

The name "Yat-Kha" was first used in 1992, when Kuvezin and Russian composer Ivan Sokolovsky released *Antropophagy*, a fusion of electronica and traditional Tuvan music. The pair parted company in 1993 and Kuvezin kept the name Yat-Kha for the band, which has undergone several changes in lineup of both instrumentation and people. Yat-Kha's music has been described as folk-rock, ethnic rock and ethno-punk, among other labels, although Kuvezin calls it Tuvan rock.

Yat-Kha's first international release was the 1995 album *Yenesei Punk*, which reached no. 2 on the European world music charts. It features traditional Tuvan instruments, guitars, and Alexei Saaia on vocals along with Kuvezin. The lyrics of each song are about Tuva's natural beauty except for the opening track "Beautiful Soviet Country," which, somewhat ironically, asserts that life began in Tuva only after its incorporation into the Soviet Union.

By 1999, the band had had a complete lineup change, with Kuvezin being the only remaining member. He was joined by his former throat-singing teacher Aldyn-ool Sevek on vocals and morin khuur and Evgeniy (Zhenya) Tkachev on percussion. Tkachev, the longest-serving member of the band other than Kuvezin, uses a mixture of traditional percussion instruments and drum kit, which helps give Yat-Kha their rock sound. In 1998 they released *Dalai Beldiri*, the cover of which depicts one of Tuva's famous postage stamps. The featured songs are a mixture of traditional and rock similar to those of their next album, *Aldyn Dashka* (2000), in which Alexei Saaia returns on morin khuur and vocals. This new lineup was completed by bassist Mikhail Skripaltshchikov, female vocalist Sailyk Ommun, and Radik Tulush. Both *Dalai Beldiri* and *Aldyn Dashka* feature songs composed by Kuvezin in addition to new arrangements of traditional songs.

After a live album in 2002, their next commercial release was *Tuva Rock* (2003), the heaviest and most "rock-like" of their work and the first to feature Kuvezin's compositions with English lyrics. By this time, Yat-Kha had toured all over Europe, North America, East Asia, and the former Soviet Union and won many awards. The influence of rock music continued into their next album *Re-covers* (2005), comprising cover versions of songs by the likes of Motörhead, Joy Division, Santana, and the Rolling Stones. Yat-Kha was then a three-piece band comprised of Kuvezin, Tkachev, and Theodore Scipio on bass.

Following another live album in 2005, the band had a five-year hiatus until the release of *Poets and Lighthouses* in 2010 under the name "Albert Kuvezin and Yat-Kha," although Kuvezin was the only remaining member. He was joined by guest musicians on instruments including percussion, clarinet, piano, harmonium, *duduk*, Scottish pipes, and the Appalachian dulcimer. The band released a "Best of" compilation called *The Ways of Nomad* and another live album in 2011, and today continue bringing Tuvan rock to concert halls and festivals throughout the world.

Lucy M. Rees

See also: Morin Khuur; Tuvan Throat Singing

Further Reading

Leighton, R. 1991. *Tuva or Bust!: Richard Feynman's Last Journey*. New York: W. W. Norton.

Levin, Theodore, and Valentina Süzükei. 2011. *Where Rivers and Mountains Sing: Sound, Music and Nomadism in Tuva and Beyond*. Bloomington: Indiana University Press.

Tuvan Throat Singing

A remarkable way of making vocal sounds allows a single person to produce clear, multiple tones at the same time, and to sing melodies with higher overtones that do not sound like a human voice. This technique, generally referred to as *overtone singing*, is practiced widely by singers from the vast grasslands and taiga of southern Siberia and northwestern Mongolia. These singers developed a stunning range of well-articulated techniques with different stylistic traits, known as *khöömei* (throat-singing). Throat-singing became a global phenomenon from the early 1990s onward, led by singers from the Republic of Tuva (Russian Federation). Several circumstances led to its rise: the breakup of the Soviet Union and the subsequent possibilities for travel and cross-cultural exchange; an urge to revive indigenous traditions among Turkic and other minorities in Russia; and curiosity of music listeners and professionals, from contemporary composers to rock bands, about overtones and timbre and their importance for the voice and for hearing. Today, throat-singing occupies a central place in the Tuvan musical landscape, where it stands side by side with Tuvan folk songs, revived shamanistic and animistic practices, and Western and Asian urban music styles.

STYLES, TECHNIQUES, AND TERMINOLOGY

Overtones, also called *harmonics*, are the component frequencies that make up the spectrum of a tone. They give the impression of sound having a color, because we usually hear harmonics together as one sound—that is, holistically. Tuvan singers (and/or their immediate neighbors, who also practice throat-singing) discovered that it is possible to select harmonics in the sound of the human voice and to make them audible as distinct tones in their own right. Over the course of time, they developed many methods to do so.

"Khöömei" is a generic term for all techniques of throat-singing together, as well as referring to one specific, basic technique. The generic term, believed to derive from the root *khö-* (throat, larynx), covers different ways in which singers employ force on the throat. These give vocal sounds a sharp and unnatural sound compared to the speaking voice or "normal" ways of singing. There are three common techniques of Tuvan khöömei and two major substyles. The technique that sounds least like any sound of the human voice is called *sygyt*, which may be compared to the sound of a high-piched flute, like a piccolo. The typical sound of sygyt is produced by rounding the lips, shaping the tongue like an L and exerting considerable pressure on the vocal folds from the chest or belly. To produce a melody, singers make very precise, small movements with the tongue, selecting one overtone after another. The technique called khöömei is characterized by a softer and usually lower-pitched sound compared to sygyt. Like the latter, there is a flute-like quality in the overtone melodies; unlike the latter, one can also clearly hear vowel sounds. Moving from lower to higher overtones, these vowel sounds go from closed, darker vowels as in wh*o* or *a*we to more open, bright ones, as in h*e*r. However, those vowel sounds only roughly indicate the actual mouth positions needed to bring out clear overtones. Singers concentrate on the overtone melody while they articulate with the tongue and lips.

A third technique, *kargyraa*, not only employs the voice's higher resonances, but also guttural ways of sound production that extend below the natural range of the human voice. The rough, "rattling" tone quality of kargyraa is very different from that of the other two techniques. It is caused by a special mode of vibration of the vocal folds that is not well understood scientifically. Here too vowels can be distinguished, along with relatively low-pitched overtones. *Borbang* or *borbbang-nadyr* is a popular substyle that combines sygyt, khöömei, or kargyraa with rapidly alternating overtones. *Borbang* means "rolling over" and emulates the sound of water flowing and splashing around rocks and pebbles, producing many different frequencies. A more demanding and less widespread substyle of the basic techniques is *ezenggileer* (from *ezenggi* [stirrup]), which has a clicking sound between the overtones linked to horse-riding rhythms. Besides these basic techniques, there are many more combinations and personal styles, some of them performed only by the singer who invented it.

Khöömei overtone melodies are not a random result of resonance: singers consciously select each overtone. Across the border, Mongolian throat-singers often sing folk melodies, which may also be rendered by instruments or a lyrical singing voice. Tuvans utilize only a few well-known melodies, having a preference for making variations on melodic patterns. They usually begin a phrase on a low or mid-range overtone (number 8, 9, or 10), move back and forth between mid-range and high overtones (from 9 to 12 or 13), and return to a low overtone (8 or 9), sometimes using the lower number 6 at some point during a phrase. Overtones 7 and 11 are avoided because they do not fit well in the pentatonic scale of Tuvan traditional music. The resultant melodies are similar to semi-improvised patterns of Tuvan instrumental music, like the Jew's harp *khomus* or horse-head fiddle *igil*. In many respects, throat-singing is like instrumental music, and this is also how many Tuvans think of khöömei. The best throat-singers (and instrumentalists, too) are capable of making ingenious improvisations within existing melodic frameworks. Khöömei, sygyt, and kargyraa are usually combined with different vocal genres, such as long songs (*uzun yrlar*), quatrain songs (*kozhamyk*), and lullabies (*öpei*). Every singer also learns to play instruments to accompany himself or herself. The most popular are the two- and three-stringed lutes, called *doshpuluur* and *chanzy* in Tuvan, respectively, and the horse-head fiddle igil.

ARTISTS AND GROUPS

The first individual Tuvans whose names have come down to us because of their outstanding musical qualities were recorded in Leningrad (now Saint Petersburg) in the 1920s and Moscow in the 1930s. Traditionally, throat-singers perform their pieces alone; in the old khöömei recordings they do not accompany themselves on any instrument, either. At the time, Tannu-Tuva was an independent republic for a brief period (1921–1944), which ended with Russia's annexation of Tuva. Ever since, the old customs of the Tuvans have been under pressure, and sometimes violently repressed, while many new ideas and practices made their entry. Starting in the 1940s, music education programs were set up, introducing theories and practices of European music. Up to that time, multipart music, the mainstay of European music, was virtually unknown in Tuva. Musicians began to perform together in collectives, eventually leading to sizable, state-run ensembles, called Sayany, Ayan, and Filarmonia. Their repertoire was based on European templates and international music styles, with a minor portion of their programs reserved for indigenous performance traditions, including throat-singing. Up to this day, however, herdsmen roaming the steppes with their sheep or yaks may be heard singing alone, expressing praise for their environment, animals, and spirits. During national throat-singing festivals, which began to be held in Tuva's capitol Kyzyl in 1992, scores of singers take the stage alone, with only a string instrument. Many emerging talents hail from Tuva's sparsely populated provinces.

These festivals took advantage of the relaxation of state regulations during the leadership of Russia's last Soviet-era president, Mikhail Gorbachev, in the 1980s. It also enabled Tuvan ethnomusicologist Zoya Kyrgys and throat-singer Gennadi Tumat to gather the best musicians for a new group: the Ansambl Tuva. This Tuvan ensemble gave priority to traditional, local songs and instrumental pieces played on indigenous instruments, and featured excerpts from older Buddhist and shamanist rituals as well. Ansambl Tuva was a new platform, not only for presenting the republic's own music, but also for boosting a sense of Tuvan identity for performers and audiences, all of whom partook in bringing old and sometimes long-lost songs back to life. The resurgence of Tuvan throat-singing reverberated strongly in other regions of the former Soviet Union, where similar vocal techniques were lost, waning, or less prominent. Several influential Turco-Mongol musicians turned to Tuvan examples for inspiration and advice. In post-Soviet Northern Asia, the unique sounds of throat-singing have become a powerful Turco-Mongol identity-marker.

Ansambl Tuva caused a stir outside Russia as well, as few people in the United States, Europe, or Southeast Asia had ever heard live throat-singing. Musicians—and throat-singers above all—were better able to benefit from the new opportunities than most other Tuvans. They frequently travelled abroad to tour, take part in

Tuvan throat singer and musician Kongar-ool Ondar. Tuvan throat singers are able to produce multiple pitches simultaneously. (Jack Vartoogian/Getty Images)

artistic collaborations, make recordings, and publish compact discs. Famous composers and musicians (for example, Frank Zappa, Ry Cooder, The Kronos Quartet) were keen to work with the best soloists. These in turn soon launched their own careers or groups.

During the 1990s, a rapid transformation took place from state-funded ensembles working within Soviet territory to independent musicians and acts operating in the global world music market, a process that paralleled the collapse and subsequent privatization of Russia's industries. Among the most successful artists following this path are Kongar-ool Ondar, Gennadi Tumat, Huun-Huur-Tu (featuring Kaigal-ool Khovalyg), Albert Kuvezin's Yat-Kha, Özüm, Chirgilchin, and Alash. When this transition began, older icons of Tuvan music, such as Khunashtaar-ool Oorzhak and Marzhymal Onder, were still alive to pass on the songs and pieces from an older epoch.

Several more progressive singers and groups also emerged around this time, the best-known being Sainkho Namchylak, an extraordinary female vocalist whose voice seamlessly merges traditional Tuvan ballads with world beats, free jazz, hip-hop rhymes, and intense vocal experimentation. Though there are traditional taboos surrounding women performing khöömei, she is not the only female publicly showcasing her ability to sing overtones.

In the late 1990s, Choduraa Tumat brought together several female throat-singers and instrumentalists in a group called Tyva Kyzy. Some Tuvan throat-singers (both male and female) successfully integrate shamanic performance styles and attributes with musical ones, leaning toward the ritual and healing side of it (Nikolai Oorzhak) or to the musical side (Gendos Chamzyryn). A female shaman, Ai Chürek, helped revive traditional healing methods, employing guttural techniques reminiscent of, yet different from, khöömei. All of these musicians added to the vitality of Tuva's musical culture and to a turn-of-the-millennium update of archaic Turco-Mongol sound ideals. The period of political and cultural turmoil also had its drawbacks. Several talented young singers, most notably Ansambl Tuva's co-founder Gennadi Tumat, died an untimely death, partly due to the many challenges these new global heroes of Tuvan culture were facing at home and abroad.

PERFORMANCE PRACTICES

The feats of throat-singers sometimes baffle listeners, making it difficult to understand its context. Nevertheless, several other performance techniques and beliefs suggest that this vocal practice did not appear out of the blue. The recitation of epics, the natural environment, animistic and shamanistic practices, and instrumental traditions help us to understand the broader sound-world these nomad tribes inhabited for centuries. Historically, Tuva has strong cultural and linguistic ties with surrounding areas, where other types of throat-singing are found. The Tuvans' close northwestern neighbors, from the Siberian Republics of Altay and Khakassia, share the tradition of throat-singing with melodies of overtones. Here throat singing is deeply embedded in performing epic stories by making use of guttural techniques called *kai* or *khai*. The emphasis in these narrative styles on words and on play with sound and timbre (or tone quality) is at times augmented by playing with overtones, and may provide one historical clue to the emergence of khöömei-like vocal techniques.

A strong preference for sound-making with a guttural quality can be found much further still in northern and western directions, among tribes speaking Turkic languages across the Eurasian plateau, such as the Sakha, Kyrgyz, Kazakhs, and Turks. According to ethnomusicologists Ted Levin and Valentina Suzukei, it was the unique combination of cultural and environmental factors that led to the development of overtone singing among tribes and clans in northwest Mongolia and southern Siberia. "The particular intersection of environment and culture—of topography, animistic beliefs, and musical practices—that provided the crucible of throat-singing was almost certainly the zone of mountains and high-grasslands that extends from the center and west of present-day Tuva into western regions of present-day Mongolia and the northwest corner of what is now Chinese Xinjiang. There, herders from a variety of Turkic and Mongolian tribal and clan groups intermingled, intermarried, and shared techniques of representing the powerful forces of their natural environment in sound" (Levin, 2006, p. 71).

The sounds of wind, rivers, and streams, of birds, and of wild and domesticated animals are not mere background noises for Tuvan ears. The forces and sounds of nature that are physically present are widely regarded by local dwellers to reflect unseen forces, such as the spirits of places and animals. The human beings living amidst this drama of nature have shaped much of their music and proto-musical sounds in response to these natural forces and spirits. Sometimes this is done in a very literal way, by making imitations of animals to lure them while hunting; at other times, environmental sounds induce imaginative and artistic musical expressions.

In modern times, many musicians still emphasize that nature is the source or at least the inspiration for their music, and also that they sing or play for the mountains, animals, and local spirits. These general, animistic attitudes overlap with shamanistic beliefs and practices. A shaman (*kham*) is a ritual specialist who establishes contact with spirits of higher and lower worlds on behalf of the local community, for example, to cure disease or influence future events. She or he often does so by playing the shaman drum (*dunggur*) and changing the normal voice to a variety of unusual, guttural timbres. This voice change supports the shaman's journey to the other world and helps to evoke the supernatural powers afflicting the sick or uninitiated bystanders. How khöömei originated is unknown, but archaic practices like these share sonic features with the more musical art of present-day throat-singing.

The last and most obvious practice that must be considered in the wider field of sonic practices surrounding khöömei is music made on instruments. Much of what makes music special globally is concerned with combining pitches in ever-new melodic, rhythmic, or harmonic combinations. Much of what makes Tuvan music special is that which happens "inside" the pitches: the internal dynamic of a single tone. Tuvan ethnomusicologist Valentina Suzukei emphasizes this important distinction by pointing out that Western music is "pitch-centered," whereas Tuvan music is "timbre-centered." The most revered of Tuvan instruments, the igil horsehead fiddle, makes abundant use of *flageolets*, harmonics played on strings. Four different types of khomus Jew's harp are known, for which all sonic material is based on harmonics. Two natural trumpets, producing tones similar to the overtone series, are used by hunters: the *amyrga* and *ediski*. In Tuvan musical culture and its cousins, the widespread use of instruments and instrumental techniques based on the overtone series have helped shape an auditory culture where players and listeners are skilled in hearing the finest details in timbres. Around the world, musicians have discovered ways to make melodies with overtones contained within a single source sound. Jew's harps are played across Eurasia and natural trumpets have been in use in ancient and modern times, such as the Australian *didgeridoo* and the *Naturtrompete* of Joseph Haydn's time; string players employ flageolets on many types of mouth-bow of sub-Saharan Africa or the musical bow *berimbao* from Brazil. But in none of these cases did a parallel art form take shape in the realm of the voice. The unique achievement of Turco-Mongol throat singers in past and present is the extension of such practices back to our most archetypal musical instrument, the human voice, and applying it in such versatile, virtuoso ways.

Mark C. van Tongeren

See also: Tibetan Buddhist Chant; Tuvan Popular Bands

Further Reading

Levin, Theodore, with Valentina Suzukei. 2006. *Where Rivers and Mountains Sing: Sound, Music, and Nomadism in Tuva and Beyond.* Bloomington: Indiana University Press.

Suzukei, Valentina. 2014. *Singing My Life: The Story of Kongar-ool Ondar, Legendary Throat Singer from Tuva*. n.p.: Bapalar.

van Tongeren, Mark. 1995. "A Tuvan Perspective on Throat Singing." *Oideion 2. The Performing Arts World-Wide,* 293–312.

U

Ukulele

The *ukulele* is a guitar-like instrument, at first played by the natives in Hawaii and Micronesia, used mainly for song and dance accompaniment. But it did not remain there. With the exception of the *sitar*, no other plucked world music instrument switched so extremely from its earlier function as an instrument of the natives to the popular culture of the Western world.

The standard (soprano) ukulele, with a length of about 54 cm, a measure of about 34 cm, and a depth of about 5.5 cm, looks like a small guitar and most commonly has four strings in a tuning similar to the four highest strings of a guitar (d-g-b-e′, the same intervals as the four-course Renaissance guitar from the 16th century), with two exceptions: first, the lowest string is one octave higher, so that it sounds only one whole tone deeper than the first string; second, its tuning is a fourth or fifth higher than that of the guitar. This tuning (g′-c′-e′-a′, resp. a′-d′-f#′-b′) gives the instrument its typical bass-less floating sound and is similar to the tuning of the Venezuelan *cuatro* (a-d′-f#′-b). In addition to this standard type, there are bigger ones ("concert," tenor, baritone, bass), which sound deeper. Some types have six strings (the first and third course are most often doubled), or eight strings (all courses are doubled). It most typically has nylon strings; only banjo-variants can use steel strings. In comparison to a guitar, the ukulele has a much more portable size and weight, the construction is similar but simpler, the production costs are much less, and tuning and playing are much easier. If you can play guitar, it is easy to learn the ukulele.

The instrument originates from similar instruments, from the *braguinha* (also named *machete*, or *machete de braga*) in size and the *rajão* in tuning, both from the Portuguese island of Madeira. From there, these instruments were brought to Hawaii by immigrants in 1879, where these instrument fused into the ukulele, which, at the latest, was used in 1886 to accompany *hula* (a typical Hawaiian dance) dancers. From Hawaii, the ukulele made its way to Micronesia. Famous Hawaiian ukulele players include Ernest Kaai (1881–1962, named "Hawaii's Greatest Ukulele Player"), Jesse Kalima (1920–1980, who developed the ukulele as a solo instrument), and Herb Ohta [Ohta-San] (1934–, who taught lots of famous ukulele players).

With the U.S. tour of the *Hawaiian Glee Club* in 1901, the ukulele became known outside of Hawaii. In 1914, a self-instruction book for it was published in Los Angeles. One year later, during the *Panama-Pacific Exposition* in San Francisco, the instrument became popular in the United States. During the 1920s and 1930s, Cliff Edwards "Ukulele Ike" (1895–1971), who sang jazzy renditions of pop standards and accompanied himself on the ukulele, helped the instrument to become more popular. From then on, lots of instructional books were published and lots of instruments were built by American guitar manufacturers. Arthur Godfrey, who during the 1940s and 1950s moderated television shows, sang and played the ukulele and promoted its popularity.

During the first decades of the 20th century, the development of the blues created a new style through the shifting of the rural blues forms from the Southern U.S. states to the ghetto-like surroundings of big cities in the Northern U.S. states. In this genre of urban blues, not only did the rural topics disappear, but also new instruments became available. Stringbands with different kinds of guitars, mandolin, fiddle, banjo, plucked double bass, and ukulele were formed. In jazz, a banjo with the tuning of a ukulele is named *banjulele, banjouke, banjo ukulele, ukulele banjo,* or *banjo uke,* as played by Al Bowlly (1898–1941) or Joe Morris (1955–).

The ukulele can be seen and/or heard in dozens of films, which can be divided into two sets. First are those in which the story of the film deals with Hawaii and the ukulele appears for regional representation (e.g., William A. Seiter's *Sons of the Desert,* 1933; and Frank Tuttle's *Waikiki Wedding,* 1937). Second are those in which the story of the film has nothing to do with Hawaii (e.g., Billy Wilder's *Some Like It Hot,* 1959; and Woody Allen's *The Purple Rose of Cairo,* 1985). In these films, the ukulele's cultural and musical roots are ignored, and it is only used as a smaller-and-easier-to-play guitar for popular Western songs. This evolution did not take place with another four-stringed instrument, the Venezuelan cuatro, because this instrument, with its bigger size and bigger depth, is not as practical and "cute" (in both mentioned films, the ukulele is played by an attractive woman) as a ukulele.

With the Hawaiian ukulele player Israel Kamakawiwo'ole and his pop-reggae-medley "Somewhere Over the Rainbow"/"What a Wonderful World," the instrument and its cultural musical roots—in this case represented by a Hawaiian musician—became very popular. The song was included in his album *Facing Future* (1993), Hawaii's first platinum musical release.

Founded in 1985 and still active today, The Ukulele Orchestra of Great Britain sings and plays as an ensemble of different ukuleles (with half-acoustic and resonator-ukuleles), added to a plucked guitar bass, performing hits such as Steppenwolf's "Born to Be Wild," Nirvana's "Smells Like Teen Spirit," and Isaac Hayes's "Shaft." Jake Shimabukuro (1976–) from Hawaii plays Queen's "Bohemian Rhapsody" or Michael Jackson's "Thriller" as an amplified ukulele solo. The attraction of these songs is the contrast of powerful rock music and the very tender sound of a small plucked instrument that includes the clichéd Hawaii associations bound with it: a truly remarkable combination.

Jörg Jewanski

See also: Cuatro; Hawaii, Music of; Polynesia, Music of; Sitar

Further Reading

Beloff, Jim. 1997/2003. *The Ukulele. A Visual History.* San Francisco, CA: Miller Freeman; revised and expanded ed., San Francisco, CA: Backbeat Books.

Tranquada, Jim, and John King. 2012. *The 'Ukulele. A History.* Honolulu: University of Hawai'i Press.

Ukulele Hall of Fame Museum. 2012. www.ukulele.org.

Vaudeville

Vaudeville was one of the most popular forms of entertainment in North America from the early 1880s through the end of the 1920s. Along with operetta, burlesque, and other 19th-century comic genres, it was highly influential in the development of American musical theater, inspiring countless Broadway composers and lyricists including George and Ira Gershwin. Vaudeville launched the careers of scores of actors, comedians, and musicians who navigated the transition from live theater performance to radio, film, and television. Its impact persists today in late-night talk shows and sketch comedy programs such as *Saturday Night Live*, whose combination of variety and comedy harks back to the vaudeville stage of more than a century ago.

The term "vaudeville" stems from various secular song traditions that developed in France between the 15th and 18th centuries. The texts of these songs often centered on love or humor and were set to simple, singable melodies with predictable forms (e.g., A B A). By the late 19th century, the term had evolved to encompass a new form of entertainment that originated in the Northeastern United States. Former ringmaster Tony Pastor (1837–1908) is credited with repurposing the word "vaudeville" in the early 1880s, in part to distinguish his family-friendly variety shows in New York from earlier, more risqué programming such as burlesque. Drawing upon existing modes of performance, including minstrelsy (blackface comedy) and the circus, Pastor's brand of vaudeville responded to demand by a newly prosperous middle class for "good clean fun" as families and women occupied a growing share of theater seats.

A central figure in vaudeville's rapid expansion was Benjamin Franklin "B. F." Keith (1846–1914), who opened several theaters in Boston and New York in the 1880s and 1890s. With his partner Edward Franklin "E. F." Albee (1857–1930), Keith managed a circuit of houses that stretched from the Eastern seaboard to the Midwest. Albee's and Keith's United Booking Office, which functioned as a middleman between theater managers and performers, exerted near-monopolistic control of the business for years. Others entrepreneurs, including Alexander Pantages and Martin Beck, further expanded the industry. Beck, a Slovakian immigrant, built or acquired dozens of theaters and eventually formed the Orpheum Circuit that dominated territories from Chicago to the West. Racial segregation in venues was common in many areas and white- and black-oriented theater chains developed regionally. By the century's end, vaudeville was performed in hundreds of cities across North America and had eclipsed comparable forms of entertainment in terms of popularity and reach.

A typical vaudeville show consisted of a dozen or so acts performed over several hours. The format was flexible and the programming highly varied. Shows usually featured some combination of popular and classical singing, comedy routines, dance numbers, illusion or stage magic, acrobatic feats, and minstrelsy. Appearances by top-billed performers were normally reserved for the latter half of the show, evidently to build anticipation. Well-known performers, many of whom would establish careers in film and television, included Harry Houdini, Will Rogers, W. C. Fields, Al Jolson, the Marx Brothers, Charlie Chaplin, Mae West, Buster Keaton, Abbott and Costello, Gracie Allen, George Burns, Bob Hope, and Rose Marie. Such star power made vaudeville a vehicle for promoting Tin Pan Alley songs, as performers frequented Manhattan's publishing houses in search of new material.

The wane of vaudeville is closely linked to the rise of other forms of entertainment, most notably radio and cinema. At the end of the 19th century, theater operators were already incorporating silent films in their shows, with or without live musical accompaniment. The share of time devoted to motion pictures steadily increased during the first two decades of the 1900s—a short-term boon for business, but the practice eventually spurred vaudeville's decline. The landscape changed dramatically with the advent of "talkies" (sound films) beginning in 1927. In just a few years' time, filmed entertainment became the main attraction for audiences at the expense of live stage performance, which was relegated to entr'actes or intermissions. As waves of performers left to pursue work in emerging media, many theaters formerly dedicated to vaudeville were reinvented as venues for screening films.

Joseph E. Jones

See also: Foster, Stephen Collins; Musicals; Tin Pan Alley; Virginia Minstrels

Further Reading

Library of Congress. 1998. "American Variety Stage: Vaudeville and Popular Entertainment 1870–1920." http://memory.loc.gov/ammem/vshtml/vshome.html.

S. D., Trav. 2005. *No Applause—Just Throw Money: The Book That Made Vaudeville Famous*. New York: Faber & Faber.

Slide, Anthony. 2012. *The Encyclopedia of Vaudeville*. Jackson: University Press of Mississippi.

Smith, Bill. 1976. *The Vaudevillians*. New York: Macmillan.

Snyder, Robert W. 1989. *The Voice of the City: Vaudeville and Popular Culture in New York*. New York: Oxford University Press.

Stein, Charles W., ed. 1984. *American Vaudeville as Seen by Its Contemporaries*. New York: Alfred A. Knopf.

Wertheim, Arthur Frank. 2006. *Vaudeville Wars: How the Keith-Albee and Orpheum Circuits Controlled the Big Time and Its Performers*. New York: Palgrave MacMillan.

Veena

A plucked stringed instrument emanating from ancient India, the *veena* (sometimes *vina*) is featured primarily in the country's classical music—both Karnatic and Hindustani genres. Viewed historically, *veena* is a generic term for all string instruments. The earliest known use of the term is contained in the Tamil people of Tirumurai's list of musical instruments dating from the sixth to the 11th centuries. Similar to other instruments (woodwinds, for example), the name represents several instruments belonging to different families, including zithers (*Rudra veena*), necked bowl lutes (*Saraswati veena*), and plucked string instruments (*Mohan veena*, ancient *veena*). An individual playing the instrument is called a *vainaka*. The Burmese harp is considered to be the earliest known form of veena; however, the term in modern usage refers to instruments of the lute genre and to certain types of guitars indigenous to India. In modern usage, the instruments designated *veena* have mainly been lutes or zithers, although recently the term has been applied to modified Western guitars. The *sitar* is considered to be a modified form of the veena, adapted to appeal to Persian musical tastes.

The Gupta veena is likely the instrument referred to in the section of the *Nātyaśāstra* devoted to instrumental music. It is described as an arched harp, played with strings parallel to the individual's body and both hands plucking the strings. This image is depicted on Samudragupta's gold coins. Although the coin's image does not clearly display the number of strings, written descriptions of a seven-string veena (*saptatantree veena*) bear a striking resemblance.

There are both fretted and unfretted types of veenas. The fretted models include the Rudra veena, which is typically associated with Hindustani classical music in the northern region of the country. The Saraswati veena is commonly used in Karnatic classical music of India's southern region. The fretless instruments include the Vichitra veena found in Hindustani music and the Chitra veena, or *gottuvadhyam*, associated with Karnatic music.

Eldonna L. May

See also: Karnatic Music; Mridangam; Sitar; Tabla

Further Reading
Khan, Mobarak Hossain, Wakil Ahmed, and Momen Chowdhury. 2012. "Musical Instruments." In Sirajul Islam and Ahmed A. Jamal (eds.), *Banglapedia: National Encyclopedia of Bangladesh*, 2nd ed. Asiatic Society of Bangladesh. http://en.banglapedia.org/index.php?title=Musical_Instruments.

Villa-Lobos, Heitor (1887–1959)

Heitor Villa-Lobos, born into a middle-class Rio de Janeiro family, became the best-known Brazilian composer of the 20th century. His prolific output reflects the vast plurality of Brazilian peoples, and he consciously sought to create a national musical style that incorporated indigenous rhythms and folk melodies into a Western classical idiom. His success during his lifetime in both Europe and the United States brought him international acclaim. He continues to inspire composers of South America and Latin American descent.

Largely self-taught, Villa-Lobos spent his childhood under the tutelage of his father, Raúl Villa-Lobos, who taught him to play the clarinet and cello. He secretly learned how to play guitar on the way to and from school, because at the time, the instrument was considered low-class and not acceptable in traditional

Heitor Villa-Lobos was one of Brazil's most prolific composers. (Bettmann/Getty Images)

Brazilian middle-class society. After an unsuccessful attempt at medical school (and after his overbearing father died), he felt free to learn as much as he could about Brazilian popular music, including street music. This street music, played by musicians called *choroes*, were the inspiration for his invented genre of *Choros*. In 1903 Villa-Lobos left home and moved in with his aunt, whose home was closer to the nightlife. He spent his formative years as a musician playing the cello in various music halls, hotels, and cinemas in Rio de Janeiro, where he met many members of the popular music scene, including Ernesto Nazareth and Anacleto de Medeiros.

Villa-Lobos spent much of the period between 1905 and 1913 traveling around Brazil. It is believed he was researching indigenous music during this time. However, no records or diaries were kept during his travels, and not much is known about exactly where he went or who he was in contact with. He traveled to the Amazon, to the northeastern state of Bahia, and south toward the border of Uruguay. Nevertheless, his musical results of these travels are better documented: this appears to be the time when he formulated the type of composer he wished to be. Many of the melodies and rhythms that he heard on his Brazilian excursions likely found their way into his music, either directly or indirectly. However, he was not nearly as meticulous an ethnographer as Béla Bartók, and he did not document his sources in any existing scores. The only exception to this is his *Guia practico* of 1932, which was a collection of folksong arrangements.

In 1913 he met his first wife, Lucilia, who was also a pianist and who premiered several of his piano works. In 1922, Villa-Lobos was chosen to represent Brazilian concert music in the "Week of Modern Art" held in São Paulo. Several of his works were performed there for an international audience. This momentous week in the life of the composer spurred him on to relocate to Paris the following year, and he lived there until 1930. While in Paris he expanded his international reputation, and connected with several notable European composers, such as Igor Stravinsky, Edgard Varèse, Maurice Ravel, and Sergei Prokofiev. By the time he returned to Brazil, he had become the most well-known living South American composer.

During the 1930s Villa-Lobos was instrumental in improving and organizing a state-sponsored Brazilian music education program, which necessitated his cooperation with the dictatorship of Gétulio Vargas. Although Villa-Lobos received criticism for generally supporting the right-wing regime, he felt it was his duty to bring the country up to date in terms of a nationalized music curriculum. The composer was, after all, primarily interested in advancing his own career, and he eventually became the Superintendent of Musical and Artistic Education for Rio de Janeiro. The Vargas regime lasted from 1930 to 1945, and during that time Villa-Lobos's goals of promoting Brazilian nationalism through music (particularly collective song) coincided with the goals of the dictatorship.

Villa-Lobos was also very successful in the United States, as both a conductor and a composer. In the 1940s he received several commissions from major orchestras, including the Boston Symphony Orchestra (Symphony no. 11), the New York Philharmonic (Cello Concerto no. 2), and the Philadelphia Orchestra. Villa-Lobos also composed a guitar concerto for Andrés Segovia, who premiered the work with the Houston Symphony Orchestra in 1951. He spent the last seven years of life back in Paris, where he continued to receive accolades, premieres, and commissions up until his death in 1959.

Villa-Lobos's catalogue is immense, and includes 12 symphonies, 17 string quartets, seven full-length ballets, more than 18 concertos, seven operas, several piano solos, a huge body of chamber works, and pieces with invented genres. Two of these genres are the approximately 14 *Choros*, and the nine works of differing mediums called *Bachianas Brasileiras*. These pieces all reveal Villa-Lobos's fascination with the music of J. S. Bach. The collective title alone gives a good indication of their intent: they are "Brazilian Bach-like pieces." The most famous of these is no. 5 for soprano voice and four cellos; the "Aria-Cantilena" movement being the composer's most recognizable and lasting melody.

Many of his works have a distinct rhythmic profile, based somewhat on the *habanera* rhythm of Afro-Cuban traditions. Some pieces include *samba*-like figurations, and *moto perpetuo* accompaniment figures, coupled with soaring melodies above. The *Choros* in particular often feature a characteristic indigenous Brazilian rhythmic background, over which quite intricate contrapuntal parts weave in and out. *Choros* no. 13 (1929) has the extremely unusual scoring of two orchestras and a band. (Sadly, the score for this was lost.) No. 10 from 1926, which is for choir and orchestra, uses enchanting ostinato rhythms and Amazonian birdsong as its primary material. In the *Choros* series of pieces, Villa-Lobos sought to combine the popular with the modern, and by translating the rhythms of street musicians into traditional classical ensembles, he was largely successful.

Christopher Gable

See also: Accordion (Americas); Brazil, Music of; Piazzolla, Astor; Samba Instruments; Samba Music; Tango

Further Reading

Appleby, David P. 2002. *Heitor Villa-Lobos: A Life (1887–1959)*. Lanham, MD: Scarecrow Press.

Behague, Gerard. 1994. *Heitor Villa-Lobos: The Search for Brazil's Musical Soul*. Austin: University of Texas Press.

Wright, Simon. 1992. *Villa-Lobos*. Oxford: Oxford University Press.

Virginia Minstrels

The Virginia Minstrels were a group of 19th-century musicians and entertainers who staged the first full-length blackface minstrel show in the spring of 1843 in New York. Comprised of Dan Emmett (1815–1904), William "Billy" Whitlock (1813–?), Dick Pelham (1815–1876), and Frank Brower (1823–1874), the group was responsible for establishing the show's standard format, instrumentation, and performing customs. Though their time together was brief, the success of the Virginia Minstrels spurred the emergence of countless minstrel troupes throughout the Northeast and ushered in the classic age of blackface minstrelsy.

The roots of the Virginia Minstrels lay in the early partnership of Emmett and Brower who, after touring together with various circus companies, formed a duo in 1842. Emmett, a self-taught fiddler and banjoist, had been performing as a blackface entertainer and songwriter for years in his hometown of Mount Vernon, Ohio, and elsewhere in the Midwest before he met Brower, a Baltimore-born comedian, singer, dancer, and the first black impersonator to play the bones. As a fiddle-and-bones duo, Emmett and Brower appeared on various New York stages before joining Whitlock and Pelham. New York-born "Billy" Whitlock had learned to play the banjo in 1838, and from then on worked as a blackface performer in local variety shows and with touring circus companies. Dick Pelham, also a New York native, was known principally as a dancer prior to his joining the group as tambourine player.

In christening themselves the "Virginia Minstrels," the quartet likely intended to impart some regional authenticity to their project. Indeed, none of the group's members were actually from Virginia, but the state's association with Southern plantation life bolstered the group's representations of black characters such as Jim Crow. Likewise, in borrowing "minstrels" from family singing groups that were popular at the time, such as the Tyrolese Minstrels and the Alpine Minstrels, the group's name also evoked a sense of respectability.

Following their New York premiere, the Virginia Minstrels staged their first full-length "Ethiopian Concert" in Boston on March 7, 1843. Unlike previous blackface acts that were performed only during intermissions for a play or as one of many acts in a variety show, the troupe presented an entire evening of entertainment divided into two parts. The first included a topical address delivered in black dialect and concentrated on Northern urban scenes; the second shifted to rural Southern plantation settings. Interspersed throughout were songs attributed to Emmett (such as "Old Dan Tucker" and "Jimmy Crack Corn"), dances, stump speeches, and parody skits.

Onstage, the Virginia Minstrels arranged themselves on four chairs in a semicircle, with tambourine and bones on the ends and fiddle and banjo in between. Such a layout allowed Brower (Mr. Bones) and Pelham (Mr. Tambo) freedom to move and interact with audiences as they performed. Emphasizing rhythm, sound, and body movement over melody and harmony, the Virginia Minstrels' instrumentation and stage action provided the model for many troupes that formed in the 1840s, such as the Ethiopian Serenaders, the Congo Minstrels, and Christy's Minstrels.

In the wake of their successes in New York and Boston, the troupe embarked on a tour to the British Isles in late spring of 1843, beginning with a performance in Liverpool on May 21. By July, however, the group had to disband in the midst of financial difficulty. Emmett went on to perform independently in Lancashire and with traveling circuses before rejoining Brower and Pelham in Dublin in April of 1844. In September of the same year, Emmett and Brower returned to the United States. In October, they began a tour of New England with replacements for Pelham and Whitlock, who had chosen to remain permanently in England.

By the 1850s, the minstrel show model and repertoire established by the Virginia Minstrels had increased in scope and changed in context. The two-part structure was supplanted by a three-part form, and older and cruder dialect tunes were replaced by popular and sentimental ballads of the "genteel" tradition of minstrel songs by composers such as Stephen Foster. However, during the early 1840s, the Virginia Minstrels were of singular importance in establishing the groundwork for minstrelsy's popularity, both nationally and abroad.

John Stanislawski

See also: Emmett, Dan; Vaudeville

Further Reading
Lott, Eric. 1993. *Love and Theft: Blackface Minstrelsy and the American Working Class.* New York: Oxford University Press.
Nathan, Hans. 1962. *Dan Emmett and the Rise of American Negro Minstrelsy.* Norman: University of Oklahoma Press.
Toll, Robert C. 1974. *Blacking Up: The Minstrel Show in Nineteenth-Century America.* New York: Oxford University Press.

Vocables

Evident in indigenous song styles throughout the world, *vocables* are musically sung syllables that contain no referential meaning. Vocables can consist of only vowels, parts of obsolete words, or "extra" vowels inserted into words to complete a melodic shape or phrase. Most prevalent in Native American musics, vocables perform a wide variety of functions because the musical system strongly reflects the entire culture.

Songs associated with task and incorporating vocables exist for virtually all activities in Native American societies. The use of vocables varies from tribe to tribe and region to region. Many Native American songs have no words at all, relying completely upon vocables to convey meaning. The length of the notes constitute a melodic line that is determined by vocalization techniques, and the use of isorhythm and/or rhythmic repetition is common.

Vocables are typically organized into sequential patterns that resemble words and recur in songs sung by speakers of several languages. One of the most common vocable patterns is *heyowicinayo*. Indians in the North and Central United States rely more heavily upon vocables than tribes in the East, South, and Southwestern regions. In instances where words occur, they are typically short and take up only a small component of the melody. For example, a song text from a Blackfoot Sun Dance ceremony consists of the following text: "Sun says to sing"; the remainder of the song consists of vocables. The clear enunciation of vocables is rare; however, when it does occur it is usually the result of a Native American mannerism not found in Western art music. For example, syllables can be used as an ostinato pattern or "root" to imply an action, such as "way" which recalls a swinging motion. In the repertoire of Peyote Cult songs, approximately 50% of the songs consist of vocables, with the proportion varying somewhat from tribe to tribe.

Current research about vocables has investigated their significance and categorized them into types, to suit the melodic flow and desired vocal style. Different genres have different proportions of vocables; by contrast with lexical text, vocables may promote solidarity among groups with mutually unintelligible languages, a particularly important function at modern pan-tribal powwows.

Eldonna L. May

See also: Blues; Jazz; Native American Music

Further Reading

Densmore, Frances. 1943. "The Use of Meaningless Syllables in Indian Songs." *American Anthropologist* 45(1) (January-March), 160–162.

McAllester, D. P. 1980. "North American Native Music." In E. May (ed.), *Musics of Many Cultures: An Introduction*, 307–331. Berkeley: University of California Press.

Myers, Helen, ed. 1993. *Ethnomusicology: Historical and Regional Studies*. New York: W. W. Norton.

Waltz

A dance in triple meter, the waltz was the most popular ballroom dance of 19th-century Europe. Though known now as one of the most elegant and graceful couple dances, thanks to the popularity of reality television shows like *So You Think You Can Dance* (2005–) and *Dancing with the Stars* (2005–), the waltz made a rather scandalous entrance onto the social dance scene in the late 18th and early 19th centuries. As a type of music, it charmed many a composer and infiltrated almost every genre of Western art music composition. Some would argue that, out of all dance forms, it had the greatest impact on Western musical history.

The origins of the waltz are shrouded in ambiguity. The term comes from the German verb *walzen*, which was a general descriptor for dancing to triple-metered music in closed position (that is, where the dancers' torsos face each other, the man's right hand rests on the woman's back or waist, and his left hand holds her right hand at approximately shoulder level). That term, in turn, is thought to have come from the *volta*, a country dance from southern France featuring rotating motion. The connection between the volta and the waltz is not stated explicitly anywhere, and so remains hypothetical. With regard to its actual steps, the waltz is closely related to the *Ländler*, a traditional country dance (also in triple meter) from Germany and Austria. The Ländler features stomping and clapping, which gradually melted away from the waltz as it moved from the country to the polished floors of urban ballrooms.

The waltz entered polite European society in the mid-1770s. Its rustic roots, close embrace, gliding motion, and quick rotation appealed greatly to people from all social classes because it differed so dramatically from the other dominant social dance: the minuet. Franz Joseph Haydn replaced the minuet with a "mouvement de Walze" in a piano sonatina dated ca. 1776, which some believe is the waltz's earliest appearance in classical music. Additionally, Martin y Soler's *Una cosa rara* (1786) was the first opera to incorporate the waltz. The circulation of a pamphlet called "A method of composing with two dice as many Waltzes and Schleifer [a Medieval German dance] as one wishes, without being musical or knowing anything of composition" (1786), supposedly written by Wolfgang Amadeus Mozart, also demonstrated attempts to legitimize the waltz. By the end of the 18th century, its popularity had spread internationally, as evidenced by journal articles and music publication sales. The term "waltz" likely made the move from general descriptive verb to specific dance style in the last decade of the 18th century.

As with many new styles of popular dance and music, the waltz was feared and embraced simultaneously. The fear was twofold: medical and propriety. It was believed the dance's spinning motion and excessive speed were harmful to the health, particularly that of women. One 19th-century exercise expert wrote, "Vertigo is one of the great inconveniences of the waltz; and the character of this dance, its rapid turnings, the clasping of the dancers, their exciting contact, and the too quick and too long continued succession of lively and agreeable emotions, produce sometimes, in women of a very irritable constitution, syncopes [the medical term for fainting], spasms, and other accidents which should induce them to renounce it" (Walker, 1836, pp. 148–149). Prior to the waltz, the closest contact that members of the opposite sex had on the dance floor was the clasping of one or both hands, and partners were frequently exchanged. Spectators, then, were quite shocked at the roaming nature of gentlemen's hands, the close and sustained body contact, and the lifting of the lady's skirts to prevent tripping. The famous English poet Lord Byron was perturbed at the dance's seemingly loose morals and, under his pseudonym Horace Horem Esq., penned a lengthy poem about the dance. Despite vocal protestations, the dance had some notable advocates in Thomas Wilson, an English dancing master and author of *A Description of the Correct Method of Waltzing*; and the famous German author/poet Johann Wolfgang von Goethe.

The waltz conquered continental Europe and Britain, but it reigned supreme in Vienna. Large dance halls such as Sperl and the Apollosaal opened in 1807 and 1808, respectively. The latter could hold up to 6,000 dancers. It was also due to the waltz that the Congress of Vienna, the 1815 conference of European ambassadors that met in Vienna following the Napoleonic Wars, gained the reputation for dancing: "*Le Congrès ne marche pas—il danse.*" (The Congress does not walk. It dances.)

In the early part of the 19th century, Michael Pamer (1782–1827) composed many Ländler and waltzes for these new dance halls. Franz Schubert was likely the first canonic composer who explicitly composed and published sets of waltzes, but Carl Maria von Weber successfully transplanted the waltz from the dance hall to the concert stage. His piano rondo "Aufforderung zum Tanz" (1819) featured a formal introduction, a sequence of waltz themes, and a coda that summarized all of the major themes. This form matured through the waltzes of Joseph Lanner (1801–1843) and Johann Strauss the elder (1804–1849).

Both Lanner and Strauss the elder started their careers as violinists in Pamer's orchestra. Though they worked together for many years, the pair split in 1825 and became friendly rivals for Vienna's affections. Both of their waltzes spun from improvisations on the violin, but they developed distinct styles. Lanner's waltzes tended to feature flowing, lyrical melodies with unexpected harmonic shifts. Strauss was the more conservative of the two, using predictable harmonic progressions and short melodic phrases strung together; however, his strength lay in surprising dotted rhythms and syncopations. The Viennese coined a phrase to describe their rivalry: "With Lanner, it's 'Pray dance, I entreat you.' With Strauss, 'You must dance, I command you'" (Carner, 1948, pp. 44–45).

Through Lanner's and Strauss's works, the waltz rose from the level of light dance music to veritable musical composition, and several aspects of the dance as a composition were cemented. Individual waltz themes expanded from eight bars to 16. One set usually consisted of five themes. Tempos settled to approximately 70 bars per minute. Introductions grew from a few short measures to longer, descriptive segments that frequently featured contrasting tempos and/or meters. In addition, Lanner and Strauss started to name their sets. At first the names usually designated the place or event for which they were composed. Later on, they marked certain personal events or creatively described the introduction's mood.

In the long run, Strauss won the "battle," as tours with his orchestra throughout Germany, France, and Britain in the mid- to late 1830s set Europe on a Viennese waltz craze. Lanner and his orchestra did not tour much. Other composers, such as Josef Gung'l (1809–1889), Philipe Musard (1792–1859), H. C. Lumbye (1810–1874), and Louis Jullien (1812–1860), further fueled the international waltz craze in Berlin, Paris, Copenhagen, and London, respectively. Incidentally, Gung'l was responsible for bringing the waltz to America.

Johann Strauss the younger (1825–1899), who is now far better known than his father, assumed Lanner's place as his father's rival when Lanner passed away. Strauss the elder originally opposed the choice of musical career for his sons, and Strauss the younger spent his early professional life as a bank clerk. However, on October 15, 1844, at the age of 19, he made his bold debut as a professional conductor and composer. The concert was a rousing success with critics and audience alike. This consequently strained his relationship with his father, and things remained tense between them until Strauss the elder's death in 1849. Strauss the younger fully assumed his father's place when he merged his orchestra with that of his father.

Through the 1850s and 1860s, the Strauss name was virtually synonymous with the waltz. Strauss the younger was joined on the concert scene by his two brothers Josef and Eduard. The waltzes of the Strauss brothers combined the best aspects of their father's and Lanner's waltzes. They maintained the rhythmic surprises of their father's style but melded them with Lanner's lyricism. Furthermore, Strauss the younger became an avid follower of Richard Wagner, Franz Liszt, and the New German School. His waltz themes increasingly featured themes of unusual bar lengths, more dissonant harmonies, and colorful orchestrations. Many of his waltzes earned continuous places in the concert repertory during this time period. These included *An der schönen, blauen Donau* (On the beautiful, blue Danube), most commonly known to mass audiences today through Stanley Kubrick's film *2001: A Space Odyssey*), *Künstlerleben* (The artist's life), and *Geschichten aus dem Wienerwald* (Tales from the Vienna woods). In the 1870s, Strauss the younger turned to operetta. For many, these works revealed a lack of understanding of vocal composition and dramatic structure. However, he wrote some of his most beautiful waltzes for his 16 operettas and, according to some, rescued them from oblivion. These included *Die Fledermaus*'s "Du und Du" and *Die Zigeunerbaron*'s "Schatzwalzer."

Besides the work of the Strausses, the waltz appeared in many canonic 19th-century works. Ludwig van Beethoven's *Diabelli Variations* (1819–1823) were originally called *33 Variations on a Waltz by Anton Diabelli*. Hector Berlioz incorporated the waltz into the second movement of his *Symphonie fantastique* (1830). Frédéric Chopin and Liszt wrote some of the most iconic waltzes for solo piano; Brahms, a good friend of Strauss the younger, also composed a set of 16 waltzes for solo piano (op. 39, 1865). In ballet, Léo Délibes included a waltz in *Coppelia*

(1870) as did Pyotr Tchaikovsky in *Swan Lake* (1875–1876), *Sleeping Beauty* (1888–1889), and *The Nutcracker* (1891–1892). Notable operas such as Charles Gounod's *Faust* (1859), Jacques Offenbach's *Les contes d'Hoffmann* (1881), Wagner's *Parsifal* (1882), and Giacomo Puccini's *La Bohème* (1896) also featured waltzes. Luigi Arditi's well-known soprano showcase piece "Il Bacio" (1860) was an homage to Strauss the younger's waltzes.

The glamour started to fade in the 20th century as the Austro-Hungarian Empire marched toward its demise. The dance halls with their glittering waltzes seemed to live in denial of the political decline happening just outside their doors. In early 20th-century art music, the waltz took on a nostalgic and sometimes grotesque air. These unsettling waltzes included the third movement of Gustav Mahler's *Fifth Symphony* (1902), Maurice Ravel's piano solos *Valses nobles et sentimentales* (1911) and La Valse (1920), and portions of Igor Stravinsky's ballet *Petrushka* (1911).

When the Austro-Hungarian Empire fell after World War I, the center of European light music moved from Vienna to Berlin. The waltz lost its grip on western Europe. However, by that time it had shed its scandalous qualities and adopted a beautiful and often romantic nostalgia, attracting the attention of American song writers. The waltz was used to great dramatic effect in musical theatre pieces such as Cole Porter's *Kiss Me, Kate* (1948), Rodgers and Hammerstein's *Carousel* (1945) and *The Sound of Music* (1959), Stephen Sondheim's *A Little Night Music* (1973), and Andrew Lloyd Webber's *Evita* (1978), to name a few. Following World War I, Soviet composers also embraced the waltz. Aram Khachaturian composed *Masquerade* in 1939, and Sergei Prokofiev composed his *Suite of Waltzes*, op. 110, in 1946.

Because jazz and popular music is predominantly written in duple meter today, the term "waltz" tends to be freely attached to any piece in triple meter. Current ballroom practitioners occasionally use the 19th-century concert repertory for their slow and Viennese waltzes. With popular reality television dance shows, any triple-meter song is fair game for the waltz. Though it may not be the king of dances anymore, the waltz has made its mark on history and lives on as a symbol of elegance and romance on musical theater stages, popular television shows, and classical concert halls.

Aya Esther Hayashi

See also: Classical Music, European; French Folk Dances; Ländler; Opera; Symphonic Poem; Symphony

Further Reading

Carner, Mosco. 1948. *The Waltz*. New York: Chanticleer Press.

Hornem, Horace, Esq. [George Gordon, 6th Baron Byron]. 1821. *Waltz: An Apostrophic Hymn*. London: W. Clark.

Knowles, Mark. 2009. *The Wicked Waltz and Other Scandalous Dances: Outrage at Couple Dancing in the 19th and Early 20th Centuries*. Jefferson, NC: McFarland.

Sachs, Curt. 1937. *The World History of Dance*, trans. Bessie Schönberg. New York: W. W. Norton.

Thompson, Allison, comp. 1998. *Dancing through Time: Western Social Dance in Literature, 1400–1918: Selections*. Jefferson, NC: McFarland.

Walker, Donald. 1836. *Exercises for Ladies; Calculated to Preserve and Improve Beauty and to Prevent and Correct Personal Defects, Inseparable from Constrained or Careless Habits: Founded on Physiological Principles*. London: Thomas Hurst.

Wayang Kulit

An ancient form of storytelling and great dramatic form closely allied with *gamelan*, the two-dimensional shadow-puppet theater known as *wayang kulit* (or, in its ancient form, *wayang purwa*), is an Indonesian performance medium employing music that has gained prominence in Javanese culture and that carries connotations of extraordinary power. *Wayang* means "shadow," or "ghost"; *kulit* means "leather." Made from buffalo hide, the flat, intricately cut and perforated puppets are part of a tradition that dates back at least 10 centuries, when it flourished in the royal courts of Java and Bali. The puppets are stylized exaggerations of human form. Plots for these plays with music are derived from Indonesian and Indian epics, and the *Mahabharata* and the *Ramayana*. With the passage of time, the epics became distinctly Javanese versions of the original Indian texts, and by the 10th century they were recited in the form of wayang kulit as court-based theater. Most likely, the Hindu stories were applied to indigenous beliefs and local shadow puppet traditions, melding into a uniquely Javanese custom.

Inspired by Indian models, the genre spread to other islands, including Lombok, Madura, Sumatra, and Borneo, serving as a conduit for the dissemination of both Hindu traditions and Islam to Indonesia. The genre is an important form both as a ceremonial ritual and a popular entertainment. It transmits history of ancestral spirits, educates youth in traditional cultures, and serves as the touchstone for the practice of meditation or semadi. Wayang kulit performances are also commissioned by villages to celebrate marriages, births, circumcisions, and other rites. Taught by oral tradition and rote, learning the practices and repertoire of wayang kulit maintains the rich traditional relationship of master and disciple. Student puppeteers learn their craft from a master puppeteer (*dhalang*) over the course of time by oral tradition and rote learning. Dhalangs operate the puppets while narrating the story, recite all of the dialogue, provide sound effects, and conduct the gamelan orchestra that provides the musical accompaniment. Because singing is an important part of Central Javanese compositions, dhalangs must be able to effectively convey the voice of a princess, a pauper, and a nobleman as indicated in the storyline. Because the central figure in a wayang kulit performance is the dhalang, he is usually recognized by the audience as a powerful figure—typically a religious leader, or shaman—who has the ability to communicate with the spirit world during the performance.

There are two principal types of puppets: three-dimensional wooden puppets (*wayang klitik* or *golèk*); and the flat leather shadow puppet (wayang kulit) projected in front of a backlit screen. Both forms are characterized by costumes, facial features, and articulated body parts. The dhalang operates the arms by the use of thin sticks attached to the puppets. Singers and musicians play complex melodies upon gamelan instruments and drums. Historically, the dhalangs were considered literary experts who disseminated moral and aesthetic cultural values. In addition, a talented dhalang can perform nearly 200 wayang stories (*lakon*) and is celebrated for his understanding of life and his role as a spiritual leader and teacher. Dhalangs reveal to others the mysteries of earthly existence and explain the philosophical and mystical composition of life, the nature of order in the world, of cosmic justice, and the laws of the universe.

The roles of comic characters representing the common man, and also celebrating Islamic heroes through the use of the puppets, have served as a vehicle for protesting socio-political issues, a function that can be attributed to the genre's continued popularity during the course of history. Although stories taken from the Indian epics, the *Mahabharata*, and the *Ramayana* have the highest popularity and prestige (especially the *Mahabharata*), stories of Javanese and Islamic origins are also performed with good result.

An Indonesian master puppeteer moves a *wayang kulit* puppet before a white screen. This form of shadow puppetry typically presents tales from the major Hindu epics. (Aman Rochman/AFP/Getty Images)

There are at least 200 wayang kulit stories in the repertoire, commonly known as the "Rama cycle" for the *Ramayana* and the "pendawa cycle" for the *Mahabarata*. The repertoire and performance practices were taught by oral tradition within the families of puppeteers, musicians, and puppet makers. The dhalang (rarely a woman) is expected to memorize a great body of stories and to recite ancient narrative passages and poetic songs creatively, performing all the roles in a particular play. He commands a thorough knowledge of *karawitan* (musical repertory and practice), is familiar with particular occasions, speaks with a wide variety of voices suited to everyone from the most refined gentleman to the crudest villain, can skillfully move the puppets to convey a variety of refinement and crudity, knows archaic languages and the complete range of contemporary social dialects, is a repository of spiritual and cultural values, and is acquainted with the latest political events and social problems. Wayang narratives involve moral and ethical challenges faced by the characters in their travails of life, love, and war. These morality plays contend with issues of good versus evil, as well as the struggle between right and wrong. They are about the pursuit of living a virtuous, noble life and the search for meaning. The structural plan for wayang kulit plays typically consists of three sections, accompanied by music performed by the gamelan ensemble that changes character or mode (*pathet*) to reflect the section breaks.

Wayang kulit takes place during the course of an entire night; the plays usually depict a battle whose turmoil is reflected in a disturbance of nature that is resolved when order is restored to human society and the world. Seated between the light source and a screen, the dhalang casts the shadows of the puppets against the screen, while at the same time signaling the gamelan ensemble (consisting of a combination of bronze gongs, xylophones, drums, and string instruments) for the musical selections necessary to accompany the scene. Sometimes he sings, too, to set the mood for an upcoming scene. Even though the stories center on Indic characters, they have been adapted in Java through the incorporation of stock comic characters who act as servants to the protagonists and serve as translators for the audience. All of the familiar characters communicate the various modes of human existence and manners of behavior.

Wayang kulit has changed significantly since Indonesia gained independence from the Dutch in 1945. For example, it was once very difficult to be accepted as a dhalang if one was not born into the family profession. In recent years, however, successful puppeteers have instead learned their craft from books and through observing other performers. Applying technology to puppet theater has been beneficial by providing better access to users, particularly children and young adults viewing wayang kulit with modern technology. Hansnul Jamal from the Universiti Sains Malaysia produced a multimedia experiment, "Borrower of the Light," incorporating cyberpunk science fiction with Malay traditional wayang kulit. Wayang kulit remains popular today primarily as a tourist attraction, catering to the island's eco-tourists and visitors. In an attempt to attract a younger, technologically facile audience, the genre also has recast itself by incorporating more comedy, references to celebrities, flashy stage spectacle, colored lights, strobe lights, synthesizers, and pop music. In 2008, the first wayang kulit animation, titled "Jala Emas Jala Perak," was produced by Art Media Production in Kota Bharu, Kelantan, capturing the narration and the story that originated from the *Ramayana* epic. In 1996, a wayang virtual research project began as an experimental version of the traditional wayang kulit under Universiti Malaysia Sarawak. The virtual version of the traditional puppet is combined with a 3D animated figure and controlled by a mouse, where the visuals were projected onto a white screen.

Eldonna L. May

See also: Gamelan Orchestra (Javanese); Indonesian Popular Music

Further Reading

Brandon, James, ed. 1993. *On Thrones of Gold: Three Javanese Shadow Plays*. Honolulu: University of Hawaii Press.

Heins, Ernst. 1970. "Cueing the Gamelan in Javanese Wayang Performance." *Indonesia* 9, 101–127.

Keeler, Ward, 1987. *Javanese Shadow Plays, Javanese Selves*. Princeton, NJ: Princeton University Press.

Kunst, Jaap. 1973 [1934]. *Music in Java: Its History, Its Theory, and Its Technique,* 3rd ed., rev. and enlarged by Ernst Heins. 2 vols. The Hague: Martinus Nijhoff.

McFee, Colin. 1936 (repr.). *Wayang Koelit and Its Music.* New York: AMS Press.

Sumarsam. 1984. "Gamelan Music and the Javanese Wayang Kulit." In Stephanie Morgan and Laurie Jo Sears (eds.), *Aesthetic Tradition and Cultural Transition in Java and Bali* (Monograph 2), 105–166. Madison: University of Wisconsin Center for Southeast Asian Studies.

Van Ness, Edward C., and Shita Prawirohardjo. 1980. *Javanese Wayang Kulit.* Singapore: Oxford University Press.

X

Xalam

The *xalam* (also spelled *khalam*) is a plucked lute with four or five strings that is played in the West African countries of Senegal, The Gambia, and Mali. It is primarily played by *griots*, professional musicians, storytellers, and oral historians who are found throughout the west African Sahel. The word "xalam" comes from the Wolof language and usually refers specifically to the instrument played by Wolof griots, called *gewel*. "Xalam" is also sometimes used as a general term for any of the closely related plucked lutes played by West African griots. It is thought to be one of the models that inspired the creation of the American banjo.

The body (or resonator) of a xalam is carved from a single piece of wood to form a hollowed-out oval with a rounded back, which is covered in goatskin or cowskin. The round neck passes approximately two-thirds of the way through the resonator, where it connects to a fan-shaped bridge that supports the strings through a hole in the animal-skin soundplane. Each of the nylon strings is a different length, and they attach to the neck with leather hoops that can be tightened or loosened to change tuning. Xalam may differ in number of strings, size, and use of an electric pick-up, but the basic features are always the same. These organological characteristics make the xalam nearly identical to neighboring West African lutes that have different names: for example, the Mande *ngoni* (or *koni*), the Fula *hoddu*, and the Moorish *tidinit*, among several others. Other West African lutes, such as the Jola *akonting* and Gnawa *gimbri*, are closely related but differ in important details such as the shape of the bridge and the passage of the neck all the way through the resonator. Based on the xalam's construction details and unusual playing style, scholars believe that xalam is one of the instruments that inspired slaves taken from West Africa to the Caribbean and United States to build gourd banjos, predecessors of the modern American banjo.

Someone who plays the xalam is called a *xalamkat*. The Wolof suffix *-kat*, which is roughly means "one who does ___," is probably the source of African American slang terms such as "jazz cat" and "hip cat" (from Wolof *hepikat* [one who sees clearly]). Traditionally, the xalam was only played by members of griot families, who acted as court musicians, storytellers, oral historians, genealogists, and advisors. The knowledge of how to play and build a xalam was passed down within families for centuries, though today it is more acceptable for musicians from non-griot families to play the instrument as well. It is far more common for men to play the xalam, though some women do play the instrument. The xalam is typically played solo or as part of a small ensemble at personal events such as weddings, infant naming ceremonies, and private parties, where it is used to accompany lyrics drawn from the griot historical repertoire. It may also be heard in larger ensembles playing for national folkloric performances, touristic presentations, and popular *mbalax* dance music. Some of the best-known xalam players today include Bassekou Kouyate, Mama Sissoko, and Cheick Hamala Diabaté, among others.

To play the instrument, the xalamkat alternately strikes the strings with the back of the index or middle finger in a downward motion and plucks upward and downward with the thumb. The two longest strings are used for most of the melodic content, and they are stopped with the fingers of the left hand to produce different pitches, as with a guitar. The two or three shorter strings are always played open, serving as repetitive drone strings or higher melody strings. Xalamkats tune their instruments in several different ways, with each tuning system—called *fodet* in Wolof—being used to accompany a specific musical and lyrical repertoire. The word "fodet" can also refer to the short, repeating musical patterns of six to 24 beats that constitute the foundational musical content of xalam music. In performance, these ostinato patterns are embellished by variations and virtuosic interjections, as well as the lyrical singing they accompany.

Scott V. Linford

See also: Griot; Jali; Kora

Further Reading

Charry, Eric. 2000. *Mande Music: Traditional and Modern Music of the Maninka and Mandinka of Western Africa*. Chicago: University of Chicago Press. [Companion CD: "Mande Music."]

Coolen, Michael Theodore. 1991. "Senegambian Influences on Afro-American Musical Culture." *Black Music Research Journal* 11, 1–18.

Coolen, Michael Theodore. 1983. "The Wolof Xalam Tradition of the Senegambia." *Ethnomusicology* 28(3), 477–498.

Durán, Lucy. 1981. "A Preliminary Study of the Wolof Xalam (with a list of recordings at the BIRS)." *Recorded Sound* 79, 29–50.

Hale, Thomas. 2007. *Griots and Griottes: Masters of Words and Music (African Expressive Cultures)*. Bloomington: Indiana University Press.

Y

Yodeling

The *yodel*, featuring rapid movement between head and chest voice, is a unique vocalization both hallowed and maligned, sacred and profane. It is as old as humankind and as contemporary as hip-hop and techno; both unique and universal and with a deeper and more global past than is generally presumed due to its association with lowest-common-denominator, inebriated, Oktoberfest, "Sound of Music" sing-alongs. What people assume about yodeling is based on this cultural template of kitsch, which marginalizes it as a sign of civilization in decline.

The reputation of yodeling suffered dating back to the 13th century when Eckhardt of Saint Gall (Switzerland) demanded the prohibition of "ugly vocal sounds" and "voices, neighing (as if the voice of a singing she-ass), lowing or bleating (like farm animals), effeminate voices, and every counterfeit, ostentation, and novelty of voices" (Plantenga, 2013, p. 16). Later, in the 15th century, Arnulf of Saint Ghislain complained that yodelers "bray with the din of their brawling bark louder than an ass" and that "they spew out harsh-sounding things," giving fuel to critics spanning Western history from Roman emperors to opera critics, popes, Mark Twain, Goethe, *Village Voice* journalists, and Nashville producers.

Yodeling's reputation is just now, over the past 20 years, recovering from being hijacked by kitsch-meisters, nationalists, and fascists in the 1930s. It is becoming acceptable again, even crucial world music, right in one's own backyard, as Austrian world musician Hubert von Goisern discovered—while touring Africa.

The yodel and such preceded language and song as humans attempted to communicate with animals and their environment—perhaps with an existential cry of awe into the wilderness. Yodelers often imitate birds. Lucretius, in *De rerum natura*, wrote: "Imitating with the mouth the liquid notes of birds came long before men were able to repeat smooth songs in melody and please the ear" (Plantenga, 2013, p. 10). The most effective bird mimicry ensured an evening meal, but sometimes humans just wanted engaging conversation. Some bird yodels may actually launch the vocalist into a state of self-inquiry—as the yodel bends to personal desires and self-enchantment. Many rites around the world include bird-call yodels, including those of Khirgiz and Yakut shamans who imitate birds visually and vocally. New Guinea's yodelers interweave bird calls into their rituals. The cuckoo is a favorite (*Kuckucks-jodler*), but other birds—nightingales, loons, doves, whippoorwills, and mockingbirds—are also imitated. The ideal conditions for a Swiss *Juutz* (nature yodel) would include the singers harmonizing with their own yodeled echoes in nature, with the echo representing early instants of recorded sound as the mountain air preserved the echo for a few ephemeral, stirring seconds.

The yodel served as a utilitarian call, as warning, or as long-distance communication among herders or herders and their herds in (often) mountainous or otherwise treacherous terrain. Author-musician Ed Sanders of the Fugs calls it "a homemade Morse code for people in the mountains" (Plantenga, 2004, p. 12). Pulitzer Prize–winning novelist Booth Tarkington described a yodeler in *Penrod* (1914) as "a lunatic whooping the lonely peace of the woods into pandemonium" and as "a code-signal to summon forth his friend" (Plantenga, 2013, p. 11).

Humans domesticated animals until herds began to heed the cowherd's yodel, leaving herders with less to do. As cattle grazed, cowherds discovered leisure; *homo faber*, meet *homo ludens*. With leisure came idleness, which led to play, and play led to engrossing vocal experiments. Hermann Hesse described this in *Peter Camenzind* (1906): "On one of the slopes where I usually drove my beasts ... I sprawled in the warmth, gazed in wonderment at the hurrying white cloudlets, and yodeled softly to myself until the goats noticed my laxness and took advantage of it" (Plantenga, 2013, p. 11).

In the Romantic era (later 18th century), the yodel, reshaped by human aesthetics and playfulness, was introduced into popular songs as a decorative refrain, "a soul-freeing flow of notes," as Eastside Dave Kline, a Pennsylvania Swiss yodeler describes it, which effectively hotwired nature to civilization (Plantenga, 2004).

A yodel is basically a powerful vocal that shifts rapidly between chest and head voice, accenting the voice break as a desirable audio effect. This jolt of air at the glottis, where the epiglottis muscles open and close the glottis flap to ensure that food goes down the esophagus and not the trachea, highlights the pitch change—and a three-octave leap can certainly be a shock to both ear and decorum. No glottal jolt, no yodel; everything else is secondary.

Whereas yodelers sharpen this transitional cleft between bass and falsetto voices at the pitch change, Western singers from pop to opera polish away that rough seam with glissando techniques to the point of imperceptibility. Musicologist Erich von Hornbostel (1877–1935) listed the yodel's chief characteristics as including: transition from chest voice to falsetto, large distances between notes, broad range extending the outer edges of sound, sung on vowels—AH, OH, OO for chest notes, AY, EE for head voice—that are often preceded by consonants, which function as "levers," propelling the yodel over long distances.

Country music's biggest star, Hank Williams, was genetically predisposed to the voice-break yodel, stretching the vowel-howl of words such as "lonesome." Irish singer Dolores O'Riordan of the Cranberries was also born with the ability to voice-break, allowing her to effortlessly wring extra soul from a simple phrase.

People usually assume that yodeling is of Swiss origin; 17th-century tales, in fact, describe Swiss mercenaries suffering from homesickness who, upon hearing certain yodels, would suffer unusual effects. A law was eventually passed that forbade hysteria-arousing yodeling in their presence.

Swiss yodeling provides a grand topographical dialogue between human and environment, inspiring deep connections to the big "out there." Manfred Bukofzer, in his 1936 *Magic & Technique in Alpine Music*, described the magical powers of the *kuhreihen*, mystical incantations consisting of yodeled tones combined with certain words and cow names, which aided in binding a herder to his herd and eradicated evil spirits and illness (Plantenga, 2004, p. 25).

Yodeling is so associated with Switzerland that many refuse to believe it originated in Africa. The earliest yodel was indeed Central African; Bantus, Bushmen, and Pygmies all yodel. Pygmies are likely the original yodelers; their deceptively simple, yet awe-inspiringly complex yodels are used to celebrate a successful hunt, lure animals into traps, influence fate, praise the forest, and simply entertain.

Recent DNA studies corroborate Alan Lomax's and Victor Grauer's pioneering Cantometric studies, which attempted to document global vocals based on a list of (shared) traits to trace their origin and dissemination. Both the DNA and Cantometrics studies reinforce out-of-Africa theories that the original humans, "a single band of 'native' Africans," migrated from Africa, carrying their characteristic vocals—including hocketed and polyphonic yodeling—in a diaspora that began more than 20,000 years ago when, as Grauer points out, "the ancestors of every human now living were a single population" (Grauer, 2006, p. 15).

They wandered, evolved, and eventually populated the world, with their music morphing with changing topographies, social systems, needs, and circumstances. Lomax and Grauer found yodeling in the farthest corners of the Earth: Taiwan, South America, Genoa, Scandinavia, Scotland, Georgia, and beyond.

African vocals likely entered the New World via slave ships. Yodeling and its rougher cousin, the field holler, no doubt nourished the roots of gospel, blues, jazz, and soul. But yodeling was probably already present before the first slaves and (Alpine) colonists arrived: the Sioux prepared for battle, and also augmented their love songs, with yodels. Black cowboys and Mexican *vaqueros* likely taught cowboys how to yodel.

Uniqueness and versatility ensure yodeling's continued vitality. Many artists became great because of—and not despite—their yodeling: Hank Williams, Jimmie Rodgers, jazz vocalist Leon Thomas, and Tuvan vocalist Sainkho (Demetrio Stratos), among others.

Yodeling is heard in literally every musical genre. Yodeling survives—even thrives—and its uniqueness is precisely why many contemporary avant-garde vocalists, beginning with the Dadaists, such as Jaap Blonk, Yma Sumac, Paul Dutton, Anna Nacher, Erika Stucky, Mij the Yodeling Astrologer, Tim Buckley, Shelley Hirsch, Christine Lauterburg, Phil Minton, Kutzkelina, and many more return to the primitive to astonish and transcend content and ordinary musical thresholds to reinvent a speculative future.

Bart Plantenga

See also: Field Hollers; Lomax, Alan and John; Rodgers, Jimmie; Vocables

Further Reading

Abbott, Lynn, and Doug Seroff. 1993. "America's Blue Yodel." *Musical Traditions* 11.

Grauer, Victor. 2006. "Echoes of Our Forgotten Ancestors." *The World of Music* 48(2), 5–58.

Koopman, John. 1999. *A Brief History of Singing and Unsung Songs*. Appleton, WI: Lawrence University.

Plantenga, Bart. 2004. *Yodel-Ay-Ee-Oooo: The Secret History of Yodeling Around the World*. New York: Routledge.
Plantenga, Bart. 2013. *Yodel in Hi-Fi: From Kitsch Folk to Contemporary Electronica*. Madison: University of Wisconsin Press.
Rose, Brandel. 1961. *The Music of Central Africa*. The Hague: Martijnus Nijhoff.
Thomas, Leon. 1971/2002. "Umbo Weti." On *Leon Thomas in Berlin* [CD]. BMG.
Wagner, Christoph, compiler. 1998. *American Yodeling 1911–1946* [CD]. Trikont.
Zemp, Hugo. 1986–1987. *Jüüzli of the Muotathal* (four-part documentary series on yodeling in Switzerland). Paris: CNRS.

Yuman Music

The Yuman people belong to one of several recognized Native American tribes located across the Mojave Desert from southern California and Arizona into northern Baja California in Mexico. They include the Grand Canyon and central Arizonan tribes (Havasupai, Yavapai, Walapai), the Colorado River tribes (in order upstream, Quechan, Cocopa, Halyikwami, Kohuana, Yuma, Halchidhoma, and Mojave); the Maricopa on the Gila River; and the California Peninsular tribes (Kumeyaay, Kiliwa, Paipai).

The California clans are dominated by the modern Kumeyaay, including the former Diegueño, Kamia, and Tipai-Ipai (in San Diego and Imperial Counties, extending down to Ensenada). They speak mutually intelligible dialects of a single language and share musical traits and ceremonies with the Yavapai and Walapai. Kumeyaay ceremonies of adolescence, mourning, religion, and marriage include singing and dancing, accompanied on musical bow and whistle, and the traditional call to ceremony was made with a bull-roarer. Singing originally played a central role in healing and managing weather, but only its use in storytelling has survived alongside modern hymn and popular singing. Young men played a traditional gambling game (known by its Spanish name, *Peon*) and performed courtship songs on the flute, but they did not use drums: other instruments include baskets (scraped or beaten with a stick) and rattles made of clay, gourds, turtle shells, deer hooves, or tin cans. Some song types were restricted to shamans and other men who took jimsonweed in order to enhance spiritual connections.

Yuman music developed a highly distinctive mode of singing, including a relaxed, flowing vocal quality with a "rise" in the center of a ternary structure (A A A ... Rise, A). One type of song unique to Yuman culture emphasizes ridicule; these were generally called "bad songs" and were directed at other clans throughout much of California and the Great Basin.

The Mojave and Quechan retain some of the large territory they formerly controlled through trade and war. Because singing was an important part of social interaction between tribes, Mojave musical traditions have been incorporated into most other Yuman song repertoires. In the Mojave tradition, dreams are believed to be the basis of everything in life, including music, so new songs are received through dreams, and singers must "dream" an old song before having the right to sing it. The Havasupai of the Grand Canyon speak a Yuman language and share the relaxed vocal quality, but their songs have many different formal structures, more specific types, and may be accompanied by drums.

The most significant structural characteristic of Yuman music is that most songs are organized into long, coherent series based on a single myth; as cycles can contain more than 100 songs, it can take several days of ceremonies or social gatherings to sing a complete cycle. Songs contains a combination of vocables and two to three character names or places from the myth (most notably in Diegueño, Quechan, and the non-Yuman language Luiseño). Trading of song cycles was common; the Mojave perform song cycles that they attribute to the Chemehuevi, the Kamia, and the Quechan. The oldest cycles include the *Akaka* (raven), *Yelak* (goose), *Ahta* (cane), and *Kapeta* (turtle). Learning and performing these cycles requires both stamina and virtuosity, and song leaders control the flow of unison singing with the assistance of a rattle. Singers may dance in rotating circles or sing to accompany two silent lines of dancers (men facing women, moving forward and backward).

The Smithsonian-Densmore collection contains cylinder recordings and transcriptions of Native American music (2,385 made by Frances Densmore herself); her selections of Yuman, Cocopa, and Yaqui music were transferred to long-playing records (LPs), held by many university music libraries. George Herzog, the first American professor of comparative musicology, also made notable transcriptions and analyses of Yuman and Maricopan music. New resources include Quechan filmmaker Daniel Golding's 2010 documentary entitled *Songs of the Colorado*, and contemporary recordings by several tribal elders and song leaders.

Laura Stanfield Prichard

See also: Densmore, Frances; Native American Music; Navajo, Music of

Further Reading

Densmore, Frances. 1932. *Yuman and Yaqui Music*. Washington, D.C.: Coyote Press.

Herzog, George. 1928. "The Yuman Musical Style." *Journal of American Folklore* xvi, 183–221.

Hinton, L. 1984. *Spirit Mountain: An Anthology of Yuman Story and Song*. Tucson: University of Arizona Press.

Hinton, Leanne. 2002. "Diegueño," "Havasupai," and "Mojave." In *The New Grove Dictionary of American Music*. Oxford: Grove.

Spier, Leslie. 1933/1978. *Yuman Tribes of the Gila River*. New York: Dover.

Z

Zajal

Zajal or *zadjal* is the name of an Arabic form of poetry that relies on dialectic oral speech rather than conventional classical language. Its origin stems from a variety of Andalusian vernacular and strophic poetry that emerged at the turn of the 11th century, and then spread to the rest of the Arab world. Etymologically, "zajal" means "to raise the voice in singing." Formed out of a rich history of intercultural and Hispano-Arabic exchanges, this new poetry developed with and was influenced by music and singing. Materializing as a form of poetry used for entertainment and debauchery, it evolved into an independent and sophisticated popular art that expresses joy as well as the difficulty of living.

Under the Almoravid rule (1031–1130 CE), Andalusia (south of the Iberian peninsula) had known two forms of poetry, the *muwashshah* and zajal. With an original strophic structure using different rhymes and dialects within the same poem, these forms introduced new prosody to classical Arabic poetry. The muwashshah was written in formal Arabic, whereas zajal was composed entirely from local dialects of the Iberian peninsula. However, the origins of these two forms are still debated. While some say that zajal developed from the muwashshah, others consider that the former preceded the latter. Some scholars trace the beginning of zajal to pre-Islamic and early Islamic times, whereas others affiliate it with the Romance lyrical poetry that existed in the Iberian peninsula. Regardless of these hypotheses, one thing is certain: zajal became a hybrid art form practiced by Muslims, Jews, and Christians in their weddings and other festive occasions.

Zajal is formed by an initial couplet (*matla'*); a closure (*Markaz*) that rhymes with the matla'; and different strophes (quatrains). Those strophes usually contain three symmetrical lines (*tercet*) called *ghusn* (pl. *aghsan*), and rhyme together in one strophe but differ from one strophe to another (Monroe, 1989, pp. 38–39). *Sajal* is based on a binary rhythmic cycle and a formal repetitive structure (*a a b b b a*), alternating—from a verbal point of view—refrain (matla') and verses (aghsan).

The Andalusian zajal became a formally established poetry art with Ibn Quzman (1080–1160), native Andalusian poet of Cordoba, who used it for his panegyrics (*madih*, poem of effusive praise), but also to sing about nature, wine, and love. Later on, zajal was adopted by Sufism. In its contemporary form today, zajal is very popular in the Maghreb, Egypt, and the Levant (especially Lebanon and Palestine). It is often used in conjunction with *shi'r 'ami* (vernacular poetry) or replaced by the term *mu'anna* in the Levant, and *malhun* in the North African context.

The lyrics of zajal are rich in themes related to the profane and the sacred. Profanity poems deal generally with daily pleasures such as love, eroticism, and wine;

nostalgia for the lover; description of nature; and satirical poems. The poet can treat different themes in one verse. With the development of Sufism, zajal lyrics took on a more religious tone, with a description of mystical experiences. Nowadays, zajal is used more to express social and political problems in society.

In Lebanon, zajal is still a popular poetry form, because of its high literary value and formal virtuosity. As an oral tradition born in the mountains and the villages and influenced by Syriac liturgy and poetry, it succeeded in gaining sophistication and popularity. It also became a national pride and an entertainment practice with annual and regional championships. This contemporary folk poetry, semi-sung and semi-improvised, is a collective form of poetry, sung on popular melodies and often accompanied by percussion instruments. It is a usually spontaneous and humorous contest between two people or two teams called *Zajalin* (zajal makers), who criticize or praise each other and exalt their abilities in the literary, poetic, and historical domains. The poet starts sometimes his improvisation with the word "*Ufff*" (an expression of pain and melancholy that is more like a warning to get the public's attention). Then, using the same meter and rhyme as the opposite group, he repeats one or more words used by his challenger to start the poetry duel. The chorus (*al-raddadah*) supports the poet and interprets his thematic refrains, accompanied by tambourine (*daff*) and clapping. These duels usually exalt the superiority of a community or a region, the beauty of the mountains, the village, the joy of love, and attack the enemy or the rival community.

From a vernacular poetry rather despised by medieval classical poets, zajal evolved into a very popular and valued poetry in the 20th century, despite its absence today from media and formal artistic representations.

Diana Abbani

See also: Andalusian Music; Kalthoum, Umm; Malhūn; Sufism, Music of

Further Reading

Corriente, Federico. 1986. "Again on the Metrical System of Muwassah and Zajal." *Journal of Arabic Literature* 17, 34–49.

Emery, Ed. 2009. *Prolegomena for a Musicology of the Aajal: A Contextualized Comparison of Forms of Colloquial Strophic Poetry in Arabic Musical Culture in North Africa, Egypt and Lebanon.* London: School of Oriental and African Studies.

Haydar, Adnan. 1989. "The Development of Lebanese Zajal: Genre, Meter, and Verbal Duel." *Oral Tradition* 4(1–2), 189–212.

Monroe, James T. 1989. "Which Came First, the Zajal or the Muwaššaḥa? Some Evidence for the Oral Origins of Hispano-Arabic Strophic Poetry." *Oral Tradition* 4(1–2), 38–64.

Semah, David. 1995. "Modern Arabic Zajal and the Quest of Freedom." *Journal of Arabic Literature* 26(1–2), 80–92.

Stern, Samuel M. 1974. *Hispano-Arabic Strophic Poetry: Studies* (selected and edited by Leonard Patrick Harvey). Oxford: Clarendon Press.

Wulstan, David. 1982. "The Muwassah and Zajal Revisited." *Journal of the American Oriental Society* 102(2), 247–264.

Zwartjes, Otto, and Henk Heijkoop. 2004. *Muwassah, Zajal, Kharja: Bibliography of Eleven Centuries of Strophic Poetry and Music from al-Andalus and Their Influence on East and West.* Leiden, The Netherlands: Brill.

Ziegfeld, Florenz, Jr. (1867–1932)

Florenz Ziegfeld, usually known as "Flo" Ziegfeld, was an influential American Broadway producer and theater manager in the beginning of the 20th century. He was notable for the series of long-running revues, the *Ziegfeld Follies* (1907–1931), inspired by the Folies Bergère of Paris, which won him the title of "Glorifier of the American Girl," and also as the producer of the musical *Show Boat* (1927) by Jerome Kern and Roger Hammerstein II.

He was born into a German immigrant family. Ziegfeld's father, Florenz Ziegfeld, Sr., ran the Chicago Musical College and later opened a nightclub called the Trocadero. Ziegfeld, Jr. was thus exposed to the business of entertainment when he was young and helped his father to recruit performers for the World Columbian Exposition in 1893.

Ziegfeld's stage spectaculars, the *Ziegfeld Follies*, which began with *Follies of 1907*, showed his ambition of "Glorifying the American Girl" (Kantor and Maslon, 2004, p. 18) and were produced annually until 1931. Through the *Follies*, enhanced with elaborate costumes and sets, he reflected an image of the most refined ideals of female beauty. "It is necessary for a girl selected for the Follies to have personality and have grace. I do not care if the hair is long or short, blond or brunette, as long as it frames the face becomingly," said Ziegfeld in 1928. "Back and shoulders, of course, should be beautiful, and a rounded neck is also essential, while graceful hands are quite necessary," and then he emphasized that "the legs must be shapely, and last but not least, the proportions of the figure must be perfect" (Kantor and Maslon, 2004, p. 18). These productions introduced beautiful women chosen by Ziegfeld and were choreographed to the works of prominent Tin Pan Alley composers such as Irving Berlin, George Gershwin, and Jerome Kern. The *Follies* also helped many performers, female and male, achieve significant successes with both their finances and their popularity: Fanny Brice, Lillian Lorraine, Ruth Etting, W. C. Fields, Will Rodgers, Eddie Cantor, Nora Bayes, Billie Burke, and Ann Pennington, among others.

Ziegfeld initially started the *Follies* for Anna Held, a Polish-born stage performer whom he discovered in London. It was Held who suggested that Ziegfeld produce a Broadway revue like the famous French Folies Bergère, with beautiful girls, music, fashion, and also comedies. The *Ziegfeld Follies of 1907*, the first revue of the long-time series, opened on July 8, 1907, with the chorus known as the Anna Held Girls, and was an instant smash hit that ran for 79 performances. The first *Follies* cost $13,800 to stage, $3,800 a week to run, and yielded a profit of $120,000 (Golden, 2000, p. 112). Ziegfeld kept bringing the *Follies* back every summer until 1925 and two more versions in 1927 and 1931 until the onset of the Great Depression.

In addition to introducing glamorous female performers, Ziegfeld also accepted African American comedian Bert Williams to the all-white show *Follies* in 1910, which was a shock to the audience as well as the cast. It was said that some cast members delivered an ultimatum to Ziegfeld that unless Williams was fired, they would leave. Ziegfeld replied, "Go if you want to. I can replace every one of you, except the man you want me to fire" (Chude-Sokei, 2006, p. 2).

Ziegfeld and Anna Held's relationship became worse and worse after the *Follies*. Ziegfeld earned a lot of money through the *Follies* but also lost a lot by gambling. Besides this, he was unfaithful to Held and although Ziegfeld and Held never actually married, they had lived together long enough to qualify as legal husband and wife. Finally, they divorced in 1913, and the following year Ziegfeld married actress Billie Burke, who played Glinda in *The Wizard of Oz* in 1939. They had one child, Patricia Ziegfeld Stephenson.

The *Follies* grew from 79 performances in 1907 to 424 in 1922, which ran for the whole year. Originally the *Follies* were produced during the summer every year, but gradually became nearly an everyday entertainment. Ultimately, Ziegfeld built his own 1,600-seat theater in 1927 and produced his own show, *Rio Rita*, in February of the same year there. At the end of year, *Show Boat* was produced in the Ziegfeld Theatre. *Show Boat* was considered a landmark in the history of Broadway, and producing it was probably one of the most challenging yet best decisions that Ziegfeld ever made. His daughter recalled, "*Show Boat* was really a step for him that was terrifying . . . he said, 'we cannot do this musical with all this sadness'" (Kantor and Maslon, 2004, p. 112). The libretto dealt with racism and mixed marriage, together with serious social issues, so this show challenged the audience in the 1920s. Nonetheless, *Show Boat* won positive reviews and was a big success. It has been revived a couple times and also filmed three times.

In his last year, Ziegfeld staged a revival of *Show Boat* and brought stars from the *Follies* to CBS radio with *The Ziegfeld Follies of the Air*, in an attempt to bring the successful revues to the new medium of radio. His half-hour series aired on Sunday evenings during 1932. After Ziegfeld died in 1932, the series returned in 1936, serving as a tribute to the showman. Ziegfeld died at a hospital in Hollywood on July 22, 1932, after a long illness. He had never recovered from an attack of pneumonia the past winter and had been ill intermittently since February, though he still tried to work as a producer.

Chloe Hsun Lin

See also: Cohan, George M.; Lenya, Lotte; Musicals; Ragtime

Further Reading

Breon, Robin. 1995. "*Show Boat*: The Revival, the Racism." *TDR: The Daily Review (1988-)* 39(2) (Summer), 86–105.

Chude-Sokei, Louis. 2006. *The Last "Darky": Bert Williams, Black-on-Black Minstrelsy, and the African Diaspora.* Durham, NC: Duke University Press.

Dunning, John. 1998. *On the Air: The Encyclopedia of Old-Time Radio.* New York: Oxford University Press.

"Florenz Ziegfeld Dies in Hollywood after Long Illness." 1932. *New York Times*, July 23.

Golden, Eve. 2000. *Anna Held and the Birth of Ziegfeld's Broadway.* Lexington: The University Press of Kentucky.

Kantor, Michael, and Laurence Maslon. 2004. *Broadway: The American Musical.* New York: Bulfinch.

Zither

Zither, both a German and an English word, describes a wide range of chordophones or stringed instruments constructed from a block of wood or board with a frame or an elongated soundbox or resonator. The frame could be as simple as a stick with one string, such as the musical bow (a monochord). It can have from one to more than 100 strings made from catgut, animal hair, leather, waxed linen, nylon, silk threads, metal such as brass, or other materials. The strings are bowed or plucked with the fingers or with a plectrum.

Zithers are found in all parts of the world. They include autoharps, dulcimers, guitar zithers, harp zithers, mandolin zithers, pianochordia, psalteries, violin zithers, and more. The resonator of the zither can either be joined or glued to the frame (such as for dulcimers and psalteries) or detached from it. Some European and American zithers were highly decorated.

The term "zither" is derived or originated from the ancient Greek word *kithara*. The zither and its related family of instruments were found as far back as in ancient times. Wooden zithers such as the *qin* or *guqin* have existed in China since the 12th century BCE. That had around seven silk strings but lacked bridges. The ancient Chinese *zheng*, a plucked zither dating from around the sixth or seventh century BCE, had movable bridges and 12 or more silk strings. (The modern zheng usually has 16 metal strings.) Zithers related to the kithara existed in ancient India as far back as the fifth century BCE. Early zithers of India included the *bīn* or *vina* and were documented from as early as 1000 BCE. The Korean *ajaeng*, a relative of the Chinese *yazheng*, is a bowed zither that made its appearance before the fourth century BCE. It had adjustable bridges, but instead of being plucked it was bowed with a stick. The 12-string Korean *kayagum* has been in existence since the eight century BCE. The Japanese *koto*, an elongated, 13-string plucked zither with movable and permanent bridges, had roots in China and was heard in Japan from the eighth century BCE. From ancient Burma came the *saùng-gauk*, an arched harp that was traced to the second century CE Buddhist rulers. The Korean *komungo*, a long plucked zither from the seventh century, had six silk strings, detachable bridges, and frets.

Zithers consist of strings stretched along a flat body. They are found in cultures throughout the world. (Bill Johnson/The Denver Post via Getty Images)

Zithers existed in Europe during the 12th century. The term "zither" was used in Europe from the 15th century for a chordophone with a neck. Its development varied regionally across Europe. Its early appearance was rectangular in design with various numbers of strings. The instrument was constructed with a wooden soundbox or resonator slightly over 19 inches in length and about two inches wide. It contained from two to three strings made from animal gut, hair, brass, or other wires. The soundbox of these early zithers was detachable. To stop the sound, a small metal bar was used to press the melody strings against the frets (Michel and Fujie, 1997). Among zithers from medieval Russia were rectangular or longitudinal zithers, instruments related to the northern lyre. These longitudinal zithers had five and sometimes four strings and a flat soundbox glued to the soundboard. They did not have sound holes in the soundboards, but the holes for the string pegs were drilled into the neck of the instrument.

The northern European *scheitholt*, a box zither with a fingerboard, played a significant role in the development of the modern zither in Europe and America. The scheitholt, which translates into English as "wooden stick," was depicted in numerous paintings from the 15th and 16th centuries onward. It was found in various European countries and regions including Austria, France, Germany, Holland, Iceland, Italy, Russia, Scandinavia, Switzerland, and Eastern Europe. Constructed of wood, the width of the soundbox of the scheitholt was around two inches and its length slightly over 19 inches. The European zither was also related to the cittern and guitar. The *cittern*, a very popular instrument during the Elizabethan era and used in England from the Renaissance period, had roots tracing to the kithara. It was usually decorative and ornamented. An arch-cittern had around 20 chromatic brass frets, a double set of melody strings with one fret, and nine bass strings with another fret.

The scheitholt had two or more melody strings and eight or more bass strings fastened with iron pins. The strings were made of catgut, animal hair, or metal such as brass. The melody strings of a scheitholt found at the Germanisches National-museum, Nürnberg, were tuned g^1 to d^1, with the bass string tuned to G and its fundamentals. This particular scheitholt also contained iron frets, with the first 14 forming a diatonic Mixolydian scale (Van der Meer, 1970). The scheitholt later developed into the *schlagzither* or *kratzzithern*. Instead of being placed on the soundbox, the frets of the kratzzithern were on the fingerboard, glued to the instrument. It was played with a plectrum or quill. Some of these later developed into the Schwyzer zither, a double zither with two diatonic fingerboards popular in Switzerland. The strings of the schlagzither were diatonic and struck with the fingers and a plectrum.

The European zither had 30 or more strings and a fretted fingerboard. A plectrum on the right thumb plucked the strings or accompaniment, while the left hand stopped the sound. Constructed with a flat soundboard, the zither was placed on a table or the performer's lap when being played. Two main types of European zithers from the 18th century were the Mittenwald zither and Salzburg zither. Both were circular in design. The edges of the Mittenwald zither were curved, whereas only the side opposite the performer of the Salzburg zither was round. Although the tuning of these zithers differed, a standard tuning of the Salzburg zither was 29 strings tuned by fifths (C, G, D, A, E, and so on) plus five melody strings tuned a´, d´, g´, g, and c (Michel and Fujie, 1997). According to Van der Meer, the Salzburg zither can have three melody strings and 12 bass strings. The Mittenwald zither by Franz Kren was shaped similar to a lyre. These zithers, created during the 1830s, had 14 bass strings fastened to pegs in the arched bridge and four melody strings fastened to hitchpins. The strings were tuned a^1-a^1-d^1-$g/a^{1\flat}$-G-b-g^1-$F^{1\sharp}$-e^1-d^1-a-$c^{1\sharp}$-e-g-d-A-c. The frets are organized diatonically, resulting in a Mixolydian scale in two octaves. There are also two shorter frets (Van der Meer, 1970).

One European country important in the development of the zither, including the bowed zither, was Holland. These box zithers were hollowed and square. They ranged in length from two to three feet or more with three to four strings. Each end had a bridge and the first string was used for the melody. In one method used to play it, the right thumb and a small stick or quill held in the left hand are used to pick the first string to produce the melody. Some players used two small quills to produce the sound: one to slide over the strings while the other produced the melody by striking the first string. A bow was sometimes used to slide over the strings as the nail of the thumb picked the first string to play the melody. These types of box zithers were found in Holland during the mid-18th century and were called *hommel* or *nordische balk*. The European zither had many names depending on the country or region: for example, *cetra da tavola* (Italy), *épinette des vosges* or *cithara* (France), *hummel* (Sweden), *langleik* (Norway), and *palaika* (Russia).

The Alpine zither, a box zither, was directly descended from the scheitholt of Germany and Austria. It was quite popular in these countries during the 18th and 19th centuries. It used more than 30 open or accompanying strings made from catgut, nylon, or metal. The melody strings had frets and were chromatic. The strings were played with a plectrum on the right thumb. During the 18th and early 19th centuries, the zither made its way from the countryside of Europe to its cities via the rich aristocrats. Most wealthy homes had zithers and aristocrats sought zither teachers for their offspring. The instrument was used for entertainment at European inns and salons.

The Alpine zither developed into a virtuoso concert instrument, the concert zither. From a folk-tradition instrument, the zither was transformed into a concert solo and accompanying instrument for various performers such as singers, guitarists, violinists, and others. By the mid 19th to early 20th centuries, the Alpine zither had also become as a concert instrument. Exercise books were printed and composers created works for it. Virtuoso zither players were frequently on the scene. These include Johann Petzmayer, who rose to frame in the mid-1820s in Vienna. In the mid-19th century, Carl Ignaz Umlauf helped to further establish the zither as a concert instrument. Another virtuoso was Germany's Adam Darr (1811–1866).

The Alpine zither also developed into the Salzburg zither, a flat wooden zither with five melody strings and 35 to 38 open strings stretched over the resonator. It contained a chromatic fretted fingerboard and its lower half was shaped in the form of an S. With the soundhole on the lower right side, the Salzburg zither had a scroll on the left side. In America, Franz Schwarzer (1828–1904), an immigrant from Austria, created and improved these instruments during the late 1860s.

The plucked zither or *psaltery* is one of the most distinguished and unique instruments in the Baltic region. It played an important role in the traditional music of Estonia, Latvia, and Lithuania. These zithers have unique regional names: *kanklè* in Lithuania, *kannel* in Estonia, and *kokle* or *kükle* in Latvia. The Baltic plucked zither or psaltery is related to the Finnish *kantele*, a zither with 36 or more strings (Muktupāvels, 2002). A block of wood was used to create the early Baltic psaltery, with the soundboard attached on the side, top, or bottom. The parts of the 19th-century Baltic psaltery were glued together. It had 17 to 33 or even 90 strings parallel to the soundboard. These were stretched over a bridge connected to the resonator (Schötz and Fujie, 1999). The Baltic psaltery had a very distinct shape and characteristic acoustic features. Similar to the psalteries from the medieval period, the Baltic psaltery is wing-shaped, or has extended wings with the strings arranged like a fan. The instrument does not have a bridge, and this contributes to a special resonant sound due to the overtones (Tëmkin, 2004).

The 19th-century German and Austrian box zither influenced the design and construction of the Baltic psaltery. This included gluing of the wood around the frame, the use of a bridge and metal tuning pegs, and the production of a chromatic scale. Nevertheless, the Baltic instrument also retained a distinct character and represented a symbol of national pride and ethnic identity. It was created with a handhole and extended wing that resulted from the soundboard protruding beyond the peg line. The handhole was placed below the peg line and resulted in a style of playing similar to that of the ancient lyre, with the instrument placed vertically. Because of the handhole, the player could pluck and mute the strings with the left hand, which also held the instrument. Instead of placing the instrument on the lap or a table, players were able to rest their arms on the wing extension and place the instrument with the back against their abdomens. This made it easy to strum the strings with the right hand and stop the sound with the fingers of the left hand (Tëmkin, 2004). The Baltic psaltery was used during the 19th century to accompany songs and dance or to perform in ensembles with other zithers or other instruments such as hammered dulcimers and violins. The development of the Baltic psaltery during the 19th century was influenced by the German and Austrian zithers already found in those countries (Schötz and Fujie, 1999).

Throughout time, zithers varied in the way they were tuned. Countries and regions each had their own method of tuning. By the late 19th century, tuning in fourths and fifths (based on the circle of fifths) for the strings that accompany developed into the standard. However, the strings that played the melody continued with nonstandard regional tuning. The melody strings of zithers in Vienna, for example, were tuned differently than those in various regions of Germany. For example, in Munich: a′–a′–d′–g–c; in Vienna: a′–d′–g′–g–c (Michel and Fujie, 1997).

Zithers that lacked fingerboards are called "fretless" zithers, whereas those with fingerboards are termed "fretboard" or "fingerboard" zithers. From around 1885 to the 1940s, zithers without fingerboards were produced in Europe, including in Germany, Switzerland, and other European countries. These instruments were related to the psaltery. Due to their popularity during the late 19th century up to the 1940s, they were commercially or industrially mass-produced and available at a low price. Such instruments included the autoharp or chord zither, guitar zither, harp zither or *aeol*, mandolin zither, pianochordia, violin zither, and others. These zithers without fingerboards had chromatic and diatonic strings. A thumb plectrum and the fingers were used to play the instrument. Friedrick Menzen obtained a patent for it in the late 1890s in Berlin and the Oscar Schmidt Company manufactured them in Germany and the United States.

The autoharp, a fretless zither, was created in 1880 by Karl August Gütter. It was constructed with wood, steel strings, and intersecting bars. It accompanied singing in homes, salons, and schools. Originally manufactured in Germany, the autoharp became a huge hit in the United States. By the late 19th century, music-making and entertainment were not only for the educated, upper-class Europeans or bourgeoisie. At that time more middle-class families were being educated and playing musical instruments (such as zithers) at home for entertainment and pleasure. These instruments were not difficult to learn, and those not trained to read music were able to play them by rote. This trend also spread to the United States.

The *harfen-zithern* (harp zither) was mass-produced in Berlin by Alwin Eichler and in New York by the Aeolian Company. These zithers only had accompanying strings and chords and lacked any melody strings. The lyre and violin zithers were really guitar zithers. The former instrument looked like a lyre; the violin zither was played with a bow similar to a violin bow. The violin and harp zithers were developed during the 1920s. Another guitar zither that lacked a fingerboard was the *sonora* zither, which had crossed strings. These zithers without fingerboards (e.g., the autoharp) were lacquered black and decorated (Michel and Fujie, 1997).

The repertoire for the fretless zithers consisted mainly of transcriptions of other works. They were much easier to play than the traditional zithers that had fingerboards. They came with diagrams that even those who did not read music could follow to successfully play the instrument. This system of playing consisted of "diagrams that are placed over the body of the instrument and underneath the strings" (Michel and Fujie, 1997, p. 80). Traditional zither players did not use these fretless zithers. By the 1940s, the popularity of the zithers lacking fingerboards declined, and so did the manufacturing of them. Some of this was largely due to World War II, which affected the production of the instruments, among other factors. These instruments are no longer of significance in Germany or other European countries (Michel and Fujie, 1997).

The zither made its way to America via various European immigrants. The early Germans who settled in Pennsylvania between the 18th and 19th centuries brought the German scheitholt to this region and further developed it. They both made and played these instruments. Two types existed: the plectrum zither and the bow zither or dulcimer. A quill or stick was used as the plectrum to pluck the strings of the plectrum zither, whereas a bow, usually from a violin or similar to it, was used to play the bow zither or dulcimer.

The dulcimer, which has been around since the Middle Ages, gained a following as a folk instrument during the 18th century in Europe. This box zither was in high demand by the 19th century in both Europe and the United States. It was brought to the American colonies during the 17th century by the English. A result of the synthesis of the scheitholt and hummel was the Appalachian dulcimer, a fretted box zither. Typical Appalachian dulcimers are elongated, rectangular or trapezoidal in shape, with one to two melody strings (treble) tuned to the same pitch and two to three drone strings (treble and bass). When playing the dulcimer, the player sits and uses the fingers or a pick or plectrum (also called a noter) in the left hand to pick out the melody. The right hand strums the drone strings and harmonizes the melody. The plectrum can be made of bone, quill, wood, or cane. The Appalachian dulcimer may have straight sides or curved sides similar to an hourglass. The latter is the more common. The strings of the hammered dulcimer can have as many as three octaves. Small mallets or beaters, called hammers, were usually used to strike the strings of the hammered dulcimer (Holmes, 1999). This dulcimer resurfaced during the folk music revival in America during the 1960s. The Appalachian dulcimer is still very popular in the Kentucky and Tennessee mountains regions.

These zithers (including bowed and plectrum zithers, dulcimers, and hummels) were very popular in the mountains of Kentucky and Tennessee and often accompanied singing of English and Scottish ballads. The early plectrum zither in America was narrower, long, rectangular, and had more strings than the bow zither. The strings were usually constructed of wire and a plectrum was used to play it. The keys and bridges of the plectrum zither differed considerably from those of the bow zither, including the manner in which they were placed on the instrument. The soundboard or rectangular box of the plectrum zither was made of wood more than three feet in length. No nails were used to make it; instead, the wood was glued and pegged together. Its head piece was more than a foot long and usually had some ornamentation. It used around eight strings made of steel wire and 15 wire frets on its left side, along with a wooden bridge (Mercer, 1923).

The minstrel shows in the United States during the mid-19th century popularized the use of the banjo, an instrument used by both black and white folk in popular traditions. English blackface minstrelsy did not use the banjo. The banjo-zither was an instrument created by Brooklyn native Alfred Cammeyer (1862–1949). It gained popularity during the late 1880s, and Cammeyer took it to England in 1888, where it was an instant hit. He created a closed-back banjo with five wire strings instead of the customary gut strings. The fifth string did not stop at the fifth fret on the peg on the side of the neck, but instead extended to the peg head. Cammeyer developed and expanded a special technique and style that emphasized the "singing" and lyrical qualities of the new banjo-zither. This classic style, also known as guitar-style or finger-style, was used not only on the banjo-zither but also on regular banjos (Winans and Kaufman, 1994).

In summary, the zither evolved over many centuries, beginning in Asia and spreading to Europe, America, and other parts of the world. This widely ranging family of chordophones continues to be performed with in various parts of the world.

Barbara Bonous-Smit

See also: Berimbau; Dulcimer; Guzheng; Koto; Psaltery; Qānūn; Qin; Sanjo; Veena

Further Reading

Armstrong, Randall. 1980. "The Adaptable Appalachian Dulcimer." *Music Educators Journal* 66(6) (February), 38–41. http://www.jstor.org/stable/3395806.

Holmes, Gillian S. 1999. "Dulcimer." In Jacqueline L. Longe (ed.), *How Products Are Made: An Illustrated Guide to Product Manufacturing,* vol. 4, 196–201. Detroit: Gale.

Mercer, Henry C. 1923. "The Zithers of the Pennsylvania Germans." Paper read at a meeting of the Bucks County Historical Society held at Doylestown, PA, January 20. Doylestown, PA: Bucks County Historical Society. http://zither.us/zithers.pennsylvania.germans.

Michel, Andreas, and Linda Fujie. 1997. "Changes in Central European Concepts of Folk Musical Instruments: Industrially Produced Zithers without Fingerboards." *The World of Music* 39(3), 71–90. http://www.jstor.org/stable/41699165.

Muktupāvels, Valdis. 2002. "Musical Instruments in the Baltic Region: Historiography and Traditions." *The World of Music* 44, 21–54. http://www.jstor.org/stable/41699450.

Pesavento, Alissa Ann Teresa. 1994. "Concert Zither in America: Its History, Performance Practice, and Repertory." Master's thesis, Kent State University.

Schötz, Franz, and Linda Fujie. 1999. "'Cultivated and 'Non-cultivated' Folk Music: On Music-Making among Traditional Dance Musicians." *The World of Music* 41(2), 41–61. http://www.jstor.org/stable/41699266.

Smith, L. Allen. 1980. "Toward a Reconstruction of the Development of the Appalachian Dulcimer: What the Instruments Suggest." *The Journal of American Folklore* 93(370) (October-December), 385–396. http://www.jstor.org/stable/539870.

Tëmkin, Ilya. 2004. "The Evolution of the Baltic Psaltery: A Case for Phyloorganology." *The Galpin Society Journal* 57, 219–230, 217. http://www.jstor.org/stable/25163802.

Van der Meer, John Henry. 1970. "Curt Sachs and Nürnberg." *The Galpin Society Journal* 23 (August), 120–125. http://www.jstor.org/stable/842076.

Winans, Robert B., and Elias J. Kaufman. 1994. "Minstrel and Classic Banjo: American and English Connections." *American Music* 12(1) (Spring), 1–30. http://www.jstor.org/stable/3052489.

Winternitz, Emanuel. 1961. "The Survival of the Kithara and the Evolution of the English Cittern: A Study in Morphology." *Journal of the Warburg and Courtauld Institutes* 24(3/4) (July-December), 222–229. http://www.jstor.org/stable/750796.

Zouk

Zouk is a type of creole dance music that arose in the French Antillean islands of Guadeloupe and Martinique in the late 1970s. It eventually gained global popularity in the 1980s through the genre's most important ensemble, Kassav'.

A complex mix of musical styles, zouk's roots are grounded in a combination of elements, including Haitian *compas direct* (*cadence-rampa*), Dominican *cadence-lypso*, *soukouss* from the Congo or Cameroon, American jazz, and Latin American or Caribbean styles from Brazil, Argentina, and Cuba. Local musical traditions evolving through European or African influences have also made their mark on the genre, including song and dance forms supported by *bèlè* or *gwo ka* drum ensembles, European ballroom dance types such as the quadrille, local *biguine* popular music, and music ensembles connected with Carnival traditions.

The term "zouk" is a Creole creation and contraction developed out of the local pronunciation of the word *mazurka*—"mazouk"—a type of European dance form found in the French Antilles and elsewhere. By the 1950s, the term was being used locally to describe a type of country dance supported by small jazz band ensembles, and by the 1960s had evolved into a term to describe dance music connected with local practitioners.

The group credited with the development of modern zouk, *Kassav'*, was also important as the style's main promoter. Kassav' formed in 1979, grounded in the vision of the Guadeloupian musician Pierre-Edouard Décimus who felt that foreign artists dominated the island's music scene, and that Guadeloupe lacked a strong Antillean musical presence or identity. With his brother (and bassist) Georges Décimus, and guitarist/vocalist Jacob Desvarieux, Kassav' began composing and recording a style of music that was polished, rhythmically complex, and internationally aware, but distinctly Antillean in sound and identity. For example, they are credited for integrating local gwo ka drumming music into their modern style as a way to put an Antillean mark on their sound. By the 1970s, gwo ka drumming was associated with rural life and thought to be unsophisticated until Kassav' collaborated with well-known gwo ka drummer Velo to play on their early albums; however, they eventually drifted away from their close connection to gwo ka drumming. After several years of refining and developing their sound, their 1984 recording *Zouk-la sé sèl médikaman nou ni* became the album that marked the peak of their international success, particularly in Europe, Africa, and the Antilles.

The band's name also reinforced their commitment to drawing on local roots; the word "Kassav'" was the local *Kweyol* (creole) word for cassava, an important tuber prepared as a staple of the Guadeloupian diet. Another important feature tying zouk to Antillean identity was its use of Kweyol lyrics. Kweyol is the language of Guadeloupian people of African descent; it is a complex mixture of French, English, Arawak, and several languages from Africa that were brought to the island and developed while its speakers labored on sugar plantations. Kassav' were pioneers in bringing Kweyol to the popular music stage; until that time, most local popular music was sung in French as a substitute for the marginalized and stigmatized local creole language and its respective culture. Song lyrics in zouk compositions are primarily centered on themes of love or other types of "light" subject matter, and always with a particularly positive message. While many substyles of zouk exist, the two most predominant are "zouk hard" and "zouk love," with the former characterized by its more popular fast dance style, and the latter distinguished by compositions made up of slower love ballads.

Writers and scholars have described zouk as a studio-based music due to its heavy reliance on technology in its production. Compositions are based on drum and bass ostinato patterns that have various types of melodic instruments—such as trumpets, guitars, or electronic keyboards—layered over it. The technical sophistication used by Kassav' in the studio was motivated by their desire to create a product that would rival French commercial recording, and influenced by Jacob Desvarieux, who had an established career as a studio musician in Paris. Zouk's electronic sound meant that it was largely a style listened to by the public through sound systems or on the radio, with only a small number of popular groups performing it live. This had a negative impact on the live music scene and would eventually become an important factor leading to its demise by the late 1990s. Recording technology had spread far and wide, thereby allowing anyone to potentially create zouk music, and the heavy reliance on technology made it difficult for the genre to evolve or progress.

Gavin Webb

See also: Jazz; Reggaetón

Further Reading

Donnelly, Laura Caroline. 2010. "Life after Zouk: Emerging Popular Music of the French Antilles." MA thesis, Michigan State University.

Guilbault, Jocelyne. 1993. *Zouk: World Music in the West Indies*. Chicago: University of Chicago Press.

Zydeco

Zydeco music is indigenous to southern Louisiana, evolving primarily in the 20th century. It is a combination of musical forms that mixes Afro-Caribbean music, African American blues, Cajun, black Creole, jazz, soul, and rhythm and blues (R & B). It is very popular as dance music, with an accordion dominating the sound, along with a *frottoir* (a washboard-type percussion vest that hangs against the player's chest) often being played with a spoon. The first star of zydeco music is generally held to be Clifton Chenier. More contemporary zydeco musicians include Buckwheat Zydeco, Chris Ardoin, and C. J. Chenier, son of pioneer Clifton.

The origin of the word "zydeco" is disputed. One theory is that it comes from the extinct language of the Atakapa Indians of southwestern Louisiana who mixed with African slaves: the words roughly translated as *shy* for "dance" and *ishol* for "youths." These were then misheard by the Spaniards who explored Louisiana as roughly sounding like "zydeco." Another theory is that the word comes from various West African languages, usually transliterated as *zari* or *zarê* for "dance," and evolved into "zydeco."

The most prevalent theory is that "zydeco" comes from a phrase in French referencing hard times: *"Les haricots ne sont pas salés"* (literally, "The beans are not salty"). It refers to persons so poor they cannot afford salt meat for the snap beans often grown by black Louisiana farmers. Spoken in Creole French, the phrase could be slurred enough to sound like "Leh-sy-di-co ne son pah salay," a contraction of which evolved into "zarico," "zodeco," and finally "zydeco."

The latter theory is given weight through the work of folklorist Alan Lomax. In the 1930s, he and his father John traveled throughout the South, were recording rural musicians for the Archive of Folk Song at the Library of Congress. Among various black musicians singing about their grinding poverty, there were references in several songs to "Les haricots ne sont pas salés." It was part of the oral tradition in a largely illiterate society.

In 1965, musicians Cleveland and Clifton Chenier made a recording which captured their bantering conversation, including what sounded like the word "zydeco." At that session, they recorded a tune listed as "Zydeco sont pas salés." The phrase is repeated several times in the song, which had the same beat that the Lomaxes captured in the 1930s but which had not yet been given a name.

Accordionist Clifton Chenier (1925–1987) of Opelousas, Louisiana, was a Creole French-speaking performer who became known as the "King of Zydeco" as well as "King of the South." Known for his dynamic live performances in which he wore a cape and a crown, he had begun recording in 1954. Reproductions of early album covers use the word "zodeco" for his music, as well as listing a cut on one called "Zodico Stomp," but by 1955, the word "zydeco" was the fairly standard usage. Chenier, the first national star of zydeco music, later claimed credit for devising the word.

In 1960, musicologist Robert "Mack" McCormick wrote notes for his album of local American folk musicians, *A Treasury of Field Recordings*. He used the spelling "zydeco," which was repeated in reviews, sometimes being associated with "Creole music." The concepts of "Creole" and "Cajun" can be confusing, but the two are not synonymous. Cajuns—named with a corruption of the word "Acadians"—descended from early French settlers who colonized Canada in today's maritime provinces of Nova Scotia, New Brunswick, and Prince Edward Island. The eastern seaboard of America, north of the Virginia colony, had been designated by mapmaker Giovanni da Verrazano as "Arcadia," from the classic Greek meaning an idyllic place. Dropping the "r," the French settlers named their region Acadia, and were known as Acadians. When the British took the region from France, their political and religious resistance led to the Acadians being forcibly expelled by the English and dispersed throughout America and the Caribbean. Some were sent to the Louisiana territory, where Acadians found a degree of acceptance in the region with its French background and Catholic heritage, having been a territory of France from 1682 to 1762. Sometimes separated family members who had been scattered throughout the Western hemisphere were reunited there, forming small, close-knit communities. The Acadians eventually became known as Cajuns, much as "Indians" were sometimes called "Injuns." The Cajuns developed their own culture in the backwoods, bayous, and swamps of south Louisiana, a region still often called Acadiana. Their music evolved as a very distinctive type which was generally performed by musicians who were white.

Creoles are not Cajuns, and are thus harder to define. A Creole might be a white person born in Louisiana of French and Spanish ancestry, or it might be a black person who descended from African, Afro-Caribbean, Native American, or European heritage, in any combination. The zydeco tradition is that of French-speaking rural black Creoles.

Zydeco bands generally include a blues accordion as the primary instrument, along with the washboard-vest frottoir. Modern zydeco bands may also include electric guitar, bass, and drums. Zydeco generally does not rely on the fiddle which is so prevalent in Cajun music, but rather leans heavily toward a bluesy sound with a pronounced backbeat. Some modern bands utilize a double kick to the bass drum to emphasize the syncopation, called "double-clutching."

Zydeco is especially conducive to dancing. The steps performed to zydeco music often look like swing dancing. The music may be sung in French or English, with the latter preferred by many contemporary bands. Although many are original, some zydeco songs rework traditional blues along with modern versions of very old Creole tunes. The lyrics may deal with love, food, and the enjoyment of life as well as serious socio-political themes.

Although Clifton Chenier is hailed as the originator of modern zydeco music, Amédé Ardoin, who made early recordings of Creole music in 1928, is credited as laying the foundation for what would become known as zydeco. The first known recording with a distinct zydeco type of sound is held to be Clarence Garlow's "Bon Ton Roula" in 1949. In 1954, Wilson "Boozoo" Chavis recorded "Paper in My Shoe," considered to be the first truly zydeco record. This was followed by the ascendancy of Clifton Chenier, still a benchmark of the zydeco form.

When Chenier appeared at California's Berkeley Blues Festival in 1966, the jazz critic for the *San Francisco Chronicle*, Ralph J. Gleason, gave a rave review to both the musician and the form of music he played. In the 1970s and 1980s, Chenier reached a national audience when he appeared on the popular PBS music showcase *Austin City Limits*. Honored with a Grammy Award in 1983, Chenier and his band toured the world, bringing Creole zydeco to a global audience.

In the 1980s, Rockin' Sidney (Sidney Simien) brought popular attention to zydeco music with his surprise hit, "My Toot Toot." Chenier, Rockin' Sidney, and Queen Ida (Ida Lewis Guillory, the first female to lead a zydeco band) won Grammy Awards for zydeco, furthering its prestige and popularity.

Accordionist Buckwheat Zydeco (Stanley Dural, Jr.; 1947–) of Lafayette, Louisiana, became a mainstream national success beginning in the 1980s. He began his career backing Clifton Chenier, but then set out on his own, gaining acclaim for his talent as well as for advancing the zydeco form itself. He won new fans by appearing in the 1987 movie *The Big Easy*, which was set in New Orleans, and he won an Emmy for his music in the 2001 CBS-TV movie, *Pistol Pete: The Life and Times of Pete Maravich*.

Zydeco continued to gain acclaim from the 1980s onward, as new artists triumphed nationally and internationally, expanding the form to include new styles and fusion music. Modern performers include Chubby Carrier, Geno Delafose, and Terrance Simien, as well as C. J. Chenier, who is carrying on the tradition popularized by his father, Clifton Chenier. Beau Jocque fused zydeco with a heavy beat and strong bass line, adding elements of funk, hip-hop, and rap. Chris Ardoin, Keith Frank, and Zydeco Force further accentuated the "double clutching" of the bass drum. Contemporary artists who have created a fusion of zydeco with other forms such as soul music include Leon Chavis, Lil' Nate, Mo' Mojo, and Kenne' Wayne, whose sound is referred to as "zydesoul." In 2007, zydeco joined Cajun music in a new Grammy Award category, currently part of Best Regional Roots Music.

With the mixing of French-speaking blacks and multiracial Creole musicians, zydeco is currently enjoyed around the world. There are numerous zydeco festivals in the United States and abroad which further its appreciation and evolution.

Nancy Hendricks

See also: Acadian Music; Accordion (Americas); Bluegrass; Blues; Cajun Music

Further Reading

Gould, Philip. 1992. *Cajun Music and Zydeco.* Baton Rouge: Louisiana State University Press.

Koster, Rick. 2002. *Louisiana Music: A Journey from R&B to Zydeco, Jazz to Country, Blues to Gospel, Cajun Music to Swamp Pop to Carnival Music and Beyond.* Cambridge, MA: Da Capo Press.

Sandmel, Ben. 1999. *Zydeco!* Oxford, MS: University Press of Mississippi.

Tisserand, Michael. 1998. *The Kingdom of Zydeco.* New York: Arcade.

About the Editors

ANDREW R. MARTIN, PhD, is professor of music at Inver Hills Community College, Inver Grove Heights, Minnesota, where he teaches courses in music history, music analysis, and percussion and directs the African music ensemble and steelband. Martin is a sought-after performer and clinician throughout the United States and internationally and he is director of Steelbands for Carifest Minnesota. Martin's research explores globalization, Caribbean music and movements, tourism, American music, and popular and folk music and musicians during the Cold War. He has published widely on these topics and presented numerous lectures and conference papers throughout the United States, Canada, Caribbean, Europe, and China. His research has appeared in several print sources, including the journals *American Music, Pan Podium: The Journal of the British Steel Band Society,* and *The Journal of New York Folklore,* and in reference works including *The Grove Dictionary of American Music*. He is the author of the books *Steelpan Ambassadors: The US Navy Steel Band, 1957–1999* and *Steelpan in Education: A History of the Northern Illinois University Steelband*. Since 2011, Martin has written the semiregular newspaper column "Pan Worldwide" in the *Trinidad Guardian*.

MATTHEW MIHALKA, PhD, is an instructor of music at the University of Arkansas, where he coordinates the music department's general education offerings and teaches courses in music history, popular music, and music in non-Western cultures. He received his MA and PhD from the University of Minnesota-Twin Cities. His research addresses the use of music in 20th/21st-century American society, particularly during sporting events. His work has been published in *The American Organist, Notes, American History through American Sports,* and *Music in the Social and Behavioral Sciences*.

Contributors

Diana Abbani
Sorbonne, Paris

Rachel Adelstein
University of Chicago

Nadia Ali
Freelance Writer

Bronius Ambraziejus
Independent Scholar

Jurgita Antoine
Independent Scholar

Christopher L. Ballengee
Anne Arundel Community College

Elizabeth Kimzey Batiuk
Western Michigan University

Erin E. Bauer
Claremont Graduate University

Emily A. Bell
Independent Scholar

Adem Merter Birson
Ipek University

Barbara Bonous-Smit
Queensborough Community College,
City University of New York

Ronda L. Bowen
Independent Scholar

Hicham Chami
University of Florida

Sutapa Chaudhuri
University of Calcutta

Morgen Chawawa
Botho University

Elizabeth A. Clendinning
Emory University

Robert Crowe
Boston University

Melissa Cummins
Sam Houston State University

Amelia Davidson
University of Kansas

James I. Deutsch
Smithsonian Institution

Antonella Di Giulio
University at Buffalo

Phillip Alexander Ducreay
West Virginia University

Felix Eid
Independent Scholar

Athena Elafros
Keuka College

Erick Falc'her-Poyroux
Independent Scholar

Maristella J. Feustle
University of North Texas

Jack W. Forbes
Cardinal Stritch University

John Forrestal
Boston University

Greg Freeman
SouthernEdition.com

Jessica Freyermuth
University of Kansas

Bradley Fugate
Independent Scholar

Christopher Gable
University of North Dakota

Christine Gangelhoff
The College of The Bahamas

C. M. Gregory-Thomas
Independent Scholar

Dr. Anna Hamling
University of New Brunswick

Ralph Hartsock
University of North Texas

John Hausmann
University of Cincinnati College-Conservatory of Music

Aya Esther Hayashi
The Graduate Center, CUNY

Dr. Nancy Hendricks
Arkansas State University, Dept. of English

Jacob Hicks
Florida State University

Phoebe E. Hughes
Independent Scholar

Justin R. Hunter
University of Arkansas
University Muenster Musikhochschule

Jörg Jewanski
Independent Scholar

Henry Johnson
University of Otago

Ayla Joncheere
Independent Scholar

David Crawford Jones
University at Albany, State University of New York

Joseph E. Jones
Texas A&M University, Kingsville

Tanner Jones
Independent Scholar

Joshua Katz-Rosene
Graduate Center, City University of New York

Broderick Kenny
Independent Scholar

Hae Joo Kim
Independent Scholar

Contributors

Jacoba Kint
Independent Scholar

Mayako Koja
Okinawa Prefectural University of Arts

Lynn C. Kronzek
Lynn C. Kronzek & Associates

Danielle M. Kuntz
Independent Scholar

Dr. Mary Talusan Lacanlale
CSU Dominguez Hills

Francisco D. Lara
University of Memphis

Silvia M. Lazo, PhD
University of Montana

Cathleen LeGrand
Independent Scholar

Chloe Hsun Lin
Calvary Bible College

Scott V. Linford
UCLA

Chia-Yu Joy Lu
Wesleyan University

Jonathan Z. Ludwig
Rice University

Christopher Lynch
Center for American Music
University of Pittsburgh

Matthew Machin-Autenrieth
Independent Scholar

Joseph R. Matson
Independent Scholar

Eldonna L. May
Wayne State University

Jacopo Mazzeo
University of Southampton

Gerry McGoldrick
Ryerson University

Emily Rose McManus
Saint Mary's College, Notre Dame

Christy J. Miller
University of Kansas

George Monger
Freelance folklorist and museum/heritage conservator and consultant

Aaron Mulvany
Habib University

Hope Munro
Independent Scholar

Jason Newman
Independent Scholar

Elizabeth Gackstetter Nichols
Independent Scholar

Ted Olson
Independent Scholar

Elizabeth Ozment
Georgia Gwinnett College

Greg A. Phelps
Lindsey Wilson College

Melanie T. Pinkert, PhD
Sandy Spring Museum

Bart Plantenga
Independent Scholar

Nick Poulakis
National and Kapodistrian University of Athens

William Price
University of Alabama at Birmingham

Dr. Laura Stanfield Prichard
Harvard University Libraries

Liz Przybylski
University of California, Riverside

Abdur Rahman
Independent Scholar

Lucy M. Rees
Independent Scholar

Timothy R. Robbins
Independent Scholar

Saul Mauricio Rodriguez-Hernandez
Universidad de Buenos Aires

Stacie Lee Rossow, DMA
Florida Atlantic University

Ivan Sablin
National Research University Higher School of Economics
University of Heidelber

Benedetta Saglietti
Università degli Studi di Milano Statale

Lola San Martín Arbide
Independent Scholar

Luis Sanchez
Independent Scholar

Amanda L. Scherbenske
Jewish Music Forum

Melanie Schiller
University of Groningen

Nico Schüler, PhD
Texas State University

Jessica A. Schwartz
Columbia University

Meredith Schweig
Independent Scholar

Ryan Shaffer
Stony Brook University

Dr. Carol L. Shansky
Iona College

John A. Shoup
Al Akhawayn University

Dr. Ravindra Pratap Singh
Department of English and Modern European Languages
University of Lucknow

Hope Munro Smith
California State University, Chico

Lorenzo Sorbo
University of Milan

Kelly St. Pierre
Youngstown State University
Case Western Reserve University

Yona Stamatis
University of Illinois Springfield

John Stanislawski
University of Illinois at Champaign-Urbana

Theresa Steward
Independent Scholar

Contributors

Travis D. Stimeling
West Virginia University

Eric S. Strother
Anderson University

Yoko Suzuki
University of Pittsburgh

Alejandra Tapia
Independent Scholar

Mark C. van Tongeren
Independent Scholar

Juliana Tzvetkova
Independent Scholar

Joshua Watkins
University of Trinidad and Tobago

Dr. Gavin Webb
Marist College

Dr. Ryan R. Weber
Misericordia University

Frances Wilkins
University of Aberdeen

Hei Ting (Hety) Wong
University of Pittsburgh

Brian F. Wright
Case Western Reserve University

Tse Chun Yan
Independent Scholar

Jun Zubillaga-Pow
King's College London

Index

Note: Page numbers in bold indicate main entries in the encyclopedia.

Abba, Dimi Mint (1958–2011), 327
'Abd al-Wahhāb, Muhammad, 34, 438, 439
Abenaki, 249
Aboriginal storytelling and song, 141
Aborigines, music by, 231–233
Abrahm, Otto, 67
Abshire, Nathan, 128
Acadia, 127, 962
Acadian Music, **1–2,** 127
Acadians, 962
A cappella vocal music, 172
Accordion
   in Acadian music, 1, 127
   in Cajun music, 128
   chromatic, 5
   in conjunto music, 191–192, 193, 195
   corrido accompanied by, 194
   in cumbia, 215
   family of instruments (*see* Bandoneón)
   in Ireland, 243
   in Tejano music, 893–894
   in zydeco music, 963
Accordion (Americas), **2–5**
Accordion, Types of, **5–8**
Acordión de botón, **6–7**
Acoustic guitar
   as accompanying instrument, 63
   conjunto music using, 192
   development of, 329
   steel-strung, 838
   traditions influencing playing of, 75
   in western swing, 203
Acuff, Roy, 270
Adams, Alton (1889–1987), 140
Adams, Yolanda, 314
Adderly, Julian "Cannonball," 186, 224, 225

Addis Ababa, music scene in, 46–47
Addy, Yacub (1931–2015), 191
Adé, "King" Sunny (1946–), **8–9,** 13
Aerophones, 240
Aerosmith, 752
Afanasyev, Alexander (1826–1871), 7
Afghanistan, music of, 659–661
Africa
   bagpipes in, 54
   music of, 190–191, 337–339
   yodeling in, 945
African American comedians, 951
African American Great Migration, 722, 749
African American influence on country music, 202
African American music and musicians. *See also individual artists, e.g.,* Lead Belly (1888/9–1949)
   blues and blues influence on, 96, 97
   composers, 425–428
   cultural value of, 508–509
   funk, 287–290
   influence of, 8–9
   instruments played in, 62
   post-World War II, 710
   white musicians influenced by, 693, 749
African American slaves, instruments built by, 326
African-Ecuadorean music, 28
African-inspired polyrhythms, 102
African instruments, 47
African nations, social structure of, 147
African slaves
   in Andes region, 25, 102
   banjo playing by, 60
   bomba music (Puerto Rico), 110

African slaves (*cont.*)
  in Bomba region (Eduador), 108, 109
  in Brazil, 114–115
  in Caribbean, 139, 177
  in Colombia, 214, 215
  in Cuba, 176, 761
  descendants of, 108
  emancipation of, 145
  gatherings, 190, 191
  instruments played by, 88
  vocals, 945
African Spirituals, **9–12**
Afrobeat (Afropop), 8, **12–15**, 491, 493
Afroblocos, 146
Afro-Bolivians, music of, 102, 103
Afro-Brazilian identity, 115, 118
Afro-Brazilian music, 113
Afro-Brazilian musical bow, 87
Afro-Brazilian religions, 133
Afro-Brazilian samba schools, 145
Afro-Caribbean rhythms, 179
Afro-Caribbeans, Carnival celebrated by, 130, 143
Afro-Cuban Jazz, **15–17**, 179
Afro-Cuban music
  culture, 764
  influence of, 140
  instruments played in, 179
  mambo, 525
  mbalax influenced by, 549
  rhythms, 180
  rumba, 177, 760–762
Afro-Eastern tradition, 23
Afro-Ecuadorian identity and culture, 108
Afro-fusion, 645
Afrofuturism, 289
Afro-Jazz era, 178
Afropop, 330
Afro-Puerto Ricans, 110
Afro-Trinidadians, 130, 838, 881
Ahmad, Fadzil (1941–), **17–19**
Ahmadinejad, Mahmoud, 796
Aita Donostia, 70
Ajnās, 32–33
Akerangu, 11
Albee, Edward Franklin "E. F." (1857–1930), 827, 925
Alberdi, Juan, 883
Albinoni, Tomaso Giovanni (1671–1741), 188
Alboka, 70
Albright, William, 716

Alejandrino, José, 665
Alencar, José de (1829–1877), 116
Alevis, 53–54
Alexander, Arthur, 834
Alexis, Clifford, 841
Al-Fārābī, 31
Al Faruqi, Lois Ibsen, 24
Algeria, music of, 716–721
Algerian singers, 459–461
Algonquin languages, 249
Al-Hafnawi, Hasan, 439
Alizadeh, Hossein, 796
Al-jadid music, 86
Allaga, Géva (1841–1913), 245
Allen, Ed, 827
Allen, O. K., 501
Allen, Tony (1940–), 14, 490
Allende, Salvador, 620
Almanac Singers, 335, 790
Al-maqam al-'Iraqi, 68
Alpine dances, 48
Alpine zither, 955, 956
Al-Qasabji, Mohammad, 439
Al-Shushtarī, 24
Al-Sunbātī, Riyād, 32, 438
"Alternative country," 205
Al-Tifāshī, Ahmad, 23
Altiplano, music of the. *See* Andean Region, Music of the
Al-Tunsi, Bayram, 438
Amadinda, **19–20**
Amaya, Carmen (1913–1963), 760
Amazon deforestation, 114
Ambach, Melchior, 50
Ambrosian chant, 319
American Indian Movement, 594
American Reform congregations, 45
Americas, bagpipes in, 54
Amirataii, Bayaz (1955–), 443
Amish Hymns (*Ausbund, Gesangbuch*), **21–22**
Ammann, Jakob (1644–ca. 1730), 21
Amos, Daniel, 314
Amplified guitar, 57
Anabaptists, 21
Andalusia, poetry in, 949
Andalusian Music, **22–25**
  flamenco, 272, 273, 274, 277, 278
  legacy of, 33–34
Andean Region, Music of the, **25–30**
  Argentina, Chile, and Bolivia, 26–27, 101, 104

Index

Cumbia, 29
Ecuador and Colombia, 28
mestizo music, 564–565
Peru, 27
precolonial, 101
Anderson, Leroy, 270
Anderson, Rita (1946–), 539, 540
Andrade, Julio, 158
Andrade, Oswald de, 119
Andrews Sisters, 132
Angelou, Maya, 133
Anglés, Higinio, 33
Anglo-Celtic ballads, 148
Angola, instruments from, 88
Animals' voices, imitation of, 231–232
Animism, 900
Anthony, Marc, 772
Anti-apartheid movement, 516, 546
Antiphonale, 319–320
Apartheid, 496, 518, 519, 545, 546, 547, 548
Appalachian dulcimer, 242, 958
Appalachian rhythm, 113
Arab Classical Music, **30–35**
  Bedouin influence on, 81
  belly dancing associated with, 86
  conceptual framework, 30–32
  European influences, 33, 34
  historical context, 32
  Iraqi musicians influenced by, 67, 68–69
  Ottoman Empire legacy of, 53
  point/counterpoint, 33–34
  sound of Arab music, 32–33
Arabic melodies, transcriptions of, 67
Arabic poetry, 949–950
Arab music, 640, 641, 642
Arabs, flamenco influenced by, 272
Arbeau, Thoinot (b. Jehan Tabourot), 282
Ar Braz, Dan (1949–), 155
Arcadelt, Jacob (ca. 1507–1568), 512
Arctic Indian music, 589, 591
'*ardhah* (war dance), 81
'*ardhah* (war songs), 82
Arditi, Luigi, 936
Ardoin, Amédé, 128, 963
Ardoin, Chris, 961, 964
Arezzo, Guido d' (ca. 992–1050 CE), 321
Argentina, music of
  cumbia in, 217
  dance in, 158, 159
  Nueva Canción, 619
  opera, 668

regional, 26
tango in, 58, 667, 882–886
Arghul, 83
Armenian Music, **35–39**
  classical music, 37
  in competitions, 261
  contemporary popular music, 38
  folk music, 37–38
  liturgical music, 36–37
  memorabilia, 546
Armónico, 121–122
Armstrong, Louis (1901–1971), **39–41**
  bebop criticized by, 409, 848
  blues influence on, 97–98
  country musician collaborations with, 202
  instruments belonging to, 546
  jazz played by, 849
  musicians performing with, 826, 827
  Native American musicians performing with, 594
  Rainey, Ma dealings with, 722
  Rodgers, J. dealings with, 755
  swing music played by, 710, 848
Arolas, Eduardo, 884
Arriaga, Juan Crisóstomo de (1806–1826), 70
Art music
  Bolivian, 104
  Brazilian, 116–117
  Caribbean, 139–141
  Chinese, 332
  classical music relationship to, 170
  dulcimer in, 243, 244, 245
  Hungarian, 474–476
  Persian, 222
  Western, 222, 932
Arvanitaki, Eleftheria, 318
Asad, Bashar al-, 84
Asch, Moses (1905–1986), 278, 279
Ashkenazi Jews, Music of, **41–46**
Asia Minor Greeks, 316
Astatke, Mulatu (1943–), **46–48**
Atatürk, Mustafa Kemal, 53
Atkins, Chet (1924–2001), 149, 204
Atkins, Mark, 232
Atonalilty, development of, 175
Atrache, Farid el- (ca. 1915–1974), 642, 643
Aubret, Isabelle, 161
Aufschnaiter, Benedict Anton, 188
Ausbund, 21–22
Aussel, Roberto, 669

Australia, music of, 141–142, 205, 231–233
Austral Islands, music of, 688–689, 692
Austria, German annexation of, 66
Austria, music of, 786–787
Austrian dances, 51
Austro-German Dances, **48–52**
Austro-Hungarian Empire, 174, 936
Autoharp, 696, 957
Autry, Gene, 3, 202–203
Axé, 118
Ayala, Castor, 110
Ayala, Pedro (1911–1990), 192, 893
Ayala, Ramon, 197
'ayalah, 82, 83
Ayla, Safiye, 643
Ayler, Albert, 187
Aymara-influenced bells, 102
Aymara people, 103
Ayoreos, songs of, 102
Azembo, Soeda (1872–1944), 252
Azkue, Resurrección María de (1864–1951), 70
Azores, dance from, 158–159
Azpiazu, Don, 761
Azuma asobi, 292
Azurmendi, Idoia (1971–), 70
Azzouz, Arnaud, 577–578

Babs, Alice (1924–2014), 610
Baby boom generation, music of, 717, 750
Bacchus (god), 143–144
Bach, J. S. (Johann Sebastian) (1685–1750), 56, 57, 116–117, 172, 188–189, 668, 842, 929
Badala, 653, 654, 660
Bagadoù, 154
Bagdad, clave pattern in, 177
Bağlama, **53–54**
Bagpipes, **54–57,** 64, 70, 83
Bahamian music, 331–332
Bahari, Ali-Asghar (1905–1995), 443
Bailecito, 26, 103
Bailes de mascaras (private masked balls), 144–145
Bailey, Mildred, 594
Bairischer ("Farmer Dance"), 51
Bajo sexto
  accordion accompanied by, 7
  in conjunto music, 192, 193, 195, 893
  corrido accompanied by, 194, 196
Bajramovic, Saban (1936–2008), 760
Baker, Theodore (1851–1934), 592, 593

Balafon, 47, 339
Balasanyan, Sako (Super Sako), 38
Balfa, Dewey, 127, 128, 129
Bali, music of, 183, 295–299, 307–310
  Balinese *gamelan gong kebyar* ensemble, 184
  Balinese *wayang kulit,* 307
  gamelan, 555–556
  Kecak, 453–456
Ball, Ernie, 329
Ballads
  Anglo-American, 202
  Anglo-Celtic, 148
  corrido, 193, 194, 195–198
  in country music, 202
  Icelandic, 367–369
Balochistan, music in, 652–653
Bals folk, 284
Baltic psaltery, 956–957
Balungan, 183
Bamboche, La, 285
Bamboo-keyed instruments, 297
Bamboula rhythms, 707
Bambuco, 28
Band, Heinrich (1821–1860), 7, 58, 668
Banda/orquesta, conjunto relationship to, 192
Bandas pelayeras, 215
Bandish, 650
Bandola, 28
Bandoneón, **58–59**
  construction, 59
  history, 58
  musicians playing, 667, 669
  origin, 7, 668
  tango music played on, 884
Bandonion (term), 58
Bandô Tamasaburô V (1950–), 433
Bandurria, 213
Banerjee, Nikhil (1931–1986), 821
Bangsawan, 17
Banjo, **59–64**
  in bluegrass, 95
  coconut, 684
  fiddle accompanying, 269
  history, 60–63
  kora relationship to, 477
  in minstrel shows, 958
  in Pashto music, 660
  playing style, 93
  prototypes and inspiration for, 326, 941
Banjo-zither, 958–959

Index

Barbat, 644
Barbosa, Domingos Caldas (ca. 1739–1800), 115
Barenboim, Daniel, 669
Bariu, Laver (1929–2014), **64–65**
"Barn dance" programs, 202
Baroque, 171–172
Barranquilla, Carnival de, 214
Barrett, Aston "Family Man" (1946–), 540
Barrett, Carleton "Carly" (1950–), 540
Barriles, 111
Barroso, Ari (1903–1964), 118
Bartenstein, Fred, 93
Bartók, Béla (1881–1945), 32, 56, **65–67,** 190, 474, 668, 928
Bashir, Munir (1930–1997), 643–644
Bashir Brothers (Munir and Jamil), **67–69**
Basie, Count, 79, 710, 849
Basque, Music of the, **69–72**
Basque Country, 69
Basque language (Batua), 69–70, 71
Basque Radikal Rock *(rock radikal vasco),* 71
Bass-button accordion, 7
Basse Bretagne, 285
Basse danse, 282–283
Bass in Cajun music, 128
Basso continuo, 171
Bassoon, 172
Batá Drums, **72–73**
Bateria, 143
Batson, Dawn, 841
Bauzá, Mario, 15, 16
Bavarian Polka, 783
Bayan, 7
Beach, Amy (1867–1944), 593
Beastie Boys, 897, 898
Beatles, The, **74–78**
  "British invasion" launched by, 717, 750–751
  Great Britain influences, 75
  in Hong Kong, 136, 163
  Indian influences, 76–78, 809, 821
  Japanese musicians compared to, 429
  Latin American influences, 75
  musicians influenced by, 246
  North American influences, 74–75, 204, 499
Beau Jocque, 963–964
Bebop, **78–80**
  Afro-Cuban jazz combined with, 16
  jazz competition with, 848

  music influenced by, 15
  origin and development of, 409, 657, 658, 848
Bechet, Sidney, 186, 722
Beck, Martin, 925
Bedouin, dances of, 81–82
Bedouin Music, **81–84**
Bee, Tom, 594
Beethoven, Ludwig van (1770–1827), 51, 173, 189, 855, 935
Beijing Opera, 414–420
Béjart, Maurice, 440
Belafonte, Harry, 132–133, 517, 518, 546, 547, 739
Bélé, **84–85**
Belizean music, 563
Bell, William, 833
Bellamy, Tony, 594
Bells
  drums accompanied by, 73
  Tibetan, 900–901
Belly Dance, **85–87,** 221
Beloved, nature-related imagery for, 31–32
Beltrán, Lola, 535
Benda, Georg (1722–1795), 817, 818
Benedict, St. (ca. 480–ca. 546 CE), 319
Benin, singers from, 465–467
Benjamin of Tudela, 793
Bennet, Michael (1943–1987), 581–582
Benton, Dave, 260
Berg, Alban, 175
Bérimbau, **87–89,** 115–116
Berlin, Irving (1888–1989), 334, 579, 580, 903, 905, 951
Berlioz, Hector (1803–1869), 174, 855, 935
Bermudez, Lucho (1912–1994), 214, 216
Bernal, Paulino (1939–), 192
Bernaola, Carmelo (1929–2002), 70
Bernstein, Leonard (1918–1990), 526
  Jewish materials incorporated by, 45
Berry, Chuck, 1–2, 74, 429
Bertsos, 70
Betz, Hans, 21
Bhagwat, Anupama, 821
Bhangra, 652
Bharti, Rais, 578
Bhojpuri song texts, 167, 168
Biafran War (1967–1970), 491
Biamegh, 11
Biblical cantillation, 42
Bidgood, Lee, 95

Big Band era
  Afro-Cuban music in, 16
  jazz ensembles, 710
  swing development in, 849
Big Band music, 79–80
Billy the Kid, 6
Biniou, 56
Birds, imitation of, 943
Biwa (gakubiwa), 294
Björk (1965–), **89–92**
Black, Bill, 694
Black cowboys, 945
Black culture, white representations of, 61–62
Blackface minstrelsy. *See* minstrel shows/minstrelsy
Black gospel, 97, 239, 311, 312–313, 314
Black New Orleans jazz, 233–234
Black Panther Party, 518
Black Power movement, 13, 288, 491, 516
Black singers in contests, 260
Black spirituals, 281
Blackwell, Chris (1937–), 465, 540, 741–742
Blades, Ruben, 772
Blake, Blind, 97
Blake, Norman (1938–), 94
Blanasi, David, 232
Blanchard, Jean, 285
Blevins, Ruby (Patsy Montana) (1908–1996), 202
Blind Abing (Hua Yanjun) (1893–1950), 256
"Blind Blake" (Blake Alphonso Higgs) (1915–1986), 331–332
Bliss, Philip (1838–1876), 311
Bloch, 45, 190
Block, Rory, 99
Blocos afros, 118
Bluegrass, **92–96**
  banjo in, 60, 63
  counterculture influence on, 205
  development of, 204
  instruments played in, 270
  steel guitar in, 837
"Blue note," 99
Blues, **96–99**
  berimbau performance fusion with, 88–89
  birthplace of, 190
  Dixieland influenced by, 233
  field holler relationship to, 271
  Mississippi Delta, 62
  musicians, 420–423
  origin and rise of, 509–510, 709–710
  rock and roll influenced by, 74
  steel guitar in, 837
  stringed instruments in, 63
Blumenthal, Nissan (1805–1903), 45
Blythe, Nat, 507
Bnegão (1973–), 120
Boeschenstein, Johannes, 43
Boethius, 321
Boethius, Severinus (ca. 480–ca. 525), 321
Bohemian folksongs, 151
Boko Haram, 466
Bol, **99–101**
Bolcom, William, 716
Boleros, 192, 708
Bolivia, Music of, **101–104**
  after European colonization, 102–104
  cumbia, 29
  before European colonization, 101–102
  folkloric music, 26–27
Bollywood Music, **105–108**, 831
Bologne, Joseph, 140
Bomba, Ecuador, 28, **108–110**
Bomba, Puerto Rico, **110–111**
Bomba drum, 109
Bombarde, 56
Bombazos, 111
Bombo (bass drum), 178
Bones (Britain and Ireland), **112–113**
Bongos, 75
Bön religion, 900
Boogie-woogie, 847
Book Binder, Roy, 99
Border music, 195
Bordes, Charles (1863–1909), 70
Bosnia-Herzegovina, music of, 260, 305, 306
Bossa nova, 75, 118–119
Bostic, Joe, 313
Boublil, Alain (1941–), 582
Boucher, William, 61
Bourrée, 284, 285
Bouzouki, 86
Bowed psaltery, 696–697
Bowed zither, 955
Bowie, David, 161
Box zither, 955, 956, 958
Boyd, Jean, 203
Bradley, Owen (1915–1998), 204
Braggs, Billy, 336

Index

Brahms, Johannes (1833–1897), 66, 189, 855, 935
Brant, Sebastian, 50
Brass-band concerts, 191
Brassens, Georges (1921–), 159–160, 161
Brass instruments
   in conjunto music, 192
   note range of, 173–174
Braveman, Mal, 79
Brazil, Carnival in, 144–145, 146–147
Brazil, Music of, **113–120**
   African influences, 115–116
   art music, post-colonial, 116–117
   bossa nova, MPB, and tropicalia, 118–119
   contemporary, 120
   dance, 158, 159
   early popular music, samba, and carnival culture, 117–118
   European colonial, 114–115
   indigenous, 113–114
   instruments, 87, 88
Brazil, religions of, 133
Breaux, Cléoma, 127, 128
Brecht, Bertolt (1898–1956), 502
Breiner, Peter, 287
Brel, Jacques (1929–), 159, 160–161
"Breton music" (term), 156
Breton pop, 285
Breuer, Katherina, 49
Brewster, James (1929–), 708
Bring Back Our Girls Movement, 466
"British invasion," 246, 582, 717, 750
Brittany
   cultures from, 156
   instruments played in, 56
   as multicultural area, 285–286
   music of, 154
Brooks, Garth (1962–), 205
Brower, Frank (1823–1874), 112, 930, 931
Brown, Clifford, 490
Brown, James (1933–2006)
   African musicians influenced by, 491
   Afro-Cuban music influence on, 16–17
   compositions, 289
   as funk founder, 288
   influence of, 13
   soul music influenced by, 835
Brown, Milton, 203
Brown, Roy, 621–622
Brown, Ruth, 98–99
Brown, Sidney, 7

Bruckner, Anton (1824–1896), 51, 856
Buarque, Chico (1944–), 119, 622
Buchanon, Elwood, 224
Buckwheat Zydeco (Stanley Dural, Jr.) (1947–), 961, 963
Buddhist chant, 815–817, 896–899
Buena Vista Social Club, **121–124**
Buenos Aires
   cumbia in, 217
   migration to, 58, 883–884
   slave trade in, 883
   tango in, 882
Buhari, Muhammadu, 492
Bukofzer, Manfred, 944–945
Bulas, 111
Buni, Vardan, 442
Bunny Wailer (Neville Livingston), 539, 541, 741
Bunraku, **124–125**
Bunraku theater, 433
Burke, Billie, 952
Burlesque, 925
Burmese harp, 927
Burnett, Chester (Howlin' Wolf), 98
Burns, George, 926
Burton, Gary, 669
Button accordion, 191–192, 193, 195
Byrd, William, 284
Byrne, David, 14
Byron, Lord, 934
Byzantine lyra, 207

Cabral, Augusto, 166
Cabral, Pedro Álvares, 113
Cadenza, 172
Caetano, Antonio da Silva, 145
Cafés cantantes, 273
Cage, John, 175
Cagney, James, 182
Cajun (concept), 962
Cajun accordion (squeezebox), 7
Cajun-French dialect, 127
Cajun Music, **127–129**
   accordion use in, 7
   development of, 962
   origin of, 4
   zydeco compared to, 964
Cajuns, origin of, 1
Cakewalk, 903
Call-and-response
   in bélé, 85
   in bomba, 111

Call-and-response (*cont.*)
   in calypso, 130–131
   in rumba, 763
   in saya, 102
   in soul, 832
   tamboo bamboo accompanying, 881–882
Calloway, Cab, 710
Calvin, John (1509–1564), 21, 571
Calypso, **129–133**
   Caribbean musical history dominated by, 331
   competitions, 170
   instruments played in, 180
   international interest in, 139, 739
   language typical of, 829
   musicians influenced by, 74, 75
   quelbe band playing of, 708
   soca compared to, 830, 831
Calypso Rose (born McArtha Lewis) (1940–), 133, 828–829, 830
Camacho, Apolinar (1917–2002), 102
Cambrensis, Giraldus (ca. 1146–ca. 1223), 153
Canales, Laura, 894
Cancio-corridos, 194
Candomblé, 115, **133–136**, 147
Canetti, Jacques, 160
Canmeyer, Alfred (1862–1949), 958–959
Cannon, Gus, 62
Cantigas, 23, 33, 34
Cantometrics, 509, 945
Cantonese language, 136
Canto orfeônico (Orpheonic singing), 116
Cantopop, **136–139**, 161, 162–163
Cantwell, Robert, 95
Capoeira, Brazilian art of, 88, 89, 115–116, 147, 195
Cárdenas, Lázaro, 535
Cardin, Pierre, 868
Caribbean, exotic image of, 133
Caribbean Art Music, **139–141**
Caribbean music
   calypso, 129–130
   genres, 215
   goombay, 331–332
   influence of, 74
   instruments, 330
   quelbe, 707–708
   salsa, 771
   soca, 829–830

Cariso melodies, 707
Carlo Gesualdo, Prince of Venosa, 513
Carmagnole, 282
Carmichael, Stokeley, 518
Carmody, Kevin Daniel "Kev" (1946–), **141–143**
Carmos, Carlos do (1939–), 264–265
Carmos, Lucília do (1919–1998), 264–265
Carnavalito, 26, 103
Carnival, Music of, **143–147**
   African folklore influence, 115
   Brazilian Carnival destinations, other, 146–147
   calypso, 131, 132, 133
   creolization of, 130
   cumbia performed in, 214
   ensembles and parade, 145
   history and development, 143–145
   instruments in, 838–839
   international, 147
   samba role in, 118
   samba schools, 145
   soca, 133
   women performers, 169
Carnyxes (war horns), 152
Carpio, Luzmila, 104
Carranza, Venustiano, 196
Carrier, Chubby, 129, 963
Carson, Fiddlin' John, 202
Carter, Rubin, 247
The Carter Family, **148–150**, 753
   blues songs recorded by, 202
Carter Sisters, 148
Caruso, Enrico, 182
Casas do fado (houses of fado), 263, 264
Cash, Johnny (1932–2003)
   Lead Belly songs covered by, 499
   performers working with, 149, 150
Cash, June, 150
Castanets, 112
Castanyoles, 112
Castro, Fidel, 210–211, 699
Catholicism, 133, 134
Catholic Lenten season, festivals preceding, 143
Catlett, Sid, 80
Caucasian tar, 888
Cavaquinho, 212
Caxixi rattle, 88
Cazzati, Maurizio, 187–188

Index

Čechomor, **150–152**
Cellarius, Henri, 706–707
Celtic folk groups, instruments played by, 56
Celtic language, 156
Celtic Music, 148, **152–157**
Central Europe, herding instruments in, 56
Cepeda, Rafael, 110
Chabrier, Jean-Claude, 68
Cha-cha-cha, 525, 526
Chacón, Emma (1886–1972), 70
Chaguoro, 73
Challenger space shuttle, 197
Chamamé, 58
Chamarrita, **157–159**
Chamber music, 173
Chambers, Paul, 224
"Champagne Music," 680
Chan, Eason, 138
Change, music as tool for, 789
Chanson (Urban/Modern), **159–161**
Chants. *See also* liturgical chants
    Buddhist, 815–817, 896–899
    Jewish, 43, 793
    Navajo, 597
Chantwèl, 85
Chapman, Tracy (1964–), 945
Char (b. Cherilyn Sarkisian), 38
Charango, 102
Charbeta, 659–660
Charles, Ray (1930–2004), 204, 832
Charles VI (1711–1740), 50
Charrango, 26
Charro, 534
Charro movies, 535
Chaurasia, Hariprasad, 821
Chavez, Carlos (1899–1978), 895–963
Chavis, Wilson "Boozoo," 963
Cheng, Sammi, 138
Chenier, C. J., 961, 963
Chenier, Cleveland, 962
Chenier, Clifton (1925–1987), 2, 4, 961, 962, 963
Cherry, Don, 88
Cheung, Jackie (Jackie Cheung Hok Yau), 137
Cheung, Leslie (Leslie Cheung Kwok Wing), 137, 138
Chiang Kai-shek (1887–1975), 872–873
Chicano country, 894
Chicano movement, 893

Chicanos, 193
Chicha, 29
Chile
    cumbia in, 217
    music of, 25, 26
    Nueva Canción, 620
Chinese Civil War, 137
Chinese dulcimer, 243
Chinese music
    guoyue, 332–333
    instruments, 254–257, 336–337, 672–674
    opera, 414–420
Chinese Pop, **161–164**
Choates, Harry, 1, 128
Chopin, Frédéric (1810–1849), 174, 935
Chopi People, Music of the, **164–167**, 551–552
Choral music
    African, 495–496, 552
    Basque, 70–71
    in opera, 172
Choro, 117
Chottin, Alexis, 32
Chow, Adrian (Adrian Chow Pok Yin), 138
Christian, Charley
    blues influence on, 97–98
    improvisations by, 79
    recordings of, 80
Christian church, art music influenced by, 140
Christian festival, Carnival as, 144
Christianity in Armenia, 36
Christian Missionaries, 553
Christian music, contemporary, 314
Christy, Edwin P., 112, 281
Chromatic accordion, 5
"Chucu Chucu" rhythm, 214
Chukhajian (Tchouhadjian), Tigran (1837–1898), 37
Chutney, **167–169**
Chutney Soca, 168, **169–170**, 830
Çifte telli, 85–86
Cimbalom, 242, 243, 244, 245
Cinquillo, 179
Cittern, 954
Civil rights, 516, 518, 627, 789, 835
Clapton, Eric, 420, 499, 742
Clarinet, 131, 223
Clarke, Stanley, 289
Classical cumbia, 215

Classical music, American
 banjo in, 60
 blues influence on, 98
 ragtime influence on, 716
Classical music, Arab, 30–35, 53, 67,
  68–69, 81, 86
Classical music, Eastern, 243, 245
Classical Music, European, **170–176**
 Armenian, 37
 Baroque, 171–172
 classicism, 172–173
 contemporary, 174–175
 origins, 170–171
 Romanticism, 173–174
Classical music, Hindustani, 99–100
Classical music, Indian, 443–448,
  462–464
Classical music, Iranian. *See* Iranian
  Classical Music
Classical music, Javanese, 302–303
Classical music, Ottoman, 637–640
Classical music, Pakistani, 649–650, 651
Classical music, Persian, 222, 795
Classical music, South Asian, 711–715
Classical music, Western, 317
Classical period, 172–173
Claves and Clave Rhythm, **176–180**
 definition and overview, 176–177
 rhythm, 177–180
 in rumba, 762
Clawhammer, 60
Clerc, Julien, 161
Cliff, Jimmy (1948–), 538
Cline, Patsy (born Virginia Hensley)
  (1932–1963), 204
Clinton, George, 289
Cobain, Kurt, 752
Coffee preparation, songs/poems
  accompanying, 82
Cohan, George M (1878–1942), **180–183**,
  579, 904
Coimbra fado, 264
Coleman, Jaybird, 272
Coleman, Ornette, 187
Collier, William, 181
Collins, Albert, 98–99
Colombia, music of, 25, 28, 29
Colometry/Colometric, **183–185**
Colón, Willie, 772
Colonialism, military bands and, 740
Coltrane, John (1926–1967), **185–187**,
  224, 491, 610

Columbia, 760, 762–763
Comenius, John Amos (1592–1670), 571
Commercial urban blues, 97
Common, 14
Concertina, instruments related to, 2, 58,
  668. *See also* Bandoneón
Concertino
 instruments constituting, 188–189
 ripieno compared to, 172, 188
Concerto, 6, 172, **187–190**
Concerto grosso, 172, 188
Conch shell, 140
Conch-shell trumpets, 685
Conductus, 171
Conga, 16, 75
Congolese-African customs, 147
Congo Square, **190–191**
Conjunto, **191–192**
 in Andean region, 26
 origin of, 4
 rise of, 892–893
 Tejano influenced by, 894
 western swing influenced by, 203
Conjunto (Norteños), **193–195**
Consumer culture, 750
Contemporary corridos, 197
Contemporary news stories, compositions
  about, 202
Contino, Dick (1930–), 2, 3
Contredanse, 283, 285, 524–525
Convivencia (Spain), 792
Cooder, Ry, 121, 123, 499, 910
Cooke, Sam (1931–1964), 833, 835
Cook Islands, music of, 687–688, 691
Cool jazz, 80, 409–410
Copeland, Shemekia, 99
Copland, Aaron (1900–1990)
 Afro-Cuban music influence on, 764
 American touch, 857
 blues influence on, 98
 fiddle played in music by, 270
 McPhee, C. cited by, 554
Coplas, 109
Corea, Chick, 467
Corelli, Arcangelo (1653–1713), 188,
  189
Cornamusa, 57
Corrido, **195–198**
 contemporary, 197
 instruments accompanying, 194
 norteña music as vehicle for, 193
Cortes, Joaquin (1969–), 760

Index

Cortijo, Rafael (1928–1982), 110
Cossacks, Music of, **198–201**
Costuming in bélé, 85
Cotillon, 284
Countercultural upheavals, 204–205
Counterculture movement, 288, 751
Counterpoint, 172
Country and western, 75, 201, 694–695
Country dance, 960
Country Music, **201–207**
    banjo in, 60
    blues influence on, 96
    Brazilian, 120
    Cajun music influenced by, 128
    conjunto fusion with, 192
    first family of, 148–150
    guitar in, 75
    rock and roll influenced by, 74
    subsets of, 63
    Tejano music, 894
Country-rock, 204, 205
Courlander, Harold (1908–1996), 278
Courville, Sady, 128
Cowboys, yodeling by, 945
Cowboy songs, 202–203, 507, 508
Cowell, Henry (1897–1965), 554
Cowherd's yodel, 944
Cox, Ida, 97
C-pop, 161–164
Crabb, Jason, 312
Cramer, Floyd (1933–1997), 204
Creole (concept defined), 962, 963
Creole art music, 140
Creole culture, 85
Creole culture in Caribbean, 139, 169
Creole dance music, 140, 960–961
Creole folk dance, 84
Creole language, 130, 131
Creoles of color, music by, 191
Cretan Lyra, **207–209**
Croatia, music from, 260
Crockett, Davy, 269
Crosby, Bing, 202
Crosby, Fanny (1820–1915), 311
Crossley-Holland, Peter, 32
Crouch, Andrae, 314
Crowe, J. D., 95
Cruz, Celia (1925–2003), **209–212**
    Afro-Cuban music influence on, 16–17
    music themes, 771–772
    Puente, T. introduction of, 699

Csárdas, 66
Cuá, 111
Cuatro, 131, **212–213**
Cuba, music of
    black populations, 761
    instruments from, 72, 176, 177, 179, 761–762
    mambo, 524–527
    nueva trova, 621
    rumba, 760–765
    salsa, 771
    singers, 209–212
    social clubs, 121–124
Cuban Revolution, 1959, 621, 699, 763–764
Cubop movement, 179
Cueca, 26, 102, 104
"Cultural cannibalism" (term), 119
Cumbamba, 109
Cumbia, **213–217**
    in Andean region, 29
    Colombian, 215
    Latin American variations, 216–217
    performers, 215–216
    rise of, 25
    Santafesina, 217
    sonidera, 216
    villera, 217
Cumbia andina, 29
Cumbiamba, 215
Cumbia sabanera, 215
Cumbia vallenata, 215
Cyclic gong, 183, 184, 298
Cylindrical drums, 864
Cyprien (Cipriano) de Rore (ca. 1515–1565), 512
Cyrus, Miley, 596
Czech dances, 680, 681
Czech Republic, music of, 150–152
    bluegrass in, 95
    country music in, 206

Da, Stefane, 260
Daddy Yankee (Ramón Luis Ayala Rodriguez), 744, 745
Daff, 81, 378
Dagar brothers, 230
Dagda (Irish deity), 153
Daibyoshi, 865
Dairo, I. K., 13
Dalaras, George, 318
Dalida, 161

Dameron, Tadd, 16, 224
Dance
  African, 191
  Austrian, 51
  Balinese, 454
  Bedouin, 81, 83
  bélé accompanying, 84–85
  bomba accompanying, 111
  in Brazil, 117
  Breton, 154
  Cajun music accompanying, 127–128
  of Chopi people, 165–166
  country music accompanying, 148
  creole, 960–961
  Cretan, 208–209
  in cumbia, 215
  dhol accompanying, 228
  Flamenco music accompanying, 274–277
  French, 282–286
  gamelan music performed with, 303
  German, 50, 496–497
  Hawaiian, 684, 923
  Irish, 381–388
  Irish music accompanying, 113
  Japanese, 436
  Korean, 607–610
  Pakistani, 653
  Pashtun, 653
  Polish, 676–683
  Polynesian, 684
  salsa, 772
  Swedish, 783
  women in, 235
Dance-drama, Balinese, 454–456
Dancehall, **219–221**, 742, 744
Dances anglaises, 283
Dance troupes, 11
Daniels, Charlie, 205
Danielson, Virginia, 32
Danse du ventre, la, 86
Daramad, 223
Darbuka, 31, **221–222**, 235
Darbukah, 81
Darr, Adam (1811–1866), 956
Darweesh, Sayyed (1892–1923), 32
Dastgah, **222–224**
David, Ferdinand, 189–190
Davies, Sir John, 283
Davis, Bill Evans, 225
Davis, George, 503
Davis, Jesse Ed, 594

Davis, Miles (Dewey, III) (1926–1991), **224–226**
  African musicians influenced by, 490, 547
  funk influence on, 289
  new directions embraced by, 80, 411
  Parker, C. playing with, 658
  quintet, 185–186
DeBussy, Claude (1862–1918), 66, 185, 716
Décimus, Georges, 960
Décimus, Pierre-Edouard, 960
Dehlavi, Amir Khusro, 650
Deiro, Guido (1886–1950), 3
Deiro, Pietro (1888–1954), 3
Dekker, Desmond (1941–2006), 538
Delafose, Geno, 963
De la Rosa, Tony, 193, 893
Delgado, Justino, 331
Délibes, Léo, 935–936
Delmore Brothers, 98
Delta blues, 420
Dem Bow, 744
Demian, Cyrillus (1772–1847), 5
Demófilo (Antonio Machado Álvarez) (1848–1893), 273
Denny, Sarah, 250
Densmore, Frances (1867–1957), **226–227**, 507, 593
Derksen, Cris, 594
Desert blues, 909
Desvarieux, Jacob, 960, 961
Detwiler, Russell, 503
Deutscher Dreher, 48, 51
Dhadd (drum), 651–652
Dhal (drum), 38
Dhalang, 937–938, 939
Dhantal, 169, 170
Dhol, **227–229**, 652, 653, 661, 889, 891
Dholak, 169, 170
Dhrupad, **229–230**, 808, 821
Diabaté, Cheick Hamala, 326, 942
Diabaté, Toumani (1965–), 92, 326
Diablada, 27
Diawara, Manthia, 325
Díaz, Aniceto, 525
Diddley, Bo, 179–180
Diddley bow, 96
Didgeridoo, **231–233**
Dilruba, 77
Dindial, Rasika, 168–169
Dion, Célne, 161, 257, 259
Dionysius (god), 143–144

Discépolo, Enrique Santos, 884
Disco in China, 163
Distler, Marian (1919–1964), 278
Dittersdorf, Carl Ditters von (1739–1799), 817, 818
Diwali, 228
Dixieland, **233–234**, 635–637, 847, 848
Djembe, **234–236**
Dmitri Pokrovsky Ensemble, **236–237**
Dodecaphonic technique, 175
Dodson, Annie Grace Horn, 271
Dominican music and dance, 561–563
Domino, Fats, 1–2
Donga (Ernesto Joaquim dos Santos, 1890–1974), 117–118
Donizetti, Gaetano, 281
Donso ngoni, 310
Doobie Brothers, 180
Doo-wop, 287, 288, 313
Dorje, 900–901
Dorsey, Thomas A. "Georgia Tom" (1899–1993), 97, **237–240**, 312–313
Dorsey, Tommy (big band leader), 237, 848
Double-action instruments, 5
Doucet, Michael, 129
Douglas, Frederick (1818–1895), 281–282
Dranes, Juanita "Arizona" (1889/1891–1963), 312
Drehtanz, 51
Dr. Oloh (Israel Olorunfeh Cole) (1944–2007), 331
"Drum circle," 234, 236
Drums
 in Acadian music, 1
 African, 304–305, 338
 in Afrobeat, 14
 in Armenian music, 38
 bagpipe competition with, 57
 Batá, 72–73
 in Bedouin music, 81–82
 in bomba, 111
 in Cajun music, 128
 in Caribbean, 330
 in conjunto music, 192, 193
 in cumbia, 214, 215
 in gamelan orchestra (Javanese), 301
 griot use of, 327
 Indian, 443, 574–576
 Japanese, 863–869
 in Middle East, 221–222
 Pakistani, 651–652
 in rumba, 762
 in South Asia, 859–861 (*see also* Tabla)
 in Southeast Asia, 456–459
 steelpan and, 839
 tassa drumming, 169, 888–892
 in West Africa, 234–236, 330–331, 529
Drupatee (born Drupatee Ramgooni) (1945–), 168, 169, 830, 831
Dub music, 219, 742
Du Bois, W.E.B., 9
Duda (dudy), 56, 57
Duduk, 35, 38, **240–241**
Dulcimer, **242–245**, 958
Dultzaina, 70
Dundun (dunun), 235
Duterte, Jean-François, 285
Dvořák, Antonín (1841–1904), 593, 856
Dylan, Bob, **246–248**
 bluegrass musician interest in, 94
 influences on, 507
 instruments preferred by, 63, 75
 musicians influencing, 335, 336, 420, 791
 recordings of, 718
 rock and roll played by, 751

Earp, Wyatt, 6
Easter Island (Rapanui), music of, 688, 692
Eastern European nations, 260–261
Eastern Polynesia, music of, 687–689
Eastern Polynesia hymns, 690–693
Eastern sacred music, ancient, 11–12
Eastern Woodland Native American Music, **249–250**, 589, 590
Eckstine, Billy, 224
Ecuador, music of, 28, 29
Edict of Expulsion (Spain), 792–793
Edo Period (1603–1868), stories set in, 433
Edwardes, Georges (1852–1915), 579
Edwards, Cliff "Ukelele Ike" (1895–1971), 923–924
Egypt, music of
 instruments, 642–643
 singers, 268, 437–441
Eichler, Alwin, 957
Einheitsbandoneon, 59
Eisenkeilnest (Kingfisher's nest), 51
Electric amplification in Acadian music, 1
Electric bass in conjunto music, 192, 193, 195

Electric guitar
  in Afrobeat, 12, 13
  sounds produced by, 77
  in tango, 668
  in Tejano music, 894
  in West African popular music, 327, 331
  in western swing, 203
Electric organ, 83
Electro-acoustic techniques in music, 117
Electronic music, 810
Electronic sound, 961
Ellington, Duke
  Afro-Cuban music influence on, 16–17
  in big band era, 849
  blues influence on, 97–98
  chord progressions played by, 79
  Davis, Miles compared to, 224
  musicians collaborating with, 46–47
  Scandinavian musician collaboration with, 610
  swing music played by, 710, 848
Elliott, "Ramblin" Jack (born Elliot Adnopoz) (1931–), 335, 336
El Roumi, Halim (1919–1983), 266
Emerick, Geoff, 74
Emmett, Dan (Daniel Decatur) (1815–1904), 61, 112, **250–252**, 477, 930
Engel, Joel, 45
Enka Music, **252–254**, 428
Eno, Brian, 14
Entaala, 19
Entenha (art-popular song), 315, 316, 317
Enthogens, 585
Entrudo, 144
Enya (1961–), 155
Epinette de voges, 242
Erentxun, Mikel, 71
Erhu, **254–257**
Escudero, Francisco (1912–2002), 70
Esnaola, Secundino (1878–1929), 70
Essex, John, 283–284
Estonia, music of, 260, 765–766, 956
Ethio-jazz, 46
Ethiopia, music in, 46–47
"Ethiopian Melodies," 279–280, 281–282
Ethnomusicologists, 226–227
Europe
  bagpipes in, 54
  Jewish immigration to, 794

European Broadcasting Union (EBU), 258, 259, 260
European musical theory, 33–34
European Renaissance guitar, 213
Europeans in Caribbean, 139–140
European Union, 258
Eurovision Song Contest, **257–261**, 782
Euskadi (term), 69
Eustache, Pedro (1959–), 241
Evans, Gil, 224, 225
Exoticism in music, 274
Expulsion (Spain), 792–793, 794

Fado, **263–266**, 755, 756–757
Fairuz (1935–), 68, **266–268**
Falcon, Cleoma, 1
Falcon, Joe, 1, 127, 128
Falla, Manuel de (1876–1946), 273
Faltl, Hans, 787
Fandango, 159, 264
Farabi, al-, 644
Farahani, Mirza Abdollah (1843–1918), 222
Farajpouri, Saeed (1961–), 443
Farandole chain dance, 282
Farhangfar, Nasser, 908
Farmer, Henry George, 32, 33–34
Farouk, King of Egypt, 438, 439
Feather, Leonard, 79
Felipe, Julian, 665
Felsted, Samuel (1743–1802), 140
Feminist movement, 751
Ferdinand, Emperor (1637–1657), 50
Ferguson, 61
Fernandes, André, 165
Ferré, Léo (1916–1993), 159–160, 161
Ferrer, Horacio, 267
Ferrer, Ibrahim (1927–2005), 122
Festa, Costanzo (ca. 1485–1545), 512
Feuillet, Raoul, 283–284
Feynman, Richard, 913
Fiddle, **268–271**
  Acadian music using, 1, 4
  chamarrita accompanied by, 158
  in Iran, 441–443
  in Ireland, 243
  in Mongolia, 573–574
  in western swing, 203
Field Hollers, **271–272**, 945
Fields, W. C., 926
Fillmore, Henry, 716
Filmi, 105

Film industry, Indian and American compared, 105
Filmi songs, 107–108
Film music, 107–108
Fingerboard zithers, 957
Fingerpicking style
  on acoustic guitar, 75
  banjo playing in, 60, 63
Finland, music of, 782
Firqat al-Harbiyyah, 83
Fitzgerald, Ella, 41, 710, 825–826
Flamenco Music, **272–278**
  dance, 274–277, 759–760
  future trends, 277–278
  history, 272–274
  oscillation in, 225
  songs, 759, 760
Flanders, music of, 782
Flatt, Lester (1914–1979), 93, 204
Flayfel, Mohammed, 266
Fleck, Béla, 63
Fletcher, Allice Cunningham (1838–1923), 226, 593
Fleuret, Maurice, 285
Floren, Myron (1919–2005), 2, 3
Flores, Lola (1958–), 760
Flute
  in Andean region, 26, 27, 101–102
  Basque, 70
  Bedouin, 83
  in calypso, 131
  in classical music, 172
  in cumbia, 214, 215
  Native American, 586–588, 589
  in Polynesia, 685
  Slovakian, 286–287
Folk dances
  of Azores, 157–159
  French, 282–286
  German, 49–50, 496–497
  Renaissance, 49–50
Folk instruments
  duduk, 241
  dulcimer, 243, 244, 245
  in Sardinia, 498–499
Folklore, local, instruments from, 190
Folkloric ensemble (Andean region), 25
Folkloristic music (Austria), 786–787
Folk music
  Albanian, 64
  American, 61, 253, 509, 789–792, 962
  American revival of, 204, 958
  Anglo-Celtic, 148
  Argentine, 58
  Armenian, 37–38
  art music compared to, 139
  Austro-German, 50
  banjo in, 60
  blues as, 96
  Brazilian, 119
  Chinese, 162, 332
  Cuban, 122–123
  Filipino, 664–665
  French festivals, 285
  global tradition, 265
  Greek, 316, 317
  Indian, 228, 369–371
  Iranian, 441
  Italian, 389–392
  Japanese, 253, 434
  Korean, 779–781
  Latin American, 212
  Mexican, 329, 532
  Norwegian, 614–618
  Pakistani, 652–653
  political commentary in, 246
  Portuguese, 725–727
  postwar revival of, 63
  Russian, 236–237
  Scots-English, 280
  Serbian, 911–913
  Swedish, 622–624
  Turkish, 53
  U.S. Virgin Islands, 707–708
  Yiddish, 45
Folk rock, 56, 751
  American, 63
  Scandinavian, 57
Folk songs
  American, collecting, 507, 508, 509
  American, hymnody, 811–815
  Estonian, 765–766
  Hungarian, 65–67
  Japanese, 568–569
  Liverpool, 75
  Moravian, Bohemian and Silesian, 151
  Serbo-Croation, 66
Folkways Records, **278–279**
Ford, Willie Mae (1904–1994), 313
Forró, 118
Forud, 223
Fosse, Bob (1927–1987), 581–582

Foster, Stephen Collins (1826–1864), 62, **279–282,** 931
Frame drum, 748
France, music of
  castanets in, 112
  instruments, 56
  popular music, 159–161
Francisco, Slinger (Mighty Sparrow) (1935–), 132, 827, 828
Franco, Francisco (1892–1975), 71, 274, 794
Frank, Keith, 964
Frankish Gallican chant, 319
Franklin, Aretha (1942–), 834–835
Frederick the Great of Prussia, 676
Freedom and People's Rights Movement, Japan (1874–1890), 252
"Free jazz" ("The New Thing"), 411
  emergence of, 80
French Baroque, dances of, 283
French-Cajun language, 128
French colonies in North America, 1
French Folk Dances, **282–286**
French military bands and quadrilles, 233
French mourning song, 42
French Polynesia, music of, 688
French Quadrille, 706
French Romantic operetta, 44
Fretless zithers, 957–958
Frevo, 118, 146–147
Friedländer, David (1750–1834), 44
Frishkopf, Michael, 24
Fritts, Donnie, 834
Frosini, Pietro (1885–1951), 3
Frugé, Ernest, 128
Frye, Theodore, 239
Fugue, 171–172
Fujara, **286–287**
Fuju music, 13
Fulson, Lowell, 98
Funk, **287–290**
  Afrobeat compared to, 13
  conjunto fusion with, 192
  formation of, 835
  soca development aided by, 828
Furi, 436
Furstenberg, Florian Daule von, 50
Fusion
  in Arab classical music, 34
  bands, 15
  and beyond, 411–412
  components of, 225
  emergence of, 80

Gabriel, Charles H. (1856–1932), 311
Gabriel, Peter, 35, 461, 462
Gabrieli, Giovanni, 187, 852–853
Gagaku, **291–295,** 864–865
Gaita, 56, 57, 214, 215
Gaither, Bill, 315
Gajde, 64
Gaku-daiko, 865–866
Gakusô, 294
Galan, Francisco "Pacho" (1906–1988), 215–216
Galdo, Joseph, 465
Galpin, Francis, 243
Gambus, 17–18
Gamelan music
  colometry in, 183, 184
  gamelan gong kebyar, 184, 451–453
  influence of, 185
  publications on, 556
  transcribing of, 555
  wayang kulit allied with, 937, 938–939
Gamelan Orchestra (Balinese), **295–299**
Gamelan Orchestra (Javanese), **299–304**
  associated arts, 303
  geography, history, and culture, 300
  instruments and ensembles, 300–301
  musical structure, 302–303
  tuning, 302
Gandhi, Mahatma, 807
Ganga, **304–305**
Ganga Singing, **305–307**
Gangtai, 163
Gao Ming (ca. 1305–1359), 673
Garbarek, Jan (1947–), 610, 611
Gardel, Carlos (1890–1935), 669, 885
Garland, Hank (1930–2004), 204
Garland, Red, 224
Garlow, Clarence, 963
Garrett, Kenny, 225
Gasparyan, Jivan, Sr. (1928–), 241
Gauchos, 883–884
Gay artists, 260
Geer, Will, 334
Gender-based violence and discrimination, campaign against, 646
Gender family, metallophones in, 297
Gender identities for instruments, 176
Gender roles, World War II, 203
Gender Wayang, **307–310**
Genre mixing, 32
Genyi, 11
Geremia, Paul, 99

Gerena, Manuel (1945–), 274
German immigrants, music of, 3, 191, 280, 958
German Renaissance folk dances, 49–50
German-speaking minority groups, dances by, 51
Germany
  accordion in, 58
  bagpipes in, 57
  bandoneón in, 59
  miracle play genre in, 817
Gerovitsch, Eliezer (1844–1913), 45
Gershwin, George (1898–1937)
  accordion used in songs by, 3
  Afro-Cuban music influence on, 764
  blues influence on, 98
  musicians influencing, 579
  as song plugger, 904
  as Tin Pan Alley composer, 903, 951
Gershwin, Ira (1896–1983), 579, 903
Getz, Stan, 119
Geza ongaku, 434–435
Ghalib, Mirza (1797–1869), 651
Ghanaian highlife, 180
Gharana playing style, 100, 230, 820–821
Ghazal, 17, 18, 31–32, 651
Gherardello da Firenze (ca. 1320–ca. 1362), 511
Gholi, Mirza Hossein (1853–1916), 222
Ghost Dance, 592
Gidayû-bushi, 124
Gifford, Paul M., 243
Gilbert, Henry F. (1868–1928), 191
Gilbert, Ronnie, 790
Gilberto, Gil (1942–), 119
Gilberto, João (1931–), 119
Gillespie, Dizzy
  Afro-Cuban jazz, involvement with, 15, 16
  band, 185
  bebop played by, 79, 80
  Davis, Miles playing with, 224
  Parker, Charlie playing with, 657–658
Gillis, Tanya "Tagaq," 92
Gimbri, **310**
Ginastera, Alberto, 667, 669
Ginsberg, Allen, 467
Giovanni da Cascoa (1340–1350), 511
Girinya, 11
Gitanos, 272, 273, 274, 276, 277, 759
Glass, Philip (1937–), 232, 810, 898
Glass slide, 89

Gleason, Ralph J., 963
Glinka, 32
Global popular music, 131
Gluck, Christoph Willibald Ritter von (1714–1787), 853
Glykeria, 318
Gnawa, 705
Goadeg sisters, 285
Gobbi, Alfredo (1912–1965), 561
Godfrey, Arthur, 924
Godoy, Carlos Mejía (1943–), 622
Goethe, Johann Wolfgang von, 934, 943
Goisern, Hubert von, 943
Gold, Nick, 121
Golding, Daniel, 947
Goldner, George, 698
Goldsmith, Thomas A., 94
Gomes, Antônio Carlos (1836–1896), 116
Gong
  in gagaku, 294
  in gamelan music (Balinese), 184, 297–298
  in gamelan music (Indonesian), 183
  in gamelan music (Javanese), 300, 301, 302–303
Gong cycle, 302–303
González, Juan de Marcos, 121
González, Rubén, 121, 122
González, Sara (1951–2012), 621
González Mina, Leonor (1934–), 214, 216
Goodman, Benny, 697, 826, 847, 848, 849
Goodman, Steve, 94
Goombay, 331–332
Gore, Albert, Sr., 270
Gospel Music, **311–315**
  black, 97, 239, 311, 312–313, 314
  contemporary, 313–315
  industry, 315
  musicians specializing in, 13
  rural, 148, 149, 202
  soul influenced by, 832–833, 834, 835
  southern, 311–312
Gottlieb, Stephanie (1741–1800), 818
Gottschalk, Louis Moreau (1829–1869), 191, 593
Gounod, Charles, 936
Grad und Ungrad ("pass/fail"), 51
Graham, Trevor, 142
Grand Coolee Dam, 335
Grand Ole Oprey, 3, 93, 149, 202, 204
Granz, Norman, 16, 79, 80
Grappelli, Stéphane, 203

Grauer, Victor, 945
Gray, Macy, 14
Great Basin Indian music, 589, 590–591
Great Depression, 128, 202, 203, 710, 723
Great Highland Bagpipes, 54–56
Gréco, Juliette, 160–161
Greco-Byzantine chant, 319
Greece, Ancient, 143–144
Greek Military Junta, 1967–1974, 317
Greek music, influence of, 321
Greek music genres, 601–603
Greek Popular Music, **315–318**
Green, Keith, 314
Gregor, Christian (1723–1801), 570, 572
Gregorian Chant, 42, 170–171, **318–322**
Gregory I, Pope (ca. 540–604 CE), 144, 319
Gregory II, Pope (669–731), 170
Gregory of Narek (950–1010), 37
Gregory the Illuminator (ca. 257–ca. 332), 36
Grimm, Willi, 233
Griot, 219–220, **322–328**, 941
Grupo, 192, 893
Grupo tejano, 894
Guache, 214–215
Guaguancó, 760, 763
Guettat, Mahmoud, 23, 34
Guéye, Bira, 549
Guillén, Nicolás, 140
Guinea-Bissau, music of, 330, 331
Guitar. *See also* acoustic guitar; amplified guitar
 accordion *versus,* 4
 in Andean region, 26, 28
 Azorean, 158
 banjo displaced by, 63
 as blues instrument, 96–97
 in calypso, 131
 corrido accompanied by, 196
 in country music, 148
 in Cuba, 121–122
 Hawaiian, 838
 in Latin America, 212
 in Mexico, 329
 Native American music played on, 270
 in Polynesia, 684
 in Portugal, 263
 in Puerto Rico, 213
 in West Africa, 529–530
Guitarrón Mexicano, **328–330**
Gullin, Lars (1928–1976), 610

Gumba, **330–332**
Gunga, 88
Gung'l, Josef (1809–1860), 935
Guoyue, **332–333**
Gupta veena, 927
Guridi, Jesús (1886–1961), 70
Gurruwiwi, Djalu, 232
Gusheh, 222, 223
Gusli, 696
Guthrie, Arlo, 335, 336
Guthrie, Woody (1912–1967), **333–336**
 Dylan, Bob influenced by, 246
 influences on, 507
 Klezmatic singing of songs by, 467
 Lead Belly performances with, 501
 recordings by, 278
 Seeger, P. singing of songs by, 791
Gütter, Karl August, 957
Guy, Buddy, 98–99
Guzheng, **336–337**
Gyil, **337–339**
Gypsies. *See also* Romani people
 dances by, 66, 86
 flamenco influenced by, 272, 273, 274
 instruments played by, 244, 245
 music of, 577–578, 737–739
 origin of, 577
"Gypsy jazz," 203

Habanera, 16, 117
Habanera-style bass lines, 131, 132
Hachiro, Kasuga (1924–1991), 253
Hackbrett, 242, 243, 244
Hadith, 842–843
Hadith, 31
Hadjidakis, Manos, 317
Hafez, 796, 846
Haggard, Merle (1937–), 203–204
Haig, Al, 80
Haile Selassie, Emperor of Ethiopia (1892–1975), 539, 741
Haitian festivals, 733–735
Hajhouj, 310
Halévy, Fromental (1799–1862), 44
Haley, Alex, 323
Haley, Bill, 749
Half-tone, 842
Halk Evleri (People's Houses), 53
Hallyday, Johnny, 161
Hamasaki Ayumi and Misia, 430
Hambo, 51
Hamburg Reform Temple, 45

Hammer dulcimer, 242, 378, 650, 696, 958
Hammerstein, Oscar, II, 182, 579
Hammond, John, 246, 826, 849
Hanamichi, 435
Hancock, Herbie
  funk influence on, 289, 411–412
  Klezmatics, work with, 467
Handel, G. F. (George Friedrich) (1685–1759), 57, 172, 189
Handy, W. C. (1873–1958), **341–344**
  as blues figure, 97, 721–722
  train imitations recalled by, 6
Haney, Carlton, 94
Han music, 874–876
Hanson, Elizabeth, 249
Hapsburg monarchy, 50
Harana and Kundiman, **344–345**
Hardanger Fiddle (Hardingfele), **345–347**
Hard bop, 410
"Hard gospel," 313
Hardin, Lil, 202
Harding, Frank, 904
Harfen-zithern (harp zither), 957
Hargrove, Roy, 14
Haridas, Swami, 229
Harjo, Joy, 594
Harmonica, 6, 7
Harmonic rhythm, slackening of, 225
Harmonium, 168, 169, 170, **347–350**
Harp
  in British isles, 153–154, 243
  Burmese, 927
  kanun, 38
  Mande hunters', 310
Harpsichord, 172, 173
Harrington, George (Christy), 112
Harris, Corey, 99
Harris, Sam, 181
Harrison, George (1943–2001), 74, 76, 77, 78, 241, 809, 821
Harrison, Lou (1917–2003), 185
Hart, Alvin Youngblood, 99
Hart, Lorenz, 903
Hartford, John (1937–2001), 205
Has, Kuntz, 50
Hattori Ryōichi, 428
Haute Bretagne, 285
Haute danse, 282–283
Havana shipyards, music from, 176, 177
Havasupai, 946–947

Hawaii, Music of, **350–354**
  dance, 684
  hymns, 689–690
  instruments, 212, 684, 838, 923–924
  steel guitar in, 837
Hawaiian guitar, 838
Hawaiian styles in country music, 202
Hawaiian ukulele, 212, 684
Hawkins, Coleman
  blues influence on, 97–98
  swing music played by, 710, 848, 849
Hawkins, Edwin, 313
Hawkins, Tramaine, 314
Hayashi, 434
Haydn, Franz Joseph (1732–1809), 173, 817, 853, 854, 933
Hays, Lee, 790
Hebenstreit, Pantaleon, 243
Hébert, Germain and Louise, 284–285
Hebrail, Jean, 466
Hegarty, Antony, 92
Heine, Heinrich, 706
Heinz-Schickhause, Karl, 243
Held, Anna, 951, 952
Hellerman, Fred, 790
Hempson, Denis (1695–1807), 153
Henderson, Fletcher, 826, 827, 848, 849
Hendrix, Jimi, 491, 595
Hensley, Virginia (Patsy Cline) (1932–1963), 204
Herding instruments, 56–57, 286–287
Herding yodel, 944
Hermann, Hugo (1896–1967), 6
Hernandez, Joe, 893
Hersart de La Villemarqué, Théodore, 154
Herzog, George, 947
Hesse, Hermann, 944
Heyowicinayo, 932
Hibari, Misora (1937–1989), 253
Hibera, 102
Hichiriki, 293
Hickman, Hans, 32
Higgs, Joe, 539
Highlife, 12, 13, **354–356**, 490
Hijaz, music of, 81
Hikawa Kiyoshi (1977–), 253–254
Hilali, Abu Dzyd al-, 81
"Hillbilly" (term), 63
"Hillbilly music," 201
Hiller, Johann Adam (1728–1804), 817
Himmel, Friedrich Heinrich (1765–1814), 817

Hindemith, Paul, 190, 857
Hindu life-cycle ceremonies, 168
Hindu rituals, 307
Hindu society, Balinese style of, 295
Hindustani classical music, 99–100
Hindustani language, films in, 106
Hines, Earl, 849
Hip-hop
   in gospel music, 314, 315, 318
   Native Americans in, 595
   New York, 744
   rap and, 727–733
HIV/AIDS prevention, 646
Ho, Denise, 138
Hodges, Johnny, 185
Hoff, Jasper Van't (1947–), 465
Hoffmann, E. T. A. (1776–1822), 817
Hōgaku, **356–358**
Hogan, Ernest (1865–1909), 715–716
Hohner, Matthias, 6
Holiday, Billie, 41
Holland, zither in, 955
Holly, Buddy, 74, 180, 429
Hollywood, 105
Homophobia, 219
Homosexuals *(adés)*, 134
Hong Kong
   British occupation of, 163
   music in, 136–137, 138, 162
   repatriation of, 138
Honky-tonk, 203, 204, 205
Hooker, John Lee, 98, 910
Hope, Bob, 926
Hopkins, "Lightnin'," 98
Hörburger, Felix, 51
Hornbostel, Erich Moritz von (1877–1935), 67, **358–361**, 944
Hosono Haruomi, 429
"Hot new country," 205
Hou, Philemon, 547
Houdini, Harry, 926
House Un-American Activities Committee, 790
Houston, Gilbert "Cisco," 335
Hovhannes, Alan (1911–2000), 37
Hovhannes Mandakuni, Catholicos (?–490), 37
Howe, Jemima, 249
Howlin' Wolf (Chester Burnett), 98
Huapano norteño, 7
Huayno, 101, 103, 104, 216, **361–363**
Hubban (habban), 83

Hughes, Jimmy, 834
Hui, Sam (Sam Hui Kwun Kit), 137
Hula, 684, 923
Hulak-Artemovsky, Semen (1813–1873), 199
Human rights activism, musician involvement in, 465–466
Hungary
   art music, 474–476
   bagpipes in, 57
   Nazi occupation, 65
   peasant music, 66
Hunter, Alberta, 709
Hunter's music, 528
Huqin, **363–366**
   family of instruments, 254, 332
   term, 255
Hurt, "Mississippi" John, 97
Hus, Jan (1369–1415), 570
Husička, 51
Hussein, King of Jordan, 83
Hymns
   American, 811–815
   Amish, 21–22
   Polynesian, 689–693

Ialorixá, 134
Iamboo bamboo, 131
Iberian Peninsula, Moorish culture on, 31
Ibn al-Kalbi, Hisham (d. 819 CE), 644
Ibn Gabriol, Sholom, 793
Ibn Quzman (1080–1160), 949
Icelandic Ballads, **367–369**
Icelandic musicians, 89–92
Idá (fardela), 72
Idelsohn, Abraham Zvi (1882–1938), 792
Idiophones
   in Asia, 899
   in bomba, 111
   marimba, 536–538
Iglesias, Julio, 259
Immigrants to United States, music of, 3, 191, 269, 280, 958
Inca Empire, 25, 26
Incas, 101
Independence movements, music influenced by, 174
India, cinema in, 105–108
India Connection Theory, 577
Indian-African fusion, 828
Indian-Caribbean music, 167–169
Indian Folk Songs, **369–372**

Indianismo movement, 116
"Indianist" movement, 593
Indian music
   bagpipes in, 54, 57
   bones in, 112
   dhol in, 227–229
   drums in, 574–576
   Karnatic music, 443–448
   key figures, 807–811, 861–863
   khayal, 462–464
   Musafir, 577–578
   rhythm in, 99–100
   Thumri, 895–896
   veena in, 926–927
   vocal styles in, 229–230
Indian-Trinidadian culture, 169
Indigenous cultures, 201
Indigenous instruments, 140
Indigenous music
   in Philippines, 663–664
   in Taiwan, 873–874
   vocables in, 931–932
Indo-Caribbean folk drumming, 888–892
Indonesia
   gamelan music, 183
   geography, history, and culture of, 300
   independence, 939
   performance medium, 937–940
Indonesian Pop Music, **372–374**
Infante, Blas, 274
Instrumental music, 172, 196
Intangible Cultural Heritage of Humanity, 265, 277, 286, 536, 607
International, Dana, 260
International pop music, 318
"Interpunctuating" (term), 184
Iranian *bandari* music, 83
Iranian Classical Music, **375–380**
   composed classical pieces, 376–377
   history, 375–376
   instruments played in, 243, 245, 377–378
   key figures, 795–797
   radif, 222, 376
   20th century performance, 378–379
Iraq, music of, 643–644
Ireland
   bagpipes in, 54
   cultures from, 156
   "Irish music" (term), 156
   stringed instruments in, 153, 154, 243
   traditional music, 113, 154, 155
Iriondo, Lourdes (1935–2005), 71

Irish American Vocal Music, **380–381**
Irish Dance Music, **381–385**
Irish rhythms, 61
Irish Step Dancing, **385–388**
Isaacs, Bud, 837
Islam, 31, 324
Isorhythmic Motet, 557
Israel, Jewish immigration to, 794
Israel, music of, 259–260, 794
Italian Folk Music (Various Regions), **389–392**
   central area, 391
   Mediterranean area, 389
   northern area, 390–391
   Sardinia, 391–392
Italian opera, 280–281
Italy, herding instruments in, 56–57
Itólele, 72, 73
Iyá, 72
Iyor-gheer, 11
Iztueta, Juan Ignacio de (1767–1845), 70

Jackson, Aunt Molly (1880–1960), 334
Jackson, Mahalia (1911–1972), 239, 240, 313, **393–395**
Jackson, Michael, 693, 752, 924
Jacobsen, Israel (1728–1828), 44
Jacopo da Bologna (1340–1386), 511
Jaegerhuber, Werner (1900–1953), 140
Jai, Rikki (Samraj Jaimungal), 170, 831
Jali, **396–398**
Jamaica, music in, 219–220, 330
Jamal, Hansnul, 939
James, Nehemiah "Skip," 97
Janggu, **398–399**
Janowski, Max (1902–1991), 45
Japan, Music of, **399–406**
   bluegrass in, 95
   court music, 183
   drums, 863–869
   enka, 252–254
   gagaku, 291–295
   kabuki, 433–434
   koto, 478–481
   mikagura, 292, 293, 567–568
   min'yô, 568–569
   puppet theater, 124–125
   rockabilly influence, 428–429
   shakuhachi, 797–801
   shamisen, 805–807
   shômyô, 815–817
   theater, 603–607

Japanese American music, 864
Japanese popular music, 253, 449–451.
    See also J-Pop
Japanese theater, 433–436
Jara, Victor (1932–1973), 620
Jared, St., 47
Jargy, Simon, 68
Jarmusch, Jim, 47
Jaroff, Serge, 200
Jarre, Maurice, 287
Java
    geography of, 300
    music of, 183, 299–304
Jazz, **406–412**. *See also* Bebop
    Afrobeat compared to, 13
    Afro-Cuban, 15–17
    American, 39–41, 161
    bands, 635–637
    blues influence on, 96, 97–98
    in China, 161
    concerto influenced by, 190
    conjunto fusion with, 192
    cool jazz, 80, 409–410
    development of, 179, 656–659
    Ethiopian, 46, 47
    European, 826
    fusion and beyond, 225, 411–412
    hard bop, 410
    landmarks, 190–191
    Lebanon, 268
    Milo, 331
    modal jazz, 410–411
    musicians, 224–226
    Native Americans in, 594
    beyond New Orleans, 407–408
    in New Orleans, 179, 190–191,
        233–234, 635, 847
    "The New Thing" ("free jazz"), 80, 411
    Nordic, 610–611
    origins and rise of, 406–407, 709
    post-bop, 185–187
    racial issues in, 233–234
    Shanghai, 162
    South African, 546
    stringed instruments in, 60, 63
    styles of, 78, 80, 233–234 (*See also*
        Bebop; Dixieland)
    Swing Era, 408–409
    swing relationship to, 847, 849
    tango combined with, 668
    western swing connection to, 203
Jazz-fusion, 289

Jazz-rock, 225
Jefferson, Blind Lemon, 61, 500, 709
Jefferson, Thomas, 61, 269
Jehan, Noor (1925–2000), **412–414**
Jeliya, 528–529
Jero (Jerome White, Jr.) (1981–), 254
Jesuits, 103, 114
"Jesus Movement," 313–314
Jewish Americans, music by, 903
Jewish music, 41–46, 467–474
Jews, flamenco influenced by, 272–273
Jew's harp, 87
Jhal, 890, 891–892
Jhanjh, 889
Jidaimono, 124
Jim Crow (fictional character), 930
Jimenez, Leonardo "Flaco" (1939–), 2, 4,
    192, 195, 893
Jimenez, Santiago, Jr., 195
Jimenez, Santiago, Sr. (1913–1984), 192
Jingju (Beijing Opera), **414–420**
    characters, 416–417
    important repertoires, 418
    music, 417–418
    origins and development, 414–415
    schools, 419
    symbolism, 415–416
Joachim, Joseph, 189
Jobim, Antônio Carlos (Tom), 119
Johansson, Jan (1931–1968), 610
Johnson, Emory, 239
Johnson, James P., 827
Johnson, James Weldon, 9–10
Johnson, Robert (1911–1938), 97, **420–423**,
    709
Johnson, Susannah, 249
Joik, **423–424**
Jola people, 60
Jolson, Al, 903, 926
Jones, George (1931–2013), 204
Jones, Philly Joe, 224
Joplin, Janice, 693
Joplin, Scott (1867–1917), 62, **425–428**,
    715, 903, 905
Jordan (country), 83
Jordan, Esteban "Steve" (1939–2010), 192,
    195
Jorgy, Simon, 32
Joropo, 212
Jorrin, Enrique (1926–1987), 525
Jôruri, 124
Joseph II, Emperor of Germany, 818

Index

Joyce, P. W., 243
J-Pop, **428–431**
   American popular music influence on, 400
   Cantopop relationship to, 138
   C-pop compared to, 162
   defined, 404
   development of, 403
   rise of, 450
Jublag, 184
Judeo-Arabic language, 793
Judeo-Spanish (Ladino) language, 793
Juju music, 8, 9, 13

Kaai, Ernest (1881–1962), 923
Kabuki, **433–436,** 865–866, 868
Kagel, Mauricio, 669
Kagurabue (yamatobue), 293
Kaipo, Joe, 202
Kakko, 294
Kalhor, Kayhan (1963–), 443
Kalima, Jesse (1920–1980), 923
Kalthoum, Umm, 268, **437–441**
Kamakawiwo'ole, Israel, 924
Kamancheh, 31, 222, 377, 378, **441–443**
Kamancheh'I, Mirza Mohammad, 442
Kamkar, Ardeshir (1962–), 443
Kantele, 696
Kanun (harp), 38
Karaoke songs (K-song), 138
Karnatic Music, **443–448**
   fundamental elements of, 444–446
   in practice, 446–448
Kartâl, 112
Kartomi, Margaret, 31
Kasagi Shizuko, 428
Kaser, 82
Kassav', 960, 961
Kata, 436
Kathak dance, 100
Kay, Monte, 79
Kayokyku, 253
Kayokyoku, 253, **449–451**
Kayumas, 309
Keb' Mo', 99
Kebyar, 184, **451–453**
Kecak, **453–456**
Keil, Charles, 10
Keita, Salif (1949–), 325, 327
Keita, Sundiate (ca. 1217–1255 CE), 324
Keith, Benjamin Franklin "B. F." (1846–1914), 925

Kekuku, Joseph, 836, 837
Kelly, Paul (1955–), 141, 142
Kemenche (violin), 38, 442
Kempul, 302
Kena, 26
Kendang, 301, **456–459**
Kennedy, John F., 197, 518, 717
Kennedy, Robert F., 751
Kenong, 302
Kent, Stephen, 233
Kenton, Stan, 15–16
Kenya, musicians from, 645–647
Kérékou, Mathieu, 465
Kern, Jerome (1885–1945), 579, 903, 951
Kerr, Anita (1927–), 204
Kershaw, Doug, 127, 128
Kes the Band, 831–832
Ketama, 277
Kethuk, 302–303
Keyboard instruments, 172, 189
Khachaturian, Aram (1903–1978), 37, 936
Khaled, Cheb (1960–), **459–461,** 716, 718–719, 720
Khali, 100
Khan, Ali Akbar, 809–810, 811, 821
Khan, Allauddin, 808, 821
Khan, Darvish (1872–1926), 222
Khan, Esmail, 442
Khan, Naimat, 649
Khan, Nusrat Fateh Ali (1948–1997), **461–462,** 650
Khan, Vilayat, 820–821
Khan Kawa, Hameed, 577–578
Khatchadourian, Eileen, 38
Khayal, 230, **462–464,** 649–650
Khaz, 37
Khene, **464–465**
Khonakol, 100
Kidjo, Anglique (1960–), **465–467**
Kifi, 651
Kincaid, Bradley (1895–1989), 202
Kindi, al-, 644
King, Carole, 429
King, Martin Luther, Jr., 240, 751, 835
King, Pee Wee (1914–2000), 2, 3
King, Riley "B. B.," 98–99
King Kong (musical), 517
King Radio (Norman Span), 132
King Wellington (Hawthorne Quashie), 828
Kisumu, Kenya, 645
Kitsch, 943

Kittredge, George Lyman, 508
Kjarkas, Los, 26
Klezmatics, 467
Klezmer, **467–474**
  history, 468–470
  music, 42, 472–473
  social practice, 470–472
Kline, David, 944
Knight Caraballo, Pedro (1921–2007), 211–212
Knopfler, Mark, 247
Kobzar string band, Ukranian, 7
Kodály, Zoltán (1882–1967), 65, 66, 68, 190, 245, **474–476**
Kohandani, Hossein, 908
Kojs, Juraj, 287
"Ko-Ko" (chord progression), 79
Kol Nidre (song), 42, 45
Kol nidrei chant, 43
Komagaku, 292
Kongo/Angolan instruments, 88
Kongo/Angolan musical bow, 87
Kora, 327, **476–478**
Korean dance, 607–610
Korean folk music, 779–781
Korean vocal folk genre, 654–656
Koto, **478–481,** 953
Kotsuzumi, 865
Kouyate, Bala Faseke, 324, 942
Kouyate, Bassekou (1966–), 326
K-Pop (Korean Pop), **481–486**
  contemporary, 485–486
  C-pop compared to, 162
  history, 481–483
  J-pop influenced by, 430
  Korean Wave, 484–485
  style and characteristics, 483–484
  Western influence on, 163–164
Krakowiak, 676, 679
Krauss, Alison (1971–), 94
Kremer, Gideon, 669
Kretschen, 45
Krupa, Gene, 697, 848
Kuban People's Republic, 200
Kubitschek, Juscelino, 118
Kuczynski, Frank Julius Anthony. *See* King, Pee Wee (1914–2000)
Kuhreihen, 944–945
Kulintang, **486–490**
Kulthūm, Umm, 32, 34, 642
Kumeyaay, 946
Kumi-daiko, 866, 868

Kunst, Jaap, 183, 184
Kuor, 338
Kushner, Tony, 467
Kussundé, 331
Kuti, Fela (1938–1997), 8, 12, 13–14, 46, **490–493**
Kuti, Fema (1962–), 14, 493
Kuti, Seun, 493
Kweyol lyrics, 960
Kwok, Aaron (Aaron Kwok Fu Shing), 137
Kyrie, 319–320

Labéguerie, Michel (1921–1980), 71
Laboa, Mikel (1934–2008), 71
Labor (defined), 182
Lachari, 168
Lacy, Rufino (1795–1847), 70
Lady Gypsy, 831
Ladysmith Black Mambazo, **495–496,** 553
LaFarge, Peter, 594
Lai, Leon (Leon Lai Ming), 137
Laika, 315, 316–317
Lama, Sege, 161
Lamothe, Ludovic (1882–1953), 140
Lampell, Millard, 790
Lancaran, 302
Lancers quadrille, 707
Land, Arnhem, 231
Landini, Francesco (ca. 1325–1397), 171
Ländler, 48–49, 50–51, **496–497,** 933, 934
Lane, Edward, 221
Langolette, 242
Lanner, Joseph (1801–1843), 934, 935
Lanois, Daniel, 247
Lapinha, Joaquina, 115
LaRocca, Nick, 635
Latin America
  instruments associated with, 58, 176
  interconnectedness in, 102
Latin American New Song (Nueva Canción), 104, 618–622
Latin culture, 321
Latin jazz, 15, 16, 697, 698
Latin Liturgy, vocal music of, 318–319
Latin music, 697–700
Latinos, 211
"Latin-pop," 213
Latvia, music of, 956
Lau, Andy (Andy Lau Tak Wah), 137
Laúd (laoud) (laúd cubano), 122
Launeddas, **498–499**
Laure, Mike, 216

La Villemarqué, Théodore Claude Henri, vicomte Hersart de, 154
Lavoe, Hector, 110
Lavwa, 85
Lavway, 130–131, 839, 881–882
Lawa, 170
Lawson, Doyle (1944–), 94
Layālī, 30
Lazkano, Ramón (1968–), 70
Lead Belly (1888/9–1949), **499–502**
  blues influence on, 98
  musicians, later influenced by, 709
  musicians known to, 334
  recordings by, 278
  rise to prominence, 507, 508
Lebanon, music of, 266–268
Ledbetter, Huddie "Leadbelly." *See* Lead Belly (1888/9–1949)
Le Gendre, Dominque (1960–), 140
LeJeune, Iry, 128
Lennon, John (1940–1980), 74
Lenya, Lotte (1898–1981), **502–504**
Léonin, 171
Leopold I (1658–1705), 50
Lertxundi, Benito (1942–), 71
Lesbian, gay, bisexual, transgender, and queer (LGBTQ) audiences, 260
Levey, Ethel, 181
Levine, Michael A., 836
Lewandowski, Louis (1821–1894), 44
Lewis, Furry, 97
Lewis, Jerry Lee, 75, 429
Lewis, McArtha (Calypso Rose) (1940–), 133, 828–829, 830
Li Jinhui, 162
Limbak, Walter, 454
Limondijan, Hampartzoum (1768–1839), 37
Lincoln, Abraham, 6
Linda, Solomon (1909–1962), 552, 553
Lingiari, Vincent (1919–1988), 141–142
Lin Xi, 138
Lisbon fado, 264
Listopadov, Alexander (1873–1949), 200
Liszt, Franz (1811–1886), 190, 554, 855–856, 935
Litefoot, 594
Lithuanian music, **504–507**, 956
Little Richard, 74–75
Liturgical chants
  Ethiopian, 47
  Jewish, 41
  of Middle Ages, 170–171
Liturgical collections, Jewish, 45
Liturgical music
  Armenian, 36–37
  Brazilian, 114
  East European, 44
Liturgical reading, Jewish, 42
Liturgical texts, Hebrew, 45
Liturgy, reform of, 319
Liu, Benjamin, 24
Liu Tianhua (1895–1932), 256
Livingston, Neville (Bunny Wailer), 539, 541, 741
Loba, 660
Loesser, Frank, 580
Lomax, Alan (1915–2002), **507–510**
  bluegrass analyzed by, 93
  blues musicians discovered by, 98
  Cajun music recorded by, 128
  as ethnomusicologist, 38
  folk music materials collected by, 334–335
  global vocals studied by, 945
  Lead Belly, dealings with, 500–501
  Seeger, Pete connection with, 553
  zydeco studied by, 962
Lomax, John Avery (1867–1948), 500–501, **507–510**
Lomayesva, Casper Loma-da-wa, 594
Longfellow, Hanry Wadsworth (1807–1882), 592
Longhi, Vincent "Jim," 335
Longoria, Félix, 197
Longoria, Valerio (1924–2000), 192, 194, 893
López, Isidro, 893
Lopez, Joe, 893
Lorca, Frederico García (1898–1936), 273, 275
Lord Invader (born Rupert Grand) (1914–1961), 131
Lord Kitchener, 829
Lord Shorty (born Garfield Blackman) (1941–2000), 133, 169, 828
Lotfi, Mohannad Reza, 796
Louisiana, music of, 127, 129
Louis XIV, King of France, 244, 283
Lowland bagpipes, 56
Luanda, instruments from, 88
Lucía, Paco de (1947–2014), 274, 277
Lucumi, 73
Ludwig, Christian, 188
Luhrmann, Baz, 107

Lully, Jean-Baptiste (1632–1687), 853
Lunceford, Jimmie, 849
Lundu, 117, 264
Lute. *See also* Tar
   in China, 672–674
   in Japan, 805–807
   origin of, 23
   oud, 38, 640–644
   in Turkey, 53–54
   in West Africa, 941–942
Lutfi, Huda (1948–), 440
Luther, Martin (1483–1546), 21, 50, 571
Lutheranism, 571
Lutoslawski, 190
Lyons-Alvarez, Fayann, 831
Lysenko, Mykola (1842–1912), 199

Maal, Baaba (1953–), 327
Macdowell, Edward (1860–1908), 593
Macedonia, music of, 737–739
Machaut, Guillame de (ca. 1300–1377), 171
Machito (Frank Grillo), 15, 16
Maddox, Rose Lee (1925–1998), 203
Madrigal, **511–514**
   fourteenth century, 511
   musical development role of, 171
   sixteenth century and beyond, 512–514
Magnante, Charles (1905–1986), 3
Magnus, Finn, 6
Mahjubi, Reza, 441–442
Mahler, Gustav (1860–1911), 45, 51, 174, 856, 936
Mahmoud, Malek, 442
Mai, 436
Maihar gharānā, 821
Maimonides (Moshe ben Maimon), 22
Mairena, Antonio (1909–1983), 274
Makam, **514–516,** 640–641
Makarezos, Nikolaos, 317
Makeba, Miriam (1932–2008), 331, **516–519,** 546, 547
Malay-Arabic music, 17
Malay music, **519–521**
Malaysia, music in, 254
Malhūn, 32, **522–523**
Mali musicians, 909–911
Malle, Louis, 225
Mallick brothers, 230
Malm, William, 183
Malouf, **523–524**
Mambo, **524–527,** 771

Mamluk Sultan Baybars, 81
Mañachi, Ñanda, 28
Manchot, Carré, 286
Mande cultures, 325, 326, 477
Mande griots, 324, 327
Mande hunters' harp, 310
Mandela, Nelson, 496, 546, 547–548, 645
Mande Music, **527–530**
   spheres of, 528–530
Mandopop (Mandarin Chinese popular music), 136, 137, 138, 161, 162, 163
Mané, Kaba (1957–), 331
Mangeshkar, Lata (1929–), 106
Manjago community, 60
Manley, Michael, 541
Mannette, Ellie, 840, 841
Manol (Manolis Venios) (1845–1915), 642
Mansingh, Raja (1486–1517), 229
Mansouri, Ebrahim, 441–442
Mantinádes, 208
Manu Chao (1961–), **530–532**
Manuel, Peter, 12, 274–275
Maori aerophones, 685
Maori dance, 684
Mao Zedong, 163
Mapuip (mouthbow), 102
Maqaam (maqām), 17, 31, 32, 68, 640–641
Marabouts, 324
Maraca, 75, 84, 111, 214–215
Maracatu, 115, 146, 147
Marching music, 234
Marcus, Scott, 32
Mardi Gras, 143, 147
Marenzo, Luca (ca. 1553–1599), 512–513
Margaryan, Hayk (HR Hayko), 38
Marginalized peoples, songs focusing on, 620
Mariachi, 329, **532–536**
Maricopan music, 947
Marimba (American, Guatemalan, Marimba de Arco), **536–538,** 563
Marinelli, Karl (1745–1803), 818
Mariza (Mariza Nunes) (1973–), 264, 265
Marley, Bob (1945–1981), 9, **538–542,** 720, 741, 742
Marley, Damien, 539, 542
Marley, Rita, 542, 742
Marley, Stephen, 539, 542, 742
Marley, Ziggy, 539, 542, 742
Marquesas Islands, music of, 689, 692–693
Marsalis, Branford, 225
Marsalis, Wynton (1961–), 191

Marshall Islands, Music of, **542–545**
Martin, George, 74, 77
Martin, Grady (1929–2001), 204
Martin, Sallie, 239
Martin, Sean, 709
Martínez, Narciso (1911–1992), 7, 192, 893
Martínez, Oscar, 893
Martínez, Petrona (1939–), 214, 216
Martínez, Raul "El Ruco," 7
Martinique bélé, 85
Maruhon, 435
Masala film, 107
Masekela, Hugh (1939–), 46, 518–519, **545–548**
Mashak, 57
Mashtots, Mesrop (362–440 CE), 36–37
Masterpiece of the Orala and Intangible Heritage of Humanity, 552, 702, 844
Matsutoya, Yumi (Arai Yumi), 429
Matusky, Patricia, 183
Mauricio, Fernando (1933–2003), 264
Mawwāl, 32
Maxixe, 117
Mayfield, Curtis, 289
Mazurka *(mazurek)*
  as Alsatian couple dance, 285
  conjunto influenced by, 192
  as dance form, 960
  folk influence on, 174
  historic conditions, 677–678
Mbalax, **548–551**
Mbande, Venáncio (1930–), 167, 552
Mbaqanga, 546, 547
Mbila, 165–166, **551–552**
Mbube, **552–554**
McAllester, David, 597
McBane, Matt, 63
McCartney, Paul (1942–), 74, 241
McCormick, Robert "Mack," 420, 962
McCoury, Del, 95
McEntire, Reba (1955–), 205
McGhee, Howard, 16
McGuire, Barry, 314, 717
McIntire Lani, 202
McLean, Don, 791
McLeod, Alice, 187
McMahon, Charlie, 232
McPhee, Colin (1900–1964), 185, **554–556**
McShane, Ronnie, 113
Medici, Catherine de, 282
Medieval Secular Song, **556–559**
Medio, 88

Meditation, 900
Mediterranean music, 794
Megamusicals, 582
Mehr, Ebrahim Ghanbari (1928–), 443
Meidah, Malouma Mint Moktar Ouid (1960–), 327
Meir ben Isaac Nehorai of Worms, 41
Melevi Order (Sufi), 843–844
Melevi Sama, 844–845
Melisma, 832, 833
Mellits, Marc, 63
Melodeon, 5
Melody-elaborating instruments, 301
Mélusine, 285
Membertou, Henri, 249
Membranophone, 304–305
Mendelssohn, Felix, 44, 189–190
Mendelssohn, Moses, 44
Meng Tian (d. 210 BCE), 336
Mennonites, 21, 22
Mensah, E. T. (1919–1996), 12
Mento, 219, **559–561,** 739–740
Menzen, Friedrick, 957
Mercier, Peader, 113
Merengue, **561–563**
  international interest in, 139
  quelbe band playing of, 708
Meshorerim, 43, 44
Meskatian, Parviz, 796
Mestizo adaptation of sanjuán, 28
Mestizo Music, 102–103, **563–565**
Metal-keyed instruments, 300, 301
Metallophones, 297
Metaxas, Ioannis, 316
Metheny, Pat, 88
Metronome, 184
Mexican American influence on country music, 202
Mexican cumbia, 216
Mexican Regional Music, **565–567**
  guitarrón mexicano, 328–330
  mariachi, 329, 532–536
  mestizo music, 564
Mexican Revolution (1910–1917), 892
Mexican *vaqueros,* 945
Meyerbeer, Giacomo (1791–1864), 44
Micronesia, music of, 923
Middle Ages
  ballads in, 195
  Celtic music in, 152
  musicians in, 153
  music in, 170–171

Middle East
  bagpipes in, 54, 57
  culture, stereotyping of, 86
  instruments in, 67
  transformations in, 266–267
Mighty Sparrow (born Slinger Francisco) (1935–), 132, 827, 828
Mikagura, 292, 293, **567–568**
Mike, Johnny, 586
Mi'kmaq, 249
Milanés, Pablo (1943–), 621
Milhaud, Darius (1892–1974), 45, 117
Military, art music influenced by, 140
Military bands, 740
Miller, Glenn, 848
Milo jazz, 331
Milonga music, 7
Minamoto no Masanobu, 292–293
Minnesang, German, 42
Minstrel shows/minstrelsy
  African American, 721
  Cuban theater compared to, 764
  cultural exchange of ideas in, 269–270
  Ethiopian melodies, 281
  in Europe, 112–113
  instruments used in, 61–62, 958
  key figures, 250–252
  musicians influenced by, 716, 925
  roots of, 208
  in South Africa, 552, 553
  Virginia Minstrels, 477, 930–931
  white performers, 754
Minstrel songs, 60
Min'yô, **568–569**
Miracle play genre, German, 817
Miranda, Carmen (1909–1955), 118, 119
Miranda, Lin-Manuel (1980–), 118
Mi-sinai melodies, 42, 43
Mississippi delta blues, 62
Mitchell, Joni, 63, 265
Mitchell, Timothy, 273
Mitsuhashi, Kifu, 798
Mittenwald zither, 955
Mizmar, 83
Modal jazz, 410–411
Modeling as teaching method, 11
Moderate Reform movement, 45
Moderate Reform synagogues, 44
Modern urban electric groups, 529–530
Modinha, 117, 264
Mohammed, prophet (ca. 570–632 CE), 324

Mojave, 946, 947
Mongolia, music of, 573–574
Monk, Meredith, 89
Monk, Thelonious, 79, 186, 224
Monkey, imitation of, 453
Monochord, 170
Monroe, Bill (1911–1996), 63, 93, 204, 270
Monroe, James, 24
Montana, Patsy (Ruby Blevins) (1908–1996), 202
Montand, Yves, 161
Montano, Machel, 170, 831
Montaya, Ramón (1880–1949), 276
Montbel, Eric, 285
Monte, Marisa (1967–), 120
Monteverdi, Claudio (1567–1643), 171, 187, 513–514
Montjarret, Polig (1920–2003), 154
Montoya, Carlos (1903–1993), 760
Moody, Dwight (1837–1899), 311
Moore, Russell, 594
Moore, Scotty, 694
Moorish culture, 31
Moraes, Vinicius de (1913–1980), 119
Morante, José, 197
Moravian Music, 151, **570–573**
Morenada, 27
Morente, Enrique (1942–2010), 277
Morgan, Lee, 490
Morganfield, McKinley "Muddy Waters," 98, 507
Morin Khuur, **573–574**
Morley, Thomas (ca. 1577–1602), 283, 513
Morocco, music of, 522–523, 705
Morris dancing, English, 51
Morrison, Jim, 429
Morrison, Van, 499
Morton, Jelly Roll (1890–1941), 39, 507
Motet, 171
Mother Maybelle and the Carter Sisters, 148
Motrebi, 887
Moura, Ana (1979–), 265
Mouth-bow, 87
Mouth organ, 464–465
Mouvement Folk, 285
Mozambique
  ethnic groups of, 164–167
  music of, 551–552
Mozart, Wolfgang Amadeus (1756–1827), 173, 189, 817, 818, 854–855, 933

Mridamgam, **574–576**
Muddy Waters, 98, 507
Muenster, Sebastian, 43
Muffat, Georg, 188
Muhammad, Prophet, 842–843, 846
Muhammad Rashad Bey, 523–524
Muhammad Shah, Mughal emperor, 649
Mui, Anita (Anita Mui Yim Fong), 137
Mukesh (1923–1976), 106–107
Mukoyama, Eriko, 645
Mulattos in Brazil, 114–115
Müller, Wenzel (1767–1835), 817, 818
Mulligan, Gerry, 669
Munduk, 309
Munro, William, 830
Munuggurr, Milkay, 232
Muqaddam ibn Mu'āfa, 23
Murphey, Michael (1945–), 204–205
Musafir, **577–578**
Muscle Shoals music, 834, 835
Musette (folk bagpipe), 56, 284
"Music" (term usage), 896
Musical instruments
  in Africa, 337–339
  in Armenia, 240, 241
  in Australia, 231–233
  in Bali, 296, 297–298
  in Candomblé, 135
  in Carnival, 145–146
  Celtic, 152–153
  from Celtic regions, 156
  in China, 254–256, 332, 336–337, 672–674
  of Chopi people, 165
  Cuban (*see* Cuba)
  evolution of, 172
  in gamelan orchestra, 300–301
  gender wayang, 307–308
  Greek, 170, 207–209
  in Hawaii, 212, 684, 923–924
  in India, 574–576, 926–927
  in Iran, 83, 243, 245, 377–378, 441–443
  in Ireland, 243
  in Japan, 293–294, 478–481, 797–801, 805–807
  in Latin America, 212–213
  in Mexico, 328–330
  in Mongolia, 573–574
  in Polynesia, 684–685
  in Portugal, 263
  in Sardinia, 498–499
  in South Asia, 464–465
  in Sweden, 622–624
  in Trinidad and Tobago, 838
  in West Africa, 326–327, 476–478, 941–942
  in zydeco, 963
Musical notation, development of, 171
Musicals, 105, **578–583**
Musical salons, 117
Musical theater
  figures, 180–182
  milestones of, 171
  regional styles, 173
  vaudeville, 406, 925–926
Música norteña (northern music), 892–893
Música Popular Brasileira (Brazilian Popular Music, MPB), 119
Música sertaneja ("country music"), 120
Música tropical (tropical music), 29
Music theory, modern, 170, 171, 172
Music therapy, 232
Music transcription, 66–67
Musique traditionnelle, 285
Musotto, Ramiro (1963–), 88, 89
Musund, 82
Muwashshah, 23–24, 31, 32, 34

Nabati, 82
Nachsteigen, 48
Nagado daiko, 864
Nagauta, 433, 434
Nagi, Ibrahim, 32
Nair, Mira, 107
Najara, Israel, 793
Nambicuara Indians, 114
Namiki Michiko, 428
Naniwabushi/rokyoku, 253
Napoleon, 676
Narcocorridos, 194, 195, 197
Narrative singing, 433
Nascimento, Dinho (1951–), 88–89
Nascimento, Milton (1942–), 119
Nash, Johnny (1940–), 540
Nashville, country music in, 204
Nasser, Gamal Abdel, 34, 439
Nassib, Sélim, 440
Nation (concept), 156
Nationalist musical movement, 174
Native American ceremonial sites, 191
Native American Church Music, **585–586**

Native American elements in Mardi Gras, 143
Native American Flute, **586–588,** 589
Native American Music, **588–594**
   Acadian music influenced by, 1
   Arctic, 589, 591
   Eastern Woodlands, 249–250, 589, 590
   Great Basin, 589, 590–591
   instruments played in, 270
   Northwest Coast, 589, 591
   Plains, 589, 590
   Southwest, 589, 591
   study of, 226–227
   vocables, 931–932
Native American Popular Music, **594–597**
Nature and technology, relationship between, 91
Naumbourg, Samuel (1815–1880), 44
Navaira, Emilio, III (1962–), 192
Navajo, Music of, **597–599**
Nāy (Ney), 31, 222, 377, 378, 599–601
N'Dour, Youssou (1959–), 327, 548, 549, 550
Neemakai, 660
Neff, Pat, 500
Neoclassicism, 174–175
Neo kyma (new wave), 315, 316, 317
Nerses IV (Nerses Shnorhali), Catholicos (1102–1173), 37
Netherlands, music of, 782
Neue Synagoge, Berlin, 45
Neukomm, Sigismund (1778–1858), 116
Neumatic musical notation, 320–321
New Age music, 155
Newgrass, 60, 63, 205
Newman, Jerry, 80
New Orleans jazz, 179, 190–191, 233–234, 635, 847
New Orleans Mardi Gras, 143, 147
New Orleans white band culture, 233
"The New Thing," 411
Newton-John, Olivia, 259
New-wave laika, 315, 317
New World Negro (concept), 15
New Zealand Maori aerophones, 685
New Zealand Maori dance, 684
Ney, 31, 222, 377, 378, **599–601**
Neydavoud, Morteza, 796
Ngodo, 165–166, 551
Nicaragua, music of, 622
Nie Er, 162
Nielsen, Carl, 856

Nigeria, instruments from, 72, 73
Nigerian musicians, 8–9, 12, 13–14, 46, 490–493, 625–628
Nigunim, 44
911 terrorist attacks, 2001, 197
Nisiotika, **601–603**
Niue, music of, 687
Nobuo Uematsu, 155
Nomos, agrarian cults of, 143
Nongak, **607–610**
Nordic Jazz, **610–611**
Norman, Larry, 314
Norteña (term), 193, 194
Norteño Conjunto, 192
Norteño music, 6, 7, 193–195
North American pop, 133
North Indian vocal music, 895–896
North Korea, Music of, **611–614**
Northumbrian smallpipes, 56, 57
Northwest Coast Indian music, 589, 591
Norwegian Folk Music, **614–618**
Nô Theater, 433, **603–607**
Nowakowsky, David (1848–1921), 45
Nueva Canción, 104, **618–622**
Nueva trova, 621
Nukunonu, chanting on, 686
Nunes Garcia, José Mauricio (1767–1830), 116
Nyatiti, 645
Nyckelharpa, **622–624**

Obama, Barack (1961–), 645, 791
Oberek, 676, 678–679
Obey, Ebenezer (1942–), 13
Oboe, 38, 172
Ó Catháin, Rory Dall (1570–1650), 153
O'Connor, John Kennedy, 257
Octave, princple of, 842
Octave doubling, 5
Odori, 436
Offenbach, Jacques (1819–1880), 44, 936
Oganezashvili, Sasha (1889–1932), 442
Ohta, Herb (Ohta-San) (1934–), 923
Okedo, 865–866
Okie migration, 203
Oklahoma dust bowl, 334
Okónkolo (omelé), 72
Olatunji, Babatunde (1927–2003), **625–628**
Oldham, Spooner, 834
Old Roman tradition, 319
Old Spanish chant, 319
Oliver, Joe "King," 39, 722

Index

Olmsted, Frederick Law, 271
Olorum (god), 134
Olsen, Poul Rovsing, 68
Ônaobi uta, 292
Onda chicana, la, 893, 894
O'Neill, Eugene, 182
Onofriana, Maria Severa (1820–1846), 264
Opera, **628–634**
    Argentine, 668
    Chinese, 414–420
    choral music in, 172
    musical dramas resembling, 817–819
    Taiwanese, 870–872
Opera flamenca, 273–274
Operetta, 935
Oral historians and musicians, West African, 322–328
Oral tradition
    aboriginal (Australia), 141
    in Arab classical music, 30
    Pakistani, 652–653
Oratorio, 172
Orchestra
    concertos for, 190
    evolution of, 172
    piano, union with, 189
    technical improvements, 173–174
Orff, Carl, 51
Organ in Bedouin music, 83
Organum, 171
Orientalism, 86
Original Dixieland Jazz Band, **635–637**
O'Riordan, Dolores, 944
Orixás, 134–135
Orquesta, 894
Orquesta tejana, 194
Ory, Kid, 39–40
Oskar, Paul, 260
Ossman, Vess, 62
Oteiza, Jorge (1908–2003), 71
"Other," masked individuals as, 144
Otis, Johnny, 180
Ōtsuzumi, 865
Ottoman Classical Music, **637–640**
Ottoman Empire, 53, 198, 316, 793
Ottoman influence in Arab classical music, 31–32
Oud, 38, **640–644**
Oulman, Alain (1928–1990), 756–757
Owens, Buck (1929–2006), 203–204
Owiyo, Suzanna (1975–), **645–647**
Ozuna, Sunny, 893

Pablo, Luis de (1930–), 70
Pacheco, Johnny, 211, 772
Páez, 28
Pagani, Federico, 698
Paganini, Niccolò (1782–1840), 189
Page, Jimmy, 232
Pahinui, Cyril, 595
Pahinui, Philip Kunia "Gabby," 595
Pakavaj (pakhawaj), 77, 228
Pakistan, Music of, 461–462, **649–654**
Palestine, liberation of, 439
Palestrina, Giovanni Luigi da (1525–1594), 171
Palm, Jan Gerard (1857–1907), 140
Palma, José, 665
Palm-wine music, 12–13
Pamer, Michael (1782–1827), 934
Pan-Asian regional pop, 163
Pan-Indianism, 592
Pan-Pacific Pop, 684
Panpipes (in Samoa-Tonga area), 685
Panpipes *(zampoñas),* 26, 27
Pan-Polynesian Pop, 684
Pansori (P'ansori), **654–656**
Pantaleon, 244
Papadáki, Aspasía, 209
Papadopoulos, George, 317
Parang, 131
Pareja, 28
Parisian Varietées quadrille, 707
Parker, Charlie (1920–1955), **656–659**
    Afro-Cuban jazz, involvement with, 16
    band, 195
    bebop played by, 79, 80
    blues influence on, 97–98
    Davis, Miles playing with, 224
Parker, 'Colonel' Tom, 695
Parra, Violeta, 620
Parsons, Squire, 312
Paschal, Janet, 312
Pashto Music, **659–661**
    badala, 653
    genres, 659–660
    instruments, 660–661
Pasillo, 28
Pastor, Tony, 925
Pastoral instruments, 56–57
Patriotic music, Chinese, 162
Pattakos, Stylianos, 317
Patton, Charlie, 97, 710
Patton, Mike, 92

Paul, Sean, 220
Pavan, 283
Payvar, Faramarz, 796
Peasant music, Hungarian, 66
Pelham, Dick (1815–1876), 251, 930, 931
Peña, Manuel, 194
Penn, Dan, 834
Penn, William, 21
Pennywhistle, 905–907
Pepin the Younger (ca. 714–768), 170
Pepper, Jim, 586, 594
Pepys, Samuel, 244
Percussion instruments
  in cumbia, 214–215
  in gagaku, 294
  of South Asia, 859–861 (*see also* drums; Tabla)
Perestroika, 200
Performance techniques, Japanese, 436
Perkins, Carl, 74
Perkins, Rachel, 142
Perlinpinpin Folk, 285
Perlman, Itzhak, 467
Pérotin, 171
Perry, Lee "Scratch" (1936–), 540
Persia, instruments originating in, 243
Persian art music, 222
Persian classical music, 222, 795
Persian-influenced classical music, 53
Peru, music of
  cumbia in, 216–217
  folkloric ensemble in, 25
  Mestizo music, 564, 565
  regional, 26, 27
Perviz, Husrev, 644
Peter, Paul, and Mary, 314
Petrarca, Francesco, 511
Petrassi, Goffredo, 190
Pettiford, Oscar, 594
Petty, Tom, 499
Petzmayer, Johann, 956
Peyote music, 594
Peyote songs, 585–586, 932
Philippines, Music of, **661–667**
  folk music, 664–665
  indigenous, 663–664
  kulintang, 486–490
  modern, 665–666
Phillips, Sam (1923–2003), 694
Piano
  compositions on, 669
  concertos, 190
  orchestra union with, 189
  precursors of, 242
Piano accordion, 2, 5
Piazzolla, Astor (1921–1992), 7, 58, **667–670,** 886
Picasso, Pablo, 329
Pickett, Wilson, 834
Pietism, 571
Piffero, 57
Pikelny, Noam, 63
Pimba, **670–672**
Pine Grove Boys, 1
Pinkillu, 26
Pino, Geraldo (1938–2008), 13
Pinto, Luiz Álvares (1719–1789), 115
Pipa, 294, **672–674**
Pipes, Bedouin, 83
Piphat, 183, **674–676**
Pixinguinha (Alfreda da Rocha Viana, Jr.) (1897–1973), 117
Piyyutim, 793
Plains Indian music, 589, 590
Planno, Mortimer, 539
Plant, Robert, 232
Plantation songs, 279–280
Poché, Christian, 30, 68, 701
Poindexter, Buster, 830
Pokok, 298
Pokrovsky, Dmitri (1944–1996), 200, 236–237
Polish Americans, dances performed by, 680, 681
Polish National Dances, **676–680.** *See also* Austro-German Dances; Polka
Political commentary in music. *See* social and political themes in music
Political song, Greek, 315, 316, 317
Polka, **680–683**
  accordion use in, 2, 3, 4, 7, 58
  as Alsatian couple dance, 285
  Austro-German, 48, 51
  conjunto influenced by, 192
  corridos in polka rhythm, 196
  introduction of, 706
  schottische compared to, 783
  Tejano music, 894
Polonaise (polonez), 174, 676–677
Polynesia, Music of, **683–689**
  eastern Polynesia, 687–689
  geography, 685
  western Polynesia, 685–687

Polynesian Hymns, **689–693**
   eastern Polynesia, 690–693
   Hawaii, 689–690
   western Polynesia, 690
Polyphony, 171, 233
Polyrhythmic dance style, 288
Ponche (punch), 178
Poor whites, Dixieland appeal to, 234
Popo, Sundar (1943–2000), 168, 169
Popular music, American, 205. *See also* Tin Pan Alley
Popular music, Asian
   in Hong Kong (English), 136
   in Japan, 253
   in Taiwan, 876–878
Popular music, calypso influenced by, 131
Popular music, European
   Armenian, 38
   bagpipes in, 57
   concerto influenced by, 190
   dulcimer in, 244
   French, 159–161
   Serbian, 911–913
Popular music, Mexican, 193
Popular song *(minyō)*, 428
Popular songs, Schlager, 781–782
Portable recording equipment, 507
Porter, Cole (1891–1964), 579, 580, 936
Portugal, Carnival in, 144
Portugal, Marcos (1762–1830), 116
Portugal, music of, 725–727, 755–757
Portugal, song in, 263–266
Portuguese colonizers, 114
Portuguese pop music, 670–672
Portuondo, Omara (?–1930), 122
Post-bop jazz, 185–187
Potter, Tommy, 658
Powell, Bud, 16, 658
Pozo, Chano, 15, 16
Prado, Dámaso Pérez (1916–1989), 525–526
Prayer, call to (Islam), 31
Presley, Elvis (1935–1977), **693–696**
   African American influence on, 721, 749
   Beatles coverage of songs by, 74
   Lead Belly songs covered by, 499
   Marley, B. influenced by, 540
   performers working with, 149
   on television shows, 239–240
Previn, André, 810
Primaeux, Verdell, 586
Primera, Alí (1942–1985), 622

Prine, John, 94
Prison songs, 500, 501
Profanity poems, 949–950
Programmatic music, 856
Progressive bluegrass, 205
Progressive conjunto, 192, 893, 894
Prohibition of music, 31
Prokoviev, Sergei (1891–1953), 857, 929, 936
Protestant Reformation, 21, 50
Provençal troubadour tradition, 23
Prudencia, Cargio (1955–), 104
Psaltery (Bowed, Unbowed), **696–697**
Psychedelec rock, 288, 289
Puccini, Giacomo, 936
Puente, Tito (1923–2000), **697–700**
   Afro-Cuban music influence on, 16–17
   musicians collaborating with, 211
   salsa music, 772
Puerto Rico
   cuatro in, 212, 213
   nueva canción in, 621–622
   reggaetón in, 743, 745
Pulido, Roberto, 893
Punhab, music in, 651–652
Punk, 90, 205
Puppet theater, 303, 937
Puro, 109
Putin, Vladimir, 260
Pututu, 27
Pygmies, 945
Pythagoras of Samos (ca. 570–ca. 495 BCE), 170

Qānūn, 31, 222, **701–702**
Qasabji, Muhammad (1892–1966), 642
Qasīdah, 31, 32, 81
Qaum, 243
Qawwali, 461–462, 650–651, 846–847
Qin (Guqin), **702–705**
Qin-pipa, 672–673
Qissa, 652, 654
Qoli, Mirza Hossein (1854–1916), 888
Qraqeb, **705**
Quadrille, **706–707,** 708
Quarter-tone, 842
Quartet music (gospel), 312, 313
Quechan, 946, 947
Quechua language, 101
Queen Ida (Ida Lewis Guillory), 963
Quelbe, **707–708**
Quichua people, 28

Quiñones, José Luis, 329
Quiñones, Sam, 194
Qur'anic recitation, 31

Rabab (rababah), 81
Race music, 749
Race Records, **709–711**, 761, 825, 826
Rachmaninoff, Sergei, 190
Racial politics, 79–80
Racial segregation, 925
Racial stereotypes in text and music, 281, 715–716
Racine, Julio (1945–), 140
Racism, 234
Racy, A. J., 31–32, 33
Racy, Ali Jihad, 68
Rácz, Aladár, 245
Radif, 222, 376, 795, 796, 887
Radio, 202
Raducanu (1931–), 760
Raffi (Cavoukian), 38
Raga, 77, 229–230, **711–715**, 808, 879, 895
Ragga, 742
Ragtime
  banjo in, 62
  Dixieland influenced by, 233
  rise of, 191
  royalties, 425
  Tin Pan Alley, relationship to, 903
Rahbani, Assi and Mansour, 266–267, 268
Rahbani, Ziad, 268
Rahzel, 92
Rai, **716–721**
  backlash and future directions, 719–720
  key figures, 459–461
  youth culture, 717–719
Rainey, Gertrude "Ma" (1886–1939), **721–723**
  commercial records, involvement with, 97
  music by, 238
  musicians performing with, 237, 312, 825
  in 1920s, 709
Rajasthan, music of, 577–578
Rajasthani folk music, 228
Rakha, Alla (1919–2000), 230, **723–725**
Rameshgar, Bagher, 442
Rami, Ahmad, 438
Ramírez, Alnaldo, 194
Ramos, Ruben (El Gato Negro), 894
Ramsawak, James, 169

Ranchera
  in conjunto, 192
  rhythm in, 329
Rancho Folclórico, **725–727**
Raoni, Kayapó chief, 114
Rap
  in gospel music, 314–315
  in Greece, 315, 318
Rap/Hip-Hop, **727–730**
Rap/Hip-Hop in Africa and Middle East, **730–733**
Raqs sharqi, 85–86, 221
Rara, **733–735**
Rastafarianism, 539–540, 741
Ravel, Maurice (1875–1937), 70, 174, 929, 936
Ray, Satyajit, 106
Razif, 83
Razzano, José, 885
Reagan, Ronald, 752
Reagen, Bernice Johnson, 791
Rebab, 301, **735–737**
Rebetika, 315, 316, 317
Recife, Carnival in, 146–147
Recording equipment, 507
Recording technology, 961
Redding, Otis (1941–1967), 834, 835
Reddy, Helen, 751
Rediwaire, 51
Redman, Don, 710, 848
Redova (redowa), 192, 193
Redzepova, Esma (1943–), **737–739**, 760
Reels á bouche, 1
Reeves, Jim (1923–1964), 204
Reform Movement (Judaism), 44
Reggae, **739–743**
  Caribbean musical history dominated by, 331
  dancehall music and, 219
  international interest in, 139
  rai compared to, 720
  Trinidad youth preference for, 133
Reggaetón, 742, **743–745**
Regina, Elis (1945–1982), 119
Regional *versus* national music, 236
Reich, Steve (1936–), 185
Reichardt, Johann Friedrich (1752–1814), 817
Reichert, Louise, 285
Reinhardt, Django, 203
Religio-medicinal songs, 11
Renaissance, music in, 171, 512–513

Renan, Ernest, 156
Republic of China (ROC), 872
Requinto, 28
Reser, Harry, 62
Resonator guitar (Dobro), 837
Reuchlin, Johannes, 43
Reyna, Fredy, 212–213
Reynolds, Dwight, 720
Rhythm and blues (R & B)
   bebop compared to, 80
   black and white artists in, 694
   influences on, 96, 180
   performers of, 314
   post-World War II, 710
   soul influenced by, 832, 835
Rhythmic oddity property, 178
Ribera y Tarragó, Julian, 33–34
Riddle, Lesley (1905–1980), 202
Rieser, Bob, 791
Rigaudon, 285
Right and wrong, struggle between, 938
Riley, Terry (1935–), 185
Rimsky-Korsakov, Nikolai, 37
Rímur, **745–747**
Rio de Janeiro
   Carnival, 118, 143, 144–145
   music in, 116, 146
Ripieno, concertino compared to, 172, 188
Riq, 31, 33, 222, **747–748**
Ritornello (concept), 188
Ritsos, Yiannis, 317
Rivera, Ismael, 110
Rivera, Jenni (1969–2012), 197
Rivero, Carmen, 216
Roach, Max, 224, 658
Road-march calypsos, 131
Robbins, Ed, 334
Roberts, Dink, 62
Robeson, Paul, 790
Rocha Viana, Alfreda da, Jr. (Pixinguinha) (1897–1973), 117
Rocheman, Lionel, 285
Rock
   conjunto fusion with, 192
   funk fused with, 289
   influences on, 179–180
   in Japan, 253
   traditional music blended with, 63
Rockabilly, 428–429
Rock and Roll, **748–753**
   African Amerian influence on, 749
   baby boom and consumer culture, 750
   bands, 74
   Beatles impact on, 750–751
   blues influence on, 96
   calypso competition with, 132
   conjunto fusion with, 192
   in France, 161
   influences on, 179
   Japanese music influenced by, 428–429
   key figures, 693–696
   musicals impacted by, 581
   rise of, 4, 694
   1970s to 1990s, 751–752
   traditional music blended with, 1–2
   21st century, 752–753
   Woodstock, 751
   young Latino preference for, 211
Rockin' Sidney (Sidney Simien), 963
Rocksteady, 739, 740
Rococo melodies, 43
Rocolera music, 28
Rodeheaver, Homer A. (1880–1955), 311
Rodgers, Jimmie (1897–1933), **753–755**
   blues influence on, 98
   impersonations of, 202
   yodeling by, 945
Rodgers, Richard (1902–1979), 580, 903
Rodgers and Hammerstein, 186, 411, 579, 580, 581
Rodrigues, Amália (1920–1999), 263, 264–265, **755–757**
Rodríguez, Arsenio (1911–1970), 525
Rodríguez, Silvio (1946–), 621
Rôei, 292
Rogers, Will, 926
Roldán, Amadeo (1900–1939), 140
Rolling Stones
   influences on, 420, 499
   recordings of, 718
Roman chant, 319
Romani Music, 737–739, **758–760**
Romani people
   dances by, 86
   klezmorim performance with, 470
Romantic era
   concertos during, 189–190
   flamenco during, 273
Romantic quadrille, 707
Roman times, bagpipes in, 54
Rome, ancient, Saturnalias in, 144
Rondalla, 664–665
Ronkin, Mary Cohan, 181

Roosevelt, Franklin, 182
Root, George F. (1820–1895), 311
Ropars, Loeiz, 154
Rosa, Noel (1910–1937), 118
Rosas, Juan Manuel de, 883
Rosenfeld, Monroe H., 903–904
Ross, "Black Face" Eddie, 62
Rossi, Salamone (1570–1630), 42
Rubayi, 660
Rub board, 1
Rumba, 16, 180, **760–765**
Rumi, 637, 796, 846
Runo Song, **765–766**
Rural blues ("country blues"), 97
Rural samba, 117
Russell, Curley, 80
Russia, music of
  medieval, 954
  post-Soviet, 201
  regional *versus* national, 236
Russian Civil War (1917–1922), 200
Russian Orthodox Church Music, 200, **767–770**
Ryukoka, 252–253

Saba, Abolhasan (1902–1957), 222, 796
Sabar, 327
Sabri, Sharif, Pasha, 438
Sachs, Carl, 48
Sachs, Curt, 701
Säckpipa, 57
Sacred Harp singing, 811–815
Sacred music, Jewish, 43
Sa'd, Masoud-e (1046–1121), 441
Safi al-Din, 177
Sahak I (Isaac the Great), Catholicos (348–439), 37
Sahak III Dzoraporetsi, Catholicos (?–703), 37
Saibara, 292
Sainko (Demetrio Stratos), 945
Sainte Marie, Buffy, 594–595
Sakamoto Kyū, 429
Sakamoto Ryūichi, 429
Salas y Castro, Esteban (1725–1803), 140
Salazar, António de Oliveira (1889–1970), 265, 757
Saldívar, Mingo, 195
Saldívar, Yolanda, 894
Saljuq music, 637
Sallaberry, Jean Dominique Julien (1837–1903), 70

Salsa, **771–772**
  clave in, 178–179
  Cuban, 209–210
  cumbia competition with, 216
Salterio, 242
Salvador, Brazil, 146
Salzburg zither, 955, 956
Sama, 844–845
Samba enredo, 143, 145
Samba Instruments, **773–774**
Samba Music, **774–779**
  Afro-Brazilian, 113
  alternatives to, 118–119
  contemporary, 778–779
  emergence and rise of, 117–118
  ensembles and parade, 145–146
  history and development, 775–777
  musical styles, 775
  socio-cultural context, 777–778
Samba-reggae, 120
Samba schools, 118, 143, 145
Sammari (love songs), 82
Sammartini, Giovanni Battista (ca. 1700–1775), 854
Samoa, music of, 685–686
Samurai, 124
Sánchez, Chalino, 194, 197
Sand, George, 284
Sanders, Ed, 944
Sanders, Pharoah, 187
Sangalo, Ivete (1972–), 118
Sanjo, **779–781**
San Jose Taiko, 864
Sanjuán, 28
Sanjuanito, 28, 29
Sankey, Ira D. (1840–1908), 311
San no tsuzumi, 294
Sanshin, 434
Santamaria, Ramon "Mongo," 699
Santana
  Afro-Cuban music influence on, 16–17
  debut of, 699
Santería, 73, 210
Santur, 242, 243, 245, 377, 378
Sanxian, 434
Sarangi, 650
Sardinia, Folk music in, 391–392, 498–499
Sargam syllables, 99–100
Sarisözen, Muzaffer (1899–1963), 53
Sarkissian, Karnig, 38
Sarmiento, Domingo, 883

Sarod, 77, 107, 650
Saron family of instruments, 301
Satie, Erik, 716
Saudade, 263, 757
Saura, Carlos, 266
Savopoulos, Dionysis, 317
Ṣaworo, 73
Saya (genre), 26–27
Sayakian, Harutyun (Sayat Nova) (King of Song) (1712–1795), 38
Saya music, 102, 103
Scandinavia, bagpipes in, 57
Scheitholt, 954–955
Schenk, Johann, 819
Schikaneder, Emanuel (1751–1812), 818
Schiller, Friedrich, 855
Schlager, **781–783**
Schlesinger, Kathleen, 33–34
Schliefer (slide), 51
Schliessinger, Sigmund (1835–1906), 45
Schneider, Bernard, 21
Schneider, Michael, 21
Schoenberg, Arnold (1874–1951), 45, 89, 175, 857
Schönberg, Claude-Michel (1944–), 582
Schottische, **783–786**
  accordion use in, 4, 7
  as Alsatian couple dance, 285
  conjunto influenced by, 192
  Germanic versions of, 48
  introduction of, 706
  steps, 785–786
Schrammel, Johann (1850–1893), 786
Schrammel, Josef (1852–1895), 786
Schrammelmjusik, **786–787**
Schröter, Gottleib, 244
Schubert, Franz, 51, 934
Schuhplattler, 48–49
Schuman, Clara, 190
Schuman, Robert, 190
Schwarz, Stephen, 582
Schwarzer, Franz (1828–1904), 956
Scofield, John, 225
Scotch Snap, **787–789**
Scotland
  cultures from, 156
  music in, 54–56, 153
  pipebands in, 154
Scots-English folk music, 280
Scots-English tradition, 281
Scott, Milly, 260
Scottish Highland Bagpipes, 57

Scottish-Irish descended persons, bagpipes at funerals for, 55
Scottish-Irish music, Acadian music influenced by, 1
"Scottish music" (term), 156
Scruggs, Earl (1924–2012), 63, 93, 204
Seck, Thione (1955–), 548, 549–550
Secola, Keith, 595
Secular music, 171
Seeger, Peter (1919–2014), **789–792**
  banjo championed by, 63
  Guthrie, W., dealings with, 335
  influences on, 334, 335, 336, 507, 552–553
  Lead Belly influence on, 501
  Lead Belly songs covered by, 499
  musician and activist, 790–791
  publications, 791–792
  recognition, 791
  recordings by, 278
Segovia, Andrés, 929
Segundo, Compay (1907–2003), 122
Seiz, 213
Seldom Scene, 63, 94
Selena (Selena Quintanilla), 894
Senegalese music, 548–551
Sephardic Jews, 306
Sephardic language, 42
Sephardic Music, 43, **792–795**
September 11, 2001 terrorist attacks, 55
Sepultura, 120
Setar, 377–378, 819, 887
Seven Years' War (1756–1763), 127
Sewamono, 124
Shaan, 660
Shabalala, Joseph (1941–), 495, 496, 553
Shādhiliyya tarīqa, 24
Shadow puppet theater, 303, 937
Shaheen, Simon (1955–), 643
Shahnaz, Jalil (1921–2013), 796
Shahnazi, Ali Akbar (1897–1985), 888
Shajarian, Mohanned-Reza (1940–), **795–797**
Shakespeare, William, 112
Shakuhachi, **797–801**
  manufacture, 799
  music, 800–801
  performance traditions, 799–800
  types, 797–799
Shamanic Music in Mongolia and Inner Asia, **801–805**
Shamanism, 900

Shamisen, 124, 434, **805–807**
Shamma, Naseer (1963–), 643–644
Shanghai Jazz, 162
Shanghai popular music, 162–163
Shankar, Ravi (1920–2012), 77, 106, 230, 241, 724, **807–811**, 819, 820, 821–822
Shape-Note Singing (Sacred Harp Singing), **811–815**
  current practice, 814–815
  history, 812–813
  style and notation, 813–814
Shaqwa, 82
Sharagan (sharakan), 36–37
Sharif, Mahmoud, 438
Shaw, Artie, 848, 849
Shawqi, Ahmad, 32
Shchurov, Vyacheslav (1942–), 200
Shehnai, 77
Shelton, Robert, 246
Shem Tov, Israel Baal (1698–1760), 44
Sheng
  Europe, introduction into, 5
  instruments resembling, 293
Sherman, Nick, 594
Sheyr, 653, 654
Shidaiqu, 162–163
Shihāb al-Dīn, 32
Shiloah, Amnon, 22, 31, 33
Shimabukuro, Jake (1976–), 924
Shitende, 165
Shivelan, 165
Shô, 293
Shofar, 41
Shôga, 291–292
Shôko (metal gong), 294
Shômyô, **815–817**
Shorter, Wayne, 412
Shosagoto, 436
Shostakovich, Dmitry (1906–1975), 45, 857
Showboat (show), 579–580, 952
Shunda, József, 245
Shunyo, Tottori, 252
Sibelius, Jean (1865–1957), 174, 190, 856
Siemanowoski, Richard, 503
Sierra Leone, music of, 330–331
Siku, 27
Silesian folksongs, 151
Simien, Terrance, 129, 963
Simon, Paul, 495, 496, 518–519, 546, 553, 742
Simon and Garfunkel, 63

Simone, Nina (1933–2003), 161, 945
Sims, Jules, 131
Sinatra, Frank, 16–17, 202, 499
Sindh, music in, 651
Singapore, music in, 163, 254
Singing bowls, 899–902
Singing Sandra, 133
Singspiel, **817–819**
Sinhô (José Barbosa da Silva, 1888–1930), 118
Sioux, yodeling by, 945
Sioux women, songs of, 226
Sissoko, Mama, 942
Sitar, 76, 77, 78, 107, 225, 650, 660, **819–822**, 923
Ska, **822–825**
  Beatles and, 74
  dancehall drawing on, 219
  reggae influenced by, 739, 742
  rise of, 740
Ska-punk, 742
Skeletal melody instruments, 301
Skyladika (dog music), 315, 317
Skynyrd, Lynyrd, 205
"Slack"/"slackness" (term), 220
Slaves. *See also* African slaves
  in ancient Rome, 144
  in Argentina, 883
  in Caribbean, 707
  in Cuba, 763
  instruments built by, 326
  instruments played by, 59, 61
  in Jamaica, 330
  slave trade, 177
  spirituals, 9–10
  in Trinidad, 130
  vocals, 945
  white depiction of, 62
Sledge, Percy, 834
Slendro scale, 308
Slide guitar, 89
Sloane, Hans, 60
Slovakian flute, 286–287
Sly and the Family Stone, 288
Smallpipes, 57
Smetana, Bedřich (1824–1884), 51, 174, 856
Smith, Bessie (1894–1937), **825–827**
  Armstrong, L. dealings with, 40
  classic blues of, 203
  commercial records, involvement with, 97

Dorsey, T. A. influenced by, 238
Rainey, Ma dealings with, 722
in 1920s, 709
Smith, Buster (1904–1991), 657
Smith, Joe, 827
Smith, Lucius, 62
Smith, Mamie, 709
Smith, Velma (1924–2014), 204
Snipes, John, 62
Snoa, 51
Soca, **827–832**
chutney, 133, 168, 169–170
emergence of, 133
Socarras, Alberto, 15
Social and political themes in music
African, 467, 491–493, 545–548, 645, 646
Algerian, 718
American, 246, 717, 789–792
Australian, 142
Brazilian, 119
Iranian, 796–797
Jamaican, 540, 541–542
Japanese, 252, 253
Latin American, 618–622, 772
Lebanese, 267
Native American, 594–595
Spanish, 274
zydeco, 963
Social issues, puppet theater addressing, 938
Social issues, songs addressing, 131, 132, 219–220
Socially engaged music, Basque, 71
Society Islands, music of, 687, 688, 691
Soghomonian, Soghomon (Komitas) (1869–1935), 38
Solkattu, 100
Solo concerto, 189
Solo instruments, whole orchestra compared to, 172
Soloist, orchestra relationship with, 189
Sonata, 173
Sondheim, Stephen (1930–), 580, 581, 582, 936
"Song demonstrators" (term), 904
"Song pluggers" (term), 904
Son House, 98, 272, 710
Son jalisciense, 532, 534, 566
Son music
Cuban, 560, 561
Guatemalan, 537
in mambo, 525

mariachi, 532, 533
mestizo, 564
Mexican regional, 565–566, 567
Sorozábal, Pablo (1897–1988), 70
Sosa, Mercedes (1935–2009), 619, 620, 622
Soto, Gary, 329
Soukous, 180
Soul, **832–836**
conjunto fusion with, 192
funk fused with, 288, 289
influence of, 8
soca development aided by, 828
Sousa, John Philip, 716
South Africa, music of, 495–496, 516–519, 545–548
South Asia, music of, 464–465
South Asian music, 464–465, 711–715
Southeast Asian music, 183, 185, 254
Southern, R. W., 23
Southern gospel, 311–312
Southern whites, rural, musical traditions of, 201
South India, music in, 100
Southwest Indian music, 589, 591
Soviet Union, 36, 200
Soweto uprising, 1976, 547
Spain, music of
bagpipes in, 57
castanets in, 112
flamenco, 272–278, 759–760
herding instruments in, 56
Roma and Romani music in, 758, 759, 760
Spendiaryan, Alexander (1871–1928), 37
Spies, Walter, 454
Spike fiddle, 573–574
Spirituals, African, 9–12
Sprachinseltänze, 51
Springsteen, Bruce, 751–752, 791
Square dance, 270, 706, 707
Srravinsky, Igor (1882–1971), 175
Sruti box, 107
Stafford, Tom, 834
Stamitz, Johann (1717–1757), 854
Stanley, Ralph, 94–95
Starr, Ringo (1940–), 74
Stax Records, 833
Steelbands, 143
Steel Guitar, **836–838**
in Acadian music, 1
in Cajun music, 128
in country music, 203–204

Steel orchestras
- after World War II, 840–841
- in calypso, 131, 827

Steelpan, **838–841**
- in Caribbean art music, 140
- international interest in, 139
- soca compared to, 831

Steelpan tuner, 839–840
Steel-strung guitar, 838
Stevens, Sufjan, 63
Stichometry, 183
Stivell, Alan (1944–), 154, 156, 285
Stonehill, Randy, 314
Stookey, Paul, 314
Stowe, Harriet Beecher (1811–1896), 281
Stradella (Standard) bass system, 7
Strauss, Johann the elder (1804–1849), 934, 935
Strauss, Johann the younger (1825–1899), 935, 936
Strauss, Richard (1864–1949), 174, 781, 856
Stravinsky, Igor, 190, 245, 668, 716, 929, 936
Street cries, 271
Streisand, Barbara, 837
String band, 60, 204
String bass, 203
Stringed instruments
- Celtic, 153
- chamarrita accompanied by, 158
- hegemony of, 172
- Swedish, 622–624
- West African, 476–478

String quartet, 173
Struck chordophone, 242
Sufism, Music of, **842–847**
- history, 842–843
- instruments played in, 705
- *kafi* ties to, 651
- Melevi Order, 843–844
- Melevi Sama, 844–845
- Qawwali and, 650, 846–847
- use of, 843

Sufism, zajal influenced by, 950
Sugar, Dick "Ricardo," 698–699
Suite in baroque period, 172
Sukawati, 309
Sulayman, ʿUmar, 84
Suling, 301
Sulzer, Salomon (1804–1890), 44

Sunbati, Riyad el- (1906–1981), 642
Sunday, Billy, 311
Sun Ra, 289
Superblue (Austin Lyons), 830–831
Surakarta, music of, 300
Suso, Foday Musa (1950–), 326
Suyá Indians, 114
Svarmandal, 77
Swamp pop, 1–2
Swange, 11
Sweden, music of
- bagpipes in, 57
- dance in, 783
- string instruments in, 622–624

Sweeney, Joel Walker, 61
Swing, **847–850**
- Afro-Cuban influence on, 16
- bebop compared to, 78, 79, 80
- Cajun music influenced by, 128
- departure from, 656, 657
- era of, 408–409
- race music and, 710

Swinging Addis, 46–47
Swiss yodeling, 944–945
Sylvester, Mark, 63
Symphonic form, 174
Symphonic Poem, 850–852
Symphony, **852–858**
- 18th century, 853–855
- innovative, 174
- 19th century, 855–856
- origins, 852–853
- rising importance of, 189
- 20th century, 856–857

Synthesizer
- in tango, 669
- in West African popular music, 327, 331

Syria, nationalism in, 83
Syrian Bedouin singers, 83–84

Tabla, 77, 106, 107, 225, 228, 378, **859–861**
Tabla dayan, 100
Tagalog, 665
Tagaq, Tanya, 595
Taghrudah, 83
Tagore, Rabindranath (1861–1941), 230, **861–863**
Tahiti, music of, 687, 690, 691–692
Taiko, **863–869**
Taiwanese Opera, **870–872**

Index

Taiwanese Traditional and Popular music, **872–878**
  enka, 254
  historical and sociopolitical contexts, 872–873
  popular music, 876–878
  traditional music, 873–876
Taj Mahal (musician), 910
Takht, 31, 33, 222
Tala, 100, **879–881**
Taliban, 653–654, 661
Tam, Alan (Alan Tam Wing Lun), 137
Tama, 327
Tamboo Bamboo, 839, **881–882**
Tambour bélé, 84
Tambourine, 748
Tampura, 77
Tanburah (simsimiyyah), 81
Tango, **882–886**
  dances, other compared to, 159
  development of, 667, 668
  instruments associated with, 58, 59
  musicians, 669
  music utilizing, 7
  swing orchestras utilizing, 16
Tango brasileiro, 117
Tanrikorur, Cinuçen (1938–2000), 643
Tansen, 229
Tap dancing, 113
Tapia, Roberto, 197
Tappa, 659
Taqs, 17
Taqsīm, 17, 30, 31, 33, 67, 68, 643, **886–887**
Tar, 81, 221, 222, 377, 748, **887–888**
Tarab, 30, 31, 33, 68
Targan, Şerif Muhittin (1892–1967), 643
Tarka, 26
Tarkington, Booth, 944
Tassa Drumming, 169, **888–892**
Tavener, John, 89
Tawfiq, Samirah (1935–), 83–84
Taylor, Creed, 186
Taylor, James, 94
Taylor, Koko, 98–99
Tchaikovsky, Pyotr (1840–1893), 174, 936
Teagarden, Jack, 826
Teague, Liam, 841
Teatro variedades, 764
Technocumbia, 29
Technology and nature, relationship between, 91

Tehrani, Hossein (1912–1974), 908
Tejano music, **892–895**
  accordion use in, 4, 6, 7
  conjunto, 193, 195
  importance of, 192
  origin of, 4
  predecessor to, 194
  western swing influenced by, 203
Telemann, Georg Philipp (1681–1767), 188
Teló, Michel (1981–), 120
Tent calypso, 131
Tenzer, Michael, 183
Terreiros (farmyards), 134
Texas-Mexicans, music by, 193–194
Texas swing, 128
Thailand, music of
  piphat ensemble, 183
  wong piphat, 674–676
Thalberg, Sigismond (1812–1871), 189
Theater companies in Caribbean, 140
Theka, 100
Theodorakis, Mikis, 317
Thile, Chris (1981–), 95
Thomas, Carla, 833
Thomas, Henry, 97
Thomas, Leon, 945
Thornton, Big Mama, 721
Thumri, **895–896**
Tibetan Buddhist Chant, **896–899**
Tibetan Singing Bowls, **899–902**
Tibwa, 84
Tickell, Kathryn, 57
Tigranian, Armen (1879–1950), 37
Tigres del Norte, Los, 194–195, 197
Tihai, 100
Tillman, Charles (1861–1943), 311, 312
Time-cycle instruments, 301, 303
Time Unit Box System (TUBS), 177
Timpan, 243
Tindinit, 310
Tindley, Charles Albert (1851–1933), 311, 312
Tin Pan Alley, **902–905**
  ballads, 847
  composers and songwriters, 181–182, 951
  songs, 848, 926
Tin/Pennywhistle, **905–907**
Tinya drum, 27
Tiple, 28
Tippett, 190
Tiv songs, 10–11

Tobin, Robert Deam, 260
Todd, Oliver (1916–2001), 657
Tōgaku, 292
Tombak, 377, 378, **907–908**
Tonality, breakdown of, 174, 175
Tonality, modern, 171, 172
Tonga, music of, 686–687, 690
Torelli, Giuseppe (1658–1709), 187–188
Toro, Yomo (1933–2012), 213
Torun, Mutlu (1942–), 643
Tosh, Peter (1944–1987), 539, 541, 741, 742
Toto la Momposina (1940–), 214, 216
Touma, Habib Hassan, 30–31, 32, 33, 34, 222
Touré, Ali Farka (1939–2006), 327, **909–911**
Tracey, Hugh, 166
Traditional music, dulcimer in, 244
Train imitations, 6
Trans-Atlantic slave trade, 177
Transcendence, 11–12
Transsexual musicians, 260
Travis, Randy (1959–), 205
Tremulos in accordion, 5
Trepak, 147
Tresillo, 178, 179
Tridates (Tridat III), 36
Trikitrixa, 70
Trinidad
   Carnival, 143
   identity, 133, 170
   music of, 133, 167, 168, 839
Trinidad and Tobago, music of, 129–130, 169, 827, 830, 838, 840
   tamboo bamboo, 881–882
   tassa drumming, 888–889
   United States influence on, 131
Trio eléctrico, 146
Tri Yann, 285
Troilo, Anibal (1914–1975), 7, 667, 669
Tropicália, 119
Trote, 27
Troubadours
   Arab influence on, 33
   Armenian, 38
   Provençal troubadour tradition, 23
Trujillo, Chico, 217
Trump, Donald, 82
Trump in calypso, 131
Tse, Kay (Kay Tse On Kei), 138
Tsudi, 165
Tsuzumi drums, 864

Tubb, Ernest (1914–1984), 149
Tuning systems, 842
Tunisia, music of, 523–524
Turbo-Folk, **911–913**
Turkey, music of, 245, 260, 643
Turkish Alevis, 53–54
Turkish duduk, 241
Tuvalu, music of, 684, 686, 690
Tuvan Popular Bands, **913–916**
Tuvan Throat Singing, **916–922**
   artists and groups, 918–920
   performance practices, 920–921
   styles, techniques, and terminology, 916–918
Twain, Mark, 943
Twitty, Conway (1933–1993), 204
Two-step dance music, modification of traditional, 233–234
Txalaparta, 70
Txistu, 70

Ubago, Alex, 71
Übern Fuaß ("over the foot"), 51
'ūd, 31, 67, 68, 222, 377
Uganda, music in, 19–20
Uhlig, Carl Friedrich, 58
Uilleann pipes, 56, 57, 243
Ukulele, 212, 684, **923–924**
Ulanov, Barry, 79
Umbanda, 135
Umlauf, Carl Ignaz (1746–1796), 818, 956
UNESCO, 265, 277, 278, 286, 536, 552, 607, 702, 704, 844
United Kingdom, dulcimer in, 244–245
United States
   Carnival in, 143, 147
   dulcimer in, 242–243, 245
   Jewish immigration to, 794
   rumba in, 761, 764
Urban blues, 97
Urban mestizo music (in Bolivia), 103
Urban samba, 117–118
U Roy, 219
Uruguay
   dance in, 158, 159
   music of, 619–620
Usta, Mahmut, 701
U.S. Virgin Islands, music of, 707–708
Utada Hikaru, 430

Valdés, Ramón ("Bebo"), 16
Valen, Richie, 75

Valentino, Rudolph, 885
Vallenato, 215
Van Eps, Fred, 62
Vaqueros, 945
Varèse, Edgard (1883–1965), 555, 929
Vargas, Getúlio, 116, 145, 929
Varoujian, Sonya, 38
Vasconcelos, Naná (1944–), 88
Vaudeville, 406, **925–926**
Vaughan, James D., 312
Vaughan, Sarah, 825–826
Vaziri, Ali-Naqi (1887–1979), 222, 223
Vedder, Eddie, 462
Veena, **926–927**
Vegas, Lolly, 594
Vegas, Pat, 594
Veloso, Caetano (1942–), 119, 622
Venezuela
   cuatro in, 212, 213
   music of, 25
Verbunkos, 66
Verdelot, Philippe (ca. 1480–1530), 512
Verdi, Giuseppe (1813–1910), 174
Viadana, Lodovico Grossi da, 187
Vibraphone, 47
Vielle (hurdy-gurdy), 284
Vienna, Austria
   folkloristic music in, 786–787
   singspiel in, 817–818
Viglietti, Daniel (1939–), 619
Vihuela, 212, 329
Villa, Beto, 893
Villa, Pancho, 196
Villa-Lobos, Heitor (1887–1959), 113, 114, 116–117, **927–930**
Villarreal, Bruno (1901–1976), 192
Vinson, Eddie "Cleanhead," 185
Viola, 88
Violence, celebration of, 219
Violin
   Acadian music using, 1, 127
   in Andean region, 27
   Arab classical music using, 31, 33
   Armenian music using, 38
   in Bolivia, 102
   in calypso, 131
   chamarrita accompanied by, 158
   in classical music, 173
   concertos for, 189
   dastgah using, 223
   fiddle compared to, 269
   in Iran, 441–442

   musical instruments resembling, 207, 208
Virginia Minstrels, 250, 251, 477, **930–931**
Virgin Islands, music of, 707–708
Virtuoso, 189–190
Vissi, Ana, 318
Vivaldi, Antonio (1678–1741), 188, 853
Vocables, **931–932**
Vocal styles, unique, developing, 693
Volanis, Sotis (1971–), 760
Volta, 933
Voodoo, 191
Vuletic, Dean, 260
Vuvuzela, 734

Wabenaki, 249
Wagner, Richard (1813–1883), 174, 935, 936
Wagon, 294
Wajid Ali Shaw of Oudh (1847–1856), 895
Wakrapuku (pututu), 27
Walden, Phil, 834
Wales
   cultures from, 156
   harp in, 154
Walker, Frank, 826
Walker, Jerry Jeff (1942–), 204–205
Wallace, Sippie, 709
Waltz, **933–937**
   accordion use in, 4, 7
   as Alsatian couple dance, 285
   Austro-German, 48, 50
   conjunto influenced by, 192
   corridos in waltz time, 196
   introduction of, 706
   music derived from, 28
   schottische compared to, 783–784
Wang Sengqian (425–485), 672
Wang Zhaojun, 674
War, Rossy, 29
War horns, Celtic, 152
Warren, Guy (Kofi Ghanaba), 180
Was, David, 247
Was, Don, 247, 718
Wasla (musical suite), 24
Watson, Doc, 93
Wayang Kulit, 307, 309, **937–940**
"Wayang wong," 308–309
Wayno, 27, 29
Wayñu, 26
Weavers, 335, 552–553, 790
Webber, Andrew Lloyd (1948–), 582, 936

Weber, Carl Maria von, 934
Webern, Anton, 175
Weelkes, Thomas (1576–1623), 513
Weigl, Joseph, 819
Weill, Kurt (1900–1950), 502, 503
Weisenburg, Heinrich, 188
Weisse, C. F. (1726–1804), 817
Wei Wende, Queen, 672
Welk, Lawrence (1903–1992), 3, 680
Wells, Kitty (born Muriel Deason) (1919–2012), 203
"Welsh music" (term), 156
Wenders, Wim, 122, 123
West African music
   instruments, 59, 60, 62, 72, 234–236, 330–331, 941–942
   mande, 527–530
   musicians, 322–328, 396–398
   practices, 177
West African popular music, 12–15. *See also* Afrobeat (Afropop)
West African slaves in Brazil, 114–115
Westerman, Floyd Red Crow, 594
Western instruments
   Arab classical music using, 33, 34
   in Bolivia, 103
   in dastgah, 223
Western music
   in Cajun format, 128
   Japan influenced by, 252, 253
Western Polynesia, music of, 685–687
Western Polynesia hymns, 690
Western pop songs, 108
Western popular music
   Greek popular music influenced by, 317
   Japanese pop influenced by, 428–429
   Korean pop influenced by, 163–164
Western swing, 203
West Indies, banjo playing in, 60
Wexler, Jerry, 835
Whitaker, Frank, 251
White gospel, 312
White image of country music, 201–202
Whiterose, Julian, 131
Whitlock, William "Billy" (1813–?), 61, 251, 930
Whittaker, Hudson "Tampa Red," 238
Wiesse, Michael (1488–1539), 570–571
Willaert, Adrian (ca. 1490–1562), 512
William IX, Duke of Aquitaine (1071–1126), 447
Williams, Bert, 951
Williams, Clarence, 825, 826
Williams, Gaughan, 32
Williams, Hank (1923–1953), 128, 203, 944, 945
Williams, Larry, 74
Williams, Tony, 840
Wills, Bob, 203
   blues influence on, 98
Wilson, Thomas, 934
Wilson, Winston "Spree," 839
Wilson, Woodrow, 33, 333
"Wimoweh" (song), 552–553, 554
Winans, BeBe and CeCe, 314
Wind instruments
   in Andean region, 101
   concertos for, 189
   in cumbia, 214, 215
Wolof, 60
Women
   amateur music-making by, 168
   changing roles of, 235
   as chutney soca performers, 169
   as griots, 325, 326–327
   as rock and roll performers, 751
   sexualization of, 219, 220
Wonder, Stevie, 13, 289
Wong, Anthony (Anthony Wong Yiu Ming), 138
Wong, Wyman (Wyman Wong Wai Man), 138
Wong Jum Sum, 137
Wong piphat, 674–676
Wood-combed harmonica, 6
Woodstock Music Festival, 1969, 285, 699, 751, 809, 822
Wooten, Art, 270
Working-class culture, corrido role in, 197
Working-class whites, 201
Workman, Creed, 186
"World music," 792, 795
World War I, 96, 198
World War II
   recorded music during, 710
   steel orchestras after, 840–841
   western swing during, 203
Wu Man, 673
Wynette, Tammy (1942–1998), 204

Xalam, 310, **941–942**
Xylophone, 19
Xylophone, African, 165–166, 337–339, 551–552

Index

Yacoub, Gabriel, 285
Yambú, 760, 762
Yang qin, 243, 245
Yang Yinliu (1899–1984), 256
Yankaran, Anand and Rakesh, 168
Yankaran, Isaac (1932–1969), 168
Yankovic, Albert "Weird Al" (1959–), 2, 4
Yankovic, Frankie (1915–1998), 2, 4
Ybarra, Eva (1945–), 192, 195
Yeahquo, Ed Tiende, 586
Yellowman, King, 219–220
Yesayan, Nune, 38
Yé-yé song, 161
Yiddish folksongs, 45
Yiddish language, 42
Yoakam, Dwight (1956–), 205
Yodeling, 754, 755, **943–946**
Yogyakarta, music of, 300
Yoruba music
  instruments played in, 72, 73
  lyrics in Yoruba, 467
  traditional, 8, 9
Youch, Adam (1964–2012), 897, 898
Young, Lester (1909–1959), 79, 657
Yo-Yo Ma, 669
Yugoslavia, music of former, 260, 782, 912
Yuman Music, **946–947**
Yung, Joey (Joey Yung Cho Yee), 138
Yungas region, 103
Yupanque, Atahualpa (1908–1992), 619, 620

Zajal, 23, 33, 34, 83, **949–950**
Zampogna, 56–57
Zampoña, 57
Zapata, Emiliano, 196
Zappa, Frank, 16–17

Zawinul, Joe, 412
Zazpi, Ken, 71
Zé Carlos (José Carlos Schwarz) (1949–1977), 331
Zemirot, 43–44
Zhou Shaomei (1885–1938), 255–256
Ziegfeld, Florenz, Jr. (1867–1932), **951–953**
Ziegfeld Follies, 951, 952
Zimbabwe, independence of, 542
Zimmerman, Carl Friedrich, 58
Zimmerman, Robert Allen. *See* Dylan, Bob
Zinzendorf, Nicholas Ludwig von, Count, 570, 571–572
Ziporyn, Evan, 556
Ziryāb, 22–23
Zitarrosa, Alfredo (1936–1989), 619–620
Zither, 336–337, 478–481, 696, 702–705, **953–959**
Zouk, 830, **960–961**
Zubeldia, Emiliana (1888–1987), 70
Zulaika, José Gonzalo (1886–1956) (Aita Donostia), 70
Zulu lyrics, 547
Zulu migrant workers, 552
Zumsteeg, Johann Rudolf (1760–1802), 817
Zurna (oboe), 38
Zwaninul, Joe, 289
Zwiefacher, 48, 51, 285
Zwingli, Ulrich (1484–1531), 21, 571
Zydeco, **961–964**
  accordion use in, 7
  Cajun music compared to, 127
  contests, 129
  origin of, 4
Zydeco Force, 964